SELF-OWNERSHIP, PROPERTY RIGHTS, AND THE HUMAN BODY

How ought the law to deal with novel challenges regarding the use and control of human biomaterials? As it stands the law is ill-equipped to deal with these. Quigley argues that advancing biotechnology means that the law must confront and move boundaries which it has constructed; in particular, those which delineate property from non-property in relation to biomaterials. Drawing together often disparate strands of property discourse, she offers a philosophical and legal re-analysis of the law in relation to property in the body and biomaterials. She advances a new defence, underpinned by self-ownership, of the position that persons ought to be seen as the prima facie holders of property rights in their separated biomaterials. Amongst others, this book will appeal to those interested in medical and property law, philosophy, bioethics, and health policy.

MUIREANN QUIGLEY holds the Chair in Law, Medicine, and Technology at Birmingham Law School. Before moving to academia she was a medical doctor. Her research is explicitly interdisciplinary and focuses on the philosophical analysis of law and policy. She is particularly interested in biotechnological advances and innovations, and how these can and ought to be dealt with by society. She has previously held a number of research grants, including from the Wellcome Trust and the Leverhulme Trust. She is a member of the editorial board of Medical Law International. In 2012, she won the Mark S. Ehrenreich Prize in Healthcare Ethics Research.

CAMBRIDGE BIOETHICS AND LAW

This series of books was founded by Cambridge University Press with Alexander McCall Smith as its first editor in 2003. It focuses on the law's complex and troubled relationship with medicine across both the developed and the developing world. Since the early 1990s, we have seen in many countries increasing resort to the courts by dissatisfied patients and a growing use of the courts to attempt to resolve intractable ethical dilemmas. At the same time, legislatures across the world have struggled to address the questions posed by both the successes and the failures of modern medicine, while international organisations such as the WHO and UNESCO now regularly address issues of medical law.

It follows that we would expect ethical and policy questions to be integral to the analysis of the legal issues discussed in this series. The series responds to the high profile of medical law in universities, in legal and medical practice, as well as in public and political affairs. We seek to reflect the evidence that many major health-related policy debates in the UK, Europe, and the international community involve a strong medical law dimension. With that in mind, we seek to address how legal analysis might have a trans-jurisdictional and international relevance. Organ retention, embryonic stem cell research, physician-assisted suicide, and the allocation of resources to fund health care are but a few examples among many. The emphasis of this series is thus on matters of public concern and/or practical significance. We look for books that could make a difference to the development of medical law and enhance the role of medico-legal debate in policy circles. That is not to say that we lack interest in the important theoretical dimensions of the subject, but we aim to ensure that theoretical debate is grounded in the realities of how the law does and should interact with medicine and health care.

Series Editors

Professor Graeme Laurie, University of Edinburgh

Professor Richard Ashcroft, Queen Mary, University of London

SELF-OWNERSHIP, PROPERTY RIGHTS, AND THE HUMAN BODY

A Legal and Philosophical Analysis

MUIREANN QUIGLEY

University of Birmingham

CAMBRIDGE
UNIVERSITY PRESS

CAMBRIDGE
UNIVERSITY PRESS

University Printing House, Cambridge CB2 8BS, United Kingdom

One Liberty Plaza, 20th Floor, New York, NY 10006, USA

477 Williamstown Road, Port Melbourne, VIC 3207, Australia

314-321, 3rd Floor, Plot 3, Splendor Forum, Jasola District Centre, New Delhi - 110025, India

79 Anson Road, #06-04/06, Singapore 079906

Cambridge University Press is part of the University of Cambridge.

It furthers the University's mission by disseminating knowledge in the pursuit of education, learning and research at the highest international levels of excellence.

www.cambridge.org
Information on this title: www.cambridge.org/9781107036864
DOI: 10.1017/9781139568326

© Muireann Quigley 2018

First published 2018

A catalogue record for this publication is available from the British Library

ISBN 978-1-107-03686-4 Hardback

Do Bhrian, cuisle mo chroí.

CONTENTS

ACKNOWLEDGEMENTS

This book owes debt to many people who have influenced and helped my thinking on various aspects of it over the years. My interest in property in the body goes all the way back to my initial foray into bioethics and law as an undergraduate in the Centre for Social Ethics and Policy (CSEP) at the University of Manchester. I was introduced to questions relating to this, as well as to self-ownership and rights theories, by Charles Erin. This interest deepened later; when working at the CSEP I decided to do my PhD on the topic. Margot Brazier, John Harris, and Charles Erin supervised this, and I am indebted to them for their support and insights. I am also grateful for the initial encouragement of Graeme Laurie and Richard Ashcroft, who were my examiners, to continue to pursue this area of research in book form. This book builds on work started then. In the process of researching and writing the book, I came to see some of my earlier arguments as wrongheaded and in need of revision. This evolution in thinking is reflected in the book. As such, it contains ideas and arguments that readers might detect as having moved on from earlier published work.

In researching and writing this book, I have benefited greatly from discussions with many colleagues. These include those at the CSEP and law school at the University of Manchester; the Centre for Ethics in Medicine and the law school at the University of Bristol; and the law school at Newcastle University, especially colleagues in the Law, Innovation, and Society Research Group. A few years ago, I was lucky enough to spend a couple of months as a visiting researcher at the University of Edinburgh's law school where I did some initial research into Scots law for the book. I am grateful to the Mason Institute, and to Graeme Laurie in particular, for hosting me. I am also greatly obliged to Edinburgh's Kenneth Reid, who at short notice kindly provided me comments on the Scots property law sections of the book. In January 2014, I co-organised, along with Imogen Goold, a workshop titled 'Evolution or Revolution? The Biomaterials Property Debate and

Changing Ethical, Legal, and Social Norms ' at the Brocher Foundation in Geneva. The attendees deserve thanks for intense discussions which had a lasting influence on the approach taken in the book.

Too many people to individually mention have found themselves over the years engaged in conversations pertaining to parts of this book, but deserving of special mention are Semande Ayihongbe, Imogen Goold, Imogen Jones, and Daithí Mac Síthigh who, along the way, read near enough full drafts of the manuscript. My thanks also go to TT Arvind, Nicky Priaulx, Gill Haddow, Hillel Steiner, Luke Rostill, Derek Whayman, and Jamie Glister. They all offered invaluable comments – and sometimes extended discussions – on chapters in the book or on ideas contained within it. I would also like to thank Craig Purshouse and Kathryn MacKay who provided much needed research assistance at various points during the writing and editing process.

The support and patience of Finola O' Sullivan, Rebecca Jackaman, and colleagues at Cambridge University Press has been greatly appreciated. I am also grateful to John Wiley and Sons for permitting me to use portions of Quigley, M., 'Propertisation and commercialisation: On controlling the uses of biomaterials' (2014) 77 *Modern Law Review* 677. This article represents the genesis of some of the ideas which can be found in the book. In particular, Section 4 of Chapter 9 reworks and extends my analysis relating to property and income rights which can be found in this article.

Finally I could not have done this without the love and support of my husband Brian Willis. He encouraged me to stick with it and push on through, even through what became known as the chapter of doom. My love to him always.

TABLE OF CASES

UK

ECHR

Australia

TABLE OF LEGISLATION

UK Statutes

Statutory Instruments

Human Tissue Act Codes of Practice

European Directives

Foreign Statutes

Bodies of Value

1 Introduction

Human biomaterials can be valuable in different ways: valuable for their contribution to science and medicine, valuable commercially, and valuable to the persons from whom they are removed. The values attached to such materials have evolved over time; something that, in no small part, has been driven and mediated by advances in biotechnology and medicine. One consequence of this is the emergence of novel challenges for the law, including questions of how the law ought to resolve disputes over the use and control of biomaterials. It is the transformation in the use and value of biomaterials which prompts the enquiry at the heart of this book. This, along with recent legal decisions, means that questions of what ought and ought not to be done to and with our bodies and bodily tissues need to be more fully explored. In particular, questions regarding who ought or ought not to be able to control the uses (and abuses) of these are important.

Property, as we will see, is one way of securing control over biomaterials; albeit often this has been utilised to the benefit of third parties. When we say that a resource falls within the domain governed by property relations we are acknowledging a particular way of controlling that resource. This recognition brings such resources within the purview and protections of existing property institutions. Those who argue that persons should be seen as having property in their separated biomaterials think that individuals ought to have this type of control therein, as well as any consequent protections in their exercise of that control. The effect of being denied property in, and ownership of, our separated bodily tissues, is that we are prevented from having adequate control over (our interests in) them. This is a pressing concern where that control is ceded to other parties, such as researchers and biotech companies. This book is thus an exploration of property as applied to human biomaterials. Specifically, it offers a new, philosophically grounded, defence of the position that persons ought to be seen as the holders of property rights in their separated biomaterials (at least initially).

2   On Control and Conflict

Below are two stories: one of a woman and one of a man whose respective cells and blood revolutionised medical science and medicine. Both stories are about control; control over one's body and bodily tissues, and control over one's legacy. To be more exact, one of the accounts given is really about *lack* of control over these things and how it can be lost at the hands of medicine and medical research. I also outline several legal cases, from three common law jurisdictions – the United States, England and Wales, and Australia – all of which involve disputes over human tissue. Together these stories and cases reveal how, with advancing technology, human tissues, cells, and other biomaterials can be put to a multitude of novel uses, often not foreseen by the person who is the source of those materials. Through them we can see how this changing biotechnological landscape creates and confers new value(s) on these materials, something which is brought into sharp focus by the commercial and quasi-commercial interests of a variety of actors.

2.1   *Immortal Cell Lines and Antibodies*

In January 1951, Henrietta Lacks was diagnosed with cervical cancer. It turned out to be a particularly aggressive form of the cancer, from which Henrietta died within nine months.[1] Three months earlier when she had given birth to her fifth child, there had been no mention of the tumour in her medical notes.[2] During the investigation of her signs and symptoms and subsequent treatment at Johns Hopkins hospital several tissue samples were taken of the cancerous cervical tissue. These samples were given to George and Margaret Gey who were, at the time, working on creating an immortal cell line. Attempts to do this with human cells had not been successful up to this point.[3] However, Henrietta's cells (called HeLa) were unlike any others the Geys had worked with; they simply grew and grew and grew (at an almost alarming rate).[4] It would later emerge that the cells grew so prolifically that they could get carried on dust particles and

---

[1] For the story of Henrietta Lacks and the HeLa cell line see R. Skloot, *The Immortal Life of Henrietta Lacks* (London: Pan Books, 2010).
[2] *Ibid.*, p. 20.   [3] *Ibid.*, pp. 40–48.   [4] *Ibid.*, p. 47.

infect other cell cultures.[5] Within a short time, HeLa cells were being mass produced and shipped around the country for use in research. At first they were used for research on the poliovirus and later for other kinds of research. To name but a few, the use of HeLa cells has contributed to advances in cell culture techniques,[6] the discovery of the number of chromosomes in cells and, consequently, chromosomal abnormalities,[7] the understanding of how viruses function,[8] and the discovery that strains of human papillomavirus cause cervical cancer.[9] They are currently used for research and traded all over the world.[10] Henrietta Lacks never knew that her cells were being used for these purposes. The first time her name appeared in print in connection with the cells was twenty years later.[11] Additionally, her family only found out about the cells in 1973.[12]

In 1970, before Henrietta Lacks' name was published in relation to the HeLa cell lines, Ted Slavin started selling his blood to different biotech companies. Ted's blood serum had extremely high levels of Hepatitis B antibodies; this had been caused by repeated exposure through blood transfusions in the 1950s. Ted suffered from haemophilia, which was the reason for the repeated transfusions.[13] Around the early 1970s, companies began developing testing kits for Hepatitis B. In order to conduct research into these, they required a supply of serum with antibodies to the Hepatitis B virus. As such, Ted realised that his blood was valuable to these companies; he contacted several companies and started selling his blood for up to $10/ml. Furthermore, he set up a company to collect and sell blood from other people in similar situations.[14] Since Ted's

---

[5] *Ibid.*, pp. 176–180.   [6] *Ibid.*, pp. 114–115.   [7] *Ibid.*, pp. 116–117.   [8] *Ibid.*, p. 113.
[9] *Ibid.*, pp. 242–243.   [10] *Ibid.*, pp. 108–121.   [11] *Ibid.*, pp. 198–199.
[12] *Ibid.*, pp. 206–217. In saying this I am attentive to the comments regarding the historical context made recently by Duncan Wilson. He cautions against assessing the historical circumstances surrounding the HeLa cell line through our contemporary ethical lens. He argues that to do so 'projects a current view of the world backwards and overlooks how historical actors lived and worked in a different moral climate' ('A troubled past? Reassessing ethics in the history of tissue culture' (2016) 24 *Health Care Analysis* 246, 256). Nevertheless, by contrasting the Lacks story with that of Ted Slavin, as well as contemporary legal cases, we can appreciate how different historical contexts and times can impact on issues of use, control, and conflict which are central to the analysis in this book.
[13] B.S. Blumberg *et al.*, 'Ted Slavin's blood and the development of the HBV vaccine' (1985) 312 *New England Journal of Medicine* 189. See also Skloot, *Immortal Life*, pp. 230–231 and R. Skloot, 'Taking the least of you', *New York Times Magazine* (16 April 2006), www.nytimes.com/2006/04/16/magazine/16tissue.html?pagewanted=all (accessed 27 November 2017).
[14] Blumberg *et al.*, 'Ted Slavin's blood'. For a legal case involving the sale of blood see *Green v. Commissioner* 74 TC 1229 [1980]. The case involved Margaret Green who repeatedly

haemophilia often meant he could not work, this provided him with a means to earn some money.[15] In addition to the companies which were trying to develop commercial testing kits, public laboratories were also conducting research into blood-borne viruses. Accordingly, Ted contacted Dr Baruch Blumberg at the National Institutes of Health (NIH) and agreed to provide samples at no cost for research purposes. Dr Blumberg was the Nobel Prize-winning scientist who had discovered the Hepatitis B virus.[16] Along with colleagues at the NIH, he used Ted's blood 'in research on the radioimmunoassy test, tissue fluorescence techniques, the development of a vaccine against Hepatitis B virus, and the prevention of primary cancer of the liver'.[17] Ted Slavin died in 1984.

2.2   Spleens, Genes, and Prostates

In 1976, around the time that Ted Slavin was selling his blood to biotech companies, John Moore was diagnosed with hairy cell leukaemia. At the time, he lived in Alaska working on the oil pipeline.[18] The form of leukaemia that Moore had was rare. For this reason, he was referred to Dr Golde at the University of California, Los Angeles (UCLA) medical school where Dr Golde removed his spleen. Later, John Moore moved to Seattle, but for nearly seven years he continued to make regular trips to UCLA to see Dr Golde. At these visits samples of blood and bone marrow, amongst other tissues, were collected; Moore thought that this was part of his ongoing care. When, during visits, he started being asked to sign consent forms, which included a waiver of his pecuniary interests, he began to ask questions. Eventually, he contacted a lawyer, whereupon he discovered that Dr Golde and colleagues had been conducting research on his tissue.[19] As it turned out, in 1979, they had created a cell line (the 'Mo' cell line) from Moore's tissue. On the 30 January 1981, the regents of UCLA filed for a patent covering the cell line itself, along with a variety of methods for producing products from the cells.[20]

---

sold her blood to a blood bank. The issue in the case was whether expenses incurred as a result of this were tax deductible. The Court concluded that some expenses were eligible. For a discussion of this see A. Hyde, *Bodies of Law* (Princeton: Princeton University Press, 1997), pp. 57–62.

[15] Skloot, *Immortal Life*, p. 231.   [16] *Ibid.*   [17] Blumberg *et al.*, 'Ted Slavin's blood'.
[18] Skloot, *Immortal Life*, p. 227.   [19] *Ibid.*, p. 229.
[20] *Moore* v. *Regents of the University of California* 51 Cal.3d 120 at 127 [Cal, 1990] [*Moore*, Supreme Court].

Dr Golde and his colleague Shirley Quan, a researcher at UCLA, were listed as the inventors of the cell line. Subsequently, the patent was issued on the 30 March 1984.[21]

In 1984, the year that Ted Slavin died, John Moore filed a lawsuit against Dr Golde, the researchers, the regents of UCLA, and the pharmaceutical companies who bought the patent licences. The case was tried on thirteen causes of action; these included an action in conversion:[22] '[c]onversion involves an intentional dealing with "goods" that is seriously inconsistent with the possession or right to immediate possession of another person'.[23] Thus, for Moore's claim in conversion to succeed, the Court would have had to have found that his tissues were in fact his property or, at least, that he had immediate rights of possession with regards to them. Moore claimed that 'he continued to own his cells following their removal from his body, at least for the purpose of directing their use'.[24] The majority in the Court of Appeal of California (second district) seemingly agreed with his submission and upheld the action in conversion, maintaining that a 'patient must have the ultimate power to control what becomes of his or her tissues'.[25] However, the Supreme Court of California subsequently overturned the ruling.[26] The reasoning of the Court in reversing the appellate decision largely rested on the perceived negative impact on research that permitting individuals to claim property in their own tissues might have. It was the opinion of the Court that imposing a liability in conversion on researchers could hamper research and its potential benefits to society.[27] The fidelity of this reasoning, as we will see later in the book, is questionable. The defendants were not conducting gratis research solely for wider societal benefit; they had, in fact, filed a number of patents pursuant of the research, which restricted access to its benefits (at least in the absence of the ability to pay for it). Somewhat ironically, the majority in *Moore*, in their judgment

---

[21] *Ibid.*

[22] See *ibid.* at 128: (1) conversion; (2) lack of informed consent; (3) breach of fiduciary duty; (4) fraud and deceit; (5) unjust enrichment; (6) quasi-contract; (7) bad faith breach of implied covenant of good faith and fair dealing; (8) intentional infliction of emotional distress; (9) negligent misrepresentation; (10) intentional interference with prospective advantageous economic relationships; (11) slander of title; (12) accounting; and (13) declaratory relief.

[23] C. Witting, *Street on Torts*, 14th edn (Oxford: Oxford University Press, 2015), p. 280.

[24] *Moore*, Supreme Court at 134.

[25] *Moore* v. *Regents of the University of California* 249 Cal. Rptr. 494 at 508 [1988] at 508 [*Moore*, Court of Appeal].

[26] *Moore*, Supreme Court at 134–147.   [27] *Ibid.* at 144.

regarding conversion, referred to the continued use of the HeLa cell lines as support for the lack of authority for imposing a tortious liability. Justice Arabian, concurring with the majority decision, commented that Moore 'has asked us to recognize and enforce a right to sell one's own body tissue for profit'.[28] However, as will also become apparent later, this is to misconstrue the nature of Moore's claim. Instead, the Court of Appeal seemed to get to the nub of the issues when it stated the 'appeal raises fundamental questions concerning a patient's right to the control of his or her own body'.[29]

The next case is that of *Greenberg* v. *Miami Children's Hospital Research Institute*.[30] The Greenbergs had two children, both of whom suffered from Canavan disease and died. Canavan disease is a degenerative disease of genetic origin predominantly affecting those of Ashkenazi Jewish origin. It usually results in severe neurological symptoms and early childhood death. Having had an affected child, the Greenbergs wanted a way to identify carriers of the gene in order to facilitate prenatal testing and so approached one of the defendants, Dr Matalon.[31] The causal gene was identified in 1993 by researchers at Miami Children's Hospital. Obtaining the tissue samples in order to conduct the research and compile the resultant database was largely made possible due to the efforts of the Greenbergs. They had spent much time and effort recruiting other families suffering from the disease so that they could provide tissue samples and family medical histories. Furthermore, the Greenbergs, along with the other plaintiffs in the case, had provided financial backing for the research. They did this on the 'understanding and expectations that such samples and information would be used for the specific purpose of researching Canavan disease and identifying mutations in the Canavan disease which could lead to carrier detection within their families and benefit the population at large'.[32] However, in 1994, the researchers filed for patents relating to the gene for Canavan disease and any applications relating to prenatal testing.[33]

The plaintiffs alleged that the Miami Children's Hospital had also threatened to take action against other centres offering testing for Canavan disease. Further, the Miami Children's Hospital was 'negotiating exclusive licensing agreements and charging royalty fees', the effect of which would have been to restrict access to the test.[34] The plaintiffs claimed several causes of action, including one for conversion. In relation

---

[28] *Ibid.* at 148.   [29] *Moore*, Court of Appeal at 498.   [30] 264 F.Supp.2d 1064 [2003].
[31] *Ibid.* at 1066.   [32] *Ibid.* at 1067.   [33] *Ibid.*   [34] *Ibid.*

to this, the Court denied that the plaintiffs had a property interest in their tissue samples and genetic information, citing the judgment in *Moore* in support of this.[35] The Court claimed that to allow the claim 'would cripple medical research as it would bestow a continuing right for donors to possess the results of any research conducted by the hospital'.[36]

In 2007, the US Eighth Circuit Court of Appeals gave its ruling in the case of *Washington University* v. *William J. Catalona*.[37] Unlike the previous two cases, this case involved an action by a university against a former researcher and participants in his research. Dr Catalona had previously worked at Washington University. During his time there he collected samples both from healthy patients and those with prostate cancer for his research on the genetic basis of prostate cancer. These samples formed part of the collection held in the Genito-Urinary Biorepository at the University. In 2003, Dr Catalona moved to Northwestern University, whereupon he wrote to his patients and others asking for their permission to transfer their samples. Of these, approximately 6,000 agreed.[38] Unlike in *Moore* and *Greenberg*, in this case, whether or not the samples could be or were property was not at issue. The judgment in *Catalona* even acknowledged certain rights of ownership for the *sources* of the tissue, referring to them as *inter vivos* gifts. According to the District Court, '[t]he elements of an *inter vivos* gift are: 1) present intention of the donor to make a gift; 2) delivery of property by donor to donee; and 3) acceptance by donee whose ownership takes effect immediately and absolutely.'[39] The question at hand, therefore, was whether Dr Catalona or any of the research participants *retained* a property interest in the materials such that they could direct its use. The Court of Appeals, in agreement with the District Court, held that they did not and that these interests had passed to Washington University upon donation of the material, which now owned the samples held in the Biorepository.[40] The consequence of this, as explained by Graeme Laurie and colleagues in the context of *Moore*, is that 'while persons are denied recognition of a property interest in excised parts of our bodies, third parties may not only gain such an interest but can go on to protect it using forms of property law'.[41]

---

[35] *Ibid.* at 1074.   [36] *Ibid.* at 1076.

[37] 490 F.3d 667 [2007] [*Catalona*, Court of Appeals].   [38] *Ibid.* at 672.

[39] *Washington University* v. *William J. Catalona* 437 F.Supp.2d 985 [2006] at 997 [*Catalona*, District Court].

[40] *Catalona*, Court of Appeals at 673–677.

[41] G.T. Laurie, S.H.E. Harmon, and G. Porter, *Mason and McCall Smith's Law and Medical Ethics*, 10th edn (Oxford: Oxford University Press 2016), p. 494.

2.3   Sperm as Property

Sometime on the evening of the 28th or early morning of the 29th of June 2003, a refrigerated storage system at Bristol Southmead Hospital malfunctioned. The supply of liquid nitrogen, which ordinarily maintained the system at minus 196°C, fell below the required level. Tanks within the system contained samples of frozen semen which subsequently thawed and the sperm contained therein were irreversibly damaged. Among the damaged samples were those of Jonathan Yearworth and five other men who had undergone chemotherapy treatment for cancer at the hospital. Since the hospital has a fertility unit licensed under the Human Fertilisation and Embryology Act 1990,[42] the men had been offered the option of having samples of their semen frozen and stored for use at a later date due to the potential damaging effect of the chemotherapy on their fertility. Acting on the advice received, the six men produced samples for storage. Five of the men, and the widow of the sixth, subsequently brought an action against North Bristol NHS Trust seeking a remedy in negligence. Personal injury and property-based arguments were heard in this respect. The case reached the Court of Appeal whereupon counsel for the claimants was asked to present arguments in bailment in addition to personal injury and property.[43] Generally speaking, a bailment can occur where a party takes possession of an item of another's personal property. This possession brings with it a duty of care in respect of the goods/chattel in question. Where goods which have been bailed are subsequently damaged, an action can be brought. In *Yearworth*, a landmark ruling was made; it rejected the personal injury arguments, but concluded that 'the men had ownership of the sperm for the purposes of their present claims'[44] and, as a result, that the Trust was liable for the damage caused. As we will see in Chapter 4, this case has challenged the previous (seemingly entrenched) legal position that individuals could not have property rights in their own tissues. While not the first time that the courts have determined that body parts or tissues are capable of being treated as property at law, *Yearworth* is the first time that the person who is the tissue's source has been unequivocally recognised as the legitimate holder of property rights. *Yearworth* is also

---

[42] At the time of the ruling, the amendments contained in the Human Fertilisation and Embryology Act 2008 were not in force, but they would not have had any substantive effect on the judgment if they had been.

[43] *Yearworth and Others* v. *North Bristol NHS Trust* [2009] EWCA Civ 37.

[44] *Ibid.* at [45 (f)(v)].

significant for opening the door to property determinations in other cases.

Three recent Australian cases, *Bazley* v. *Wesley Monash IVF Pty Ltd*,[45] *Jocelyn Edwards; Re the estate of the late Mark Edwards*,[46] and *Re H, AE*[47] draw on and extend the reasoning developed in the *Yearworth* case.[48] All three involve applications by the wives of the deceased for the posthumous possession of sperm, which they intended to use for the purposes of *in vitro* fertilisation (IVF). In *Bazley*, the deceased died of liver cancer and had been undergoing chemotherapy before his death. Prior to commencing the chemotherapy he had samples of his semen stored.[49] Upon being told that the IVF unit could not continue to store the semen after death, an application was made to the Court by the wife of the deceased requesting that they be required to continue doing so.[50] In *Edwards*, the deceased had been seeking IVF treatment with his wife. After his death she obtained a court order for the extraction and storage of the sperm.[51] She then sought a further order for the release of the stored samples specifically for the purposes of IVF.[52] However, this did not proceed as the New South Wales Assisted Reproductive Technology Act 2007 requires the express consent of gamete providers for the use of their gametes after death for these purposes.[53] Subsequent to this a different order was sought to the effect that Ms Edwards was entitled to possession of the sperm samples.[54] The order did not deal with what might happen to the sperm afterwards. The facts of the third Australian case, *Re H, AE*, are similar to those in *Edwards*. In this case, following his death in a motor accident, an order had been made for the extraction and storage of the deceased's sperm.[55] This was then followed by an order releasing the sperm to the applicant (the deceased's wife) for IVF purposes.[56] The courts in all three cases held that rights of possession to the sperm vested in the applicants;[57] although, as we will see in Chapter 4, the scope and implications of these decisions are quite narrow.

3 Uses and Values of Biomaterials

These stories and cases begin to illustrate how advancing biotechnology has fundamentally altered the way we view the human body and its parts

---

[45] [2010] QSC 118.   [46] [2011] NSWSC 478.
[47] No 2, [2012] SASC 177, (No 3) [2013] SASC 196.   [48] See Chapter 4, Section 3.
[49] *Bazley* at [1].   [50] *Ibid.* at [4]–[12].   [51] *Edwards* at [13]–[15].   [52] *Ibid.* at [17].
[53] s. 23(a); *Edwards* at [20].   [54] *Edwards* at [22]–[24].   [55] *R H, AE* (No. 2) at [2].
[56] *Ibid.* at [69].
[57] *Bazley* at [21], *Edwards* at [88] and [91], and *Re H, AE* at [58] and [60].

and products. We have moved from being simply the end users of medicine and research to each of us being a potential purveyor of it. This is due, as Margaret Brazier argues, to 'the diverse means by which we ourselves may be used as medicine'.[58] Human biological materials can be used to treat illness and disease.[59] These include blood and blood products for transfusions, organs for transplantation, and gametes and embryos for IVF and pre-implantation genetic diagnosis (PGD). PGD coupled with Human Leukocyte Antigen (HLA) typing literally allows us to create a child whose umbilical cord blood can be life-saving for their brother or sister. Stem cells represent another avenue of potentially life-altering, if not life-saving, human medicine, and may yield treatments for a huge variety of diseases. Cell therapies (including those which are stem cell based) use either modified or unmodified autologous (from the patient themselves) or allogenic (not from the patient) cells in the treatment of disease. These encompass a range of applications including a burgeoning new class of products which draw on tissue-engineering expertise,[60] combining human biomaterials with artificial scaffolds; for example, cartilage for repairing joints,[61] bladders grown from a patient's own cells,[62] and biohybrid vaginas for transplantation.[63] There are also less media-worthy and exciting uses of human biomaterials, such as those used in research into the aetiology, pathology, and treatment of disease. Meanwhile, cells and tissues are frequently used for basic medical research which is not yet near clinical application. Brazier has called these diverse uses of persons and their bodies the 'notion of humans as medicines'.[64]

---

[58] M. Brazier, 'Human(s) as medicine(s)' in S. McLean (ed.), *First Do No Harm* (Aldershot: Ashgate Publishing Ltd, 2006) pp. 187–202, p. 188.

[59] For a comprehensive overview of the use of human biomaterials see Nuffield Council on Bioethics, *Human Bodies: Donation for Medicine and Research* (London: Nuffield Council on Bioethics, 2011), Ch. 1.

[60] For an in-depth analysis focused on tissue engineering see J. Kent, *Regenerating Bodies: Tissue and Cell Therapies in the Twenty-First Century* (London and New York: Routledge, 2012).

[61] T. Simonite, 'Lab-grown cartilage fixes damaged knees' *New Scientist* (5 July 2006), www .newscientist.com/article/dn9483-lab-grown-cartilage-fixes-damaged-knees/ (accessed 27 November 2017).

[62] R. Khamsi, 'Bio-engineered bladders successful in patients' *New Scientist* (4 April 2006), www.newscientist.com/article/dn8939-bio-engineered-bladders-successful-in-patients/ (accessed 27 November 2017).

[63] C. de Lange, 'Engineered vaginas grown in women for the first time' *New Scientist* (2014), www.newscientist.com/article/dn25399-engineered-vaginas-grown-in-women-for-the-first-time/ (accessed 27 November 2017).

[64] Brazier, 'Human(s) as medicine(s)', p. 187.

Attempting to get a handle on the sheer scale of activities involving human biomaterials, and on the humans as medicines enterprise, is challenging. The aforementioned research and therapeutic uses only scrapes the surface in terms of getting to grips with the growing place of the body, its parts, and products in biomedicine. In a review of human tissue storage in the United States, Elisa Eiseman and Susanne Haga estimated that '[c]onservatively, more than 307 million specimens from more than 178 million cases of stored tissue exist'.[65] These figures are now nearly twenty years out of date and it is difficult to try to determine what the current figure might be. Their projection at the time that they wrote this was that the number of specimens was 'accumulating at a rate of over 20 million per year'.[66] If this was correct, then the potential total size of current collections of human biomaterials in the United States alone is staggering. As Robert Weir and colleagues note, regarding the United States:

> Gathering reliable data about stored tissue samples is difficult because of the various types of human biological materials being stored, the diverse places (ranging from national repositories to private companies to pathology departments to the freezers in numerous researchers' labs) in which they are stored, and the sheer number of stored tissues and other biological materials.[67]

Evaluating the total numbers of samples held by various organisations, public or private, in the United Kingdom is also no easy task. We can only surmise, given the growth in the numbers of organisations (including the NHS, universities, and other institutions) that have tissue banks of one form or another, that it is likely to be an impressive number.

The evolving, ever increasing, and different uses of human biological materials come hand in hand with a change in the values that attach to organs, tissues, cells, and even the whole body. These values range from the emotional to the scientific, and public to private. Included in these are 'the public health importance of post mortem examinations. . .; the medical value of human tissues taken from both the dead and the living. . .; the value of important biotechnological interventions using human material. . .;

---

[65] E. Eiseman and S.B. Haga, *Handbook of Human Tissue Sources: A National Resource of Human Tissue Samples* (RAND Corporation, 1999), p. 133, www.rand.org/content/dam/rand/pubs/monograph_reports/MR954/MR954.chap10.pdf (accessed 27 November 2017).
[66] *Ibid.*
[67] R.F. Weir, R.S. Olick, and J.C. Murray, *The Stored Tissue Issue: Biomedical Research, Ethics and Law in the Era of Genomic Medicine* (Oxford: Oxford University Press, 2004), p. 23.

a broader commercial value of organs and tissues' and 'the ethical value of the body'.[68] Other uses undoubtedly give rise to other values. For instance, exhibitions such as Body Worlds,[69] which feature plastinated bodies and body parts, have educational value as anatomical specimens. They also have aesthetic value or value as objects of art, as do more explicit artistic pieces such as Orlan's 'Harlequin Coat' which contains skin cells from the artist's own body.[70]

Significantly, human biomaterials are now valuable as objects of commerce.[71] In this respect, powerful drivers of the 'humans as medicines' enterprise are the commercial and quasi-commercial activities of medicine, scientists, pharmaceutical companies, and other industry actors.[72] Human tissue has, as Donna Dickenson notes, 'become big business'.[73] This business side to what is ostensibly a medical endeavour has been termed the 'tissue economy',[74] and commentators refer to the 'biovalue' of biomaterials.[75] These phrases perhaps tells us more about the changing face of biomedicine than the most comprehensive of lists of the uses and applications of human biomaterials. Nils Hoppe uses the word 'bioequity' in talking about property in human biomaterials.[76] This phrase is used idiosyncratically in his proposal for the application of the law of equity to biomaterials in order to create a new property class.[77] However, it also brings to mind equity in terms more usual to the financial sector; that is, bioequity as denoting the latent value that lies in our bodies and their tissues and cells.

---

[68] J.K. Mason and G.T. Laurie, 'Consent or property? Dealing with the body and its parts in the shadow of Bristol and Alder Hey' (2001) 64 *Modern Law Review* 710, 712–713. They do point out that any potential values rely on a number of factors such as the circumstances of the removal of parts and tissues, as well as the methods employed (712).

[69] www.bodyworlds.com/en.html (accessed 27 November 2017).

[70] See www.fact.co.uk/projects/sk-interfaces/orlan-harlequin-coat.aspx (accessed 27 November 2017).

[71] Mason and Laurie, 'Consent or property?', 712–713.

[72] M. Quigley, 'Property and the body: Applying Honoré' (2007) 33 *Journal of Medical Ethics* 631.

[73] D. Dickenson, *Body Shopping: The Economy Fuelled by Flesh and Blood* (Oxford: One World Publications, 2008), p. 18.

[74] See C. Waldby and R. Mitchell, *Tissue Economies: Blood, Organs and Cell Lines in Late Capitalism* (Durham and London: Duke University Press, 2006), pp. 31–34. See also A. Webster, 'Stem cell research and society: Lessons from social science' *Bionews* (18 August 2008), www.bionews.org.uk/page_38010.asp (accessed 27 November 2017).

[75] C. Waldby, 'Stem cells, tissue cultures and the production of biovalue' (2002) 6 *Health* 305.

[76] N. Hoppe, *Bioequity: Property and the Human Body* (Farnham: Ashgate Publishing, 2009), p. 138.

[77] *Ibid.*, Chs 11 and 12.

In relation to organ and tissue donation, David Price argued that '[t]his "value" enhances the vulnerability and prospectability of our bodies and the need for donor, and indeed often community, interests to be properly protected.'[78] Such vulnerability and prospectability is starkly revealed in the illegal market in human body parts and materials. Consider the theft of thigh bones from the deceased BBC journalist Alastair Cooke. It was alleged that these had been subsequently sold to a dental implant company for more than $7,000.[79] Other body parts are also reportedly sold for high prices. In her book *Body Brokers*, Annie Cheney lists some underground prices for body parts: $550–900 for a head, $500–600 for a brain, $350–850 for each hand, and $4,000–5,000 for a whole cadaver.[80] Yet theft is not itself the driver. As Klaus Hoeyer argues, 'if it is legitimate to buy a given ubject, somebody will probably at some point find a way to procure it, legally or illegally. Buying makes theft an option.'[81] We, therefore, do not need to look as far as the illicit body (part) trade in order to appreciate the commercial worth of biomaterials.

Certain tissues and cells are not subject to the restrictions on sale which, for example, govern human organs for transplantation. This is because materials removed outwith transplant purposes are not captured by the Human Tissue Act 2004 provisions on the prohibition of commercial dealings. And even within the transplant context, the Act

[78] D. Price, *Human Tissue in Transplantation and Research* (Cambridge: Cambridge University Press, 2010), p. 3.

[79] For the story see Anonymous, 'Alistair Cooke's bones "stolen"', *BBC News* (22 December 2005), http://news.bbc.co.uk/1/hi/4552742.stm (accessed 27 November 2017), and M. Smit, 'Alistair Cooke body snatch leader pleads guilty', *The Telegraph* (18 March 2008), www .telegraph.co.uk/news/worldnews/1582092/Alistair-Cooke-body-snatch-leader-pleads-guilty.html (accessed 27 November 2017). The bones had been stolen as part of an underground tissue trafficking ring run by Michael Mastromarino under the guise of Biomedical Tissue Services. He was subsequently convicted of 'numerous charges in connection with his participation in the sale of human body parts from 244 corpse, including corrupt organization, conspiracy, theft by unlawful taking (for the theft of body parts), deceptive business practices, and abuse of corpse' (*Com. v. Mastromarino* 2 A.3d 581 (2010), 581). For an investigation into aspects of the illegal body part trade by the International Consortium of Investigative Journalists see *Skin and Bone: The Shadowy Trade in Human Body Parts* (Centre for Public Integrity, 2012), https://cloudfront-files-1.publicin tegrity.org/documents/pdfs/SkinBone.pdf (accessed 27 November 2017).

[80] A. Cheney, *Body Brokers: Inside America's Underground Trade in Human Remains* (New York: Broadway Books, 2006), p. xv.

[81] K. Hoeyer, *Exchanging Human Bodily Material: Rethinking Bodies and Markets* (Dordrecht: Springer, 2013), p. 127. Hoeyer uses the term 'ubjects' to denote those which 'leave the space identified as body', but are associated with a subject (p. 68). He uses it in order to explore the ambiguities which often attend discussions relating to both separated biomaterials and inserted parts and medical devices (p. 5).

exempts from the prohibition material which is the subject of property because of an 'application of human skill'.[82] It also exempts those which have been created outside the body such as cell lines.[83] The result is that some biomaterials can be legally traded and, thus, contribute to a flourishing and lucrative global market.[84] This is illustrated, perhaps most vividly, by considering cell lines and cell therapies.[85]

In 2011 it was declared that the cell therapy industry had 'come of age'[86] and was set to exceed the $1 billion mark in terms of annual revenue.[87] By 2013, commentators were claiming that the industry represented a 'distinct healthcare sector'[88] which formed a 'unique investment opportunity… distinct from biotech'.[89] The types of therapies and activities covered within this broad sector are diverse and wide-ranging. They include:

> permanent cell replacement therapies (hematological and nonhematological), tissue engineering (cells plus scaffolds), transient cell therapies that disrupt or reduce natural disease progression, immunomodulatory cell therapies, cell therapies that protect cells and tissues at risk, gene therapy (via cell delivery vehicles) and cell cancer vaccines.[90]

We also need to appreciate that a wealth of research is needed before therapies can be brought to market, much of which requires a supply of the relevant raw (bio)materials. In this respect, this and other unrelated types of basic research regularly use cell lines which are created from the relevant source biomaterials. For this reason, the production, processing, and distribution of human cell lines is also a thriving industry and is one

---

[82] s. 32(9)(c).
[83] s. 54(7) and Explanatory Notes, s. 10. See also the Human Tissue Authority's supplementary list which outlines materials that do and do not fall within the remit of the Act, www.hta.gov.uk/_db/_documents/Supplementary_list_of_materials_200811252407.pdf (accessed 27 November 2017).
[84] Although difficult to estimate the worth of the global industry due to the diverse and multiple uses of biomaterials, looking at individual sectors can give us an idea of its scale. For example, regarding cell therapies, Mason *et al.* estimate that there is now an annual turnover in excess of $1 billion. See C. Mason, D.A. Brindley, E.J. Culme-Seymour, and N.L. Davie, 'Cell therapy industry: Billion dollar global business with unlimited potential' (2011) 6 *Regenerative Medicine* 265, 266.
[85] This is also discussed in I. Goold and M. Quigley, 'Human biomaterials: The case for a property approach' in I. Goold, K. Greasley, J. Herring, and L. Skene (eds), *Persons, Parts and Property: How Should We Regulate Human Tissue in the 21st Century?* (Oxford: Hart Publishing, 2014), pp. 231–262.
[86] Mason *et al.*, 'Cell therapy industry', 265.   [87] *Ibid.*, 266.
[88] C. Mason *et al.*, 'Cell therapy companies make strong progress from October 2012 to March 2013 amid mixed stock market sentiment' (2013) 12 *Cell Stem Cell* 644, 644.
[89] *Ibid.*, 646.   [90] Mason *et al.*, 'Cell therapy industry', 267.

which spans both the public and private sectors. For example, the Health Protection Agency (a part of Public Health England) Culture Collections sells a range of cell lines. These come with a variety of price tags depending on which cell line is required and whether fresh or frozen samples are needed. For instance, HCA-46, which is a human colon adenocarcinoma, was available at the time of writing for £495 frozen and £545 fresh/growing. HeLa cell cultures can be obtained for £305 and £55, respectively.[91] Although this example is of cells available from a public agency, many more are available to buy from both public and private organisations.[92]

The research and therapeutic endeavours which utilise human biomaterials may be more or less removed from the process of acquiring the biomaterials from the source, as well as from the original sample obtained. Catherine Waldby and Robert Mitchell have remarked that biomaterials exist within an 'institutional complex':

> With the exception of some organs, donated tissues are not simply transferred intact from one person to another, but rather diverted through laboratory processes where they may be fractionated, cloned, immortalized, and multiplied in various ways. Tissue sourced from one person may be distributed in altered forms along complex pathways to multiple recipients at different times and at different locations throughout the world... Tissue donation is thus transformed from an act of direct civic responsibility between fellow citizens into a complex network of donor–recipient relations heavily mediated by biotechnical processes and an institutional complex of tissue banks, pharmaceutical and research companies, and clinics.[93]

The worry within such an institutional complex is that the sources of the biomaterials, their interests, and their contributions to the various undertakings (be they research- or therapy-based) become marginalised. This concern becomes more marked when we consider that tissue handling and processing is an institutionalised activity in another sense. It takes place in certain well-demarcated domains where those using cells and tissues have the requisite skills and resources. Furthermore, it only

---

[91] www.phe-culturecollections.org.uk/products/celllines/index.aspx (accessed 27 November 2017).
[92] See, for example, the following companies which all sell biomaterials in the United Kingdom (although the samples may originate elsewhere): Tissue Solutions (www.tissue-solutions.com/products.html), Seralab (www.seralab.co.uk/human-animal-matrices/normal-human-animal-tissues), and Amsbio (www.amsbio.com/home.aspx), (accessed 27 November 2017).
[93] Waldby and Mitchell, *Tissue Economies*, p. 22.

(legitimately) occurs where those involved can meet the necessary legal requirements; for example, compliance with European legislation and the licensing requirements of the Human Tissue Authority (HTA).[94] The practical effect of this, as will become apparent in Part 1 of this book, is that researchers and biotech companies can gain a level of control over tissue samples and cells which is ordinarily denied to the very source of the biomaterials. To wit, they can acquire property rights in those materials.

The diverse medico-scientific and commercial values and uses of human biomaterials, along with the legal landscape through which these are mediated and regulated, give rise to the concern that is at the core of this book; that is, the adequate protection of an individual's interests in and control over their bodies and bodily materials.[95] Throughout this book, this control is something which I will argue we each ought to have over our own bodies and bodily tissues. While there are a variety of contextual historical facts which separate them, the Lacks and Slavin stories are illuminating in this respect. They demonstrate that although control might be lost over the fate and uses of our separated biomaterials, this is not inevitable. Whether or not individuals have, and retain, such control, however, is to a large extent dependent on how the acquisition, storage, use, and transfer of these materials are regulated. Imogen Goold has said:

> What makes human tissue and organs particularly difficult to regulate is that they have different significances depending on the type of tissue, how it is used, from whom it is taken and why. People have very complicated interests in tissue and the intersection of these interests can itself be tremendously complex.[96]

The cases, which will be revisited in more depth in different parts of this book, indicate some of these difficulties and complexities. The recent sperm cases demonstrate both the challenges that biotechnological developments present to the law as applied to human biomaterials. Prior to having the

---

[94] See, for example, the HTA guidance on 'Licensing under the Quality and Safety Regulations', www.hta.gov.uk/licensingandinspections/licensingunderthequalityandsafe tyregulations.cfm (accessed 27 November 2017). This is wider than the scope of the European Union Tissue and Cells Directives (2004/23/EC, 2006/17/EC, and 2006/86/EC). For a commentary on the European context see Kent, *Regenerating Bodies*, Ch. 3.

[95] For the purpose of this book, the term 'biomaterials' will be taken to include separated body parts, organs, tissues, cells, and other derivative biological components, and is used interchangeably with these other terms. Where necessary, for the purposes of argument or clarity, I will differentiate between them.

[96] I. Goold, 'Why does it matter how we regulate the use of human body parts?' (2014) 40 *Journal of Medical Ethics* 3, 5.

technical ability to freeze and store semen for later use in IVF treatments, it was a moot point whether or not there were any legal remedies available for damage done or whether the samples could be considered as part of a person's estate. While disputes involving commercial interests have not yet come before the English courts, the US cases reveal that the challenges of advancing biotechnology are not limited to situations which have issues of remedial action at their core. The research, commercial, and quasi-commercial activities of medicine, scientists, and industry can lead to conflicts over the use (and abuse) of human biomaterials.

4 Structure of the Book

In *Yearworth*, Lord Judge CJ said that 'developments in medical science now require a re-analysis of the common law's treatment of and approach to the issue of ownership of parts or products of a *living human body*, whether for present purposes (viz. an action in negligence) or otherwise'.[97] I entirely agree. This book offers just such a re-analysis. My conclusion is that persons ought to be seen as the prima facie holders of property rights (moral and legal) in their separated biomaterials. This position, I will argue, is underpinned and justified by a recognition of persons as being self-owners (morally speaking). In making this case, I take a broad approach, drawing together often disparate strands of property discourse from the law and philosophy (in particular political philosophy and ethics). I do this because, often missing from the legal scholarship in debates regarding property in biomaterials is a philosophically grounded analysis of the underlying justification for having property rights in, and ownership of, those materials. Meanwhile philosophical discussions in this area are frequently blind to the realities of the legal landscape and how the application of the law of property to biomaterials does and could work. While these discourses take place in parallel, each could be enriched by taking a wider view.

I deliberately leave aside what Lawrence Becker identifies as the problem of the general justification of property: 'why should there be any property rights at all – ever?'[98] Becker rightly notes that this is where the

---

[97] *Yearworth* at [45] [emphasis added].
[98] L.C. Becker, 'The Moral basis of property' in J.R. Pennock and J.W. Chapman (eds), *Property: Nomos XXII* (New York: New York University Press 1980), pp. 187–220, p. 187. See also L.C. Becker, *Property Rights: Philosophic Foundations* (London, Henley and Boston: Routledge and Keegan Paul 1980), p. 3. Although he said this nearly forty years ago, it is still true of current debate in the area.

majority of the philosophical debate on property has focused its attention. Such writings are frequently concerned with the rationalisation of particular theories of property, such as first occupancy, labour theory, utility arguments, instrumental theories, and so on and so forth. Alternatively they focus on arguments regarding specific systems of property ownership (private, common, or collective). They are interested in justifying the very existence of property (rights). In this book, however, I take it as a necessary starting point that property represents a powerful and ubiquitous institution around which significant parts of our political and legal system are organised. Hence the analysis is more closely aligned with what Becker terms the specific and particular justifications of property; that is, asking 'what sorts of things should be owned and in what ways' and 'who should have title to existing pieces of it'.[99] This book sheds light on these questions expressly in the context of biomaterials separated from living persons.

In Part I, I examine the law and relevant judicial reasoning pertaining to the use of human biomaterials. In Chapter 2 we will see that the law of consent currently forms the bulwark of protections accorded to individuals regarding their bodies and separated biomaterials. This, I argue, is inadequate, both conceptually and practically speaking, for the task at hand. Moreover, we will see that these protections are more robust in relation to the deceased, than the living, a situation which is also not satisfactory. Although historically governed by the 'no property' rule, in chapters 3 and 4 it will become apparent that parts of the body are already treated as property for a variety of purposes and legal ends,[100] and that recent cases have extended property's scope in relation to human biomaterials. A key issue that will emerge from cases examined (historical and contemporary) is the fact that the law in this respect has developed in a piecemeal fashion. Moreover, if the body and its parts are not capable of being property, then relevant prosecutions or actions regarding their (ab)uses must proceed either on different bases or creative ways sought to make them subject to property considerations. What will emerge, in respect of the latter route, is that there are few, if any, coherent property principles to be gleaned from the relevant jurisprudence in respect of human bodies and biomaterials.

---

[99] *Ibid.*, p. 187.
[100] Laurie, Harmon, and Porter, *Mason and McCall Smith's Law and Medical Ethics*, p. 490. See also M. Quigley, 'Property in human biomaterials: Separating persons and things?' (2012) 32 *Oxford Journal of Legal Studies* 659, 660–666.

A consequence of the law as it stands is that the source is often the least adequately protected party in respect of the interests they may have in their biomaterials. A more explicit recognition of persons as the prima facie holders of legal property rights in their separated biomaterials could help to address this. It is not simply that there are good policy reasons to do this, but that a *presumption* in favour of this is a morally defensible position. By including the body and its parts in the list of things which we call property, we place it within a normative legal framework which can help to identify wrongs committed. It also gives us an already established framework for remedial action.[101] Yet, in attempting to do this, there is a need for a coherent property approach with justified and clear philosophical foundations. It is doubtful that the law as it currently stands in relation to property in biomaterials can provide this. Parts II and III of the book offer arguments in this respect.

In this opening chapter we have already begun to see that considerations of *use* and *control* of biomaterials are at the very core of the challenges and conflicts which can arise. My contention in this book will be that this necessarily brings them into the purview of property and ownership. However, if we are to make sense of property, we must give some sort of characterisation of the types of things that can appropriately be subject to property considerations. Chapters 5 and 6 are directed towards this task. In so doing, they examine the question of what property and ownership consist of. It will become evident in these chapters, and as the book proceeds, that the arguments offered are underpinned by normative commitments which could loosely be classed as a type of liberal egalitarianism. This emerges most strongly in Chapter 7 when I move on to look at and defend the idea of self-ownership. A central claim is that self-ownership interests mirror (morally speaking) the property interests (legal and moral) that persons can be said to have in their biomaterials after separation. Self-ownership thus forms part of the justification for recognising property in separated biomaterials.

In Part III, I move beyond self-ownership to look more closely at property rights in separated biomaterials. In Chapter 8 I argue that self-ownership creates a presumption that the source of separated biomaterials ought to be considered their owner upon separation (at least initially). I examine a variety of rationales for this, settling on an account which centres on the normative continuity that exists between the rights which persons have regarding the materials in their embodied and separated

---

[101] Goold and Quigley, 'Human biomaterials'.

states. To wit, I posit that no moral magic occurs upon separation. Persons' normative authority over their biomaterials thus remains fundamentally unchanged. In Chapter 9, the final substantive chapter, I examine the transfer of bodily property. I return to consent and argue that, in relation to biomaterials, the proper function of consent is either to authorise certain uses within the scope of the sources' property rights, or, where they wish to give up those rights, as legitimating the transfer of the relevant property rights to third parties. I look briefly at gratuitous transfers, such as donations, before looking at the selective moral disquiet that exists regarding the effect of the commercialisation of human biomaterials by their source. Chapter 10 draws the book to a close, bringing together the main themes and arguments.

PART I

Human Tissues and the Law

2

Regulating the Uses of Biomaterials

Consent and Authorisation

1 Introduction

The stories and cases outlined at the beginning of Chapter 1 illustrate two important points regarding human biomaterials. The first is that the way we think about and treat the body, and its tissues and cells, has changed with biotechnological developments and advances. The second is that these advances give rise to new and unexpected challenges and conflicts. Given this, how should we regulate the uses of human biomaterials? And how can we protect the interests which the source of the biomaterials (and indeed other parties) might have in these? The approach advocated and defended in this book is a property-based one. It is only by recognising persons as the holders of legal property rights in their separated biomaterials that we can adequately protect their interests in these. However, apart from certain exceptions, which we will see in the next two chapters, this is not the principal approach of the law in the United Kingdom. Instead the law predominantly relies on the twin guiding principles of consent and authorisation. These are given effect primarily through the Human Tissue Act 2004 (England, Wales, and Northern Ireland) and the Human Tissue Act (Scotland) 2006. In this chapter I set out and critique this legislative framework, examining the background to the two Acts, as well as their specific provisions. What we will see is that consent and authorisation-based frameworks do not, on their own, effectively protect source interests in biomaterials, especially in the light of expanding and novel medical, scientific, and commercial uses of these.

2 Human Tissue Regulation: Historical Failures

During the course of an enquiry into the deaths of children following cardiac surgery at the Bristol Royal Infirmary, it was discovered that large collections of organs and other materials were routinely being retained and stored (often for no particular purpose) following post-mortems.[1] It subsequently transpired that there were similar collections of these all around the country. Common practice at the time was to retain pieces of tissue and even whole organs after a post-mortem had been carried out. The collections included the largest in the country, which was held at the Royal Liverpool Children's Hospital (Alder Hey).[2] The scale of the collections at Alder Hey was immense. At the hospital there had been 'the wholesale systematic retention of organs between 1988 and 1995'.[3] Nearly every organ removed at post-mortem was retained.[4] As outlined in the Redfern Report:

> The large majority of retained organs were not subjected to histological examination. Rarely do they appear to have been used for medical education or research purposes. The organs were largely ignored, with the consequence that there was a remorseless increase in the number of organs stored in containers. There was some limited use of the organs for research purposes. However, the large majority of organs remained untouched throughout the period.[5]

This led to a public outcry, not in the least because many of the collections included children's tissues and organs. Margaret Brazier and Emma Cave explain:

> In some cases, infants were literally stripped of all their organs and what was returned to the families was an 'empty shell'. In a horrifying number of cases, organs and tissue retained were simply stored. They were put to no good use. In some instances, the whole foetus or still born infant was kept and stored in pots.[6]

In these cases the consent of the parents had not been sought and they did not know that parts of their deceased children had been retained.

---

[1] See Bristol Royal Infirmary Inquiry, *Inquiry into the Management of Care of Children Receiving Complex Heart Surgery at the Bristol Royal Infirmary: Interim Report* (London: The Stationery Office, 2000) [*Interim Report*].
[2] *The Royal Liverpool Children's Inquiry Report*, HC 12–11 (London: The Stationery Office, 2001) [Redfern Report]; Department of Health, *Learning from Bristol: The Report of the Public Inquiry into Children's Heart Surgery at the Bristol Royal Infirmary 1984–1995* (London: Stationery Office, 2001); Department of Health, *Human Bodies, Human Choices: The Law on Human Organs and Tissues in England and Wales* (London: The Stationery Office, 2002); and Independent Review Group, *Retention of Organs at Post-Mortem Final Report* (Edinburgh: The Stationery Office, 2001), p. 16 [*Final Report*].
[3] Redfern Report, p. 444.   [4] *Ibid.*, p. 39.   [5] *Ibid.*, p. 4.
[6] M. Brazier and E. Cave, *Medicine, Patients and the Law*, 6th edn (Manchester: Manchester University Press, 2016), p. 547. See also M. Brazier and S. Ost, *Bioethics, Medicine and the Criminal Law: Medicine and Bioethics in the Theatre of the Criminal Process* (Cambridge: Cambridge University Press, 2013), pp. 55–57.

The widespread practice in pathology of retaining tissues and even whole organs following a post-mortem was enabled, or at least not explicitly disallowed, by the law at the time. This had developed in a disjointed and piecemeal fashion, often in response to biomedical developments; in particular, corneal grafting, organ transplantation, and *in vitro* fertilisation. This resulted in numerous statutes which governed different aspects relating to the use of human tissue (and bodies) across the United Kingdom.[7] Of these, it is the regulatory gaps left by the Human Tissue Act 1961 and the Human Organs Transplant Act 1989 which were arguably the most problematic and which made the retention of organs possible in the first place.

The 1961 Act was a vague affair and has been duly criticised for this.[8] In general, the lack of consent provisions in the Act have been seen to be the root of the problems which ensued. Section 1(1) permitted 'the person lawfully in possession' of the body of the deceased to 'authorise' the removal of organs and tissue if that person had 'expressed a request' that this take place for therapeutic, educational, or research purposes.[9] Section 1(2) allowed such authorisation to take place even if such a request had not been explicitly made. In such circumstances the only obligation placed upon the person lawfully in possession of the body was that they should have 'no reason to believe – (a) that the deceased had expressed an objection to his body being so dealt with after his death, and had not withdrawn it; or (b) that the surviving spouse or any surviving relative of the deceased objects to the body being so dealt with'.[10] All that was required to verify this was that they had 'made such reasonable enquiry as may be practicable'.[11]

In truth, the absence of any explicit consent provisions is not surprising. The Act, like much of the law relating to the human body and tissue, was enacted as a result of medical advances. It was created to regulate particular uses of deceased human tissue: the transplantation of organs

---

[7] The acts were: (1) Human Tissue Act 1961, (2) Anatomy Act 1984, (3) Corneal Tissue Act 1986, (4) Coroners Act (Northern Ireland) 1959; (5) Coroners Act 1988, (6) Human Organs Transplant Act 1989, and (7) Human Fertilisation and Embryology Act 1990. There was also the Human Tissue Act (Northern Ireland) 1962, as well as a variety of orders relating to Northern Ireland: Corneal Tissue (Northern Ireland) Order 1988 (SI 1988/1844 (NI 14), Human Organ Transplants (Northern Ireland) Order 1989 (SI 1989/2408 (NI 21), and Anatomy (Northern Ireland) Order 1992 (SI 1992/1718 (NI 11).

[8] For example, see D. Price, 'From Cosmos and Damian to Van Velzen: The human tissue saga continues' (2003) 11 *Medical Law Review* 1; B. P. Block, 'A tissue Act not to be sneezed at' (2004) 168 *Justice of the Peace* 291; and Mason and Laurie, 'Consent or property?'

[9] Human Tissue Act 1961, s. 1(1).   [10] s. 1(2).   [11] *Ibid.*

and tissues, medical education and research, post-mortems, and to allow the cremation of bodies which had been used for anatomical examination. As the preamble to the Act and the parliamentary debate of the time make clear, the actual purpose of the Act was to ensure that in certain circumstances the removal of human organs and tissues was not unlawful.[12] As such, it was an Act that served to legitimise certain activities, not one which was there to protect a person's autonomy or control over their tissues. It was in this way an Act of its time. Patient autonomy and consent had not yet come to the fore in medical practice or in the law that governed that practice.

Since the Act only governed tissues removed from the deceased, this left the living mainly to the remit of the common law. And here there were also gaps. While the common law provided a remedy for unauthorised touchings and for cases of negligence during medical treatment, this was where its protection ended.[13] Once a patient had consented to and undergone a surgical procedure to remove their tissue, there was nothing that required the patient's consent in order to keep hold of that tissue and put it to further use. While the issue was not tested at common law, an individual's tissue was to all intents and purposes considered to have been abandoned.[14] This was the case regardless of the use to which it might have been put, such as research, education, public health, etc., and regardless of the potential commercial value of that tissue. As we will see in Chapter 9, it is not clear why abandonment would be presumed in the case of biomaterials since it is far from easy to abandon anything as far as the English common law is concerned.[15] In any case, the practical assumption made was that the individual's interests in their tissue ceased once it was separated from their body. Yet as we saw in the first chapter, given the diversity of interests and values that can vest in the body, its parts, and its products, this is not something that ought to be presumed. The practical consequence of this was that the individual had a lack of control over the fate of their organs and tissues, either while they were alive or after their death.

---

[12] See the comments of The Parliamentary Secretary to the Ministry of Health (Edith Pitt), *Hansard* HC Deb (1960), vol. 632, cols 1231–1258. In particular she said, 'The Bill is one which is mainly concerned with the removal of doubt... Because the Corneal Grafting Act specifically authorised the removal of eyes, there has been a natural doubt about the legality of removing other parts' (col. 1231).

[13] Mason and Laurie, 'Consent or property?', 727.

[14] Nuffield Council on Bioethics, *Human Tissue: Ethical and Legal Issues* (London: Nuffield Council on Bioethics, 1995), p. 67.

[15] See Chapter 9, Section 3.1.

One might have expected the Human Organs Transplant Act 1989 to fill some of the lacunae. Yet while this Act did encompass the removal of organs from both the living and the deceased, again consent was not its driving concern. Indeed, the Act does not mention consent. Instead, the purpose as set out in the Act was to 'prohibit commercial dealings in human organs intended for transplanting; to restrict the transplanting of such organs between persons who are not genetically related; and for supplementary purposes connected with those matters'.[16] Hence, the *actual removal* of organs for transplantation was governed by the common law. The Human Organ Transplants (Unrelated Persons) Regulations 1989 did contain consent provisions.[17] But their purpose was to make further stipulations regarding the transplant of organs between genetically unrelated individuals. The regulations did not, in any case, add anything to the existing common law, essentially codifying already existing requirements. In this regard, it obliged that a full explanation of the transplant procedure be given, that this be fully understood, and that consent be freely given without coercion or inducement.[18] The regulations, covering only solid organs for transplantation, had nothing to say on the matter of the retention of other tissues or even uses of solid organs removed outside the transplant arena.

The consequence of the retained organs scandals, and the enquiry reports which followed, was comprehensive legislative reform in which consent and authorisation took centre stage: the Human Tissue Act 2004 (England, Wales, and Northern Ireland) and the Human Tissue (Scotland) Act 2006. The presumption underpinning these Acts is that provisions relating to consent and authorisation would safeguard individuals' interests regarding their bodies and separated tissues. As we are about to see, however, while the Acts go some way to plugging some of the holes inherent in the previous legislation, there are still some concerning gaps. Consent and authorisation do not, and indeed cannot, on their own give effective protection to source interests. In this respect the Acts do not properly address the fundamental problem of the lack of control that individuals have over the use of their separated tissues. The English Act, in particular, presents a veneer of control, but, as I am about to argue, the protections that consent offers in the Act are in some respects illusory, especially in relation to living persons. It contains exemptions which weaken the control that individuals can exercise over the uses of their removed materials, while strengthening that of third parties such as researchers and industry actors. The Scottish Act is silent on how to

---

[16] Human Organs Transplant Act 1989, introductory text.   [17] SI 1989/2480.
[18] Reg. 3(2).

deal with biomaterials from the living. This is because, barring transplantation, its provisions do not cover living persons. These statutory lacunae are problematic because, as we saw in Chapter 1 and will become more evident in the next two chapters, the common law is not well-equipped to deal with the challenges of advancing biotechnology in respect of biomaterials.

3   The Human Tissue Acts: Filling Regulatory Gaps?

3.1   The English Act: Consent

The Human Tissue Act 2004 has a wide remit and is intended to govern activities in relation to the uses of human bodies, organs, and tissues. Whereas the 1961 Act just over ran to two pages, the 2004 Act is sixty pages long and consists of three parts and seven schedules. Moreover, the Act must be read in conjunction with the seven Codes of Practice which have been issued by the Human Tissue Authority (HTA).[19] These are supplemented by four additional guidance documents relating to licencing standards.[20] The creation of the HTA was mandated by the 2004 Act.[21] Its function is to regulate activities involving human tissue and, as such, it is enabled to issue Codes of Practice for the purposes of 'giving practical guidance on activities' and 'laying down standards' relating to the activities within its remit.[22] The end result is a long and complicated piece of legislation.[23] The real substance is contained within Part 1 of the Act which focuses on the consent provisions.[24]

---

[19] The Codes of Practice are Code of Practice A: Guiding Principles and Fundamental Principle of Consent Code of Practice B: Post Mortem Examination; Code of Practice C: Anatomical Examination; Code of Practice D: Public Display; Code of Practice E: Research; Code of Practice F: Donation of Solid Organs and Tissue for Transplantation; and Code of Practice G: Donation of Allogeneic Bone Marrow and Peripheral Blood Stem Cells for Transplantation. These can be found at: www.hta.gov.uk/codes-practice (accessed 27 November 2017).

[20] Code of Practice B: Post Mortem Examination Standards and Guidance; Code of Practice C: Anatomical Examination Standards and Guidance; Code of Practice D: Public Display Standards and Guidance; and Code of Practice E: Research Standards and Guidance.

[21] s. 13.   [22] s. 26(1).

[23] The 1961 Act has been referred to as 'complex and obscure' (Bristol Royal Infirmary Inquiry, *Interim Report*, para. 64). However, this seems somewhat of a mischaracterisation. While there was certainly some ambiguity surrounding the Act's provisions, there was nothing complex or particularly obscure about it. It could be claimed that it was its sheer lack of complexity which led to the subsequent problems. In this respect, such a description would appear to be more apt for the lengthy 2004 Act.

[24] Parts 2 and 3 of the Act, respectively, deal with the regulatory system required by the Act and various miscellaneous issues including definitions. Since my concern is with the consent provisions, the discussion will mainly be confined to the terms of Part 1 of the

The explanatory notes are explicit about the importance of consent, saying:

> The purpose of the Act is to provide a consistent legislative framework for issues relating to whole body donation and the taking, storage and use of human organs and tissue. It will make consent the fundamental principle underpinning the lawful storage and use of human bodies, body parts, organs and tissue, and the removal of material from the bodies of deceased persons.[25]

Appropriate consent thus forms the central focus of the Act and is required for particular purposes pursuant to Schedule 1 of the Act. The activities contained within Schedule 1 are only lawful if 'appropriate consent' has been obtained. These activities include the storage and use of whole bodies;[26] the removal, storage and use of 'relevant material' (organs, tissues, and cells) from the bodies of deceased persons;[27] and the storage and use of relevant material from the living.[28] Note that while the Act governs the removal, storage, and use of tissues taken from the deceased, it only covers *storage* and *use* from the living. The *removal* of tissue from the living continues to be the concern of the common law.

Schedule 1 of the Act stipulates the purposes for which appropriate consent is required. Part 1 of the schedule covers both the living and deceased and lists the purposes for which consent is required as: (1) anatomical examination; (2) determining the cause of death; (3) establishing after a person's death the efficacy of any drug or other treatment administered to him; (4) obtaining scientific or medical information about a living or deceased person which may be relevant to any other person (including a future person); (5) public display; (6) research in connection with disorders, or the functioning, of the human body; and (7) transplantation. Part 2 applies only to the deceased and lists further purposes requiring consent in that context: (1) clinical audit; (2) education or training relating to human health; (3) performance assessment; (4) public health monitoring; and (5) quality assurance.

Appropriate consent for scheduled purposes is required with respect to all 'relevant materials'. Relevant materials are any human cells excluding hair and nails from the body of a living person, as well as gametes and embryos outside the body;[29] the latter fall within the remit of the Human

---

Act. The discussion will also be limited to provisions relating to the competent adults; children and incompetent adults will not be dealt with here.
[25] Explanatory notes, para. 4.   [26] s. 1(1)(a) and s. 1(1)(b).
[27] s. 1(1)(c), s. 1(1)(e), and s. 1(1)(g).   [28] s. 1(1)(d) and s. 1(1)(f).   [29] s. 53.

Fertilisation and Embryology (HFE) Act 1990 (as amended 2008). This later Act is also heavily consent focused, requiring the consent in writing of the providers for the use and storage of their gametes and for the creation, use, and storage of their embryos.[30] Matters relating to Coronial activities are not covered by the 2004 Act. These fall under the Coroners and Justice Act 2009 (England and Wales) and the Coroners Act (Northern Ireland) 1959.[31] Moreover, transplant activities within Wales are covered by the Human Transplantation (Wales) Act 2013.[32] This Act, which came into force at the end of 2015, makes provisions for the use of 'deemed consent' in Wales in relation to the transplantation of organs and tissue from deceased persons. In addition to these exclusions within the Human Tissue Act 2004, materials created outside the body do not count as relevant materials either.[33] The effect of this is that any cell lines created are not covered by the Act.[34] The full implications of this are discussed later in this chapter.

The Act, in making appropriate consent its focus, is largely concerned with *who* can give this consent. With respect to the competent living adult, this means the person themselves.[35] Where an individual has died without making a decision about the subsequent use of their body and tissues, the decision can either be taken by a person nominated by them while they were alive (a nominated representative),[36] or a person in a 'qualifying relationship'.[37] Those persons considered to be in a qualifying relationship are specified by the Act.[38] Furthermore, the persons in a qualifying relationship with the deceased are ranked in a hierarchy (spouse or partner, parent or child, brother or sister, grandparent or grandchild, nephew or niece, step-parent, half brother or sister, and friend of longstanding).[39] The exceptions to this are public display and anatomical examination. The express written and witnessed consent of the person prior to their death is required for these purposes.[40]

---

[30] Schedule 3.

[31] Prior to the 2009 Act coming into force, coronial activities in England and Wales were governed by the Coroners Act 1988.

[32] In what follows, I do not discuss the details of the Welsh Act as I am, in the main, focused on non-transplant-related activities.

[33] s. 54(7).

[34] Explanatory notes, para. 10. See also the HTA's supplementary list which outlines materials which do and do not fall within the remit of the Act. Available at: www.hta .gov.uk/_db/_documents/Supplementary_list_of_materials_200811252407.pdf (accessed 27 November 2017).

[35] ss 3(1) and (2).   [36] ss 3(6) and 4.   [37] s. 3(6)(c).   [38] s. 54(9).   [39] s. 27(4).

[40] ss 3(4) and 3(5).

Arguably, these provisions address some of the most serious lacunae that existed under the preceding human tissue legislation. First, the scheduled purposes clearly set out activities which will be unlawful unless appropriate consent is obtained in the case of deceased bodies and tissues. In this respect, it is more specific than the old Act, which simply referred to the transplantation of organs and tissues, medical education and research, post-mortems, and cremation. Second, whereas the old Act contained no mechanisms for redress if its provisions were breached, the new Act allows for the prosecution of those who contravene it. The courts are empowered to give fines, a term of imprisonment, or both.[41] Third, gone is the loose wording of the old Act regarding 'the person lawfully in possession of the body'. The 2004 Act is clear about who can consent for purposes within its remit. Finally, whereas the previous legislation had nothing to say on the further use of human tissues and cells once they had been removed from the living body, the 2004 Act appears to have addressed this, offering some protection in relation to the interests of living individuals. On the face of it, therefore, the Human Tissue Act 2004 looks to be a piece of comprehensive and thoughtful legislation, aimed at giving real substance to the interests that individuals might have in controlling their bodies, organs, tissues, and cells. Yet, if we look at the detail of some of its provisions we can see that there are some problems.

3.1.1   Differential Protections

One difficult aspect of the 2004 Act lies in the fact that there is a critical disparity between the protection and control offered to the individual regarding the storage and use of their tissues while alive and once deceased. Since individuals have more interests over their body and their tissues whilst living, one might presume that this is where the weight of the law ought to lie. But the reverse is true in this Act. Although this is a function of the origins and history of the Act, it still seems somewhat amiss. As we saw above, the purposes laid out in Schedule 1 all apply to the deceased; however, only Part 1 of the Schedule is applicable to living persons. Appropriate consent is required for certain scheduled purposes using tissue samples taken from the deceased: clinical audit, education or training relating to human health, performance assessment, public health monitoring, and quality assurance. Yet, no consent is required for these

---

[41]   ss 5(7) and 25(2). For a discussion of the Act explicitly in the context of its place and role within the criminal law see Brazier and Ost, *Bioethics, Medicine and the Criminal Law*, pp. 52–65.

purposes whilst the person is alive. The fact that tissue from the living is not covered for audit, education, and so on might be understandable in cases where the tissue is being taken *exclusively* for these purposes. This is because consent to the activity involved would be part and parcel of the consent given for the *removal* of the tissue in the first place and, hence, covered by the common law.[42] In the majority of situations though, where living tissue is used pursuant to Part 2 of Schedule 1, it is unlikely that the removal itself is actually being done for the purpose of audit, training, and so on. More likely is that the tissue will be removed in the course of medical treatment. Thus, the consequence of Part 2 of Schedule 1 is that no consent for these activities need be sought from individuals who have had tissue removed as part of their medical treatment.

It has been suggested to me that perhaps we simply do not care as much about tissues and other biomaterials removed from the living or during the course of treatment, and that this perhaps explains these differential protections.[43] While this view has some merit, I am unpersuaded that it is true (or at least true all the time) that persons care more about the uses of biomaterials in the deceased context. Whether living or deceased uses are at issue, it may well depend on the particular uses, as well as *how* they come to be used. The disparity in protections is better understood as being historically contingent; that is, an Act which grew out of a scandal involving deceased bodies and their parts. Margaret Brazier and Suzanne Ost point to this underlying rationale when they note that while living persons can give consent prior to any removal taking place, and simply refuse to give it if they have objections to future uses, the 'dead cannot speak'.[44] However, since the Act does not require consent to be obtained from the living for Part 2 purposes, there is no reason (legally speaking) why patients need be told about possible retention of tissues for these purposes (when they are removed in the course of treatment).

Perhaps a good case can be made for the exemption of activities in Part 2 of the Schedule from any consent requirements. Such an argument might be made on public health grounds or on the basis that the activities circumscribed here represent a general societal good. Nevertheless, it seems that, if such an argument is to be made at all, it must apply to both the living and the dead. Taken in the context of the retained organs

---

[42] D. Price, 'The Human Tissue Act 2004' (2005) 68 *Modern Law Review* 798, 806.
[43] My thanks to Imogen Goold for this.
[44] Brazier and Ost, *Bioethics, Medicine and the Criminal Law*, pp. 58–59.

enquiries, it is understandable why Parliament wanted to ensure that organs and tissues from the *deceased* be tightly regulated for these purposes. Even so, it is not so clear why tissue from the *living* is excluded from having the protections that this provision provides. The explanatory notes state that it is because the uses of tissue from the living for such purposes 'are ones considered intrinsic to the proper conduct of a patient's treatment... or necessary for the public health of the nation'.[45] As already alluded to, if these activities are in the interests of public health, tissue samples from the deceased will have as much value in this respect (if not more, especially in cases where the aim is to shed light and gather epidemiological data on causes of death). Furthermore, it is difficult to see how any of these activities have a bearing on the treatment of individual patients. The diagnostic benefit of using patients' tissue samples is something quite apart from the uses we are talking about here. If the uses set out in Part 2 of Schedule 1 are to be considered 'intrinsic' to treatment, it can only be in the sense that activities such as audit, education and training, and public health monitoring are of benefit to *all* patients. In which case there is no obvious difference in the value of these activities whether using tissue from the living or the deceased.

3.1.2   Problematic Exemptions

Further difficulties arise because, within the activities set out in Part 1 of the Schedule, there are various exemptions which have the potential to impact negatively on the interests which persons might have in controlling the uses of their separated biomaterials.

First, pursuant of s. 7 of the Act, the consent of *living* individuals is not needed for the storage and use of their tissue if:

> (a) it is ethically approved in accordance with regulations made by the Secretary of State, and (b) it is to be, or is, carried out in circumstances such that the person carrying it out is not in possession, and not likely to come into possession, of information from which the person from whose body the material has come can be identified.[46]

---

[45] Explanatory notes, para. 13. For more on this see K. Liddell and A. Hall, 'Beyond Bristol and Alder Hey: The future regulation of human tissue' (2005) 13 *Medical Law Review* 170, 194–197.

[46] ss 1(7)–(9). See also Human Tissue Act 2004 (Ethical Approval, Exceptions from Licensing and Supply of Information about Transplants Regulations) 2006, SI 2006/1260 and Code of Practice on which states: 'There may be occasions when a clinician involved in research may also have access to a secure database that would permit identification of a sample used in research and the identity of the patient whose material is being used. Providing the research material is not identifiable to the researcher (coded

Price has commented that 'this law as a whole is underpinned by the safeguarding of informational privacy interests, tied to potential harm to the tissue source'.[47] But the interests that the source (and other parties) have in biomaterials encompass much more than just privacy. Individuals may have a range of interests which pertain to controlling the uses and fate of their separated biomaterials. Regardless of whether research gains ethical approval or the tissue samples remain unlinked to identifying data, allowing such an exemption subverts one of the supposed fundamental functions of the consent provisions; that is, respecting the autonomy of individuals. Further, the Secretary for State is empowered to dispense with the consent of living persons in circumstances where that person cannot be traced and 'it is desirable in the interests of another person (including a future person) that the material be used for the purpose of obtaining scientific or medical information about the donor'.[48]

Note the language employed here. The section designates 'the person from whose body the material has come' as *'the donor'*.[49] This is entirely inappropriate. In what sense can living persons who cannot be traced and, therefore, cannot actively engage in the process, reasonably be viewed as donors? I would suggest that they cannot. We ought not to couch activities in such language in an attempt to make them seem more benign and less problematic. The Act then goes on to say that 'there shall for the purposes of this Part be deemed to be consent of the donor to the use of the material'.[50] This, however, is a fiction. No such consent exists. Consent at least implies some form of respect or account for the autonomy of the person from whom the materials came. These exemptions do not even minimally do this, because the person in these circumstances does not exercise any choice or control over the fate of their tissues. The formulation of the exemptions simply does not recognise the interests they might have in this respect.

In saying this, it is not my intention to suggest that using biomaterials without consent cannot be justified. There may be balancing acts to be done; for instance, by taking account of the need for research that would benefit society at large. As noted section 3.1.1, there are many medical and scientific activities which benefit us all. These should be assessed on their own merits.

---

by a laboratory accession number, for example) and the researcher does not seek to link the sample to the patient, it will still be regarded as non-identifiable and the research will be permissible without consent if approved by a recognised REC [research ethics committee]' (para. 64).

[47] Price, *Human Tissue*, p. 178.   [48] ss 7(1)(a)–(c).   [49] s. 7(1)(b) [emphasis added].
[50] s. 7(3).

But, as I also remarked there, if such activities are justifiable with regards to tissue samples from living individuals, then they are also defensible in respect of materials from the deceased. This section of the Act, however, is another example of differential protections being applied. Although the Secretary of State is empowered to make exemptions for materials for the living, this can only be done for materials from the deceased via regulations which enable the High Court to make specific orders.[51] Thus, there is an extra (and most likely unnecessary) layer of protection for the deceased.

The second category of exemption which is potentially concerning is contained in s. 54(7). Here the Act exempts materials created outside the body. As a result, cell lines do not fall within the Act's remit. As put by Kathleen Liddell and Alison Hall, '[t]he implication is that people who donate material which is subsequently used to create cell lines have significantly fewer rights than donors of other tissue.'[52] They point out that such a broad exemption had not been part of the proposals in the run up to the Act, although the idea of exempting anonymised cell lines from the consent provisions had been suggested.[53] The historical background to the Act, and the consequent privileging of the interests of the deceased, rather than those of living persons, may partially explain how this aspect changed during the passage through Parliament.[54] The other factor suggested by Liddell and Hall is that there was 'a disproportionate focus on industry interests'.[55] We can see why this might have been the case given that a significant part of the global biomaterials industry consists of a trade in cell lines. As we saw in the previous chapter, they are used for countless purposes and are of immense commercial value. The HeLa cell line, which is just one such line, exemplifies the extent to which this is true. Although initially created over sixty years ago, the cell line (and its derivatives) has gone on to be traded and used for research all over the world.[56]

---

[51] s. 7(4).   [52] Liddell and Hall, 'Beyond Bristol and Alder Hey', 201.

[53] *Ibid.*, 202. See Department of Health, *Human Bodies, Human Choices*, paras 17.22–17.23 for comments regarding anonymised cell lines.

[54] There are other questionable aspects of this Act, such as the exemption which permits the non-consensual analysis of DNA from tissue samples where the 'who has it is not in possession, and not likely to come into possession, of information from which the individual from whose body the material has come can be identified' [s. 45(2)(b)]. However, due to the constraints of space I do not discuss these here.

[55] Liddell and Hall, 'Beyond Bristol and Alder Hey', 202.

[56] A quick search of the United States Patent and Trademark Office Database using the search term 'HeLa' returns with over 30,000 patents involving research which has utilised the cells in some shape or form. See http://patft.uspto.gov/(accessed 27 November 2017).

The third notable exemption in the 2004 Act is contained in s. 32(9). It exempts, from a prohibition on commercial dealings, 'material which is the subject of property because of an application of human skill'.[57] This is a somewhat strange provision. It is the one and only mention of property in the Act.[58] And in so being, it codifies in statute a questionable common law rule, the consequence of which is that third parties can gain property rights in (and thus possession and control) of biomaterials. This rule, the so-called work/skill exception, will be discussed in-depth in Chapter 3 so I will not detail its wide-ranging difficulties here. I do want to consider, however, why an exception, which is not uncontroversial at common law, was incorporated into this part of the Act and to what ends. Moreover, what are the potential problematic implications of the exception and s. 32 as a whole in the context of the Act?

To begin with, it is striking that this section is limited to 'human material for transplantation'. Neither here nor in the rest of the Act is there a general prohibition on commercial dealings. Thus, materials removed for other purposes can be traded, bought, and sold. It is clear from the title of s. 32, as well as the mainstay of its contents, that the overall concern is with prohibiting trafficking relating to organ donation and transplantation. The prohibition itself is something which is carried over from the Human Organs Transplant Act 1989 (repealed by the 2004 Act), although the work/skill exception is not. This is not surprising since the exception was only developed within the contemporary jurisprudence at common law subsequent to the 1989 Act. There is nothing in the newer Act nor the explanatory notes to suggest why the exception was imported from the common law. One reason, suggested by Liddell and Hall, is that there is a wider range of materials at issue under the 2004 Act than in the 1989 Act.[59] The 2004 Act encompasses not only organs, but cells and tissues for transplantation.[60] Discussion from Hansard reveals that Parliament was not minded to 'interfere with commercial activities that had been lawfully and ethically carried on for many years';[61] that is, the commercial trade in cells and tissues other than whole organs.

---

[57] s. 32(9)(c).
[58] Although we will see in Chapter 9, Section 2.2 that arguably Hansard reveals a proprietary undercurrent to the Act as a whole.
[59] Liddell and Hall, 'Beyond Bristol and Alder Hey', 206.   [60] s. 32(8).
[61] R. Winterton, *Hansard* HC Deb (2004), vol. 423, col. 115. See Liddell and Hall, 'Beyond Bristol and Alder Hey', for a discussion of this and the trafficking section of the then Human Tissue Bill, 205–206.

If we think about this, we can see how fossilising the work/skill exception in statute might prove problematic as technology in the transplantation arena advances; take, for example, what might be termed organ optimisation. These are techniques or technologies which have been developed to improve organ recipient outcomes by optimising the condition of transplanted organs. Accordingly, one might think that they involve work and a not inconsiderable degree of skill on the part of those utilising the technologies or applying the techniques. Consider one such optimisation system: the TransMedics Organ Care System (OCS). According to the company which developed the system, it 'is designed to maintain organs in a warm, functioning state outside of the body to optimize their health and allow continuous clinical evaluation. Hearts beat, lungs breathe, kidneys produce urine, livers produce bile'.[62] The OCS involves placing the organs in a sterile perfusion module, as well as the use of donor blood and specialist perfusion fluids to maintain the organ. Would organs which have been maintained using this or other organ care systems be deemed to have had work or skill applied to them?

The 2004 Act itself gives no guidance on potential answers this question. We, therefore, need to rely on the common law to interpret what counts as the relevant work or skill. This, however, is no easy task. The common law position, as will become apparent in the next chapter, is far from clear regarding the scope and application of the exception.[63] Regardless of whether or not we think that the exception could apply in this specific example, advances in medicine and the biosciences have challenged, and will continue to present challenges for, the regulation of human biomaterials. The preservation of the work/skill exception may turn out to be one of the future hurdles that will need to be surmounted or circumvented. As Laurie and colleagues observe with respect to this section of the Act, the consequence is now that the law 'simultaneously recognises not only that property rights *can* accrue in human material but that these can endure'.[64]

---

[62] See www.transmedics.com/wt/page/organ_care (accessed 27 November 2017). The system for hearts has been dubbed 'Heart in a Box'.

[63] Without pre-empting too much later discussion, it is reasonable to think that the heart in the situation just outlined would not be deemed to be property, or at least not that of those exercising the presumed work or skill. The fact that the purpose of organ optimisation techniques is to prepare organs with the intention of transplanting them into a recipient could be decisive in this situation, though this is not certain.

[64] Laurie, Harmon, and Porter, *Mason and McCall Smith's Law and Medical Ethics* p. 487.

The work/skill exception aside, there are two other issues with s. 32 which bear mentioning in brief at this point. The first is that the section elides the notion of property with that of market alienability.[65] It does this by association, by exempting from the prohibition on commercial dealings materials which have become 'property' through the application of skill. The idea that property rights include the right to income will be dealt with in more detail in Chapter 9, where we will see that there is nothing in the former that necessarily entails the latter. I, therefore, leave it aside for now. There is another potentially troublesome exemption contained in this section. The Act allows that permission can be gained from the HTA to engage in the otherwise prohibited activities. This is interesting and concerning, perhaps in equal measure.

The interesting part is that this potentially opens the door in the future for limited markets in organs; perhaps, for example, an NHS single purchaser (monopsonistic) market such as that suggested by Charles Erin and John Harris.[66] Whether or not this would ever happen would depend on the political and policy climate with regards to organ donation. The concerning part is that it is unlikely that it would be the individual themselves who would ever be granted permission to engage in the activities covered by this section. As we saw in Chapter 1, biomaterials are removed, handled, and processed within an institutional complex. The provisions for exemptions contained in this and other sections of the Act are thus practically operative at an institutional level, be that the NHS, individual hospitals, research institutions (public or private), biotech companies, and so on. Collectively, therefore, the consequence of the provisions contained in this section, as well as those pertaining to cell lines, is that the source can be readily excluded from transactions (commercial or otherwise) involving their biomaterials.

All of this amounts to a problem of internal coherency for the 2004 Act. At least outwardly, in making consent its guiding principle, the 2004 Act is committed to protecting individuals in the use and control of their biomaterials. But a tension arises because the permitted exclusion, by various means, of the person themselves from this use and control runs

---

[65] Price, *Human Tissue*, pp. 246–247.

[66] See C. Erin and J. Harris, 'A monopsonistic market: Or how to buy and sell human organs, tissues, and cells ethically' in I. Robinson (ed.), *Life and Death under High Technology Medicine* (Manchester: Manchester University Press, 1994), pp. 134–153. A similar proposal has been made by Cecile Fabre. See *Whose Body Is It Anyway? Justice and the Integrity of the Person* (Oxford: Oxford University Press, 2006), pp. 149–152. Erin and Harris' arguments do, however, precede this.

contrary to the overarching purpose of the Act. Hence even if consent could do the job asked of it (which I will suggest later that it cannot), any such commitment is weakened by the exemptions contained in the Act.

3.1.3 Specious Consent?[67]

The issues just outlined are compounded by the fact that the 2004 Act does not give a clear account of what the requirement to obtain such consent amounts.[68] Although it goes into detail about *who* can give consent and *for what purposes* under its remit, this is not the same as setting out the nature of that consent. This is rather surprising for a comprehensive piece of legislation which treats as foundational such a concept.[69] Nowhere in the Act, explanatory notes, or Codes of Practice (including the one on consent) is a definition of consent offered. Liddell and Hall questioned this prior to the Codes of Practice being drafted. They commented that the Act neither defined the meaning of consent nor stipulated the steps that ought to be taken in order for consent to be valid.[70] The authors referring to the Hansard debate during the passage of the Bill through Parliament suggested that this would be remedied once the Authority developed guidance on the issue.[71] Similarly, David Price commented that 'the Act identifies only the *locus* and not the *nature* of such consent'.[72] He also noted that guidance was to be issued by the Authority. Even after the draft guidance was available, other commentators expected that the issue of 'what, precisely, is meant by consent' would be clarified.[73] Such clarification has never materialised.

The Authority has produced guidance on consent, but this does not engage with the meaning of consent. Price argued that this 'would not be problematic, if consent had a clear core agreed meaning. But it does not'.[74] Considering that one of the criticisms levied at the 1961 Act was the vagueness of the language employed, it seems to be a conspicuous omission. Sections 53 and 54 define several key terms for the purposes of the Act, but not consent. Any understanding of consent must, therefore, be imputed

[67] This phrase is taken from Price, 'From Cosmos and Damian to Van Velzen', 15.

[68] Price, *Human Tissue*, p. 105.

[69] It might have been assumed that consent was a sufficiently well-delineated and understood concept within the common law, however, as we will see in Section 4, this is not the case.

[70] Liddell and Hall, 'Beyond Bristol and Alder Hey', 189–190.   [71] *Ibid.*, 190–191.

[72] Price, 'The Human Tissue Act', 805.

[73] J. McHale, '"Appropriate consent" and the use of human material for research purposes: The competent adult' (2006) 1 *Clinical Ethics* 195, 196.

[74] Price, *Human Tissue*, p. 105.

from the guidance given in the explanatory notes and the Codes of Practice. The explanatory notes state that the Act 'defines consent by reference to who may give it, and provides for a "nominated representative" who may make decisions about regulated activities after a person's death'.[75] Detailing *who* can consent and *for what purposes* does not by itself elucidate what consent in the law relating to biomaterials is to be taken to mean.[76] Where more detail is given, the relevant Codes of Practice invariably describe good consent *processes* rather than explaining what consent is or the justification for its usage.[77] Unfortunately, there is nothing to indicate the *content* of the concept. Perhaps this omission was deliberate. If it was, it was misguided. For the sake of legal clarity, and given the controversy that led to the legislative change, it ought to have been made clear what it means for the purposes of this Act.

3.2   The Scottish Act: Authorisation

The Human Tissue (Scotland) Act 2006 is in many ways similar to the English Act. It repeals the earlier 1961 Act and its main purpose is to regulate the use of whole deceased bodies, as well as the removal, use, and storage of deceased tissue.[78] Living transplantation also falls within its remit. This Act employs the term 'authorisation' rather than consent.[79] The reason for this distinction is because it was thought that 'the use of the word "consent" as currently legally understood is inappropriate and misleading in the context

---

[75] Explanatory notes of the Human Tissue Act 2004, s. 8. This is repeated in Code of Practice A: Consent, paras 18 and 30.

[76] This is despite the fact that the word consent is mentioned 133 times in the Act itself and 75 times in the explanatory notes.

[77] See, for example, Code of Practice A: Consent.

[78] There are also a number of statutory instruments which operate in Scotland in relation to human tissue: Human Tissue (Removal of Body Parts by an Authorised Person) (Scotland) Regulations 2006 (SSI 2006/327); Human Organ and Tissue Live Transplants (Scotland) Regulations 2006 (SSI 2006/390); Adults with Incapacity (Removal of Regenerative Tissue for Transplantation) (Form of Certificate) (Scotland) (No. 2) Regulations 2006 (SSI 2006/368); Human Tissue (Scotland) Act 2006 (Maintenance of Records and Supply of Information Regarding the Removal and Use of Body Parts) Regulations 2006 (SSI 2006/344); Approval of Research on Organs No Longer Required for Procurator Fiscal Purposes (Specified Persons) (Scotland) Order 2006 (SSI 2006/310); Human Tissue (Specification of Posts) (Scotland) Order 2006 (SSI 2006/309); Anatomy (Specified Persons and Museums for Public Display) (Scotland) Order 2006 (SSI 2006/328); Anatomy (Scotland) Regulations 2006 (SSI 2006/334); and Human Tissue (Scotland) Act 2006 (Anatomy Act 1984 Transitional Provisions) Order 2006 (SSI 2006/340).

[79] s. 3.

of post-mortem examination and the removal, retention and use of organs/ tissue'.[80] Authorisation in the 2006 Act means the authorisation of the person themselves or their nearest relative,[81] and, like the English Act, these are listed in a hierarchy (spouse or civil partner, partner, parent, child or step-child, half-brother or sister, grandparent, grandchild, uncle or aunt, cousin, nephew or niece, and friend of longstanding).[82]

The Act mandates that authorisation is required for materials removed from deceased bodies for the purposes of transplantation, research, education or training, and audit.[83] Authorisation is also required for post-mortems.[84] Tissue samples removed in the course of these become part of the deceased's medical record and can be used for research, education and training, and audit.[85] Post-mortems conducted within the jurisdiction of the procurator fiscal (similar to coroner in England and Wales) do not fall under the 2006 Act. There is no right of objection to these and authorisation is not needed. Samples removed in the course of a procurator fiscal's post-mortem also become part of the medical record once they are no longer required.[86] These samples may then 'be used for the purposes of – (i) providing information about or confirming the cause of death; (ii) investigating the effect and efficacy of any medical or surgical intervention carried out on the person; (iii) obtaining information which may be relevant to the health of any other person (including a future person); [and] (iv) audit'.[87] If the samples are to be used for education, training, or research, then explicit authorisation must be obtained.[88] Unlike its counterpart south of the border, the Scottish Act amends rather than repeals the Anatomy Act 1984. The effect, however, is the same: only persons themselves may authorise the use of their body for either anatomical examination or public display. This must be done in writing and be witnessed.[89]

For the purposes of the Act, authorisation generally covers both adults and children.[90] This is important in understanding the genesis of this Act. First, as we saw earlier, a significant driver of legislative change was not simply the retention of organs, but the retention of children's organs. Second, and relatedly, in the drafting of the Scottish Act, this had considerable impact on the terminology of authorisation that was adopted. In this respect, Sheila McLean and colleagues, have stated that the 'term was chosen because, after consideration of both the evidence and the law, it was felt that

---

[80] Independent Review Group, *Final Report*, para. 3.   [81] ss 6, 7, 29, and 30.   [82] s. 50.
[83] s. 3.   [84] ss 24 and 26.   [85] s. 28(3).   [86] s. 38.   [87] s. 39(a).   [88] s. 39(b).
[89] See generally Part 5 of the 2006 Act, ss. 53(5) and 53(9).
[90] Although the specific citations above are to the adult provisions.

the traditional concept of consent was inappropriate in the case of babies and young children and might be unduly burdensome for relatives'.[91] The legal consent requirement in relation to children hinges on a best interests assessment and this standard was deemed to be inapplicable regarding post-mortems. Furthermore, according to the authors, the adoption of 'authorisation' has the added benefit of encompassing those situations where parents of deceased children did not want to be informed of the details of the post-mortem; something which could be seen as being in contradistinction to the demands of consent.[92] McLean was the Chair of the Scottish Independent Review Group which recommended the implementation of the requirement for authorisation.[93] Yet, like appropriate consent in the English Act, nowhere in the 2006 Act, nor its accompanying explanatory notes, is the term defined. With the English and Scottish Acts adopting two seemingly different guiding principles, and given that neither Act adequately defines these, we are prompted to ask what the difference is between them.

3.3   Is There a Relevant Difference?

Consent, as often presented in much of the literature, suggests something like 'agreement, permission, authorization'.[94] Ruth Faden and Tom Beauchamp note that in this sense consent is 'a specific kind of autonomous choice (or action), an autonomous authorization by patients or subjects'.[95] They go on to say that this 'suggests that a patient or subject does more than express agreement with, or acquiesce in, yield to, or comply with an arrangement or proposal. He or she actively *authorizes* the proposal in the act of consent'.[96] Consent gives another 'both permission to proceed and the *responsibility* for proceeding' in relation to certain acts;[97] for example, a particular medical treatment. Proceeding without this authorisation (without consent) of the person towards whom the action is directed is viewed as morally (and potentially legally) wrong. As Mason and Laurie point out, in the health care setting consent is seen as 'the key principle that serves to legitimise dealings between health care

---

[91]   S.A.M. McLean, A.V. Campbell, K. Gutridge, and H. Harper, 'Human tissue legislation and medical practice: A benefit or a burden?' (2006) 8 *Medical Law International* 1, 15.
[92]   *Ibid.*   [93]   Independent Review Group, *Final Report*, p. 16.
[94]   N. Manson, 'Consent and informed consent' in R.E. Ashcroft *et al.* (eds), *Principles of Health Care Ethics* (Chichester: John Wiley and Sons, 2007), pp. 297–303, p. 298 [emphasis omitted].
[95]   R. Faden and T. Beauchamp, *A History and Theory of Informed Consent* (Oxford: Oxford University Press, 1986), p. 277.
[96]   *Ibid.*, p. 278.   [97]   *Ibid.*, p. 280 [emphasis added].

professionals or researchers and patients or research subjects'.[98] In their examination of consent, Faden and Beauchamp also discuss consent in the sense of 'legally or institutionally effective authorization'.[99] Here, it is not the act of consent itself which is the focus, but the procedures and rules that are in place for obtaining the consent. One sense of consent centres on the person giving consent and the other on the person or institution obtaining it. This is essentially the distinction between what we might call *substantive* consent and *procedural* consent. As such, it is obvious to note that obtaining consent in the procedural sense does not ensure that substantive consent has been given. For instance, a hospital's procedure prior to surgery might be that all patients are required to sign a consent form acknowledging that they understand the surgery and its consequent risks. Having a formal procedure in place, nevertheless, does not ensure that the patient has actually attained this understanding. Neither does it ensure that they have voluntarily consented nor that they are free of coercion or undue influence. Likewise, in the realm of tissue donation, for example, a person could authorise the use of their tissue and thus meet the formal consent requirements, but doing so does not entail that anything more substantive has been achieved.

In adopting different terminology, the opportunity could have been taken with the Scottish Act to emphasise the importance of substantive consent; that is, consent as an active authorisation which is something more than mere acquiescence. Indeed, McLean and colleagues note that 'by and large professionals on both sides of the border preferred the concept of authorisation, seeing it as being stronger than that of consent'.[100] But stronger in what sense? It cannot be stronger conceptually since, by McLean's own explanation, which we saw in Section 3.2, part of the purpose of adopting authorisation in Scotland was that it was seen as less demanding than consent; in particular that the same standards of

---

[98] Mason and Laurie, 'Consent or property?', 711.

[99] Faden and Beauchamp, *A History and Theory of Informed Consent*, p. 284. The term 'informed consent' has achieved much greater penetration into legal language in the United States than in England. In English law it has, in the past, been more usual to simply talk about 'consent', although 'informed consent' has in recent times achieved more authority in case law (see, for example, *Chester* v. *Afshar* [2005] 1 AC 134 at [57] per Lord Hope and [14] per Lord Steyn). Brazier has pointed out, 'it acts as useful shorthand to refer to the multi-faceted debate of who ultimately takes the decision on an individual's medical treatment, and how much information concerning that treatment doctors should give to their patients' ('Patient autonomy and consent to treatment: The role of the law?' (1987) 7 Legal Studies 169, 172).

[100] McLean *et al.*, 'Human tissue legislation', 16.

information giving (and thus presumably of understanding that information) do not need to be met. This, therefore, suggests that the operational conception of authorisation implicit in the final wording and implementation of the Act is not as rich as, say, Faden and Beauchamp's one set out above. It may be that this looser notion of authorisation is more practicable if it permits individuals to consent to particular courses of action without imposing an unduly burdensome process. There may even be situations where this is rationally preferred by patients, their families, and health care professionals. Yet the manner in which appropriate consent and authorisation are approached within official documents suggests that at a regulatory level this difference has not materialised.

Shortly after both Acts were enacted, McLean and colleagues said, 'it will be interesting to see whether or not there is a real, as opposed to a perceived, difference between "consent" and "authorisation"'.[101] As it currently stands there is no discernible difference between consent and authorisation to be found. In their guidance for NHS Scotland, the Scottish Executive noted that '[a]uthorisation equates to the principle of "consent" on which the Human Tissue Act 2004 is based. The equivalence of the 2 principles is an essential part of the continuation of the arrangements for sharing organs and tissue across the UK'.[102] Although the HTA Codes of Practice do not cover Scotland,[103] an earlier iteration of the Code of Practice on consent explicitly said, '[w]hile provisions of the HT (Scotland) Act are based on authorisation rather than consent, these are essentially both expressions of the same principle.'[104] Consent and authorisation are thus treated together, with little attempt to deal with them as distinct concepts. Whether or not there is a difference on the ground is a separate question and one for which empirical evidence would be needed in order to be answered. But if there is the conceptual parity (as far as law and policy considerations are concerned) ascribed by the HTA and Scottish Executive, this raises a question about why separate terms were employed in the Acts. Price observed that the distinction between the terms with regards to the Acts may just 'be a matter of semantic inference. . . rather than any formal terminological difference'.[105] Be that as

---

[101] *Ibid.*
[102] Scottish Executive Health Department, 'Human Tissue (Scotland Act) 2006: A Guide to Its Implications for NHS Scotland' (2006), available at: www.sehd.scot.nhs.uk/mels/HDL2006_46.pdf (accessed 27 November 2017).
[103] Code of Practice A: Consent, Annex A, para. 9.
[104] Code of Practice 1: Consent (July 2014), para. 19.   [105] Price, *Human Tissue*, p. 120.

it may, for the sake of clarity in an already contested area, it would have been better for the same term to be utilised on a UK-wide basis.

Given the elision of consent and authorisation by the Scottish Executive (and HTA's earlier Code of Practice), I am going to use the term consent as a catch-all in the book from this point onwards.

4 Consent: Problems of Principle

Those opposed to granting property rights over the human body and its parts and products might argue that consent provisions of both Human Tissue Acts do much of the necessary work in protecting persons' interests. As Liddell has pointed out in relation to the 2004 Act, '[c]onsent was lauded by policymakers as *the* mechanism for protecting individuals. Its importance was stressed repeatedly to the exclusion of other issues. Moreover, policymakers would not speak of its limitations or problems.'[106] As it stands, however, the Acts cannot take account of the multitude of interests that persons may have in controlling the uses of their biomaterials. This is because, as we have already begun to see, there are problems both at the level of principle and application with relying solely on consent.

The principal problem is self-evident and flows directly from the provisions of the two Human Tissue Acts; namely, the two pieces of legislation go to greater lengths to protect our interests in the use of our bodies and biomaterials once deceased than they do while we are alive. This is unambiguous as far as the Scottish Act is concerned; it almost exclusively governs the deceased (save for living transplantation). In relation to the English Act, the numerous exemptions it contains undermine the commitment to consent which it supposedly embodies. The consequence of this is that, once initial common law consent has been given for the removal of biomaterials from the living, they are left in an

---

[106] K. Liddell, 'Beyond a rebarbative commitment to consent' in by O. Corrigan *et al.* (eds), *The Limits of Consent: A Socio-Ethical Approach to Human Subject Research in Medicine* (Oxford: Oxford University Press, 2009), pp. 79–98, p. 95. Preceding the draft of the Human Tissue Bill and the subsequent passage of the 2004 Act, this was certainly the tone in the Parliamentary debate. See, for instance, HC Deb (2000–2001), vol. 362, col. 178. This focus has to be understood, as I argued in Section 2, against the historical background of the organ retention scandal. See also Valerie M. Sheach Leith's analysis in which she notes the prevalence of the informed consent discourse. Through documentary analysis she demonstrates that there are a range of issues and interests at play which go beyond consent ('Consent and nothing but consent? The organ retention scandal' (2007) 29 *Sociology of Health and Illness* 1023).

uncertain legal and regulatory space with regards to future uses. This seems unsatisfactory both from the point of view of the source of those biomaterials and third parties who may come into possession of these. As I have noted with Imogen Goold elsewhere:

> [I]t is notable that few remedies are available to the person whose biomaterials are misused or misappropriated beyond the initial consent stage. While non-consensual use per se is captured by the 2004 Act, it is silent on who has the right to possess samples, who can control their uses and to what extent, and what ought to happen downstream if transfers are undertaken (for example, to other institutions). There are also no clear protections for researchers whose research samples are damaged or taken, or for holders of biomaterials outside the research or certain therapeutic areas.[107]

While an appreciation of the prior legislative failure and organ retention scandals can give us an understanding of why consent and authorisation are the supposed guiding principles of the Acts, it remains unclear what the requirement to obtain such consent or authorisation actually amounts to. Campbell and colleagues note, 'each legislative provision firmly espouses the need for agreement to be reached before tissue and/or organs are removed, retained or used'.[108] This is all well and good, but agreement to what and for what purposes? As we have seen, the two pieces of human tissue legislation fail to define their central terms. Without specific guidance on the meaning of consent for the purposes of human tissue legislation, we are left to interpret their (legal) essence from existing common law. In this respect, the legislation does not function in a vacuum, but 'operates against the backdrop of the general law'.[109] But while cases pertaining to consent are plentiful in medical law, they do not offer much assistance in elucidating the nature and basis of consent. As we are about to see, there is in essence a lack of principled foundations. This can lead to problems when we attempt to resolve conflicts over biomaterials using consent as the touchstone for protecting source interests.

4.1   The Basis of Consent?

On the whole, philosophical accounts of the role, purpose, and justification of consent emphasise the autonomy of persons as the key

---

[107] Goold and Quigley, 'Human biomaterials', p. 246.
[108] A.V. Campbell, S.A.M. McLean, K. Gutridge, and H. Harper, 'Human tissue legislation: Listening to the professionals' (2008) 34 *Journal of Medical Ethics* 104, 104.
[109] Price, *Human Tissue*, p. 105.

underlying interest.[110] There is a plausible argument to be made that this is also how the law views things.[111] Nevertheless, even if it does, it is far from clear what kind of autonomy or whose autonomy is being protected. At a very general level we can point to self-determination as central to the approach of the common law vis-à-vis persons and their bodies. As Laurie and colleagues explain, '[b]ased on the strong moral conviction that everyone has the right to self-determination with regards to his or her body, the common law has long recognised the principle that every person has the right to have his or her bodily integrity protected against invasion by others.'[112] This is the core of the law (criminal and tort) relating to assault and battery which proscribes non-consensual touchings and gives legal redress to persons where bodily boundaries are crossed.[113] The law in this area applies to health care professionals much as it does to the average person on the street; non-consensual treatments will be considered a battery in the eyes of the law (and potentially criminal assault depending on the harm inflicted).[114] An individual's putative right to self-determination extends to refusals of treatment, even where such treatment might be life-saving. Famously, Lord Donaldson in *Re T* said that individuals with capacity have an

> absolute right to choose whether to consent to medical treatment, to refuse it or to choose one rather than another of the treatments being offered. . . This right of choice is not limited to decisions which others

[110] See, for example, Faden and Beauchamp, *A History and Theory of Informed Consent*; N. Manson and O. O' Neill, *Rethinking Informed Consent in Bioethics* (Cambridge: Cambridge University Press, 2007); O. O' Neill, *Autonomy and Trust in Bioethics* (Cambridge: Cambridge University Press, 2002).

[111] Although note Lord Donaldson's comment about consent being 'the legal "flak jacket" which protects the doctor from claims by the litigious' (*Re W (a minor) (medical treatment)* [1992] 4 All ER 627 at 635). Whilst the comment was made in the context of a case involving a minor, Margaret Brazier and José Miola have commented that the issue was who could provide the flak jacket. In the case of 'a mentally competent adult, only the patient can' ('Bye-bye Bolam: A medical litigation revolution?' (2000) 8 *Medical Law Review* 85, 94).

[112] Laurie, Harmon, and Porter, *Mason and McCall Smith's Law and Medical Ethics*, pp. 67–68.

[113] In tort, assault and trespass, along with false imprisonment, are sometimes referred to as trespass to the person.

[114] The defence of necessity can sometimes be invoked in emergency situations. See Brazier and Cave, *Medicine, Patients, and the Law*, pp. 126–128. For a discussion of assault and battery (tort and crime) in the medical context see Brazier and Ost, *Bioethics, Medicine and the Criminal Law*, pp. 40–52.

might regard as sensible. It exists notwithstanding that the reasons for making the choice are irrational, unknown or even non-existent.[115]

He went on to note that '[t]he patient's interest consists of his right to self-determination – his right to live his own life how he wishes. . . It is well established that in the ultimate the right of the individual is paramount.'[116] Lady Justice Butler-Sloss, in the same case, outlined her agreement with the decision in the Canadian case of *Malette* v. *Shulman*, quoting the following: 'The right to determine what shall be done with one's own body is a fundamental right in our society. The concepts inherent in this right are the bedrock upon which the principles of self-determination and individual autonomy are based.'[117] This position endorsed in *Re T* has received positive treatment in subsequent cases.[118] Thus, autonomy, at least qua self-determination, seems to play a central role in the law of consent.

It is notable that Lord Donaldson and Lady Justice Butler-Sloss did not speak of autonomy, but of self-determination. As John Coggon points out, direct references to 'autonomy' in the relevant case law are not common. Instead what we find are 'references to (at least what are thought to be) synonyms: "self-determination" or the right to govern bodily integrity, or the like'.[119] There are some exceptions to this. For instance, in *Chester* v. *Afshar*, Lord Steyn briefly discusses autonomy and dignity as conceptualised by Ronald Dworkin.[120] Generally, however, rather than being explicit, different understandings of autonomy have to be read into the various cases.[121] Later cases, insofar as they endorse the

---

[115] *Re T (adult: refusal of medical treatment)* [1992] 4 All ER 649 at 652–653.

[116] *Ibid.* at 661.   [117] (1990) 72 OR (2d) 417 at 432.

[118] See, for example, *Re C (adult: refusal of medical treatment)* [1994] 1 All ER 819 and *Re B (adult: refusal of medical treatment)* [2002] 2 All ER 449.

[119] J. Coggon, 'Varied and principled understandings of autonomy in English law: Justifiable inconsistency or blinkered moralism?' (2007) 15 *Health Care Analysis* 235, 236.

[120] *Chester* v. *Afshar* at [18]. See also the comment in *Re S (hospital patient: court's jurisdiction)* [1995] 3 All ER 290: 'The law respects the right of adults of sound mind to physical autonomy. Generally speaking, no one is entitled to touch, examine or operate upon such persons without their consent, express or implied. It is up to such persons to give or withhold consent as they wish, for reasons good or bad' at 302). See also *Re B (adult: refusal of medical treatment)* [2002] 2 All ER 449 where the discussion centres on autonomy rather than self-determination.

[121] Coggon identifies three understandings present in the case law: '(1) *Ideal desire autonomy* – Leads to an action decided upon because it reflects what a person should want, measured by reference to some purportedly universal or objective standard of values. (2) *Best desire autonomy* – Leads to an action decided upon because it reflects a person's overall desire given his own values, even if this runs contrary to his immediate desire. (3) *Current desire autonomy* – Leads to an action decided upon because it reflects a person's

position in *Re T* have not substantively added to our understanding of the autonomy (as the potential principled basis for consent) within the law. This may simply be a function of the facts of the particular cases that have come before the courts, which have tended to focus on issues such as information provision and legal competence. The majority of relevant cases, before and after, have elaborated on the scope and boundaries of consent, or the conditions required for consent to be legally valid, rather than its underpinnings.[122] They established and reaffirmed, for example, that signing a consent form and going through the procedural motions is not enough for a competent individual's consent to be considered valid. Patients must be 'informed in broad terms of the nature of the procedure'.[123] They must not be deceived as to the nature of the medical procedure[124] and relevant information, which has a bearing upon their proper understanding of the procedure, must be given to them.[125]

Even the recent Supreme Court decision in *Montgomery* v. *Lanarkshire Health Board* does not add in substantive terms to our understanding of the basis of consent. It is reiterated, in particular in Lady Hale's comments, that autonomy is important. She says: 'It is now well recognised that the interest which the law of negligence protects is a person's interest in their own physical and psychiatric integrity, an important feature of which is their autonomy, their freedom to decide what shall and shall not be done with their body'.[126] However, this is not elaborated on. The

---

immediate inclinations, i.e. what he thinks he wants in a given moment without further reflection' ('Varied and principled understandings', 240).

[122] For a discussion of some of these cases see J. Coggon and J. Miola, 'Autonomy, liberty, and medical decision-making' (2011) 70 *Cambridge Law Journal* 523.

[123] *Chatterton* v. *Gerson* [1981] QB 432, 443. In this case, Bristow J. maintained that, if a doctor fails to explain the nature of the medical treatment, this invalidates any consent given and can give rise to an action in trespass. However, on the particular facts of this case, it was found that the patient had been informed 'as to the general nature' of the treatment (at 442–443). See also Department of Health, *Reference Guide to Consent for Examination or Treatment*, 2nd edn (Crown Copyright, 2009), pp. 16–17.

[124] See, for example, *Potts* v. *North West Regional Health Authority* (1983) *The Guardian*, 23 July and *Appleton* v. *Garrett* (1995) 34 BMLR 23.

[125] See, for example, *Sidaway* v. *Bethlem Royal Hospital Governors and Others* [1985] 1 All ER 635; *Pearce* v. *United Bristol Healthcare NHS Trust* (1999) 48 BMLR 118; *Chester* v. *Afshar* [2005] 1 AC 134; and *Montgomery* v. *Lanarkshire Health Board* [2015] UKSC 11. Although note there has been a shift over time in these cases from a doctor-orientated, professional standard test to a more patient-orientated test regarding what counts as sufficient and relevant information (Brazier and Cave, *Medicine, Patients, and the Law*, pp. 138–144).

[126] *Montgomery* v. *Lanarkshire* at [108]. For commentaries on the case see A.M. Farrell and M. Brazier, 'Not so new directions in the law of consent? Examining *Montgomery v*

consequence is that we are left to infer potential principled bases from a set of narrow common law rules.

In this respect, we can see that the HTA's Code of Practice on Consent reflects the general common law position, stating that '[f]or consent to be valid it must be given voluntarily, by an appropriately informed person who has the capacity to agree to the activity in question.'[127] It goes on to add that the 'person should understand what the activity involves, any reasonable or variant treatment and, where appropriate, what the material risks are'.[128] The addition of the word 'material' is an update from previous versions of the Code and reflects the position set out in *Montgomery*, something which the HTA interpret as representing a reasonable patient standard:

> The test of materiality is 'whether, in the circumstances of the particular case, a reasonable person in the patient's position would be likely to attach significance to the risk, or the doctor is or should reasonably be aware that the particular patient would be likely to attach a significance to it'.[129]

Thus, in the main, well-established common law stipulations are reproduced with respect to the removal, storage, and use of biomaterials. Given this, it is questionable to what extent, as Brazier and Cave put it, 'the legal rules truly represent the ethical value of autonomy'.[130]

4.2   Against Free-standing Consent

The state of the common law with respect to consent has led, in some quarters, to a sort of autonomy scepticism. By this I do not mean that commentators do not think that autonomy is important; in general they do. But there is scepticism about the relationship between autonomy and consent. There is doubt about whether the application (and effect) of consent-related legal rules can protect autonomy in any substantive sense. McLean thinks not. She contends that 'the legal doctrine of consent lacks credibility in a number of ways as a protector of autonomy'[131] and that the law of consent is 'incapable of elucidating

Lanarkshire Health Board' (2016) 42 *Journal of Medical Ethics* 85, and J. Montgomery and E. Montgomery, 'Montgomery on informed consent – An inexpert decision? (2016) 42 *Journal of Medical Ethics* 89.
[127] Code of Practice A: Consent, para. 40.   [128] *Ibid.*   [129] *Ibid.*
[130] Brazier and Cave, *Medicine, Patients, and the Law*, p. 150.
[131] S.A.M. McLean, *Autonomy, Consent, and the Law* (London: Routledge-Cavendish, 2010), p. 86.

and defending the coherent concept of autonomy that theorists (and patients) would want to see'.[132] Insofar as the law seems to be concerned with often narrow doctrinal rules, we might think this to be accurate. Part of the disquiet here revolves around the reduction of autonomy to mere procedural aspects of the consent process. There is concern on this front, not just with the law's treatment of consent, but with the manner in which consent and consent processes are conceived and conducted within health care practice.

Onora O' Neill argues that the measures used 'for securing or respecting autonomy in medical contexts are in fact generally no more than informed consent requirements'.[133] While Laurie maintains that 'the conflation of autonomy with consent robs the former of much of its meaning and strips it of much of its ethical credibility'.[134] Obtaining consent from patients or research subjects may be seen as upholding autonomy, but, as any ethicist (or even lawyer) would point out, mere procedure cannot safeguard autonomy in any meaningful manner. The law in focusing on essentially procedural aspects, such as information and competence, may unwittingly be encouraging an impoverished process. It is, as Price remarked,

> principally concerned with the *adequacy* of consent in any particular context, as opposed to the meaning of consent. What is required either way is something which entitles a person to assume that the legal relationship between them has changed and justifies their action, i.e. is transformative.[135]

Adequacy in this sense is undoubtedly important, but without probing the question of meaning, without a sufficient and satisfactory foundation to which to anchor consent, we encounter a problem.

When consent is detached from any principled foundations, it can end up operating as a principle in and of itself. If we have no clear idea of the relevant interests which are at stake, then it ends up being treated 'as an independent value'[136] and attributed unwarranted status and normative force. Roger Brownsword argues that we must guard against overvaluing consent in

---

[132] *Ibid.*, p. 228.   [133] O' Neill, *Autonomy and Trust*, p. 37.

[134] G.T. Laurie, *Genetic Privacy: A Challenge to Medico-Legal Norms* (Cambridge: Cambridge University Press, 2002), p. 184.

[135] Price, *Human Tissue*, p. 109. The transformative nature of consent and its relationship to property rights will be discussed in Chapter 9.

[136] R. Brownsword, 'The cult of consent: Fixation and fallacy' (2004) 15 *King's College Law Journal* 223, 224.

such a manner; against moving from a *culture* of consent to a *cult* of consent and thus becoming fixated with it.[137] By fixated he means that 'consent is no longer seen as an element of a larger theory of ethical or legal justification; rather, consent becomes its own free-standing justificatory standard'.[138] If consent is treated in this manner then its role in ethical, and legal, decision-making is called into question since it can prove both too much and too little. There becomes a danger that 'where there is no consent, there must be a wrong (that we do wrong if we act without consent); and, conversely, that where there is consent, there can be no wrong (that we do right if we obtain consent)'.[139] When this happens consent is treated as both a *necessary* and *sufficient* justification for action.[140] Consent itself achieves equivalence with the justification for action and risks being reduced to mere procedure. This increases the likelihood that individuals will lack understanding about the nature of what they are consenting to or that they have been coerced or deceived in some way.

Consent as embodied in the Human Tissue Acts is free-standing to the extent that it is not adequately tied to principled foundations. Divorced from solid philosophical underpinnings, it is difficult to identify the value and use of consent and consent processes contained therein. In order to assess properly the morality of certain actions we must understand the reasons and justifications which motivate them. As such, when this is set against a background in which consent lacks an established and settled meaning and is contested (legally and philosophically), the Acts may fail to be suitably action-guiding for those professionals who must comply with their provisions. Free-standing consent is also an impoverished way of protecting the interests that individuals might have in the uses of their biomaterials. This is because consent itself is a binary transaction. As Laurie and colleagues note, a 'consent model disempowers individuals to the extent that the single "right" that it gives is the right to refuse'.[141]

Individuals can give their consent here and now, but without something more it has nothing to say about any downstream interests and uses of their biomaterials. The practical inadequacy of free-standing

[137] For an account of this obsession and some of the pitfalls of attributing such a central status to consent see Brownsword, *ibid.*
[138] *Ibid.*, 226 [emphasis omitted].   [139] *Ibid.*
[140] O. O' Neill, 'Some limits of informed consent' (2003) 29 *Journal of Medical Ethics* 4, 5.
[141] Laurie, Harmon, and Porter, *Mason and McCall Smith's Law and Medical Ethics*, pp. 496–97. See also Price, *Human Tissue*, p. 232.

consent will be illustrated in the next chapter by a number of cases from other jurisdictions. In *Moore*, for example, it is presumed that informed consent and fiduciary duty are enough to protect patient interests.[142] We will see, however, that in the face of advancing biotechnology and powerful third party interests, more is needed.

5 Concluding Remarks: Biomaterials and Consent

The change in the uses and value of biomaterials that has resulted from advances in biotechnology has brought about challenges that cannot be addressed by human tissue legislation or by consent alone. We need to avoid becoming fixated on stand-alone consent procedures, on consent merely for consent's sake. Laurie and colleagues put it well when they say that 'we should not be distracted from the property debate by the illusion that consent is the sole, or optimal, ethico-legal solution to dilemmas thrown up by modern medicine'.[143] As such, when we are thinking about consent in a particular context, in essence, we need to ask: *consent to what and to what ends?* In this respect, we need to be to be clear, legally and morally, that consent is not an end in itself. We need to recognise the reasons underpinning particular consent processes.

Brazier refers to consent as shorthand, saying that 'it acts as useful shorthand to refer to the multi-faceted debate of who ultimately takes the decision on an individual's medical treatment, and how much information concerning that treatment doctors should give to their patients'.[144] This is a useful way of looking at it because, while the giving of consent can be seen as a particular kind of autonomous action, consent is really just a means to a greater end; that end being respect for and giving effect to the autonomy of persons. In this way, consent is merely a *mode* by which we express some underlying value or interest. By respecting autonomous decision-making via consent we are signalling that we recognise that persons are at liberty to control themselves and their lives, and that they have rights of non-interference against others in the exercise of that control. The extent to which the law recognises these rights of control, or can be said to give substance to autonomy through consent provisions, is thus an important question.

---

[142] *Moore*, Supreme Court at 139–140
[143] Laurie, Harmon, and Porter, *Mason and McCall Smith's Law and Medical Ethics*, p. 496.
[144] Brazier, 'Patient autonomy', 172.

In Chapter 9 I argue that, in relation to separated biomaterials, any consent requirements are (logically and morally) presupposed and justified by the existence of property rights over the materials in question. The proper function of consent, in this sphere, is to authorise certain uses within the scope of the legitimate possessor's property rights over those materials. There is much ground to cover before we get to that, however. To begin, over the course of the next two chapters let us consider how the law currently deals with the issue of property rights in separated biomaterials.

3

Property in the Body?

1 Introduction

Insofar as the law of England and Wales, and indeed other common law jurisdictions, is concerned, traditionally the human body was considered be a *res nullius*; that is, a thing belonging to no one. This 'no property' rule initially arose in relation to the deceased body, but over time its scope expanded, with a number of contemporary cases accepting it as the baseline position regarding separated biomaterials from the deceased (and arguably from the living too). In this chapter and the next we will see that, although we might not yet deem the rule to be entirely dead, its death knell has been tolled. The development of the case law in the area makes clear that human biomaterials can fall within the ambit property, albeit for diverse legal purposes. In this respect, the principal (and possibly only) unifying feature of cases which recognise property rights in biomaterials is that in them property is used 'as a means to other legal ends'.[1] That is to say, property rights in biomaterials are not recognised for their own sake or because the biomaterials are ordinarily viewed as chattels (personal property), but because there is something else at stake which can be achieved via their status as objects of property. It is the challenges and conflicts which have arisen in relation to biomaterials that have made utilising a property framework a necessity on occasion. This is something which we will see runs through both older and more recent cases, and which connects cases from different jurisdictions. Relevant rulings include those 'to facilitate prosecutions in theft, to establish legitimate entitlements to possess tissue samples for research and other ends, as a means to permitting remedial action and compensation for damage done, and, most recently, in order to permit possession of sperm for the purposes of *in-vitro* fertilisation'.[2]

In order for us to appreciate the transformation in legal thinking which has occurred of late, in this chapter and the following one, I

[1] Laurie, Harmon, and Porter, *Mason and McCall Smith's Law and Medical Ethics*, p. 490.
[2] Quigley, 'Property in human biomaterials', 661.

outline and begin to explore the development of the law specifically in relation to the question of property in the body and biomaterials. It will become apparent throughout these chapters that the jurisprudence has developed in a piecemeal and slightly arbitrary fashion. The consequence of this is that there are few (if any) coherent property principles which can be identified in relation to human biomaterials. Further, we will see that there are difficulties with the potential philosophical bases for the creation of property rights in biomaterials, including with old Roman (and Scots) law doctrines which some have suggested could be adapted to this end.

2 'No Property' and Creating Exceptions

The questionable and uncertain origins of the 'no property' rule have been well-documented elsewhere,[3] and so in this section I set out its history in fairly brief terms. My purpose is to begin to illustrate a theme which continues from the older cases through to the contemporary ones; that is, when a determination of no property is made, certain (potentially useful) legal avenues are foreclosed.[4]

2.1 Origins and Early Difficulties

The earliest case occasionally associated with the dictum that there is 'no property in a corpse' is the *Haynes' Case*. In this case the defendant, William Haynes, had dug from their graves the bodies of four corpses, removed the winding sheets (shrouds) within which they were wrapped, and re-buried them. He was convicted of one count of petty larceny and three of felonious taking.[5] The judgment in the case, given in 1614, was that 'the property of the sheets remain in the owners... when the dead body was wrapped therewith; for the dead body is not capable of it'.[6] The most likely interpretation of this is that the Court was stating that the corpse could not *own* property, rather than it could

---

[3] See P. Matthews, 'The man of property' (1995) 3 *Medical Law Review* 251 and 'Whose body? People as property' (1983) 36 *Current Legal Problems* 193; Mason and Laurie, 'Consent or Property?' 713–715; P.D.G. Skegg, 'Human corpses, medical specimens and the law of property' (1976) 4 *Anglo-American Law Review* 412; and A. Grubb, '"I, me, mine": Bodies, parts and property' (1998) 3 *Medical Law International* 299.

[4] For a more in-depth treatment of this aspect see Goold and Quigley, 'Human biomaterials', pp. 237–244.

[5] *Haynes' Case* (1614) 12 Co Rep 113, 77 ER 1389.   [6] *Ibid.*

not *be* property.[7] That this is correct is borne out by the later account of the case given by Sir Edward Coke who says 'for the dead body is not capable of any property, and the property of the sheets must be in some body'.[8] As such, this decision cannot be seen as the explicit basis for later statements (or misstatements) of no property.

Another early case, which is sometimes mentioned in the literature, is *Dr Handyside's* (or *Handasyde's*) case. The case supposedly involved an action in trover (that is, for the interference with personal property) for the bodies of conjoined twins. It was reported that 'the action would not lie, as no person had any property in corpses'.[9] However, we cannot be sure of either the details or the significance of this case since, as Peter Skegg comments, '[i]t was first noted early in the nineteenth century, by East, who could not have had any personal knowledge of the case.'[10] It is certainly possible, maybe even probable, that the idea of there being no property in the corpse was in the general legal consciousness of the time, yet before the eighteenth century there is little written evidence of this.

From the late eighteenth to the late nineteenth centuries a number of cases concerning the burial or disinterment of deceased bodies mention or rely on the supposed rule. For example, explicit reference to it can be found in *R* v. *Sharpe*,[11] a case in which the accused dug up the body of his

---

[7] For discussions of this, see W.F. Kuzenski, 'Property in dead bodies' (1924) 9 *Marquette Law Review* 17, 18; T.M.K. Chattin, 'Property in dead bodies' (1969) 71 *West Virginia Law Review* 377, 377–378; and Mason and Laurie 'Consent or property?', 714.

[8] E. Coke, *The Third Part of the Institutes of the Laws of England: Concerning High Treason, and other Pleas of the Crown, and Criminal Causes*, 4th edn (London, 1669), p. 110. Occasionally another passage from Coke (or part of the passage) is quoted incorrectly as evidence of the claim that there was deemed to be no property in a corpse at this time: 'It is to be observed that in every sepulchre, that hath a monument, two things are to be considered, viz. the monument, and the sepulture or burial of the dead; the burial of the cadaver (that is *caro data vermibus* [flesh to worms]) is *nullius in bonis* [no one's property], and belongs to ecclesiastical cognizance; but as to the monument, action is given at the common law for defacing thereof' (p. 203). Although the phrase '*nullis in bonis*' has been used in support of the contention that there is no property in a corpse, his comments are unlikely have been intended in this manner. Instead, the purpose was to draw a distinction between the ecclesiastical and common law jurisdictions in relation to burial monuments (sepulchres). In this respect he is simply noting that the church had jurisdiction over the burial of the body itself, whereas the actions relating to the burial chamber or grave, such as defacement, fell within the common law.

[9] E.H. East, *Pleas of the Crown*, vol. 2 (London: Butterworth and Cooke, 1803), p. 652.

[10] Skegg, 'Human corpses', 413. I am indebted to Skegg's discussion on this for unpicking some of the confusions surrounding this case. In the endnotes he explains that the date of the case is unrecorded, but notes that it was heard by Sir John Wiles 'who was Chief Justice of the Common Pleas from 1732 until his death in 1761' (421).

[11] (1857) 169 ER 959.

mother in order to re-bury her alongside his deceased father who was buried at a different site. He was indicted on grounds of removing a body from a grave without lawful authority.[12] On appeal, Erle J stated that '[o]ur law recognises no property in a corpse, and the protection of the grave at common law, as contradistinguished from ecclesiastical protection to consecrated ground, depends upon this form of indictment.'[13] Mention of the rule can also be found in the later case of *Williams* v. *Williams*.[14] This involved the question of whether one could direct the disposition of one's body by will. The deceased had directed in his will that his body was to be given to a friend to be cremated and dealt with in other ways as outlined in a letter to her. Subsequent to the body being buried in unconsecrated ground, the defendant obtained a licence for the purposes of moving it to be buried in a consecrated grave. However, instead she removed it to Italy where it was cremated.[15] It was held that there was no property in the body and, therefore, it could not be disposed of by will.[16] In reaching this conclusion, Kay J relied on *Sharpe*, 'It is quite clearly the law of this country that there can be no property in the dead body of a human being. That was declared to be the law in the case of *R v. Sharpe*.'[17]

Around the same time as *Williams* was *R v. Price*,[18] which examined the question of whether it was unlawful to cremate a body. In reaching his decision (that in fact it was not unlawful) Stephen J referred to the earlier case of *R v. Lynn*.[19] *Lynn*, like *Sharpe*: also involved the disinterment of a corpse, but on this occasion it was for the purposes of dissection. Lynn's defence argued that his actions did not fall within the jurisdiction of the criminal court since hitherto 'all the writers on this subject have considered the injury which is done to the executors of the deceased by taking the shroud, and the trespass in digging the soil; taking it for granted that the act of carrying away a dead body was not criminal'.[20] It was not explicitly stated in the case itself, but one reason why a lack of a criminal offence would have been taken for granted was if it was thought that there was no property in a corpse,[21] a position which may have been influenced by

---

[12] *Ibid.* The defendant was merely fined rather than being given a custodial sentence, since the judges were of the opinion that his motives were good.
[13] *Ibid.*   [14] (1882) 20 Ch D 659.   [15] *Ibid.* at 660–661.   [16] *Ibid.* at 663.
[17] *Ibid.* at 662–663.   [18] (1884) 12 QBD 247.   [19] (1788) 2 TR 733.
[20] *Ibid.* The report also says that '[t]he crime imputed to the defendant is not made penal by any statute: the only Act of Parliament which has any relation to this subject... makes it felony to steal dead bodies for the purposes of witchcraft; but that clearly cannot affect the present question.'
[21] See Kuzenski, 'Property in dead bodies', 22 and Goold and Quigley, 'Human biomaterials', pp. 237–240.

William Blackstone. In his *Commentaries on the Laws of England*, which was published prior to *Lynn* and the other cases, Blackstone noted that 'stealing the corpse itself, which has no owner, (though a matter of great indecency) is no felony unless some of the grave-clothes be stolen with it'.[22] In *Price*, Stephen J, referring to *Lynn*, said, 'the act done would have been a peculiarly indecent theft if it had not been for the technical reason that a dead body is not the subject of property'.[23]

Hence, while the 'no property' rule has somewhat questionable origins, it was embedded in the legal consciousness and case law by the end of the nineteenth century.[24] Even from these few older cases, what we can see is that challenges arise if we do not allow that the deceased body can be property. In *Lynn* and *Sharpe*, for example, the accused could presumably have been convicted for larceny (theft), but they were not. As Mason and Laurie have said, 'the definition of theft, or larceny as it was at the relevant time, involves the appropriation of "property belonging to another". If there is no property, there can be no theft.'[25] Instead, new common law offences needed to be created and the men were convicted, respectively, of disinterring a corpse for the purposes of dissection and removing a body from a grave without lawful authority. Likewise, *Williams* v. *Williams* reveals a similar issue. If only property can be disposed of by will, then the Court's hands were tied on the matter before it. Conceivably, the decision in that case might have been different absent the no property rule.

More contemporary cases have also accepted no property as the baseline position regarding the deceased human body, extending it to encompass separated materials. The consequence of this, as we are about to see, is that

---

[22] W. Blackstone, *Commentaries on the Laws of England*, 1st edn (Oxford: Clarendon Press, 1765–1769), Book IV, 236. He also says, 'But though the heir has a property in the monuments and escutcheons of his ancestors, yet he has none in their bodies or ashes; nor can he bring any civil action against such as indecently at least, if not impiously, violate and disturb their remains, when dead and buried. The person indeed, who has the freehold of the soil, may bring an action of trespass against such as dig and disturb it; and if anyone in taking up a dead body steals the shroud or other apparel, it will be felony; for the property thereof remains in the executor, or whoever was at the charge of the funeral' (*Commentaries*, Book II, 429). Here he refers to both Coke's comments and *Hayne's Case*.

[23] (1884) 12 QBD 247 at 252.

[24] Although this is somewhat strange since, as Roger Magnusson has pointed out, mentions of the rule were mainly 'confined to *obiter dicta*'. See R. Magnusson, 'Proprietary rights in human tissue' in N. Palmer and E. McKendrick (eds), *Interests in Goods* (London: Lloyd's of London Press, 1993), p. 242.

[25] Mason and Laurie, 'Consent or property', 714.

the courts have had to employ some creative judicial reasoning in order to resolve problems wrought by having no property as their starting point.[26]

2.2 Exceptions and the Application of Skill

The Australian case of *Doodeward* v. *Spence*[27] is pivotal to the understanding of the recent contemporary cases regarding human biomaterials. It is the source of the main exception to the no property rule: the work/skill exception. We briefly encountered this in the previous chapter where I noted that the Human Tissue Act 2004 has embedded the exception in statute. The case itself, dating from 1908, involved an appeal to the High Court of Australia regarding an action for detinue. This is an action for wrongful interference with items of personal property, which allows for the recovery of the chattel.[28] In this case the item in question was a jar containing the preserved body of a two-headed foetus. The appellant had come into possession of this after it had been sold at auction from the estate of the doctor who had originally preserved the body. The jar was subsequently confiscated from the appellant by a policeman when it was displayed as a curiosity in a public place.[29]

One of the issues before the Court was the question of whether or not a preserved foetus could be property. In this respect, the three judges were divided, with Higgins J arguing that the preserved foetus was not property and that there could 'be no right to recover in trover or in detinue in respect of a thing which is incapable of being property'.[30] The other two disagreed and, *per* Griffith CJ, it was held that:

> [W]hen a person has by the lawful exercise of work or skill so dealt with a human body or part of a human body in his lawful possession that it has acquired some attributes differentiating it from a mere corpse awaiting burial, he acquires a right to retain possession of it, at least as against any person not entitled to have delivered to him for the purpose of burial.[31]

---

[26] See also Goold and Quigley, 'Human biomaterials', pp. 237–244.

[27] [1908] 6 CLR 406.

[28] Note that in England the Torts (Interference with Goods) Act 1977 abolished detinue. What was previously covered by an action in this regard has been subsumed into conversion (s.). The Act equates trover with conversion (s. 1(a)). Detinue as an action still persists in Australia.

[29] *Doodeward* at 407.

[30] *Ibid.* at 417. Trover allowed for the award of damages, as opposed to recovery of the chattel itself.

[31] *Ibid.* at 414.

This was the first time that such a determination had been made. As Higgins J noted in his dissenting judgment, there was no prior 'instance of any Court asserting any property in a corpse except in favour of persons who wanted it for purposes of burial'.[32] Yet despite the peculiarity of the circumstances and the decision in this case, the work/skill exception was later to prove useful in circumventing problems presented by the general no property rule.

The earliest contemporary case to take *Doodeward* into account was the 1997 case of *Dobson* v. *North Tyneside Health Authority*.[33] Here, relatives of a deceased woman brought a case in negligence against North Tyneside Health Authority. The deceased had died of a brain tumour. During the coroner's post-mortem her brain was removed and preserved in paraffin, although no examination of the tumours took place. At some point subsequent to this, the brain was disposed of since no further instructions were received from the coroner.[34] The plaintiffs argued that 'if the tumours had been detected [earlier] the deceased would have survived if the tumours were benign; if they were malignant, she would probably have died, but the pain which she suffered could have been ameliorated with radiotherapy'.[35] Examination of the tumours was necessary to establish this either way, but this could not be done because the brain was no longer available. Part of the arguments before the Court involved the claim that the plaintiffs, as the next of kin, had a right of possession to the brain and that the hospital, in disposing of it, had interfered with it in a manner amounting to a conversion.[36] It was held that fixing the brain in paraffin did not render it as property.[37] We should note, however, that this was not because the Court rejected the work/skill exception as capable of creating property, but because, according to Peter Gibson LJ:

> There is nothing in the pleading or evidence before us to suggest that the actual preservation of the brain after the post mortem was on a par with stuffing or embalming a corpse or preserving an anatomical or pathological specimen for a scientific collection or with preserving a human freak such as a double-headed foetus that had some value for exhibition purposes.[38]

---

[32] *Ibid.* at 421–422. [33] [1997] 1 WLR 596. [34] *Ibid.* at 598. [35] *Ibid.* at 599.

[36] *Ibid.* at 599–600. Peter Gibson LJ does note that the cause of action being alleged in the case was not at all clear (at 599).

[37] *Ibid.* at 601. [38] *Ibid.*

It is not entirely clear what we should take this to mean; for instance, is it that placing something in paraffin does not count as work or skill, or is it that the work/skill was not of a sufficient degree or suitable nature, or is it something else? We will return to these questions in Section 5.

Two years later the issue of the application of work and skill arose again, but for an altogether different purpose. *R v. Kelly and Lindsay* is a case which is curious both for its facts and its reasoning.[39] Kelly was a sculptor and Lindsay a technician at the Royal College of Surgeons. At Kelly's behest, Lindsay had numerous procured body parts in order to make sculptures. There were '35 to 40 such parts, including three human heads, part of a brain, six arms or parts of an arm, ten legs or feet, and part of three human torsos were removed and taken to Kelly's home'.[40] These were never returned and were later found in different locations, including Kelly's attic, a friend's flat, and a field at his family home.[41] Defence for the men argued that they could not be convicted in theft since the body parts could not be considered as property for the purposes of the Theft Act 1968 nor could the Royal College be considered to be in lawful possession of them.[42] The Court of Appeal disagreed, holding that 'parts of a corpse are capable of being property within s. 4 of the Theft Act, if they have *acquired different attributes by virtue of the application of skill, such as dissection or preservation techniques*, for exhibition or teaching purposes'.[43] In arriving at this point, the Court drew on the decision in *Doodeward*. Moreover, the decision in *Dobson* was taken as support for the work/skill exception with Rose LJ taking the view that the judge in that case had not 'dissented from' this point.[44]

It is interesting to note the consequences that would have followed if there had been a finding of no property. Without a determination that the body parts could be property, there would not have been a route to a criminal conviction and the men may have been acquitted. Such was the crux of the men's defence. Additionally, if the body parts had not been deemed to be the property of the Royal College of Surgeons (or at the very least in their lawful possession) this would have resulted in uncertainty regarding similar collections of materials being held at other institutions.[45] Without recourse to the protections afforded by the Theft Act, museums and other establishments containing pathology and anatomy specimens would be vulnerable to having items from their collections

---

[39] [1999] QB 621.   [40] *Ibid.* at 623.   [41] *Ibid.*   [42] *Ibid.* at 622–623.
[43] *Ibid.* at 631 [emphasis added].   [44] *Ibid.*
[45] This was a point which formed part of the appellant's argument in *Doodeward* and which Griffith CJ (albeit somewhat indirectly) seemed to agree with (at 406 and 413).

(mis)appropriated.[46] Thus, to prevent this, and to provide redress in the instant case, their Lordships needed to determine that the body parts were not captured by the general no property rule and the work/skill exception proved useful in this respect.

The exception was later reaffirmed in *AB and Others* v. *Leeds Teaching Hospital NHS Trust*.[47] This case was brought by the parents of deceased children whose organs had been retained following post-mortem examinations. Actions were raised on two counts: psychiatric injury and wrongful interference with the deceased children's bodies.[48] Here, Gage J also endorsed on the work and skill exception saying:

> In my judgment the principle that part of a body may acquire the character of property which can be the subject of rights of possession and ownership is now part of our law. . . to dissect and fix an organ from a child's body requires work and a great deal of skill. . . The subsequent production of blocks and slides is also a skilful operation requiring work and expertise of trained scientists.[49]

The effect of this application of work and skill, however, was that 'the [hospital] pathologists became entitled to possess the organs, the blocks and slides'.[50] In line with this, we can imagine that, even if work/skill had been deemed to apply in *Dobson*, the consequence could have been to vest the hospital and not the relatives with the relevant possessory right.

The no property rule (whatever its origins) originally applied in respect of the whole deceased body. Why then did its influence expand to also apply to body parts and other separated biomaterials in these more contemporary cases? The answer is, at least partially, to be found in the discussion in *Dobson*. Although the main thrust of the decisions in both the County Court and Court of Appeal was that there is no property in a corpse,[51] slippage can be seen throughout the course of the decision. The discussion moves from referring to their being no property in a corpse,[52] to talking about 'no property in a dead body or part of a dead body',[53] to the specifics of fixing a brain in paraffin.[54] Therefore,

---

[46] Presumably some redress could be found in such circumstances depending on how the body parts were acquired; for example, a civil case for breach of contract in the case of employees who took items, or a criminal conviction of breaking and entering for non-employees who enter the premises to procure the items in question. These routes, however, seem overly complicated. Given the facts, theft seems not only more straightforward, but more appropriate.

[47] (2004) EWHC 644 (QB) (also known as *Re: Organ Retention Group Litigation* [2005] QB 506).

[48] *Ibid.* at [12].   [49] *Ibid.* at [148].   [50] *Ibid.* at [156].   [51] *Dobson* at 596.   [52] *Ibid.*

[53] *Ibid.* at 600.   [54] *Ibid.* at 601–602.

when the arguments came before the Court in *Kelly* the door had already been opened both for the expansion of the scope of the rule and for the necessity of an exception. The other part of the answer may be that, given the starting position of no property in a corpse, there is little reason for the courts to presume that the status of materials removed from the deceased would change *automatically* upon separation.[55] Hence there is a need for some extra activity – the application of work and/or skill – in order to bring about the requisite normative change from *res nullius* (nobody's thing) to *res* (thing).

The key is the supposedly (normatively) transformative effect of the application of skill to the body part in question.[56] What is at issue is not merely (or even) a physical change to the materials to which work or skill has been applied, but a significant and far-reaching change of legal status from *res nullius* to *res* which may be subject to property rights. One consequence of which is that the holder of the newly created property rights is conferred with a range of liberties and powers to direct and control the use of the materials. Yet the precedent set in *Doodeward* is problematic. Thorny legal and philosophical questions arise as to the function, mode of action, and scope of the work/skill principle. How exactly does the requisite normative change come about and in what does it consist? How much work and/or skill is required to be transformative? Is the application of work or skill sufficient for property to be created and is it even necessary? And, perhaps most importantly, in whom should any property rights vest and what is the justificatory basis for ascribing such rights?

As we will see later in the chapter, the case law (such as it is) does not offer satisfactory answers to these questions. By Rose LJ's own admission in *Kelly*, the origins of the work/skill exception are 'questionable',[57] a sentiment which is echoed in the Australian case of *Roche* v. *Douglas*.[58] Here a woman claimed that she was the daughter of a deceased man and therefore entitled to a share of his estate. She applied for a court order to allow paternity testing on a sample of tissue held in the hospital where the deceased had undergone surgery. It was held that the stored tissue was property and that under court rules access could be granted to it. The Master of the Rolls declared that 'it defies reason to not regard tissue samples as property... To deny that the tissue samples are property, in contrast to the paraffin in which the samples are kept or the jar in which

---

[55] My thanks to Imogen Goold for this point.
[56] Quigley, 'Property in human biomaterials', 662–664.   [57] *Kelly* at 630.
[58] [2000] WASC 146.

both the paraffin and the samples are stored, would be. . . a legal fiction.'[59] In saying this he drew attention to the scientific advances which have taken place since *Doodeward*, which in essence challenge the utility of the exception.[60] This was, however, just a preliminary hearing and the issue was principally one of access not of ownership *per se*.[61]

Notably, the decision in *Doodeward* does not exclude other means of establishing property rights in human biomaterials; Griffith CJ said '[i]t is not necessary to give an exhaustive enumeration of the circumstances under which such a right may be acquired.'[62] This was recognised in *Kelly*, where it was observed that 'the common law does not stand still'.[63] Rose LJ commented that in the future, human tissue might be deemed to be property, even where there has been no application of work or skill, 'if they have a use or significance beyond their mere existence'.[64] These comments were, however, obiter. The effect of the common law at the time (namely the conjunction of the no property rule and the work/skill exception) was, as Brazier has explained, that 'body parts become, as if by magic, property, but property owned by persons unknown, for purposes unforeseen'.[65] Moreover, there is little apparent consistency regarding the types of activities which could trigger the use of the work/skill exception. The only unifying factor up to this point was that fact that, whosoever might come to have property (rights) in biomaterials, the one person who could not was their source.[66]

3 Materials of Uncertain Significance

If the property question in relation to the deceased body, and materials removed therefrom, is not altogether clear, the position with regards to materials from the living lacks even more clarity. This is because until the sperm cases, mentioned in Chapter 1 and discussed in more depth in the next chapter, none of the cases which came before the courts dealt with materials from the living. As such, the position with regards to these materials can only be tenuously inferred from the cases discussed in the

---

[59] *Ibid.* at [24]. [60] *Ibid.* at [14].

[61] Sanderson MR concluded that 'on the *particular facts of this case* there is a compelling reason for holding the tissue samples to be property' and that it was not 'necessary for him to determine who holds the proprietary interest in the tissue' (at [23] and [25]). See also L. Skene, 'Proprietary rights in human bodies, body parts and tissue: Regulatory contexts and proposals for new laws' (2002) 22 *Legal Studies* 102.

[62] *Doodeward* at 414. [63] *Kelly* at 631. [64] *Ibid.*

[65] M. Brazier, 'Retained organs: Ethics and humanity' (2002) 22 *Legal Studies* 550, 563.

[66] Quigley, 'Property in human biomaterials', 661.

last section. For example, the decision in *Dobson* cited an earlier edition of *Clerk and Lindsell on Torts* in which the authors supposed that the work/skill exception would also apply to living materials:

> Once a body has undergone a process or other application of human skill, such as stuffing or embalming, it seems it can be the subject of property in the ordinary way; hence it is submitted that conversion will lie for a skeleton or cadaver used for research or exhibition, and the same goes for parts of, and substances produced by, a living person.[67]

There is no indication given by the Court, however, on whether or not it endorsed this position. The discussion, given the facts of the case, was firmly on the deceased context. Likewise, in *AB* v. *Leeds* there was no consideration of this point as it was not relevant to the facts at hand.

An early contemporary case which might be viewed as creating an exception to the no property rule is *R* v. *Rothery*.[68] Rothery was arrested on suspicion of driving while under the influence of alcohol. He was brought to the police station whereupon a blood sample was taken. When the police officer in attendance had turned away, Rothery procured the capsule with his blood. This went unnoticed until after he left the police station.[69] At the Crown Court he was convicted of the theft of a capsule from a police station, as well as the statutory offence of 'failing to provide a specimen for laboratory test'.[70] He subsequently successfully appealed the conviction for the statutory offence.

The first thing to note is that it is not clear from the Court of Appeal decision what the exact charge was at trial. It is variously referred to as being for 'theft of a capsule and container, the property of the Sussex Police Authority'[71] and for 'the theft of a capsule containing a specimen of his blood'.[72] At other points the decision talks of the removal of the capsule, and in the same paragraph of the 'absence of the specimen'.[73]

---

[67] *Dobson* at 600. M. Brazier (ed.), *Clerk and Lindsell on Torts*, 17th edn (London: Sweet and Maxwell, 1995), para. 13–50. Note that the most recent edition says: 'Once a body has undergone a process or other application of human skill, such as stuffing or embalming, it seems it can be the subject of property in the ordinary way... substances produced by a living person are on principle subject to the ordinary rules of property, this was made clear by the Court of Appeal in *Yearworth v North Bristol NHS Trust*.' M.A. Jones (ed.), *Clerk and Lindsell on Torts*, 21st edn (London: Sweet and Maxwell, 2014), paras 17-42–17-43.

[68] (1976) 63 Cr App R 231. See, for example, Skene's comment in 'The current approach of the courts' (2014) 40 *Journal of Medical Ethics* 10, 11.

[69] *Rothery* at 231.

[70] *Ibid.* at 232. The second of these was overturned on appeal (at 234).   [71] *Ibid.* at 231.

[72] *Ibid.* at 232.   [73] *Ibid.*

A second point is that the Court of Appeal decision does not mention the no property rule. We, therefore, need to be careful in our assessment of the significance of this decision for the jurisprudence relating to biomaterials. Without being explicitly mentioned we cannot be sure whether it played any role in the reasoning employed, let alone whether the intention had been to create an exception to the rule. The lack of discussion on this point is most probably the result of the fact that it was the statutory offence, and not the charge of theft, which was under appeal. In any event the question of whether or not the blood was the property of the appellant was likely to have been moot. Regardless of the status of the blood sample, the capsule itself constituted police property. No fine-grained discussion of the contents of the capsule was needed.

The case of *R* v. *Welsh* two years earlier is no more enlightening.[74] The facts are reasonably similar to those in *Rothery*. The accused, an ex-policeman, had been arrested under suspicion of driving under the influence. He was brought to the police station and a sample of urine obtained. When he was left alone he emptied the containers holding his urine down the sink. The defendant was convicted on three counts, including theft of the urine sample. He appealed against his sentence, but not the conviction. Although this case might be thought to support the contention that urine can be stolen, we only have the Court of Appeal decision to refer to on this. And there is not much to be gleaned here, other than a statement of the original convictions. Like *Rothery*, all we can say is that it was not an issue that needed any discussion on appeal. Moreover, when the original case was heard at the Crown Court, there may have been little or no reason for the judge to presume that urine could not be property. The consequence of this is that we cannot take the case to be a strong authority for the proposition that urine constitutes a discrete exception to the no property rule.

A case which precedes both *Rothery* and *Welsh* is *R* v. *Herbert*.[75] The defendant in this case gave a lift to a seventeen-year-old woman. In the course of the journey he offered to cut her hair (possibly misrepresenting himself as a hairdresser). When the woman declined to have her hair cut she was driven to a quiet road whereupon the defendant proceeded to cut the back of her hair with a comb and scissors. He was charged with assault under the Offences Against the Person Act 1861. He was also charged under s. 2 of the Larceny Act 1916 (the

---

[74] *R* v. *Welsh* [1974] RTR 478.
[75] Anonymous, 'The rape of the lock: Is it larceny?' (1961) 25 *Journal of Criminal Law* 163.

predecessor of the 1961 Theft Act). The 1916 Act provided that a person who 'takes and carries away anything capable of being stolen with intent' committed an offence and that this included 'obtaining the possession – (a) by any trick [and/or] (b) by intimidation'.[76] One of the questions before the Court was whether the hair was capable of being stolen.[77] The defence's argument rested on the contention that the hair was not a chattel until it was actually severed and thus 'until it is a chattel there can be no larceny'.[78] Additionally, it was submitted that the hair was of no value and that 'the law does not concern itself with trifles'.[79] The judges, however, disagreed. They convicted the defendant and imposed a fine.[80]

On the face of it, *Herbert* seems somewhat less uncertain than *Rothery* and *Welsh*. However, we cannot attribute much significance to this case either. For a start it involves hair, which might, by some, be viewed as different to other bodily materials. And indeed we saw earlier that it is exempted from the provisions of the 2004 Act. Most people's hair regrows. Whilst it is part of the body, it is also external to it. And, crucially, there is long history of hair being treated as a chattel and being traded for various purposes, including stuffing cushions and wig making. Whether or not any of these reasons bear up under scrutiny need not bother us here. The point is that, in the minds of the judges, it may have been relatively easy to view hair as a chattel, or at least there may have been little reason for them to see it otherwise. Regardless, the more important matter is the fact that the case was heard in the Magistrate's Court. It did not reach the High Court, let alone the Court of Appeal. As such, it is not a binding precedent. Likewise, neither *Rothery* nor *Welsh* are binding regarding the property issue (if present at all) since this was not under appeal in either case.

Despite this doubtful background with regards to materials from the living, s. 32(9) of the Human Tissue Act 2004 has effectively expanded the property sphere to capture such materials. This we saw in the previous chapter. The exemption from the prohibition on commercial dealings provided by this section necessarily applies to materials removed from both the deceased and the living. Therefore, materials from the living which have skill applied can become subject to property rights. Although the section specifically applies in the transplant context, it is doubtful that it would be seen as inapplicable to tissues removed from the living for other purposes. Albeit the work/skill exception was rejected in *Yearworth*

---

[76] ss 1 and 2.   [77] Anon, 'Is it larceny?', p. 165.   [78] *Ibid*.   [79] *Ibid*.   [80] *Ibid*.

for other reasons (as we will see in the next chapter), this contention is supported by the case. It was the opinion of the Court that s. 32(9) 'would fortify the view that the common law treats parts or products of a living human body as property if they have been subject to an application of human skill'. Be that as it may, as I have commented already and will be discussed further in Section 5, there is still much uncertainty regarding the circumstances in which the rule is triggered and exactly what kind or degree of work and/or skill is required.

4 Lessons from Abroad?

The general tendency for the law in relation to property and biomaterials to recognise third parties, but not the source, as capable of holding property rights in biomaterials is not unique to the domestic jurisprudence. In this respect it is worth pausing to briefly consider some cases from the United States. These are instructive because they involve dilemmas which have not yet been tested in any of the UK jurisdictions. Some of them underline the way in which property law can be used to protect third party interests, potentially to the detriment of the source's. All of them exemplify how advances in medicine and biotechnology can give rise to unforeseen conflicts and challenges with regards to human biomaterials.

4.1 Control and Conflict Revisited

Three of the key cases which illustrate the conflicts that can arise, were outlined in Chapter 1: *Moore, Greenberg*, and *Catalona*. Recall that these, respectively, involved disputes over a cell line produced from removed splenic tissue, tissue samples donated for research into Canavan disease, and tissue samples donated for research into prostate cancer.

In the first of these, as we saw in the opening chapter, John Moore brought a case alleging thirteen causes of action, including one in conversion. In this respect Moore claimed that 'he continued to own his cells following their removal from his body, at least for the purpose of directing their use'.[81] The majority in the Californian Supreme Court disagreed. Part of the reasoning given was that they considered a patient's control over their excised tissue to be so restricted by Californian statutory law that it 'eliminates so many of the rights ordinarily attached to

---

[81] *Moore*, Supreme Court at 134.

property that one cannot simply assume that what is left amounts to "property" or "ownership" for the purposes of conversion law'.[82] The Court also rejected the action in conversion on policy grounds. First, they claimed that to allow it would unduly 'hinder research in the area by restricting access to the necessary raw materials'.[83] Second, they were concerned that recognising source property rights would entail a right for persons to commercialise their biomaterials.[84] For these reasons, although the Court concluded that there was a cause of action based on a lack of informed consent and breach of fiduciary duty, it denied that Moore had property rights in his cells and other materials.

The facts in *Greenberg* are somewhat different. Unlike in *Moore*, the plaintiffs in this case had been perfectly aware that their tissues would be used for research purposes. Indeed, the Greenbergs sought out Dr Matalon with the express purpose of helping research into Canavan disease. They helped to locate other families affected by Canavan disease, and along with them, provided not only tissue samples and their medical histories, but also financial support for the research.[85] The conflict arose because the plaintiffs claimed that they had done so on the understanding that the results of the research would be publicly available and that any consequent tests developed would be 'affordable and accessible'.[86] Relying on *Moore*, the claim in conversion was denied. However, seemingly departing from the earlier case, the plaintiffs' complaint of a lack of informed consent was also dismissed.[87] This was consequent on an unwillingness to 'extend the duty of informed consent to cover economic interests'.[88] The decision stated that to do so 'would chill medical research'[89] and 'give rise to a type of dead-hand control [by] research subjects'.[90]

There is much which could (and has) been said about these cases and indeed I will return to them later in the book.[91] For now, it is enough to note that it is not clear that the two central concerns expressed in them are particularly compelling. First is the claim that recognising source property rights would have a negative impact on research.[92] The courts considered that the source would be able to restrict access to the raw materials needed for research, as well as to potentially exert control over downstream uses of both the biomaterials and associated research results, such as data and patents. Yet why, if they were concerned about the potentially restrictive effects of property rights, were they willing to grant

---

[82] *Ibid.* at 141.   [83] *Ibid.* at 144.   [84] *Ibid.* at 148–149.   [85] *Greenberg* at 1067.
[86] *Ibid.*   [87] *Ibid.* at 1068–1071.   [88] *Ibid.* at 1070.   [89] *Ibid.*   [90] *Ibid.* at 1071.
[91] Sections in chapters 8 and 9 deal with various aspects of these cases.
[92] *Moore*, Supreme Court at 144; *Greenberg* at 1076.

them to the defendants? The effect of granting these to researchers and research institutions is that they can subsequently restrict access to both the raw materials and the results of the research.

This much is also apparent in *Catalona*, where the effect of the decision is that Washington University could limit access to both the diseased and healthy prostate samples, ring-fencing them for their own researchers. That is not to say that this was necessarily inappropriate or unjustified in this particular case. Here the *initial conditions* of the transfer of samples appear to have been clear. The consent forms contained provisions whereupon the donors waived their rights to the excised tissues, as well as to any resulting 'new material or process'.[93] As such, treating the donated tissue samples as *inter vivos* gifts (and therefore as owned objects) is consistent with the finding that donors did not retain a proprietary interest in the sample and that ownership of the samples had passed to Washington University upon donation.[94] This can be contrasted with the situation in *Moore* and *Greenberg*. In the former, there was outright deception. While in *Greenberg* the plaintiffs felt that the patents which the researchers applied for were contrary to the terms of their agreement to donate their samples and participate in the research.

A second worry which can be found most explicitly in *Moore*, is that recognising source property rights would entail a right for persons to commercialise their biomaterials.[95] This is exemplified by Justice Arabian's comments when he says:

> Plaintiff has asked us to recognize and enforce a right to sell one's own body tissue for profit. He entreats us to regard the human vessel – the single most venerated and protected subject in any civilized society – as equal with the basest commercial commodity. He urges us to commingle the sacred with the profane.[96]

The unease expressed is not a general one about the commercialisation of biomaterials, but one specifically focused on the supposed wrong of the source doing so. Much like the claim regarding the potential to restrict research, therefore, there is an asymmetric understanding of the issues involved. The result of this is that, while the source is excluded from the commercial sphere, third parties are given free rein to profit from

---

[93] *Catalona*, Court of Appeals at 671.
[94] *Ibid.* at 673–677. Although see my comments in Chapter 9, Section 3.2 regarding gifting and withdrawal from the research in this case.
[95] These points, along with the reasoning in the cases, are examined in more depth in Quigley, 'Property in human biomaterials'.
[96] *Moore*, Supreme Court at 148–149.

transactions involving biomaterials. Consent is presumed to be sufficient to protect source interests in *Moore*, with the Court holding that
there was a cause of action for lack of informed consent and for breach
of fiduciary duty.[97] Yet, excluding the source from the property paradigm enables those self-same property rights to be utilised to protect
third party interests.[98] This difficulty is underscored by a more fundamental issue, which is the conflation of property rights with the right to
sell. It is presumed that property rights necessarily entail the right to
sell, or at the very least that restrictions could not be put on this aspect
of them.[99]

4.2   Other Dilemmas

The cases just discussed all involve different types of parties, in two of
them the dispute was between the tissue progenitors and researchers
(and their institutions), while in the other it was between a researcher
and his former institution. Nonetheless, to a certain extent they all
involve challenges regarding how the original materials are obtained.
In this respect, the legal ends to which property might be employed in
relation to biomaterials are not confined to conflicts which arise at the
point of acquisition.

For instance, in *USA* v. *Arora*[100] the defendant, Dr Arora, was accused
of tampering with and destroying cells at the National Institute of
Diabetes and Digestive and Kidney Diseases (NIDDK).[101] The cells,
belonging to the Alpha 1–4 cell line, were being used in research by
Drs Sei and Wong, also employees at the NIDDK. Having derived a stable
cell line, they were growing cells in a flask in order to conduct a variety of
tests on them. They subsequently found that the cells were dying or
damaged, but could find no cause for this and began to suspect that
they had been tampered with. After investigation, it was discovered that
Dr Arora had been accessing the room in which the flasks of cells were

---

[97] *Ibid.* at 148.
[98] For a general discussion of this point see Mason and Laurie, 'Consent or property?',
p. 728.
[99] In Chapter 9 we will see that property rights do not in fact analytically entail the right to
transfer for value (including sale).
[100] *USA* v. *Prince Kumar Arora* 860 F. Supp. 1091.
[101] The motivation was attributed to 'professional rivalry' (*ibid.* at 1096).

being kept. A fake set of flasks was placed in the room and the defendant's fingerprints were found on these (which had also been tampered with).[102] A lawsuit was brought alleging both conversion and trespass. The Court found that Dr Arora had indeed tampered with the cells and that this constituted a conversion. In coming to this conclusion, Messitte J accepted that the Alpha 1–4 cell line and cells were chattels capable of being converted[103] and that Dr Arora had acted in a manner inconsistent 'with Dr Sei's right to control the cells'.[104] Since trespass constitutes a lesser interference than conversion, this count was held to be 'moot'.[105] As well as court costs the defendant was ordered to pay '$450.20 compensatory damages and $5,000.00 punitive damages'.[106]

What is interesting about this decision is that an action for conversion was seemingly permitted specifically because it did *not* involve a property-based claim by *patients* or the original cell *donors*. In allowing that there had been a conversion the Court explicitly distinguished the case from *Moore*, relying on the following comments from Justice Broussard in the dissenting judgment:

> If, for example, another medical center or drug company had stolen all of the cells in question from the UCLA Medical Center laboratory and had used them for its own benefit, there would be no question but that a cause of action for conversion would properly lie against the thief, and the majority opinion does not suggest otherwise.[107]

While this passage does indicate grounds for distinguishing the cases, Justice Broussard's overall dissenting argument was aimed at highlighting some gaps in the majority's reasoning regarding conversion. The pertinent question for him was whether, prior to removal, patients have the right to decide what uses their tissues will be put to and, as such, a right to control the uses of their separated tissues in this respect.[108] The answer for him is that they do. Specifically he said that:

> If defendants had informed plaintiff, prior to removal, of the possible uses to which his body part could be put and plaintiff had authorized one particular use, it is clear under the [Uniform Anatomical Gift Act and common law principles] that defendants would be liable for conversion if they disregarded plaintiff's decision and used the body part in an unauthorized manner for their own economic benefit.[109]

---

[102] *Ibid.* at 1093–1096.   [103] *Ibid.* at 1098.   [104] *Ibid.*   [105] *Ibid.* at 1101.   [106] *Ibid.*
[107] *Moore*, Supreme Court at 153.   [108] *Ibid.* at 154.   [109] *Ibid.* at 155.

This very point was later tested in *Colavito* v. *New York Organ Donor Network*,[110] where one of the central questions was whether human organs could constitute property.

In this case the wife of a deceased man offered his kidneys for transplantation to Colavito, a friend of the family. The kidney was flown from New York to Florida, whereupon it was deemed to be damaged and unsuitable for transplantation. Colavito was unable obtain the second donated kidney as it was 'in the process of being implanted' in another patient.[111] He brought a claim for 'loss of a transplantable kidney'.[112] His claim failed, partially due to fact that the deceased's kidney was not actually compatible with the plaintiff. Nevertheless, the case is remarkable because of Colavito's use of property. He argued that because the kidney was a directed gift that he acquired property rights in the kidney. Hence, one of the claims he brought was for conversion.[113] The New York Court of Appeals considered the question of whether the plaintiff could maintain such a cause of action. Their conclusion, which was subsequently affirmed by the Second Circuit Court of Appeals, was that Colavito could not.[114] In coming to this conclusion, the New York Court essentially relied on the no property rule, noting that no preceding cases had 'strayed meaningfully' from this.[115] Interestingly, however, Rosenblatt J commented that since 'the "no property right" jurisprudence was developed long before the age of transplants and other medical advances, we need not identify or forecast the circumstances in which someone may conceivably have actionable rights in the body or organ of a deceased person'.[116] So while Colavito was not found to have property rights in the donated kidney, the possibility that such rights might be recognised in other circumstances is not ruled out.

---

[110] *Colavito* v. *New York Organ Donor Network, Inc.* [2005] 356 F.Supp.2d 237 [*Colavito* I]; *Colavito* v. *New York Organ Donor Network, Inc.* [2006] 438 F.3d 214 [*Colavito* II]; *Colavito* v. *New York Organ Donor Network, Inc.* [2006] 8 N.Y.3d 43 [*Colavito* III]; and *Colavito* v. *New York Organ Donor Network, Inc.* [2007] 486 F.3d 78 [*Colavito* IV].

[111] *Colavito* IV at 79.   [112] *Colavito* I at 241.   [113] *Colavito* IV at 79.

[114] *Colavito* III at 53 and 58; *Colavito* IV at 81.

[115] *Colavito* III at 52–53. The Court had also been asked to consider the question of whether New York Public health law would give rise to a private cause of action in this case. The judges concluded that it would not. The reason given was that the kidneys in question would not have conferred a medical benefit upon the plaintiff and, therefore, he could not be construed as being in need of *them* – as distinct from being in need of *a* functioning kidney (at 57).

[116] *Ibid.* at 53.

5   Transforming Tissues I: Work, Skill, and Labour

When cases come before the English courts, using the no property rule as the baseline position means that particular legal avenues are not available. We have seen that to get around this a degree of legal manoeuvring has sometimes been necessary. For example, as noted earlier, without a determination of property in *Kelly* a prosecution in theft would not have been successful. Indeed, the defendants tried to argue exactly this – that there was no property, therefore, there could be no theft. Work/skill reasoning was used to avoid this inconvenient outcome. The effect of the application of work and/or skill is to alter the normative status of the materials, creating property rights where none apparently existed before. At least until *Yearworth* (examined in the next chapter), it was the principal means of creating property rights in biomaterials. Yet it is uncertain exactly what counts as the relevant work and/or skill and upon what philosophical basis the requisite property rights are created.

One possible interpretation of the work/skill exception is that it represents an application of the labour theory of property. Labour theory can be traced back to John Locke and broadly holds that a person is entitled to the fruits of their labour.[117] Locke claimed that:

> [E]very Man has a *Property* in his own *Person*. This no Body has any Right to but himself. The *Labour* of his Body, and the *Work* of his hands, we may say, are properly his. Whatsoever then he removes out of the state that Nature hath provided, and left it in, he hath mixed his *Labour* with, and joyned to it something that is his own, and thereby makes it his *Property*. It being by him removed from the common state Nature placed it in, it hath by this *labour* something annexed to it, that excludes the common right of other Men. For this Labour being the unquestionable Property of the Labourer, no Man but he can have a right to what is once joyned to, at least where there is enough, and as good left in common for others.[118]

Thus, when a person 'mixes' their labour with external resources they acquire a property entitlement in that item.[119] As explained by Jeremy

---

[117] J. Locke, *Two Treatises of Government*, ed. Peter Laslett (Cambridge: Cambridge University Press, 1988). For a discussion of this in the context of human biomaterials see R. Nwabueze, 'Biotechnology and the new property regime in human bodies and body parts' (2002) 24 *Loyola of Los Angeles International and Comparative Law Review* 19, 58 and Price, *Human Tissue*, p. 256.

[118] Locke, *Two Treatises*, pp. 287–288.

[119] For a discussion of this see Becker, *Property Rights*, pp. 32–56 and J. Wolff, *An Introduction to Political Philosophy*, rev. edn (Oxford: Oxford University Press, 2006), pp. 138–143.

Waldron, 'private property rights, according to Locke, are *natural* rights – not in the sense that men are born with them – but in the sense that, though they are acquired rights, they are acquired as the result of actions and transactions that men undertake on their own initiative'.[120] Such a rationale might function to both explain and justify the work/skill exception when it comes to human biomaterials. It is explanatory since it seemingly describes what is going on. Someone, be it a hospital pathologist or a researcher, mixes their labour with the biomaterials in question. They do this in the sense that it takes work to do this and, in some cases, requires them to employ (and apply) their not inconsiderable skills; for example, to preserve whole corpses for exhibition purposes, to make prosections of body parts, to prepare slides, to create cell lines, or even just to freeze sperm. From this, if we think that people are morally entitled to the fruits of their labour, we may also see this as providing a justification for the creation and acquisition of property rights in biomaterials which have been laboured upon.

5.1   Locke's Labour Lost

The first thing to note is that if a labour analysis explains the work/skill exception, then it only does so post hoc and on exceedingly tenuous grounds. Such a rationale was not given in the original decision in *Doodeward*.[121] Nor can it be found (at least explicitly) in subsequent cases which have applied the principle. Looking for such a rationale (or indeed any rationale) is to search for a unity which is most likely not to be found in the relevant cases. The difficulty in uncovering any consistent basis for the principle has not gone unnoticed by commentators,[122] something which becomes acutely apparent once we ask what sort of labour might be required to trigger the exception and what the effect of the labour needs to be to bring about the requisite normative transformation. The decision in *Doodeward*, for example, talks of 'work or skill' not labour.[123] Hence, we need to ask whether either of these counts as labour

[120] J. Waldron, *The Right to Private Property* (Oxford: Clarendon Press, 1988), p. 138.
[121] R. Hardcastle, *Law and the Human Body: Property Rights, Ownership, and Control* (Oxford: Hart Publishing, 2009), pp. 29–30.
[122] Price, *Human Tissue*, pp. 257–258; Laurie, Harmon, and Porter, *Mason and McCall Smith's Law and Medical Ethics*, pp. 502–503; and Brazier and Cave, *Medicine, Patients, and the Law*, pp. 560–561.
[123] Price, *Human Tissue*, p. 256. Note that there is in fact a second limb of questioning which is pertinent here which centres around the issue of lawfulness. Griffith CJ's comments in *Doodeward* were not just about 'work or skill', but the '*lawful* exercise of work or skill' (at

in the relevant sense. Price thought that the judicial reasoning we have been considering was based more in the notion of 'skill than labour per se'.[124] Consequently, he argued that a 'Lockean rationale cannot properly be regarded as underpinning the existing domestic or Australian jurisprudence'.[125] He was partially influenced in this contention by the formulation in the Human Tissue Act 2004, which mentions the application of skill, but not work.[126] However, the 2004 Act aside, there is no clear line to be located in the cases. They slip between different formulations of the exception.

In *AB* v. *Leeds*, for example, Gage LJ talks of the 'work and skill' required to produce tissue blocks and slides,[127] while the decision in *Kelly* (in places) discusses 'work' and 'skilled work'.[128] At different points the various decisions use the terms together and singly. Meanwhile, in *Dobson*, their Lordships seemingly accepted that *Doodeward* represented a satisfactory authority for the proposition that the application of skill could give rise to property rights. They simply denied that this held in the case before them:

> Although a body or part of a body which had undergone a process or other application of human skill, such as stuffing or embalming, might constitute property, the lawful removal and preservation of a brain in the course of a post mortem did not transform it into an item to which the plaintiffs had a right of possession.[129]

Why was the preservation of the brain not considered to be transformative? After all, such preservation work does require both work and skill to be applied. On the face of it, this determination is all the more curious since the later decisions in *Kelly* and *AB* v. *Leeds* ostensibly deviate from

---

414). As such, whatever we might interpret work or skill to mean, we also need to ask what it means to lawfully apply it. I am minded to think that this limb of the problem is less sticky. At least in *Doodeward* the lawfulness of the exercise of work or skill appears to be soundly connected to the lawfulness of possession. Immediately preceding the comments quoted, Griffith CJ answered the prior question of whether the possession of a deceased body for purposes other than burial was unlawful. His answer was that, as a general matter, it was not (at 413–414). He accepted that there could be a public health or public decency argument against this in certain cases, but that this did not hold in this one. For that reason he was satisfied that that 'the human body is capable by law of becoming the subject of property' (at 414). Thus it is reasonable for us to presume that the lawfulness of the exercise of work or skill turns on the prior lawfulness of the possession. My thanks to Jamie Glister for prompting me to draw out this point.

[124] Price, *ibid.*, p. 257. [125] *Ibid.* [126] s. 32(9)(c). See Price, *ibid.*
[127] *AB* v. *Leeds* at [141]. [128] *Kelly* at 624. [129] *Dobson* at 596.

Dobson, making specific reference to preservation techniques being suffi-cient.[130] We, therefore, appear to have conflicting authorities.

Two factors are of potential relevance here. First, the level of work and/or skill required to process the materials could have a bearing on the assessment being conducted in these cases. If it does, then there may be a threshold level of work/skill needed in order to be normatively transfor-mative. This would appear to resolve the apparent conflict between the cases: the work/skill done in *Dobson* did not meet the threshold, whereas it did in *Kelly* and *AB* v. *Leeds*. But such an interpretation is not satisfac-tory. Even if preserving the brain was not on a par with stuffing or embalming, it is surely comparable to the work/skill in *Doodeward*. Here Price has noted that 'the mere placing of the foetus in a jar of paraffin was sufficient to invoke the exception'.[131] Hence, given that it is the earlier Australian case which gave rise to the exception, one would expect it to be the comparator. *Doodeward* itself, however, suggests that the outcome of the application of work or skill is that body parts acquire different attributes.[132] This is something which is reiterated in *Kelly*, where their Lordships emphasise that, in that particular case, the body parts held by the Royal College of Surgeons had 'acquired different attributes'.[133] Yet this simply raises the further question of what this means.

There are different ways in which materials could be deemed to have acquired different attributes. The first is legalistic – materials take on different characteristics purely in virtue of a change of legal status. Since the very purpose of the work/skill exception is to bring about such a normative legal transformation, we can easily dispense with this inter-pretation. It is the alteration of the requisite attributes which supposedly triggers the alteration of legal status. This suggests the second possibility, which is that the transformation under the work/skill principle may need to be a tangible physical one. But what sorts of changes to the physical attributes are necessary?

Arguably, the changes to the materials in both *Kelly* and *Doodeward* were fairly minimal; they were ones of *form* not character. This also holds in *AB* v. *Leeds*.[134] Recall that in this later case, Gage LJ considered that the production of tissue blocks and slides would have conferred rights of possession on the hospital pathologists.[135] Laurie and colleagues say that

---

[130] *Kelly* at 631 and *AB* v. *Leeds* at [148] and [156].
[131] Price, *Human Tissue*, p. 257, note 161.   [132] *Doodeward* at 414.   [133] *Kelly* at 631.
[134] Price, *Human Tissue*, p. 259.   [135] *AB* v. *Leeds* at [148] and [156].

'there is a world of difference between placing a brain in preservative and preparing blocks for microscopic examination'.[136] This much is surely correct when viewed in terms of the amount of work or skill which is needed to achieve these ends. However, these blocks are still constituted of essentially the same basic materials. Hardcastle explains the preservation process, saying:

> First, the biological materials are embedded into a block of wax. Secondly, the block is sliced and each slice is fixed onto a slide. Thirdly, the slices are stained to show their different aspects. These steps do not cumulatively create a new entity. Even though the biological materials undergo substantial treatment, they maintain their separate physical manifestation and essential characteristics throughout the process.[137]

As such, microscopic slices of tissue are smaller than whole prosections or entire foetuses, but they are not 'fundamentally altered in character'.[138] Indeed a close reading of *Kelly* suggests that such a change is not necessitated by the exception. It is clear that their Lordships considered that procedures and processes such as 'dissection and preservation' constituted the acquisition of different attributes.[139] This seems to represent an exceedingly minimalistic requirement for the creation of property rights, especially when the result is that third parties become vested with the consequent rights.[140] Yet if mere preservation is sufficient, this does not fit neatly with an interpretation which emphasises the *physical* alteration of the materials.

A third possible interpretation is that the acquisition of altered attributes is a functional requirement. Through the application of work and/or skill, the materials take on a different function or purpose. This reading of the requirement is perhaps suggested by both *Doodeward* and *Kelly*. In the early case, the Court deemed that the preservation of the foetus had differentiated 'it from a mere corpse awaiting burial'.[141] On a functional analysis no fundamental changes to the foetus itself is required; the placing of the foetus in a jar of spirits (which takes minimal work/skill) is sufficient to make this distinction. In being so treated the foetus took on a new function of being a curiosity and an object of display.

---

[136] Laurie, Harmon, and Porter, *Mason and McCall Smith's Law and Medical Ethics*, p. 503, note 118.
[137] Hardcastle, *Law and the Human Body*, p. 142.   [138] Price, *Human Tissue*, p. 259.
[139] *Kelly* at 631.
[140] Laurie, Harmon, and Porter, *Mason and McCall Smith's Law and Medical Ethics*, p. 503.
[141] *Doodeward* at 414.

Comments from Rose LJ in *Kelly* also point to the relevance of the function or purpose of the materials. He said that body parts might be 'capable of being property... even without the acquisition of different attributes, *if they have a use or significance beyond their mere existence*'.[142] This comment is commonly thought to go beyond the work/skill exception to indicate that property rights can be created even where no work and/or skill is applied (and thus the materials in question have not acquired different attributes). This much can be surmised from examples he offered. These were organs for transplant, materials to extract DNA, and exhibits for a trial.[143] His observations in this respect are likely no more than a recognition that property rights in biomaterials can arise in more than one way. This interpretation would also resolve the apparent conflict with the decision in *Dobson*. In his comments, Gibson LJ refers to preserving 'anatomical or pathological specimen[s] for a scientific collection' and to 'value for exhibition purposes'.[144] This suggests that the preservation of samples for a particular *purpose* has a part to play in the property question. If this is the case, then the *intention* to use for those purposes may also be relevant,[145] something which will be discussed in Chapter 4.

5.2   Labouring and Provisos

As we have just seen, there is no explicit Lockean rationale to be located in the case law regarding property and human biomaterials. But even if it could be, the application of Lockean principles to cases of human biomaterials would not be straightforward. Determining who should be the holders of property rights in such materials or even whether there should be property rights at all may not be as simple as saying that party 'X' laboured (i.e. applied work and/or skill) on those materials. It all depends on how Locke is interpreted.[146]

Consider again part of the quotation from Locke: 'Whatsoever then [Man] removes out of the state that Nature hath provided, and left it in,

---

[142] *Kelly* at 631 [emphasis added].   [143] *Ibid.*   [144] *Dobson* at 601.

[145] Grubb, 'I, me, mine', 311; Laurie, Harmon, and Porter, *Mason and McCall Smith's Law and Medical Ethics*, p. 503; Hardcastle, *Law and the Human Body*, p. 39.

[146] Price supposed that that '[a]ny "labouring" on human tissue would seemingly be sufficient in itself to satisfy the Lockean standard'. And because of this, he argued that 'the philosophical foundations of the thesis seem shaky, uncertain and unconvincing' (*Human Tissue*, p. 254). He is right to the extent, as we will see in Chapter 8, that some of Locke's own examples of labouring do not entail particularly laborious labour. However, the Lockean connection is in itself tenuous. Moreover, for the reasons which follow in the main text, we will see that such a conclusion may not follow from Locke in any case.

he hath mixed his *Labour* with, and joyned to it something that is his own, and thereby makes it his *Property*.'[147] First, if, as per the case law, labour is property generating for third parties (those who do the labouring), then it entails the premise that human biomaterials are in fact something removed out of the state of nature. It must presume that biomaterials are unowned resources, which are part of a commons which can justifiably be appropriated. This assumption, as the rest of this book aims to demonstrate, is highly questionable. Second, and importantly, Locke added a proviso. He said that when a resource is appropriated there must be 'enough, and as good left in common for others'.[148] This, according to Robert Nozick, 'is meant to ensure that the situation of others is not worsened'.[149] In relation to biomaterials, one implication of this might be that property rights in rare or unusual tissues, cells, and other materials cannot be created simply by labouring on them. Doing so would literally restrict the access that others have to these resources and may leave them worse off. To illustrate, let us consider how a Lockean analysis might have applied in the *Moore* case.

To begin we can concede (for the sake of argument) that Golde and the researchers at UCLA were entitled to patent the *processes* which resulted in the 'Mo' cell line, as well as the *products* which were derived from it. Let us also say that the justification for this was the labour and intellectual work that these new things represented. Even with these concessions, at least narrowly applied, the Lockean proviso would not be satisfied by the allocation of property rights to them over the original tissue samples. John Moore attended the UCLA medical centre for the treatment for his splenic tumour. The result of this was that this institution and its researchers held the only samples of this and his other tissues. Thus, there existed a very limited amount of tissue, and the use of it by the researchers necessarily excludes the possibility that others could use it. At first glance, therefore, there is not *enough* and as *good* left for others. Hence other researchers are left worse off than they otherwise would have been if access is restricted.

Having said this, it is not obvious what leaving others worse off might be taken to mean in such a situation. It is plausible that excluding other researchers from this scarce biological resource might have left them worse off in the sense that they could not use it for their own research, but the implications beyond this are purely speculative. If there is a lesson to

[147] Locke, *Two Treatises*, p. 287.   [148] *Ibid.*, p. 288.
[149] R. Nozick, *Anarchy, State, and Utopia* (Oxford: Basil Blackwell, 1974), p. 175.

be learned from the Lacks and Slavin stories and from the *Moore* case, it is that we cannot predict when such materials will prove useful to medical science, nor who will realise their potential, be this by design or happenstance. As such, even if others had been granted access to the samples they may not have achieved the breakthroughs of Golde and his team (thus benefitting potential patients and society more widely).

Yet this just raises the question of how far the proviso should extend. While it is far from certain that breakthroughs would have been made by others, *without* the raw materials no advances at all are possible. It would certainly not have been practically possible for all who could have used the samples to have had access to them, given the limited supply. For this reason, the Lockean proviso might entail that other ways be found to ensure that 'enough and as good' is left and that others are not made worse off by the allocation of property rights. Ways to do this might include: not creating property rights over cell lines arising from rare tissues; making resulting cell lines freely available to other researchers; or sharing and widely distributing results of research efforts on rare biomaterials via open access mechanisms.[150]

One might point out that there are some biomaterials which are so plentiful that there will always be enough and good left for others; for instance, the most common blood type or small skin or other tissue samples taken from individuals. If this is the case, then it could be argued that a Lockean work/skill position would support the creation of property rights in these materials. But even then it is not obvious that it would. Again it is a question of the interpretation, scope, and extent of the proviso. It might be correct to suppose that researchers (and hence the potential beneficiaries of their research) are not disadvantaged by other researchers gaining property rights in commonly available biomaterials. They could after all collect their own samples from donors. But this presumes that the proviso applies only to materials collected for research and there is no reason to think that it ought to be so restricted.

Take blood for example. Especially during the winter months, radio adverts regularly run, telling us that blood supplies are running low and donations are needed for life-saving transfusions. Therefore, taking the therapeutic context into account, blood is not as plentiful as it may appear; in which case supplies that are used for research rather than

---

[150] C. Erin, 'Who owns Mo? Using historical entitlement theory to decide the ownership of human derived cell lines' in A. Dyson and J. Harris (eds), *Ethics and Biotechnology* (London: Routledge, 1994), pp. 157–178, p. 170.

treatment do have the potential to leave others worse off in a very tangible sense. One response to this is that biomaterials obtained for research and therapeutic purposes are collected in different, perhaps mutually exclusive, circumstances. Consequently, they do not impact on the availability to the divergent groups of end-users. While such an argument is interesting, it merely prompts us to ask whether there is a case for the redistribution of resources from research to therapy.

Another potential response is that blood and blood products are inherently different to other types of biomaterials because they have dual uses in both the research and therapeutic contexts. Other tissue samples (e.g. skin biopsies) do not tend to have these competing possible uses. As such, we might think that biomaterials which have no therapeutic use and are not scarce are the best candidates for the application of a work/skill exception based in labour theory reasoning. But even if we were to narrow down the application of the exception to such situations, for the reasons already elucidated throughout Section 5, we ought not to be satisfied with labour theory reasoning as the basis of the legal work/skill principle.

Leaving the work/skill exception aside, therefore, we are still left with the question of finding a coherent and justified means for creating property rights in biomaterials.

6 Transforming Tissues II: Accession and Specification

Some commentators have argued that there is scope for the application to biomaterials of the Roman and Scots law doctrines of accession (*accessio*) and specification (*specificatio*).[151] These are also found in English common law, albeit they are relatively underdeveloped.[152] Both are modes of acquiring ownership which are not reliant on deriving or acquiring title from any previous owner.[153] Accession applies where 'two pieces of

---

[151] D. Johnston, 'The renewal of the old' (1997) 56 *Cambridge Law Journal* 80; N. Whitty, 'Rights of personality, property rights, and the human body in Scots law' (2005) 9 *Edinburgh Law Review* 194, 226–227; Hardcastle, *Law and the Human Body*, pp. 131–141 and 165–171; and Price, *Human Tissue*, pp. 258–262.

[152] M. Bridge, *Personal Property Law*, 4th edn (Oxford: Oxford University Press, 2015), p. 130.

[153] They are referred to in Scots law, along with *occupatio* (first occupation), *commixtio* (commixture – mixing of solids; e.g. grain), and *confusio* (confusion – mixing of liquids; e.g. wine), as being modes of 'original acquisition'. As explained by Reid, '[i]n Scots law ownership of corporeal moveable property [chattels] can be acquired by a new title or by a title derived from the title of the previous owner. Where there is a *new* title the case is

property become joined together in such a way that one (the "accessory") is considered to have become subsumed into the other (the "principal")'.[154] The accessory is said to accede to the principal. The old English case of *Appleby* v. *Myers* illustrates some instances where the doctrine would apply:

> [M]aterials worked by one into the property of another become part of that property... Bricks built into a wall become part of the house; thread stitched into a coat which is under repair, or planks and nails and pitch worked into a ship which is under repair, become part of the coat or ship.[155]

In each instance the individual identities of the constitutive elements have been merged, but not destroyed.[156] The principal and accessory are joined in such way that their individual elements cannot be subsequently separated (at least without undue difficulty, damage, and, or cost).[157] As Kenneth Reid puts it, the accessory 'is considered, in law if not in fact, to have lost its identity as a separate item of property'.[158]

referred to as "original acquisition"' (K.G.C. Reid, *The Law of Property in Scotland* (Edinburgh: Butterworths/Law Society of Scotland, 1996), para. 539 [emphasis added]). The aforementioned are modes of original acquisition in the sense that title to the thing in question does not derive from the title of another owner: 'the making is regarded as the source of the new owner's title' (ibid.). This is to distinguish them from other modes of acquisition such as derivative acquisition, which involves the transfer (formal and informal) of ownership. Here, as noted by Carey Miller, Scots law does not follow 'Roman Law in an exact way' (D.L. Carey Miller, *Corporeal Moveables in Scots Law* (Edinburgh: W. Green and Son Ltd, 2005), para. 5.01). Whereas in Roman law *commixtio* did not result in a change of property rights, in Scots law it does (R. Hickey, 'Dazed and confused: Accidental mixtures of goods and the theory of acquisition of title' (2003) 66 *Modern Law Review* 368, 371; Carey Miller, *Corporeal Moveables*, paras 5.02 and 5.04). Note the distinction between this usage of the term 'original acquisition', which is standard in civil law jurisdictions, and the way that it is used by political philosophers. In political philosophy it is generally used to mean the acquisition of previously wholly unowned things. There is some overlap since, for example, specification and accession are applicable to 'newly' created things. These might, therefore, be thought to have been previously unowned. However, these 'new things' do not come from materials which were previously unowned, as will become clear in the main discussion.

[154] Reid, *The Law of Property in Scotland*, para. 570. See also Hardcastle, *Law and the Human Body*, pp. 131–132.

[155] (1867) LR 2 CP 651 at 659–660.   [156] Price, *Human Tissue*, p. 260.

[157] Although historically the impossibility of separation was a feature of accession, in modern Scots law accession in moveables is possible even without there being an 'indissoluble union' (Reid, *The Law of Property in Scotland*, para. 589). This recognises that, for example, industrial processes could separate out the constituent parts, but that it would be very costly or difficult to do so. See also Carey Miller, *Corporeal Moveables*, para. 3.20.

[158] Reid, *The Law of Property in Scotland*, para. 574.

Specification conversely is said to be applicable where a completely *new* thing or species of thing (*nova species*) is created. The classical Roman law examples are wine produced from grapes, olive oil from olives, and the milling of flour from wheat.[159] In each of these instances the products cannot be 'reduced' to their original constituents.[160] While there is not definitive agreement on what counts as instances of specification and accession,[161] the dividing line (such as it is), and thus the application of the individual doctrines, seems to depend on the identity of the constituent parts. For specification, the idea of a character change or change in identity in the relevant materials is important.[162] A now old Scottish Law Commission Memorandum notes that acquisition by specification occurs when the new thing 'is different *in kind* to its former components'.[163]

For English law, Hardcastle suggests that 'a new thing is created where the original material ceases to exist and can no longer be restored to its original physical state'.[164] The main authority cited in support of this contention is *Borden (UK) Ltd* v. *Scottish Timber Products Ltd.*[165] This case involved a dispute about ownership of a supply of resin which had been used to make chipboard. The Court was of the view that there was 'no property in the resin distinct from the property in the chipboard produced by the process. . . for all practical purposes [the resin] had ceased to exist and the ownership in that resin must also have ceased to exist'.[166] Here a change in character of the materials is still significant since the identities of the constituent materials cannot be restored to their original forms.

This distinction between specification and accession is supported by *Hendy Lennox (Industrial Engines) Ltd* v. *Grahame Puttick Ltd.*[167] Albeit it dealing with the straightforward end of the accession spectrum, part of

---

[159] J.B. Moyle (trans.), *Institutes of Justinian*, II: 25 (Oxford, 1911).

[160] Carey Miller, *Corporeal Moveables*, para. 4.05.

[161] Reid notes that in Scots law there is disagreement about whether these are separate principles, with some taking accession to include acquisition by specification. Reid, *The Law of Property in Scotland*, para. 588. Note that the Scottish Law Commission report above refers to specification as a form of industrial accession.

[162] E. Metzger, 'Acquisition of living things by specification' (2004) 8 *Edinburgh Law Review* 115–118, 117.

[163] Scottish Law Commission, Memorandum No. 28, *Corporeal Moveables: Mixing, Union and Creation* (31 August 1976), p. 4 [emphasis added]. Available at: www.scotlawcom .gov.uk/files/4113/1350/8753/cm28.pdf (accessed 27 November 2017).

[164] *Ibid.*, p. 169.   [165] [1981] Ch 25. See also *Re Peachdart Ltd* [1984] Ch 131.

[166] *Borden* at 46.

[167] [1984] 1 WLR 485. This case never specifically mentions accession, but to the extent that it is about two pieces of property becoming joined and the extent of the incorporation of one into the other it does deal with it.

the issue in this case was the extent to which engines had become incorporated into generators. Here Staughton J specifically differentiated the attachment of essentially unaltered engines from other situations:

> [T]he proprietary rights of the sellers in the engines were not affected when the engines were wholly or partially incorporated into generator sets. They were not like the Acrilan which became the yarn and then carpet (the Bond Worth case), or the resin which became chipboard (Borden's case), or the leather which became handbags (the Peachdart case), or the grapes, olives, wheat and barley mentioned by Crossley Vaines. They just remained engines, albeit connected to other things.[168]

The accession and specification doctrines could potentially be used to cover different types of situations in which biomaterials are utilised. For instance, accession might be applicable to the kinds of situations under consideration in *Dobson, Kelly*, and *AB* v. *Leeds*: respectively, a brain preserved in paraffin, various preserved body parts and prosecutions, and the preservation of whole organs in addition to tissue blocks and slides. Each of these involves the joining of different elements to create something else, where the thing created has not involved (at least on the face of it) a fundamental character change in the constituent materials. Meanwhile, specification could cover circumstances where some deeper form of character change or metamorphosis of the materials occurs.[169] David Johnston and Niall Whitty have both proposed, for example, that specification could be apt in cases such as *Moore*.[170] Whitty says, where 'a person alters the natural pattern of development of a living thing in such a way that the developed thing can no longer be identified with its predecessor, the case is eminently suitable for *specificatio*'.[171] Likewise, Price considered that a more specification-based work/skill principle might be appropriate 'in the context of modified, *distinct* types of derived human biological materials'.[172] These are intriguing suggestions, but the application of the doctrines may not be entirely straightforward (or satisfactory).

6.1   Potential Applications

Let us start by thinking about how an accession analysis might apply to the production of tissue blocks and slides. This process, as we saw in Section 5.1, involves encasing the tissue sample in wax to produce the

---

[168] *Ibid.* at 494.   [169] See Price, *Human Tissue*, pp. 258–262.
[170] Johnston, 'The renewal of the old', 92–94; Whitty, 'Rights of personality'.
[171] Whitty, 'Rights of personality' 227.   [172] Price, *Human Tissue*, p. 259.

tissue block, removing slices of the tissue block and fixing them to a slide, and the addition of chemicals to fix and stain the sample. The key question that demands an answer in such scenarios is: when materials are thus joined, which is the principal and which is the accessory? This is not an inconsequential question since invariably the owner of the principal will become the owner of the resultant item(s).[173] Hence, determining which is the principal will determine the allocation of new property rights. An initial possibility is that the tissue has acceded to the slide, wax, and chemicals. There are after all more of these materials in the end product than the original biomaterials. If this were correct, then the resultant slides would become the property of whoever owns the principal materials. This may be those doing the preserving and fixing or their institution (hospital, university, research laboratory, etc.).

Such a construal of the doctrine might appeal given its intersection with the work/skill exception in English law. Yet it need not be interpreted in this manner. While the relative amount of the physical substances in tissue blocks and slides suggests that the additional materials are the principal ones, the accession doctrine does not inevitably necessitate 'that bulk should prevail over value'.[174] In Scots law, value is not necessarily monetary value, but relates to the role of the product; for example, a valuable gemstone will accede to the ring once incorporated into the ring, even though it might be worth more separately than the metal setting.[175] Michael Bridge argues that, in English law, context is all important in determining how 'matters of size, value, and purpose' are to be interpreted.[176] This may be especially significant in the case of biomaterials given the multi-varied value transformation which they undergo in varying and disparate circumstances. They can, as we saw in Chapter 1, be valuable as objects of medicine, science, education, commerce, and so on. Accordingly, this may impact on our assessment of the type of value at issue and the relative importance of purpose.

In the example at hand, biomaterials are valued as pathological specimens which aid in the diagnosis of disease or for educational and research purposes (by looking under a microscope at the characteristics displayed by the cells after appropriate preparation). It is at least plausible

---

[173] Reid, *The Law of Property in Scotland*, para. 57; Bridge, *Personal Property Law*, p. 131.

[174] Reid, *The Law of Property in Scotland*, para. 590. Although note that for many prosections and preserved whole organs, the biomaterials would in fact still constitute the 'bulk'.

[175] Carey Miller, *Corporeal Moveables*, para. 3.19; Reid, *The Law of Property in Scotland*, para. 590.

[176] Bridge, *Personal Property Law*, p. 131.

to suppose accession in such cases can be taken to mean the *functional* or *purposive* subordination of the accessory to the principal.[177] The purpose of addition of the wax and chemicals is to preserve the characteristics of the tissue sample in order to facilitate the activities mentioned.[178] These additional materials are, on this analysis, subordinate to the biomaterials, and the owner of the resulting pathological specimen would be the owner of the original biomaterials. The prior question then becomes one of the ownership of the original biomaterials, something we will return to shortly. What then of other types of processes?

Hardcastle argues, for example, that cell lines and amplified DNA could be appropriately encompassed by accession. His reasoning is that, for both processes, chemicals and other materials need to be added to the originals. For the cells this induces replication whereupon the original cells divide – as do their descendants – to create the cell line. In the case of DNA, the added materials and chemicals stimulate the production of copies of the original DNA sample.[179] This process, using a technique called a polymerase chain reaction, results in many thousands (or more) copies of the DNA sequence. In concluding that accession is suitable for cell lines and amplified DNA, he presumes that the original biomaterials are still present, albeit having become minor substances within the resulting products. Consequently, he considers that they have acceded to the added materials.[180] He also supposes that the property rights in the resultant cell lines and DNA accrue to those who own the additional materials (i.e. the chemicals, etc.). Although potentially promising, I remain unpersuaded that accession is a good fit here.

The production of both cell lines and amplified DNA involves the creation of a new thing. These processes entail a character change in the original biomaterials such that the end products cannot be reduced to their original constituents. In the case of amplified DNA, the original DNA sample is in fact destroyed in the process of making the copies of the sequence. The first step in the process involves *denaturing* the double helix of the original DNA sample. This means that the double strand is split into two single strands. This can be done, for instance, by heating the

---

[177] On accession and functional subordination in general see Reid, *The Law of Property in Scotland*, para. 571.

[178] Although he does not discuss accession in this context, the fact that the purpose here is preservation rather than alteration is part of why Hardcastle rejects specification as applicable in such cases. See Hardcastle, *Law and the Human Body*, p. 142.

[179] Hardcastle, *Law and the Human Body*, pp. 169–170.   [180] Ibid., p. 170.

sample. A second step to cool the sample starts the process of binding the single strands to other short DNA sequences (primers) from the added chemical solution. These form new double stranded areas which DNA polymerase (an enzyme) can then bind to in order to synthesise the copies of the original DNA sequence. The original strand of DNA cannot be recovered. It has ceased to exist. In effect, the production of amplified DNA is more suited to a specification rather than an accession-based analysis, something which I suggest is also true of cell lines.

The creation of a cell line from progenitor cells does not involve their destruction per se, though it does involve to a certain extent their alteration. Once the primary cells are isolated from a tissue sample they are placed in a culture medium which is appropriate to the particular type of cells being cultured. The primary cells then undergo cell division, effectively creating copies of the originals. Ordinary cells will stop replicating after a certain number of divisions, whilst some can be induced to replicate indefinitely. The latter ones contain so-called immortalised cells like the HeLa and Mo cell lines.

The first thing to note is that in cell lines the progenitor cell is no longer in its original form – it has become two, then four, then eight, and so on. The second point is that, particularly in the case of immortalised cell lines, the resulting cells may not be identical to the original isolated cells. This is because they may have been modified in order to render them immortal.[181] In so developing and changing, the resultant materials can be distinguished from the original samples. That cell lines can have somewhat differing characteristics to the original cells was recognised in *Moore*: 'The distinction between primary cells (cells taken directly from the body) and patented cell lines is not purely a legal one. Cells change while being developed into a cell line and continue to change over time.'[182] This potentially makes specification the more suitable doctrine to be applied. Even if we conceded that in some instances the original progenitor cells are still somewhere to be found in the resulting product, it would not be practically possible to identify and retrieve these from the resulting substances. In this respect such processes may be more comparable to the resin in *Borden*; for all intents and purposes the original sample cells cease to exist.

---

[181] See, for example, M.I. Maqsood, M.M. Matin, A.R. Bahrami, M.M. Ghasroldasht, 'Immortality of cell lines: Challenges and advantages of establishment' (2013) *Cell Biology International* 1065.

[182] *Moore*, Supreme Court at 141, note 35.

It is worth noting that, in drawing his conclusion, Hardcastle relies on the view that the production of cell lines and amplified DNA are a particular type of accession termed accession by fruits or accession by natural increase.[183] This category of accession applies to the offspring of animals and the 'fruits' of plants, trees, vegetables, and so on. The general rule in such cases is that progeny belong to the owner of the parent animal or plant.[184] On this view we could think of cell lines and amplified DNA as being the 'progeny' of the parent cells' DNA strands. However, the move from the case of live animals and plants to modified biological materials seems somewhat tenuous. There is a lack of direct English authority on which to draw on regarding accession by fruits (as Hardcastle himself readily acknowledges), let alone anything from which to impute its application to biomaterials. There is also no suggestion in Scots law that such materials would be thus treated. Indeed, the few commentators who have considered the issue tend to take it as arguable that specification would be apt in these types of situations.[185] Hence, if one of these doctrines is to be employed, specification would seem better suited.

6.2   Some Stumbling Blocks

Despite the potential applications just set out, at a doctrinal level there are difficulties with utilising either accession or specification. Strictly speaking, they apply to items which *already* fall within property's ambit. Even though the acquisition of property rights via these routes is not reliant on *deriving* those rights from pre-existing title, they are meant to deal with situations where property rights already exist. That is to say, the purpose

---

[183]   Hardcastle, *Law and the Human Body*, p. 169.

[184]   Although note that as part of a hire purchase agreement, progeny belong to the purchaser (*Tucker* v. *Farm and General Investment Trust Ltd* [1966] 2 All ER 508). See generally C. Vaines, *Personal Property* (London: Butterworths, 1967), pp. 383–384. For a general discussion of this in Scots law see Carey Miller, *Corporeal Moveables*, para. 3.02 and Chapter 6.

[185]   Whitty, 'Rights of personality', 226–227, Carey Miller, *Corporeal Moveables*, para. 4.04, K. G.C. Reid, 'Body parts and property' in A. Simpson, R. Paisley, and D. Bain (eds), *Northern Lights: Essays in Private Law in Honour of David Carey Miller* (Aberdeen University Press, forthcoming); Edinburgh School of Law Research Paper No. 2015/25, 1–18. Available at SSRN: https://ssrn.com/abstract=2644303 (accessed 27 November 2017). This is not to say that there are not situations where accession would be more suitable; for example, the production of block and slides discussed earlier. See also a novel analysis by Jamie Glister and Tony Glister who consider the potential role of accession in relation to artificial implants such as pacemakers and hips (J. Glister and T. Glister, 'Property in recyclable artificial implants' (2013) 21 *Journal of Law and Medicine* 357).

of accession and specification is to deal with situations where the materials have owners and there is no arrangement between the parties about their use, but they are nonetheless used (either by mistake or dishonesty) to make a new thing.[186] Therefore, since prior property rights are necessitated, the doctrines do not sit well with the usual supposition that separated biomaterials are initially *res nullius*. Indeed, if such materials are initially unowned then we would not be dealing with *accessio* or *specificatio*, but with appropriation by first possession or occupancy (*occupatio* in Roman and Scots law).[187]

It has been suggested to me that perhaps I should not be so doctrinaire about this point. Where an object has no owner, then the first person to pick it up will become the owner by *occupatio*.[188] Presumably this then means that further down the line, accession and specification could come into play. This may be correct, but it does not deal with the fidelity of the presumption that biomaterials are indeed *res nullius*, and thus ripe for occupation, once separated. Nor is it sufficiently attentive to issues of justice arising from it. First occupancy, at least from a justificatory perspective, is problematic. The generation of property rights which are allocated to the first person (or organisation) to possess samples of biomaterials, as Whitty contends, 'appears unfair to the source, random in its result, and generally impolitic'.[189]

It is possible that unfair and impolitic outcomes could be avoided if we consider the *source* to be the one who becomes the owner by occupation. Such is the suggestion made by Johnston with regards to *Moore*. He posits that, on a civil law analysis, if UCLA owned the patented cell line, then it must have acquired them either because (1) title was transferred from Moore via donation or abandonment, or (2) their title derived from specification. For this, according to Johnston, 'we must assume that Moore acquired title to the cells at latest when they were removed from him'.[190] A similar contention was put forward in the Scottish case of *Holdich* v.

---

[186] Reid, *The Law of Property in Scotland*, para. 559. Reid makes this point in relation to specification, but it is also true of accession. Otherwise, if arrangements (e.g. contractual) were in place, we would be dealing with a form of derivative not original acquisition.

[187] The principal example of things which can be acquired by *occupatio* in Scots law is wild animals. See Reid, *The Law of Property in Scotland*, para. 542 and Carey Miller, *Corporeal Moveables*, para. 2.03.

[188] My thanks to Kenneth Reid for his comments regarding this.

[189] Whitty, 'Rights of personality', 223–224. See also Reid, *The Law of Property in Scotland*, para. 540 and 'Body parts and property', 12–13; Hardcastle, *Law and the Human Body*, pp. 130–131; and Price, *Human Tissue*, pp. 252–253.

[190] Johnston, 'The renewal of the old', 92.

Lothian Health Board.[191] The case, which is similar enough on its facts to *Yearworth*, will be discussed in more detail in Chapter 4. For now, however, note that counsel for the pursuer (claimant) argued that Mr Holdich took his sperm into his possession by 'depositing his ejaculate in a receptacle'.[192] Whilst we can see how Holdich might be viewed as quite literally taking possession of his sperm, the same cannot be said of situations such as that in *Moore*. Anaesthetised patients who have biomaterials removed do not take possession of them as they are not doing the removing. The same is true of non-anaesthetised patients or research participants, albeit they will be aware of the ongoing procedure while it is happening. In these situations, the first person to possess the biomaterials (in a literal sense) is the person or persons doing the removing.[193]

Nevertheless it is possible that accession and specification could be used in other circumscribed cases involving biomaterials. Where biomaterials are already deemed to be the property of a researcher or institution the doctrines could be employed. For example, specification might aid in cases where cells or tissue samples are misappropriated from research institutions and used to create cell lines or other novel products, while accession might be applicable where no *nova species* is created. The doctrines might give us some structure for determining the proprietary consequences in different situations. What these consequences are will depend on the facts and context.

In Scots law, accession is objective not subjective. This means that regardless of the good or bad intention (*bona* or *male fides*) of the party who uses the items, property rights will inhere in the owner of the principal. Thus, as a matter of 'proprietary consequences', determining which materials constitute the principal will be important.[194] Intention will only be relevant to possible compensation for the owner(s) of the accessories. The proprietary consequences of specification turn, as noted earlier, on whether a resulting 'new' thing can be reduced to its original parts. If they can, then it is not specification and owner of the new thing will not be its maker, but the owner(s) of the original materials.[195] Unlike

---

[191] [2013] CSOH 197.   [192] *Ibid.* at [29].

[193] Having said this, see Chapter 4, Section 3.1 for recent sperm cases where third parties are seen as acting as the agents of the source. It is possible that acquisition by occupation could be viewed in these terms.

[194] Carey Miller, *Corporeal Moveables*, para. 3.21.

[195] Reid, *The Law of Property in Scotland*, para 562 discussing *International Banking Corporation* v. *Ferguson Shaw and Sons* (1910) SC 182 and *McDonald* v. *Provan (of Scotland Street) Ltd* [1960] SLT 231, OH.

accession, specification is limited to good faith situations. The doctrine is not engaged (no property rights are created) where the maker of a novel product uses the original materials in bad faith.[196] The position in English law qua specification is not clear, but Bridge suggests that 'the owner of the materials is not in principle entitled to the new thing'.[197] Similar uncertainty could be said to exist in relation to accession in English law.[198]

Importantly, the question of property rights and compensation need to be kept separate. Whilst there is relatively more guidance in Scots law on the former, there is very little on the latter. In instances of accession, there is provision for compensating the owner of the original accessory materials based on the value of the materials.[199] In English law, in cases of accession, a wrongdoer may be liable in conversion.[200] The compensation will depend on market value of the chattel (biomaterials), but if a value cannot be determined, 'any doubt will be resolved in the claimant's favour'.[201] Johnston notes that, in the context of specification, Roman law did not provide for compensation for the owner of the original materials. This, he rightly implies, would be an unsatisfactory approach for contemporary cases. His preferred solution (proffered specifically in his analysis of *Moore*) is to draw on German law. He suggests that:

> [T]he maker of this new product would become its owner. . . But he would come under an obligation to the patient based on unjustified enrichment in this case, to surrender the amount of the value added to the materials as at the date of their transformation into the cell-line. The result is that he would be forced to account to the patient for some enrichment but not for the whole future profits to be made from the new thing.[202]

I am not persuaded that this is satisfactory either. Depending on how the 'value added to the materials as at the date of their transformation' is calculated, it could simply open up a route for researchers to non-consensually acquire biomaterials. If the value, in monetary terms is

---

[196] Carey Miller, *Corporeal Moveables*, para 4.06; Reid, *The Law of Property in Scotland*, para. 562.

[197] Bridge, *Personal Property Law*, p. 134.

[198] Although Crossley Vaines has suggested that 'courts are inclined to lean in favour of the innocent owner of annexed property' (*Personal Property*, p. 386).

[199] Reid, *The Law of Property in Scotland*, para. 574.

[200] Bridge, *Personal Property Law*, pp. 108 and 109. See also Vaines, *Personal Property*, p. 384. Although it likely makes no practical difference, note that Vaines was writing before the Torts (Interference with Goods) Act 1977.

[201] Bridge, *Personal Property Law*, p. 114. [202] Johnston, 'The renewal of the old', 93–94.

low, it is perhaps something that researchers would be willing to pay (on the odd occasion that a case is brought).

All of this notwithstanding, accession and specification do not address the prior, and in my view fundamental, issue of how the initial property rights are generated and acquired. Without modification these doctrines do not aid us with questions regarding ownership of the original unmodified samples. While it is possible that they could be evolved by the courts to apply to newly separated (and thus *res nullius*) biomaterials, this would be a significant departure from how they currently operate. It may simply be that old Roman doctrines are ill-suited to the challenges wrought by biotechnological processes and scientific advances. Any discussion of their applications is necessarily speculative due to uncertainties both in the interpretation of the doctrines and how they might apply specifically to conflicts involving biomaterials. There is scant contemporary legal precedent *tout court* on accession and specification in either Scots or English law, and certainly none involving the kinds of technological processes relevant to biomaterials.[203] There is thus little indication of how the courts would treat them in relation to biomaterials if they were so minded.

7   Concluding Remarks: Problematic Property Principles

The question of whether or not human biomaterials can be property, and who can be the holders of the requisite property rights are not inconsequential questions. Chapter 2 demonstrated that consent and authorisation as conceptualised within and operationalised by the Human Tissue Acts cannot do the job asked of them in terms of protecting source interests in their separated biomaterials. The current chapter revealed that the approach of the common law to the issue of property in human biomaterials is also inadequate. By tracing the jurisprudence from the early origins of the no property rule to the contemporary uses of the work/skill exception, we can see that the idea of normative transformation is significant; that is, the recasting of biomaterials from *res nullius* to *res* which are capable of being subject to property rights. Despite this insight, attempts to pin down and adequately delineate the principles underlying such a transformation have proved difficult. The work/skill exception, which is the most prominent doctrinal rule, is glaringly deficient. The supposed rationales which could be said to trigger or

---

[203] Hardcastle, *Law and the Human Body*, pp. 133 and 166.

underpin it (and thus the requisite normative transformation) are lacking on both explanatory and justificatory levels. Old Roman principles fare little better. Although there is some potential for adapting and utilising them, they are fraught with interpretive, applicability, and justificatory difficulties.

One unifying factor (perhaps the only one) amongst the relevant cases is that (until recently) the only person who could not come to own human biomaterials was their source. In Chapter 1 I suggested that the exclusion of the source from having property in their separated biomaterials is problematic. Where third parties are recognised as having property rights in biomaterials, they are protected by the law in their exercise of those rights. They thus gain a degree of control over the fate of the biomaterials which is denied to their source. Without cases which establish alternative and stronger property presumptions for the *sources* of the tissue, they will continue to be excluded from its ownership. The next chapter considers whether the newer sperm cases provide a satisfactory way forward in this respect.

4

A Property (r)Evolution?

1 Introduction

A cluster of recent sperm cases, a number of which we met briefly in the introductory chapter, have reinvigorated the debate with regards to property in human biomaterials. This chapter examines some aspects of these, demonstrating that they are significant for a number of reasons. First, they further illustrate the challenge which advancing biotechnology can present for the law; that is, how to deal with unforeseen dilemmas brought about by biotechnological progress. Relatedly, they represent another instance of the diverse legal ends for which property can be utilised. Finally, and perhaps most importantly for the Anglo-Australian jurisprudence, they go beyond the bald application of work/skill exception seen in previous cases. Although the decisions are not without some difficulties, collectively, they establish further legal bases for the ascription of property rights in human biomaterials (or at least in sperm samples). What we will see is that, as a consequence of them, the dual influences of the no property rule and the work/skill exception are in decline. This is a welcome evolution in the law in relation to property and biomaterials. What we will also see, however, is that we are left with a number of (legal) philosophical questions, which as yet have not been adequately addressed by the law.

2 *Yearworth* and Ownership of Sperm Samples

Yearworth, as we have already seen, involved claims relating to damage caused to stored sperm samples. Here causes of action relating to personal injury, property, and bailment were considered by the Court of Appeal. The decision is noteworthy, because in disputes over human biomaterials it is the first time that the *source* of those materials has been unequivocally recognised as the legitimate holder of property rights with respect to them. Yet the most significant aspect of this lies, perhaps, not in the decision itself, but in how it was reached.[1]

2.1 Property Not Personal Injury

Fundamentally, *Yearworth* illustrates the utility of employing a property approach and the related difficulty with considering novel challenges involving separated biomaterials outside such a framework. This is most evident if we consider the arguments relating to personal injury which were put forward.

Counsel for the men argued that had the sperm been damaged due to injury of the scrotum this would have been a personal injury and, further, that the mere fact of ejaculation should not make a difference to such a determination.[2] This is because the samples were being kept for use at a later date and the 'intended function of the stored sperm was identical to its function when formerly inside the body, namely to fertilise a human egg'.[3] Lord Judge CJ, however, noted some anomalies that would arise from upholding a claim in personal injury, including that (1) a personal injury would still have arisen even if the sperm had been damaged after the men had recovered their natural fertility, and (2) destruction of the sperm after the statutory limit on storage had been reached would also have to be deemed an injury in this respect.[4] In making this determination, the destruction of sperm was differentiated from unwanted pregnancy which is 'a physical event within the woman's body'.[5] In the eyes of the Court,

---

[1] M. Quigley, 'Property: The future of human tissue?' (2009) 17 *Medical Law Review* 457. See also M. Quigley, 'Propertisation and commercialisation: On controlling the uses of biomaterials' (2014) 77 *Modern Law Review* 677.

[2] *Yearworth* at [19].

[3] *Ibid.* Here the Court considered the German *Bundesgerichtshof* case in relation to a claim for damages due to destruction of frozen sperm. The German court held that damage to frozen sperm could be a personal injury as it retained a functional unity with the body; that is, was intended to be used to procreate (BGHZ 124, 52 VI. Civil Senate (VI ZR 62/93); translation of the case is available at: https://law.utexas.edu/transnational/foreign-law-translations/german/case.php?id=830 (accessed 27 November 2017)). See Whitty, 'Rights of personality', 224. Lord Stewart in a recent Scottish sperm case, which will be discussed in Section 4, thought the 'theory is a plausible one' (*Holdich* v. *Lothian Health Board* [2013] CSOH 197at [7]). For reasons which follow in the main text, I tend towards agreement with their Lordships in *Yearworth*, although arguably such an extension of personal injury law would not be much more of stretch than that contained in *Yearworth* in relation to property law. For a general discussion of reproductive injury see N. Priaulx, 'Managing novel reproductive injuries in the law of tort: The curious case of destroyed sperm' (2010) 17 *European J Health Law* 81.

[4] *Yearworth* at [19]. [5] *Ibid.* at [20].

damage cannot constitute a personal injury once the substance at issue is *separated* from the body; to do so 'would generate paradoxes, and yield ramifications, productive of substantial uncertainty'.[6]

We can see the pragmatism underlying the reasoning here. A personal injury is something which ordinarily happens directly to the embodied person. Allowing things done to our separated parts to constitute a personal injury would be to lose what is distinctive about such claims; that is, physical damage done to the person.[7] It is conceivable that alternative approaches could be developed. For example, Nicky Priaulx argues that we need to reconceptualise the notion of 'injury' in such cases.[8] Rather than conceiving of the injury in physical terms, one might look instead to the specific interests that have been interfered with; for example, the loss of the chance to be a genetic parent.[9] However, what is at issue is not simply the loss of such a chance; it is the loss of such a chance *consequent on damage* to the means to make this happen. The courts do not, and ought not to, compensate for each and every instance where there is loss of a chance (like not finding a suitable reproductive partner). For this reason, it is the interests that a person has in the use and control of their reproductive biomaterials which are key.

Although the personal injury claim was rejected, it was held that 'the men had ownership of the sperm for the purposes of their present claims'.[10] In this respect, the Court adopted A.M. Honoré's account of ownership,[11] saying 'ownership is... different collections of rights held by persons over physical and other things'.[12] This collection of rights and other elements as described by Honoré consists of eleven of what he considers to be the standard incidents of ownership:[13] the right to possess; the right to use; the right to manage; the right to the income of the thing; the right to the capital (comprising the power to alienate and the liberty to consume, waste, or destroy); the right to security (in one's position as owner); the right of transmissibility; the right to absence of term (a general immunity against the expiration of the rights); the prohibition of harmful use; liability to execution (liability regarding owner's debts); and residuary character (reflects the fact that owners

---

[6] *Ibid.* at [23].
[7] It is possible to sue in negligence for pure psychiatric harm, but this is difficult to prove. Brazier and Cave, *Medicine, Patients, and the Law*, pp. 196–197.
[8] Priaulx, 'Managing Novel reproductive injuries', 92.   [9] *Ibid.*   [10] *Yearworth* at [45].
[11] A.M. Honoré, 'Ownership' in A.G. Guest (ed.), *Oxford Essays in Jurisprudence* (Oxford University Press 1961), pp. 107–147.
[12] *Yearworth* at [28].   [13] Honoré, 'Ownership'.

can create lesser rights – for example, a lease – and upon expiration these generally revert to them[14]). Together he considers that these rights and other elements give an account of full liberal ownership.[15] His account is commonly joined with Wesley N. Hohfeld's analytical vocabulary of rights (claim, privilege/liberty, power, and immunity).[16] On this analysis of property, the incidents of ownership include: claim-rights of possession; liberty-rights to use and to consume or destroy; the power to manage, alienate, and transfer one's property; liabilities to execution and the expiration of their ownership; immunity from expropriation; the duty not to use the property in a way that harms others; and the right to the income of the thing.[17] Ownership, for Honoré, is 'the greatest possible interest in a thing which a mature system of law recognizes'.[18]

For the Court in *Yearworth*, a central feature which indicated ownership was the men's liberty to use, and to control the uses of, their sperm samples. Counsel for the Trust argued that, under the HFE Act, 'the men could not have *directed* the unit to use their sperm in any particular way... [they] could only have *requested* the unit to use their sperm in a particular way'.[19] The consent provisions of the Act mainly confer negative control regarding the use of one's gametes (and embryos).[20] The Trust, therefore, considered the men's rights thus-conceived to be so

[14] Occasionally they may become vested in other parties such as the state. *Ibid.*, pp. 126–127.

[15] *Ibid.*, p.111.

[16] W.N. Hohfeld, *Fundamental Legal Conceptions of a Right as Applied in Judicial Reasoning* (New Haven: Yale University Press, 1919, reprinted 1966). He also described their respective correlatives: duty, no-right, liability and disability. Note that many commentators use the term 'liberty' in place of the Hohfeldian 'privilege'. In this book I use the terms interchangeably. Additionally, we should note that Hohfeld thought that claim-rights are rights 'in the strictest sense' (*Ibid.*, p. 36). See S.R. Munzer's *A Theory of Property* (Cambridge: Cambridge University Press, 1990) for arguments on why Hohfeld's terminology is better conceived of as providing the vocabulary for analysis rather than constituting an analysis in itself.

[17] I will return to this list as part of the analysis in Chapter 6. Here I follow Munzer in the way he set out the incidents. However, we diverge in the Hohfeldian classification of some of the incidents. On this I have mostly followed Becker. For example, Munzer classifies the right to manage as a claim-right; I would argue that it is in fact a power since it essentially gives the holder the rights to alter the legal status of others with regards to the property. We can also see from this that the various rights can be divided into first-order and second-order rights. Second-order rights are those which modify first-order rights. Thus, powers and immunities modify claims and liberties. For example, I might have the liberty to use my book and a claim against other persons that they not use it; however, if I also have a power in relation to the book, I can use it to waive the duty of third parties to refrain from using the book.

[18] Honoré, 'Ownership', p. 108.   [19] *Yearworth* at [43].

[20] That this is the scope was confirmed in *Evans* v. *Amicus Healthcare Ltd* [2005] Fam 1.

attenuated as to 'eliminate any rights of ownership of the sperm otherwise vested in the men for the purpose of an action in negligence'.[21] The Court disagreed, instead viewing the negative control conferred by the Act as indicative of property rights. Lord Judge CJ identified this control (bestowed via the informed consent requirements) as one of the twin pillars of the Act.[22] Indeed, as we will see in Chapter 6, it is this negative control (exercised as an exclusionary right) which is one of the indicia of having a property right properly so-called.

In determining that the sperm samples could be considered as property, Lord Judge CJ accepted that the work/skill exception could apply to sperm stored in liquid nitrogen,[23] but said:

> [W]e are not content to see the common law in this area founded upon the principle in *Doodeward*, which was devised as an exception to a principle, itself of exceptional character, relating to the ownership of a human corpse. Such ancestry does not commend it as a solid foundation.[24]

His Lordship also said that 'a distinction between the capacity to own body parts or products which have, and which have not, been subject to the exercise of work or skill is not entirely logical'.[25] This is significant because it opens up other justificatory bases for the creation of property (rights). While it is the HFE Act which governs gametes, the Court commented on the inclusion of the work/skill exception in s. 32(9) of the Human Tissue Act 2004. In this respect, their Lordships were of the view that 'the effect of the subsection could not be to confine the common law's treatment of such parts or products as property *if otherwise it would rest on a broader basis*'.[26] Interestingly, the Court failed to recognise that if it had applied the work/skill exception, the requisite rights would be conferred upon the Trust or the fertility unit, not on the men.[27] This would have been in line with the previous cases outlined in Chapter 3. Some other additional reasoning would have been needed for the property rights to vest in the men (a step which, we will see shortly, a number of Australian cases have taken).

---

[21] *Yearworth* at [41].

[22] *Ibid.* at [44]. See also S. Devaney, 'Tissue providers for stem cell research: The dispossessed' (2010) 2 *Law, Innovation, and Technology* 165, 184 and *Stem Cell Research and the Collaborative Regulation of Innovation* (Abingdon: Routledge, 2014), pp. 93–95.

[23] *Yearworth* at [45(c)].   [24] *Ibid.* at [45(d)].   [25] *Ibid.*

[26] *Ibid.* at [38] [emphasis added].

[27] Price, *Human Tissue*, p. 257. This point was also made by the defenders in *Holdich* at [33]. This will be discussed in the next section.

In their discussion on property, their Lordships were influenced by the decision in the US case of *Hecht v. Superior Court (Kane)*.[28] In this 1993 case, a deceased man (Kane) had deposited sperm with Cryobank, Inc. In a suicide note to his girlfriend (Hecht), he stated that she should have the vials of sperm and that he wished her to have his child. This wish was also expressed in his will and the contract with the cryobank. Kane's children opposed the use of the sperm by Hecht and initially the Los Angeles Superior Court ordered the samples to be destroyed. Hecht appealed, seeking a peremptory decision to set aside the Superior Court's order. One of the questions to be resolved by the Court was whether sperm is the type of thing which can be disposed of at will and which is property for the purposes of probate. The judges viewed both of these in the positive:

> [A]t the time of his death, decedent had an interest, in the nature of ownership, to the extent that he had decision making authority as to the sperm within the scope of policy set by law. Thus, decedent had an interest in his sperm which falls within the broad definition of property in Probate Code section 62, as 'anything that may be the subject of ownership and includes both real and personal property and any interest therein.'[29]

Subsequently, the probate court ruled that Hecht be given three out of the fifteen vials of sperm. This was based on her 20 per cent entitlement to Kane's assets as set out in his will. Despite this, the administrator of the estate did not release the vials and further wrangling ensued. At this point the Second District Court of Appeal ordered that the vials be released.[30] After unsuccessfully attempting to become pregnant using two out of the three vials, Hecht filed a petition for the release of the remaining twelve vials.[31] While the probate judge initially denied the petition, the Californian Court of Appeal ordered the release of the twelve vials.[32]

Of this case their Lordships in *Yearworth* said that it was of 'considerable interest' and 'hard to regard ownership of stored sperm for the purpose of directing its use following death as other than a step further than that which the men invite us to take in the present case'.[33] I have argued elsewhere that the ruling in *Hecht* lends some support to the contention that the relevant proprietary interest must arise before death; it does not simply become operative post-mortem. The reason for this is

---

[28] (1993) 16 Cal.App.4th 836.   [29] *Ibid.* at 846.

[30] *Kane v. Superior Court* [1995] 37 Cal.App.4th 1577 at 1587.

[31] *Hecht v. Superior Court* [1996] 59 Cal.Rptr.2d 222 at 225.   [32] *Ibid.* at 225 and 228.

[33] *Yearworth* at [40]. Note that the HFE Act would empower those in a similar situation to Hecht to utilise their partners' sperm *if* the relevant written consent provisions are in place.

that 'the judgment was concerned with the disposition of the sperm at Will and as such it is concerned with the legitimacy of a decision which took place pre-mortem'.[34]

Successfully establishing that the sperm samples were capable of being property for the purposes of the men's claims also entailed that they had 'such lesser rights in relation to it as would render them capable of having been bailors of it'.[35] A bailment can arise where another party takes 'possession of a chattel in relation to which another person has rights'.[36] Bailors need not be owners, but do need to have possessory rights to the thing in question. In taking possession, the bailee acquires related duties in respect of the goods/chattel in question. The Court concluded that there was a gratuitous bailment (bailment without payment)[37] and that the Trust had breached its duty to take reasonable care of the samples.[38] What is significant is that without the recourse to the law of bailment, a useful avenue for remedial action would have been foreclosed. By finding that there had been a bailment, damages could be awarded, including for psychiatric injury and mental distress.[39]

Note that the Court found that the unit was liable to the men in tort for negligent damage to the sperm (damage to property). However, the damages available under tort are less favourable than those available for actions arising out of bailment (a particular legal relationship which gives rise to duties of care regarding the goods bailed). While there is some controversy over liability regarding gratuitous bailments, the Court was of the opinion that 'liability is sui generis';[40] that is, neither confined to liability arising in tort nor precluded from giving rise to liability akin to contract.[41]

---

[34] Quigley, 'Property: The future of human tissue?', p. 463.   [35] *Yearworth* at [47].
[36] *Ibid.* at [48].
[37] *Ibid.* The Court, in its assessment, relied on the judgments in *Coggs* v. *Bernard* (1703) 92 ER 107, *Wilson* v. *Brett* (1843) 152 ER 737, *Midland Silicones Ltd* v. *Scruttons Ltd* [1959] 2 QB 171, [1961] 1 QB 106, *Gilchrist Watt and Sanderson Pty Ltd* v. *York Products Pty Ltd* [1970] 1 WLR 1262, and *Port Swettenham Authority* v. *T.W.Wu and Co. (M) Sdn Bhd* [1979] AC 580.
[38] *Yearworth* at [48]   [39] *Ibid.* at [57]–[59].   [40] *Ibid.* at [48(h)].
[41] For a discussion of these aspects see C. Hawes, 'Property interests in body parts: *Yearworth v North Bristol NHS Trust*' (2010) 73 *Modern Law Review* 119, 134–136. Interestingly, Hawes argues that, although this is a novel approach given the men's situation a claim in conversion may have offered a better route, avoiding the issue of the quasi-contractual nature of gratuitous bailments (136–139). She bases this on the provisions of s. 2(2) of the Torts (Interferences with Goods) Act 1977: 'an action lies in conversion for loss or destruction of goods which a bailee has allowed to happen in breach of his duty to his bailor'. I do not pursue this here, but think that, given the difficulties

2.2 Narrow Scope and Shaky Foundations?

The decision in *Yearworth* has been met with mixed reactions.[42] Some, such as myself, have welcomed the case as an explicit step away from both the questionable work/skill exception and from the previous situation where the source was excluded from holding property rights in their own tissues. The use of bailment in opening up previously foreclosed remedial avenues has also been welcomed.[43] In spite of these advances, however, commentators have been cautious about the significance of the case and the reasoning contained therein. James Lee, for example, says that the scope of the decision is narrower than it might have been, noting that it might not be of help in cases of donation. The reason he gives for this is that donors might be taken to have abandoned their entitlements to the sperm.[44] This is an interesting suggestion. However, I will argue in Chapter 9 that donation does not entail an abandonment of entitlements; it is a transfer of them. As such, ownership could still be relevant to both donors and donees. Whether or not property-based legal avenues would be of use to either party would likely depend on the exact nature of disputes arising.

Shawn Harmon has also criticised the case for its narrowness. He is particularly troubled by the lack of elaboration regarding the scope of the rights at issue:

> What if no documents amounting to gratuitous bailment had been involved? What of the situation where the institution is not licensed

which attend liability and gratuitous bailments, her argument has appeal. Conversion generally will be discussed in Chapter 5. For a discussion on liability and gratuitous bailments see N. Palmer (ed.), *Palmer on Bailment*, 3rd edn (London: Sweet and Maxwell, 2009), pp. 58–61 and 91–96. Palmer's analysis had a strong influence on the route taken by the Court in *Yearworth* (at 48(h)–(i)).

[42] See Quigley, 'Property: The future of human tissue?'; S.H.E. Harmon, '*Yearworth v. North Bristol NHS Trust*: A property case of uncertain significance?' (2010) 13 *Medicine, Health Care, and Philosophy* 343, 346; S.H.E. Harmon and G.T. Laurie, '*Yearworth v. North Bristol NHS Trust*: Property, principles, precedents, and paradigms' (2010) 69 *Cambridge Law Journal* 476; Hawes, 'Property interests in body parts'; J. Lee, 'The fertile imagination of the common law: *Yearworth v North Bristol*' (2009) 17 *Torts Law Journal* 130; L. Rostill, 'The ownership that wasn't meant to be: *Yearworth* and property rights in human tissue' (2013) 40 *Journal of Medical Ethics* 14; and L. Skene, 'Proprietary interests in human bodily material: *Yearworth*, recent Australian cases on stored semen and their implications' (2012) 20 *Medical Law Review* 227.

[43] See Quigley, 'Property: The future of human tissue?', 466; Harmon and Laurie, *Yearworth*: Property, principles, precedents, and paradigms, 484; and Goold and Quigley, 'Human biomaterials', pp. 254–255.

[44] Lee, 'The fertile imagination of the common law', 137.

under the HFEA? What other rights does the claimant have with respect to the tissue other than return for his own agreed functional use? How far does the case and its finding of property go?[45]

These are all important questions, but it would have been extraordinary if this one case had answered them. The specific issues before the Court were, given the facts, whether damage to the sperm was a personal injury, whether it was the property of the men, whether there had been a bailment of the sperm to the Trust, and what damages might be recoverable in each of these situations.[46] Given this, the Court rightly confines its judgment to the particulars at hand.[47] The decision, as suggested by Lee, might have gone as far as to indicate that gametes broadly are to be considered as property.[48] Anything much above and beyond this would have lain well outside the facts of this case. And while the Court did not, in fact, go that far, the judgment did realise the potential, presaged in both in *Doodeward* and *Kelly*, for determinations of property in human tissue to rest explicitly on more extensive bases than had hitherto been possible. It is perhaps here that the stronger criticisms lie.

The problem with the decision is well-stated by Harmon and Laurie who say:

> [T]he conceptual foundation of the Court's finding of a (new) property interest is not entirely clear, and neither the brief reference to Honoré, nor the discussion of statutory consent adequately fill the lacunae. From whence does this property interest derive and why has it been so late in its recognition?[49]

For a case which turns on the property question, more attention to the law of property was perhaps needed. Harmon observes that property in the case seems to be acting as little more than a metaphor.[50] Meanwhile, Luke Rostill argues that the case should not be interpreted as actually vesting the men with property rights.[51] He contends that:

---

[45] Harmon, 'A property case of uncertain significance?', 347.   [46] *Yearworth* at [15]–[17].

[47] Something similar was explicitly expressed by Lord Stewart in *Holdich*. He said: 'Academics may be irritated by the opinion's apparently narrow knowledge base and by my failure to address the philosophical, ethical and policy considerations: but court judgments are about particular disputes and have to be based on the arguments and material presented' (at [5]).

[48] Lee, 'The fertile imagination of the common law', 137.

[49] Harmon and Laurie, 'Property, principles, precedents, and paradigms', 485.

[50] Harmon, 'A property case of uncertain significance?', 346.

[51] Rostill, 'The ownership that wasn't meant to be', 14.

[T]he conclusion that the men had 'ownership' for the purposes of their claims against the defendant was not a deduction from or an incident of the more general statement that they had legal ownership or possessory title for the purposes of a claim in negligence. Rather, the conclusion was confined to those particular purposes, to those specific claims.[52]

Thus, for him, the narrow context within which the decision was taken means that 'the men could have had "ownership" against the defendant *and only against the defendant* [the Trust]'.[53] He argues that the version of 'ownership' advanced by the Court cannot be considered to be a property right.[54] The particular reason, which we will see further in Chapter 6, is that for a right to count as a *property* right it must be enforceable against the world (a right *in rem*); that is, against all other persons.[55] If this is a necessary condition of a property right and, *if* the specifics of the decision in *Yearworth* are to be interpreted as Rostill suggests, then current analyses of the case which interpret it as vesting the men with property rights in their sperm are mistaken. While this is thought-provoking, we will see in Chapter 6 that it is a doubtful interpretation of the case.

Albeit for slightly different reasons, a related concern was raised in the Scottish case of *Holdich* v. *Lothian Health Board*.[56] As we will see shortly, in this case the defenders (defendants) claimed that the English case 'elides the concept of legal ownership and possessory title'.[57]

3 Sperm in Australia and Canada

3.1 Acting as Agents

While is not yet clear whether the scope of the decision in *Yearworth* will be extended to encompass other biomaterials in the future,[58] three Australian cases are germane to the question of the proprietary status of sperm samples: *Bazley* v. *Wesley Monash IVF Pty Ltd*,[59] *Jocelyn Edwards; Re the estate of the late Mark Edwards*,[60] and *Re H, AE*.[61] As

---

[52] *Ibid.*, 16.   [53] *Ibid.* [emphasis in original].   [54] *Ibid.*, 18.

[55] See, for example, S. Douglas and B. McFarlane, 'Defining property rights' in J. Penner and H. Smith (eds), *Philosophical Foundations of Property Law* (Oxford: Oxford University Press, 2013), pp. 219–243, pp. 223–224.

[56] [2013] CSOH 197.   [57] *Ibid.* at [33].

[58] Quigley, 'Property: The future of human tissue?', 464–466.   [59] [2010] QSC 118.

[60] [2011] NSWSC 478.

[61] No. 2, [2012] SASC 177, (No. 3) [2013] SASC 196. Re s. 22 of the Human Tissue and Transplant Act 1982 (WA); *Ex Parte C* [2013] WASC 3 is another recent Australian case relating to an application for the removal of sperm. However, the application was not

we saw in Chapter 1, in all three of these cases it was held that rights of possession to the sperm vested in the applicants.[62] The facts are, however, slightly different in each case, as are the jurisdictional contexts.

In *Bazley*, the samples had been stored prior to the deceased's death, but there is no legislation in Queensland which governs the storage and use of gametes after death. The IVF unit, therefore, stated that they would follow National Health and Medical Research Council guidelines on the matter. These advised against storing gametes for the purposes of IVF against the express wishes of the deceased.[63] In *Edwards*, although the deceased and his wife had previously had infertility tests and had an appointment to attend an IVF clinic, Mr Edwards had a fatal accident at work before they could attend the appointment.[64] There were, therefore, no samples held at the time of his death. As such, Ms Edwards first made an application – which was granted – for the extraction and storage of sperm samples.[65] A subsequent order was then sought for possession of the samples in order to undergo IVF treatment.[66] This case fell within the jurisdiction of New South Wales. Here, under the Assisted Reproductive Technology Act 2007 (ART Act), there is a prohibition on the provision of assisted reproductive treatment after the death of a gamete provider without their express consent.[67] This precluded the granting of the order in which Ms Edwards sought both the release of the sperm *and* permission to use it for IVF purposes.[68] As such, she brought an amended motion, seeking a declaration that she was 'entitled to possession of the sperm. The Court [was] being asked, in effect, to put aside any consideration of what she might do with it as a result of such possession.'[69] In both of these cases the orders were granted. The Court in *Bazley* drew on the decision in *Yearworth* in determining that the samples were property and that ownership of them passed to his personal representatives upon death.[70] While, in *Edwards*, Hulme J found *Yearworth* and *Bazley*, along with some other cases, 'persuasive of the view that the law should recognise the possibility of sperm being regarded as property'.[71]

---

decided on a proprietary basis (at 11) and the discussion of property does not add to that of the other cases.

[62] *Bazley* at [21], *Edwards* at [88] and [91], and *Re H, AE* at [58] and [60].

[63] *Bazley* at [4]–[6].   [64] *Edwards* at [9]–[10].   [65] *Ibid.* at [12]–[15].   [66] *Ibid.* at [29].

[67] *Ibid.* at [99]–[100]. Assisted Reproductive Technology Act 2007, s. 23(a).

[68] *Edwards* at [17].   [69] *Ibid.* at [24].   [70] *Bazley* at [33].

[71] *Edwards* at [84]. In reaching these conclusions, the courts in both *Bazley* and *Edwards* noted Master Sanderson's comments in *Roche* (discussed in Chapter 3).

Re H, AE is a South Australian case. The facts are similar to those in *Edwards*, with the deceased having died following a fatal accident. The deceased's wife applied for an order for the removal and possession of sperm samples, with the Court noting that 'it is apparent that the applicant intends to use the sperm to procure pregnancy by *in vitro* fertilisation'.[72] The application was granted subject to an exemption to the general ban on the use of gametes from deceased persons being sought from the Attorney-General of South Australia.[73] An important feature which sets this case and *Edwards* apart from *Bazley* is that the sperm samples in *Bazley* were determined to be the property of the deceased prior to death, and thus part of the deceased's estate. However they were explicitly excluded from the estates in the other two cases. The reason for this is that the samples in *Bazley* were collected prior to the death of the deceased, 'the ownership of which vested in [him] while alive'.[74] The samples in the later cases were extracted and collected posthumously, with Hulme J in *Edwards* saying that 'as Mr Edwards did not have property in his semen when he was alive, it did not form part of the assets of his estate upon his death'.[75] Given this, upon what basis were the applicants granted property rights in the samples?

Skene argues that the entitlement granted in *Edwards* was based neither on the fact that the sperm was part of the deceased's estate nor on the applicant's duty as administrator of that estate. Instead, she considers that the entitlement to possession was given due to discretionary considerations.[76] For example, the ART Act 2007 prohibits providers of assisted reproductive technology from *supplying* gametes without the consent of the other person,[77] and consent was not in place in this case.[78] Also, as we have seen, there is a prohibition in New South Wales on the posthumous use of gametes for IVF purposes. As such, these and other considerations needed to be examined to determine whether granting the order would in effect be futile.[79] While there was good reason for such discretionary considerations to be taken into account in the case, I do not share Skene's view that they form the basis of the entitlement. Instead, this seems to have been grounded in Ms Edwards' relationship to the deceased coupled with the application of work/skill exception.

---

[72] *Re H, AE* (no. 2) at [3].   [73] *Ibid.* at [69].   [74] *Bazley* at [33].   [75] *Edwards* at [87].
[76] Skene, 'Proprietary interests', 234–235.   [77] s. 21.
[78] Perhaps a little creatively Hulme J got around this point by classifying the activity in question as the 'release' rather than 'supply' of the sperm samples. See *Edwards* at [138]–[139].
[79] *Ibid.* at [127].

Regarding the first of these, the Court noted that it was open to them to recognise a 'right that extends beyond that which [Ms Edwards] would have as administrator'[80] and that she was 'the only person in whom an entitlement to property in the deceased's sperm would lie'.[81] In considering whether this was in fact the case, the Court then examined whether in applying work or skill the doctors or technicians might have property in the samples.[82] Since the decision in *Doodeward* is binding on the Australian courts, Hulme J was bound to consider the facts within its context. It was held that the exception would apply to the sperm as a result of having the samples having been preserved and stored.[83] The Court took the view that, although work and/or skill had been applied, those who preserved and stored the sperm samples were acting as *agents* of the applicant;[84] thereby, creating property rights which vested in her.[85] This extension of work/skill reasoning to allocate the consequent rights to the applicant is novel when compared to the previous usages of the exception. In England and Wales this has invariably been used to deny property rights to the sources and their representatives. Hence, although the Court did not reject the exception, it repurposed it.[86] This is a significant development in the context of the entitlements to the possession of sperm samples after their source has died. The same novel repurposing of the work/skill exception was subsequently adopted in *Re H, AE*.[87]

Like *Yearworth*, the scope of the Australian decisions is narrower than they might have been. Three particular qualifications are to be found in the cases. First, Hulme J in *Edwards* is explicit that the issue under consideration is merely that of entitlement to possession, not other proprietary entitlements that might stem from the recognition of the sperm as property.[88] A similar limit is to be found in *Re H, AE*, with Gray J saying that 'the deceased's sperm may be treated as property, at least to the extent that there is an entitlement to possession'.[89] Second, while recognising that sperm could be property within the law, the Court in *Edwards* confines it to 'certain circumstances, when it has been donated or removed for the purposes of being used in assisted reproductive treatment'.[90] Third, in *Edwards*, Hulme J was clear that the applicant

---

[80] *Ibid.* at [90].   [81] *Ibid.* at [91].   [82] *Ibid.* at [88].   [83] *Ibid.* at [79]–[82].
[84] *Ibid.* at [88].   [85] *Ibid.* at [91].
[86] See M. Quigley and L. Skene, 'Human biomaterials and property: Is the law still an ass?' in C. Stanton, S. Devaney, A.M. Farrell, and A. Mullock (eds), *Pioneering Healthcare Law: Essays in Honour of Margaret Brazier* (Abingdon: Routledge, 2016), pp. 156–167.
[87] *Re H, AE* (no. 2) at [58] and [60].   [88] *Edwards* at [78].   [89] *Re H, AE* (no. 2) at [58].
[90] *Edwards* at [84].

was 'the only person in whom an entitlement to property in the deceased's sperm would lie',[91] a position which was also endorsed in *Re H, AE*.[92] In adopting such a constrained view of the property rights involved, these cases could be subjected to a similar sort of critique to that which has been levied at *Yearworth*. Accordingly, it could be argued that what is at issue in these cases are rights of possession and that, on their own, these fall short of being full-blown property rights. Moreover, it could be thought that the rights of possession granted are exigible (that is, capable of being imposed) only against the facilities which were storing the sperm samples and were not 'good against the world'. Finally, we might also think that, in confining the right to the applicants and no one else, they carry the hallmark of personal rights rather than property rights. I think that such views, while provocative, would ultimately be misguided. The substantive arguments for rejecting such a position are set out in the Chapter 6.[93]

3.2   Further Disputes over Sperm

With regards to the issue of property in biomaterials, cases involving disputes over sperm have so far proved the most frequent to appear in front of the courts.[94] For now, therefore, they form the locus of the evolution of the law in this area. Such disputes have not been limited to ones involving either claims by the progenitors or their deceased partners. The Canadian case of *J.C.M.* v. *A.N.A.*[95] for example, involved a disagreement regarding the disposition of sperm straws held at a fertility

---

[91]   *Ibid.* at [91].   [92]   *Re H, AE* (no. 2) at [60].   [93]   See Section 4.

[94]   There have been cases involving either stored embryos or foetal tissue which have looked at the property question. Most of these have not tackled the issue straight on, either making ambiguous halfway house statements or deciding the cases on other bases. The US case of *Davis* v. *Davis*, 842 S.W. 2d 588 [1992], for instance, involved a dispute between the progenitors of a set of stored embryos. The Court maintained that 'pre-embryos are not, strictly speaking, either "persons" or "property," but occupy an interim category... any interest that Mary Sue Davis and Junior Davis have in the pre-embryos in this case is not a true property interest. However, they do have an interest in the nature of ownership' (at 597). Meanwhile other cases such as *Litowitz* v. *Litowitz*, 146 Wash. (2d) 514 [2002] and *J.B.* v. *M.B.* 783 A.2d 707 (N.J. 2001) mention property, but have no substantial engagement with it. In contrast, the Canadian case of *C.C.* v. *A.W.* 2005 ABQB 290, which entailed a dispute between AW (a sperm donor) and CC (a woman who had undergone IVF and had embryos created from the sperm), was unequivocal in its finding that stored embryos were property. The decision stating that CC owned them and that they were 'chattels that can be used as she sees fit' (at [21]).

[95]   2012 BCSC 584.

clinic. JCM and ANA, a lesbian couple who had separated, had previously given birth to two children (one each) and had joint custody of those children. Under their separation agreement, child support for both children was paid by JCM to ANA and they had divided their property. However, the sperm straws had not been included in the agreement.[96] JCM applied to the Court for sole possession of the vials so that she could have a child with her new partner. JCM had previously offered to purchase half of the vials from ANA, but ANA contended that she would prefer if they were destroyed.[97] The Court considered whether the sperm straws were property and, if so, whether they should be divided between the parties. Drawing on *Yearworth* and an earlier Canadian case involving embryos,[98] the Court concluded that the sperm straws were property and should be divided amongst JCM and ANA.[99] In so doing, Russell J was mindful of the differences between the cases; in particular, that *JCM* was not a case concerning negligence and that the decision in *Yearworth* was heavily reliant on the fact that it was the men who had *ejaculated* the sperm.[100] Interestingly, Russell J also noted an important point which can get lost in debates regarding these types of dilemmas:

> [I]t is clear to me in the context of this dispute that the sperm is the property of the parties. The sperm has been treated as property by everyone involved in the transaction, from the donor to Xytex, Genesis and the parties. It has been purchased; the parties have a right to deal with it. They have made use of it to their benefit. The respondent's moral objections to the commercialization of reproduction or the commoditization of the body seem to me to be too late. Certainly, they are interesting arguments for the respondent herself to make given she participated in purchasing and using a donation of sperm from an anonymous donor.[101]

The fact that human biomaterials can be, and indeed regularly are, treated as property, is a point that has been made previously by Imogen Goold and myself.[102] It is also something which is keenly illustrated by another couple of cases: one Canadian, one Australian.

The first of these is *Lam v. University of British Columbia*.[103] At first glance this case looks reasonably similar in its facts to *Yearworth*. It is a class

---

[96] *Ibid.* at [5]–[6].   [97] *Ibid.* at [11]–[17].   [98] *C.C.* v. *A.W.* See note 94 above.
[99] *J.C.M.* v. *A.N.A.* at [55].   [100] *Ibid.* at [61]–[63].   [101] *Ibid.* at [69].
[102] Goold and Quigley, 'Human biomaterials', p. 232. See also I. Goold, 'Sounds suspiciously like property treatment: Does human tissue fit within the common law concept of property?' (2005) 7 *University of Technology Sydney Law Review* 62.
[103] 2013 BCSC 2094.

action by a group of men who had all stored sperm with the University of British Columbia (UBC) Andrology Laboratory as they were all about to have chemotherapy. Sperm stored at the facility was damaged after the electricity supply to a freezer was interrupted.[104] The case differs from *Yearworth* because here the men had all paid storage fees. As such, the type of potential applicable legislation differed. The issue before the Supreme Court of British Columbia was whether the sperm could be considered 'goods' for the purposes of the Warehouse Receipt Act 1996 (WRA). Even though the issue of sperm as property was not explicitly considered within the Act, the Court considered the men's sperm was their property.[105] It was considered that the goods (sperm) had been bailed to UBC and that they were required to be 'careful and vigilant' bailors.[106] The defendants argued that s. 7 of the Assisted Reproduction Act 2004, which prohibits the sale of gametes, rendered certain sections of the WRA inapplicable.[107] The Court rejected this, essentially saying that limits could be placed on how items of property are dealt with (i.e. by other legislation) without creating 'an irreconcilable conflict'.[108]

The second case worth mentioning is *Clark* v. *Macourt*.[109] This case, which was on appeal to the High Court of Australia, involved a contractual dispute between two providers of reproductive technology services. The appellant (Clark) had agreed to buy stock, including straws of frozen sperm, from the respondent's company (Macourt). From the sperm straws bought, Clark averred that 1,996 of them did not comply with guidelines regarding the identification of sperm donors. She thus brought a case for breach of warranty.[110] Earlier, the Supreme Court of New South Wales had found for the appellant. Although Clark had paid Macourt's company less than $400,000, the Court held that the damages due should be the cost of buying replacement sperm from a comparator company (in this instance one in the United States). This amounted to approximately $1 million. The Court of Appeal overturned the decision on damages, holding that none were due to Clark, because her costs in buying the straws had been covered by the charges to her patients for treating them. Any losses to her were thus

---

[104] *Ibid.* at [1].   [105] *Ibid.* at [34] and [41].   [106] *Ibid.* at [42].

[107] *Ibid.* at [15] and [45].

[108] *Ibid.* at [46]. The specific point at issue was whether the warehouse could deal with the sperm as a negotiable receipt. If the sperm constituted a negotiable receipt, it 'may be sold and purchased as representation of the goods indicated on the receipt' (at [16]). The Court held, however, that it was not (at [46]).

[109] [2013] HCA 56.   [110] *Ibid.* at [1]–[3].

covered.[111] The High Court subsequently reversed the decision and held that orders should be made in line with the original ruling.

The question of whether or not the sperm *could* be property is not raised at any point in the High Court judgment. This might be seen as an artefact of the fact that it is essentially a case about breach of contract. The only mention of property or ownership in the High Court decision is when Gageler J is discussing how to measure damages. He says that the 'value to the buyer of having ownership of, and control over, contractually compliant goods that can be bought and sold in a market as at the time of delivery ordinarily equates to the market value of those goods at that date'.[112] Even so, the assumption is that the straws of sperm are just such contractually compliant goods; that they are goods or chattels that can be subject to property rights and over which sale contracts can be made and enforced.

4   Putting a Kilt on *Yearworth*?

The Scottish case of *Holdich* v. *Lothian Health Board* is reasonably similar in its facts to *Yearworth*. Prior to having treatment for testicular cancer, the pursuer (claimant) gave three sperm samples for storage by Lothian Health Board. Nine years later he requested access to the samples so that he and his wife could undergo IVF treatment, whereupon he was told that the storage unit had malfunctioned. Initially the pursuer was told that he ought not to use the sperm due to the possibility of damage. Unlike in the English case, the sperm in this one did not perish. Holdich received conflicting advice about the risks of using the sperm and ultimately decided not to use the stored samples.[113] He was seeking compensation for the damage in negligence and pursued three possible remedial avenues. These were 'a claim for mental injury consequential on property damage in breach of contract..., a claim for "pure" mental injury in delict [tort],... [and] a novel type of claim for damage to sperm, neither person nor property but something *sui generis*, with consequential mental injury'.[114] The Court of Session (Scotland's civil court) heard the preliminary pleadings for the case. The purpose of this was to look at whether the pursuer could have a cause of action under Scots law.[115] As such, certain points of law could be assessed without requiring proof of facts.[116] Permission was given for the

---

[111] *Ibid.* at [5].   [112] *Ibid.* at [67].   [113] *Holdich* at [1]–[2].   [114] *Ibid.* at [4].
[115] *Ibid.* at [3].
[116] *Ibid.* at [5]. Lord Stewart concluded that 'the claim in delict for "pure" mental injury caused by negligent out-of-body damage to sperm is apt for proof and certainly cannot be rejected out of hand'. On this basis he thought that the property claim should also be

case to go to proof (the main civil court hearing in which evidence is heard), but the case did not go to full trial and was eventually settled out of court.[117]

The defenders in *Holdich* claimed that the pursuer was 'trying to put a kilt on *Yearworth*'.[118] There are different limbs to this overall claim, not in the least the argument that the English law of bailment does not have an adequate counterpart in Scots law.[119] The crux of the matter is that bailment per se in English law need not be contractual, whereas its Scottish equivalent, termed deposit, always is.[120] However, as the sperm was stored in a NHS facility for free, it is not clear that a contract of deposit existed.[121] Some informative pieces on the finer details of Scots law in this respect can be found elsewhere[122] and so I leave these aside. Instead, I want to reflect on another claim, put forward by the defenders: that the English case 'elides the concept of legal ownership and possessory title'.[123] It is worth introducing and beginning to explore this as it will help to lay the foundations for some of the contested conceptual terrain we will encounter in the next part of the book.

4.1   Circumscribing Ownership?

In making their argument, the defenders in *Holdich* argued that the pursuer 'has none of Professor Honoré's incidents of ownership, or at least none in an unqualified way'.[124] In this respect they seemed to put

---

    heard, although he noted his reservations about whether 'the property-contract case as currently presented is sound in law'.

[117] Personal communication with the pursuer's representative, Susan O' Brien QC, Compass Chambers (16 March 2017). Given that the case settled out of court, we cannot know if the uncertainty regarding whether or not there had actually been damage to the sperm would have affected that chances of a successful outcome for the pursuer.

[118] *Holdich*. at [15]. The reasons for this are twofold, both relating to the issue of contract. First, in English law 'bailment can be "akin to contract" but is not a contract, whereas the nearest Scots equivalent, deposit, is contractual' (at [18]). Second, the Scottish Court also had to grapple with the question of whether the pursuer had contracted on an individual basis with the Lothian Health Board, a concern which would not arise for services within the NHS in England (at [18] and [53]).

[119] *Ibid.* at [18].   [120] *Ibid.*   [121] *Ibid.* at [21]–[22].

[122] For a discussion of various aspects of the case see Reid, 'Body parts and property'. See also E.C. Reid, 'Delictual liability and the loss of opportunity of fatherhood: *Holdich v Lothian Health Board*' in A. Simpson, R. Paisley, and D. Bain (eds), *Northern Lights: Essays in Private Law in Honour of David Carey Miller* (Aberdeen University Press, forthcoming); Edinburgh School of Law Research Paper No. 2015/30, 1–19. Available at SSRN: https://ssrn.com/abstract=2663063 (accessed 27 November 2017).

[123] *Holdich* at [33].   [124] *Ibid.* at [34].

forward a similar line of argument to the defendants in *Yearworth*; that the rights are so circumscribed so not to amount to ownership. While this line of argument was rejected in that case, it nonetheless raises an interesting question about the extent to which limitations on the ordinary indicia of ownership are significant. Does the circumscription of these elements diminish the rights to such an extent that we ought not to talk of property or ownership? The defenders in *Holdich* claim that Honoré's account requires that 'most if not all of the incidents of ownership' are required for there to be ownership properly so-called.[125] This, however, is a misreading of Honoré; he categorically does not say this. He suggests that a 'cardinal feature' of ownership is 'the concentration in the same person of the right (liberty) of using as one wishes, the right to exclude others, the power of alienating and an immunity against expropriation'.[126] Moreover, he goes on to say that 'it would be a distortion. . . to speak as if this concentration of patiently garnered rights was the only legally or socially important characteristic of the owner's position'.[127] Nevertheless, as we will see in the next chapter, it is correct that Honoré's account (frequently seen as a 'bundle of rights' view of property) is problematic.

Leaving this aside for now, on its own terms the defenders would seem to be incorrect in their contention that the pursuer is lacking the requisite elements. There can be no dispute that the provisions of the HFE Act, via the informed consent requirement, minimally confer and protect a gamete provider's right to exclude and power to alienate. Without their express permission no one else is permitted to use the gametes for any purpose, be that for IVF or research. Moreover, they can request that their samples be destroyed, something which would be the archetypal instance of alienation. But even if they do not go this far, they could give permission for their samples to be alienated by transfer to third parties, either as a donation to others for IVF or for research purposes. Gamete providers are, therefore, at liberty to control the uses of their samples in these circumstances, in addition to being at liberty to use them for their own IVF treatments. The fact that there are limitations on these uses does not do the work that the defenders would like. There are all manner of restrictions on things that we uncontroversially accept as being governed by property rights.[128]

---

[125] *Ibid.*   [126] Honoré, 'Ownership', p. 113.   [127] *Ibid.*
[128] For example, the fact that I cannot use my car to run over innocent pedestrians does not detract from my property rights in said car. Similarly, in relation to buildings and land, planning laws circumscribe the scope of any property rights involved. See Lyria Bennett Moses' discussion about restrictions on property as applied to biomaterials ('The

The defenders in *Holdich* claimed that the Court in *Yearworth* awarded a property remedy to the men based on a highly circumscribed *right to use*; a claim which Lord Stewart thinks they were correct to make.[129] In reaching this conclusion, his Lordship cites the following text from the English case: 'we are fortified by the precise correlation between the primary, if circumscribed, rights of the men in relation to the sperm, namely in relation to its future use, and the consequence of the Trust's breach of duty, namely *preclusion of its future use*.'[130] It is this reference to the preclusion of future uses which seems to influence Lord Stewart's understanding of the reasoning in the case. However, there is another interpretation which would fit better with the usual run of English property law; that is, what the Court was remedying was the fact that the claimants had been wrongfully dispossessed of their sperm samples.

4.2   Possession and Ownership

English law (it is commonly said) does not actually protect ownership as such. It can more accurately be described as protecting possession (or at the very least protecting individuals from dispossession): 'peaceable possession should not be disturbed by wrongdoers'.[131] Additionally, what matters for the English lawyer is relative title.[132] We can see this in operation in *AB* v. *Leeds* where it was held that 'on the assumption that the Doodeward exception applies the pathologists became entitled to possess the organs, the blocks and slides *at least until a better right is asserted*'.[133] There unfortunately is no indication about what circumstances are needed in order for a better right to be asserted. As we will see in Chapter 6, although it is true that possessory rights do not (always) equate with ownership, the person with the better right to possession

---

problem with alternatives: The importance of property law in regulating excised human tissue and *in vitro* human embryos' in I. Goold, J. Herring, L. Skene, and K. Greasley (eds), *Persons, Parts and Property: How Should We Regulate Human Tissue in the 21st Century?* (Oxford: Hart Publishing, 2014), pp. 197–214, pp. 209–211).

[129] *Holdich* at [46].   [130] *Yearworth* at [45] [emphasis added].
[131] *Jeffries* v. *The Great Western Railway Company* (1856) 5 Ellis and Blackburn 802 at 805.
[132] D. Fox, 'Relativity of title at law and in equity' (2006) 65 *Cambridge Law Journal* 330, 330; K. Gray and S. Gray, *Elements of Land Law*, 5th edn (Oxford: Oxford University Press, 2009), para. 2.2.4. We will see in Chapter 6 that there is a plausible argument to be made that English law contains a doctrine of 'deemed ownership'. See L. Rostill, 'Relative title and deemed ownership in English personal property law' (2015) 35 *Oxford Journal of Legal Studies* 31.
[133] *AB* v. *Leeds* at [156] [emphasis added].

relative to others is often considered in ordinary parlance to be the owner.[134] In *Yearworth*, therefore, it was the claimants' better right to possession, along with the duty owed to them by the Trust not to negligently damage the samples, which was the crux of the matter.

The reason this might be important in the context of *Holdich* is that, in resolving conflicts, unlike English law, Scots law is concerned with absolute rather than relative title. Ownership is one of a *numerus clausus* (fixed list) of real rights (rights in *things*).[135] It is 'the right of using and disposing of a subject as our own, except in so far as we are restrained by law or paction'.[136] Put another way it is the 'right of use, enjoyment, and abuse'.[137] Despite this, Lord Stewart thought that 'the pursuer is mistaken in thinking, apparently, that he has to demonstrate ownership in a global sense to be eligible for a Yearworth-type remedy'.[138] The reason for this is because he viewed the 'ownership' in *Yearworth* to have been predominantly derived from the men's right to use the sperm. However, as will become clear when I return to the English case in the next chapter, this is too narrow a view of the ownership at issue.

Whilst I reserve fuller discussion of the idea of property and ownership for the next two chapters, for now we can note that there is more going on in both *Yearworth* and *Holdich* than mere entitlements to possession. Clearly the fertility units have immediate rights of possession over samples for the purpose of storage. But rights of possession are not the same as having the ultimate disposition over the fate of the materials held. This is something which the progenitors have, at least until they legitimately transfer the samples and the attendant rights, or until some statutory limit (for example, time limits on storage) supersedes their rights in this respect.

---

[134] On this view of property, as Rostill explains, 'the property right, that one acquires with respect to a chattel . . . binds persons generally but not any one with a better, because pre-existing, "title" to the chattel' ('Relative title and deemed ownership', 34). See also *Waverley Borough Council* v. *Fletcher* [1996] QB 334, 345; S. Farran,' Storing sperm in Scotland: A risky business' (2011) 2 *European Review of Private Law* 258, 263; W.J. Swadling, 'Property: General principles' in A. Burrows (ed.), *English Private Law*, 3rd edn (Oxford: Oxford University Press, 2013), pp. 173–306, p. 208; and B. McFarlane, *The Structure of Property Law* (Oxford: Hart Publishing, 2008), p. 146.

[135] Reid, *Law of Property in Scotland*, para. 3; Whitty, 'Rights of personality', 222.

[136] J. Erskine, An Institute of the Law of Scotland (Edinburgh: Legal Education Trust, 1st edn 1773, reprint), II, I, 1; Reid, *Law of Property in Scotland*, para. 5.

[137] Reid, *Law of Property in Scotland*, para. 5.

[138] *Holdich* at [46]. The list of real rights in things in Scots law also includes possession so perhaps Lord Stewart thought that demonstrating a right in this respect would have been enough.

So what then are the implications of the sperm cases for how we understand the issues of property in separated biomaterials?

5 Transforming Tissues Revisited

In the previous chapter I suggested that the idea of normative legal transformation (from *res nullius* to *res*) is integral to understanding the approach of the law to separated biomaterials. This is still the case in the wake of the sperm cases. The Court in *Yearworth*, for example, accepted that the living body cannot be property. By implication this means that *in vivo* sperm cannot be subject to (legal) property rights. Upon separation, something needs to happen to bring about the requisite transformation. Given the rejection of the work/skill exception in the case, what explains and justifies the transformation of the sperm from *res nullius* to *res*?

5.1 Use Beyond Mere Existence

One thing which could reasonably be read into the existing case law (scant as it is) is that different circumstances generate property rights in different ways. Some are created by the application of the nebulous work/skill, while in other contexts something like intention and/or purpose becomes important. Hardcastle, for instance, argues that *Kelly* provides judicial support for the proposition that intention is significant (even in the absence of the application of work/skill).[139] As we saw in the previous chapter, this case suggested that property rights in biomaterials could be generated 'even without the acquisition of different attributes, *if they have a use or significance beyond their mere existence*'.[140] Consider the fact that the body parts at issue in *Kelly* had all been preserved for the purposes (educational and otherwise) of the Royal College of Surgeons. Given this, we could also presume that the requisite intention to retain the parts for such uses had been formed. If intention or purpose is significant, then it could help to explain the decision in *Dobson* where the sphere of concern was the coroner's jurisdiction. In this context there would usually be no intention or need to retain organs or tissue beyond the end of the investigation at hand. Hence the relevant purpose/intention could be viewed as missing in the case of coronial investigations. If this is correct, then work or skill applied in the course of coroner's investigations ought not to be considered relevantly transformative (even though presumably

---

[139] Hardcastle, *Law and the Human Body*, p. 151.   [140] *Kelly* at 631 [emphasis added].

no less work or skill is required here than by pathologists in other settings).

The decision in *Yearworth* could also be read in a manner consistent with an account which emphasises purpose and/or intention as being significant. The fact that the sperm was being stored for future potential IVF purposes played a central role in their Lordships' deliberations. This is a use *beyond* the mere existence of the samples. What is more, the men *intended* to preserve them for the future. As such, a plausible interpretation of the case would be that this intention to use, or the future purpose of, the sperm, along with the control bestowed within the statutory framework of the HFE Act, does the necessary work in transforming the normative status of the samples (from *res nullius* to *res*). This would also be consistent with what Hardcastle terms the 'detachment plus intention' principle.[141] He says '[f]or property rights to be created under this principle it is necessary for a person to form and express an intention to use separated biological materials as property.'[142] Although such an approach looks promising, it is not without its problems.

Before moving on to examine these, note that the elements just discussed could also be viewed as key even if their Lordships in *Yearworth* had decided to employ the work/skill exception. While the effect of the exception in all relevant instances prior to *Yearworth* was to generate property rights for third parties, the Australian sperm cases demonstrate that this need not be the case. We could instead view those doing the freezing (applying work/skill) as acting as the agents of the source. Considering it in this way might again point towards the idea of intention and/or purpose, since those doing the freezing are carrying out the intentions of the sperm progenitors.

That the exception would be applicable in the English case was disputed by the defenders in *Holdich*. They argued that 'the purpose of freezing is not to change the attributes of the thing but to preserve its attributes'.[143] For this reason they contend that the work/skill exception would not in fact have applied in *Yearworth*. The defenders are correct to note that the purpose of freezing sperm samples is for them to be available at a later date, whereupon they would need to fulfil the same physiological function as they would if they were *in vivo*. Yet they are not correct in the inference that the Court of Appeal in *Yearworth* was somehow mistaken to think that *Doodeward* would apply. As has become

---

[141] Hardcastle, *Law and the Human Body*, p. 150.   [142] *Ibid.*, p. 151.
[143] *Holdich* at [33].

apparent in the previous chapter and this one, prior case law gives little guidance on which to make detailed assessments about the scope and boundaries of the work/skill principle. Existing precedent does not rule out situations such as frozen sperm, especially if we take seriously the idea of biomaterials having a use beyond their mere existence and thus read in a purpose or intention requirement.

5.2   Intention and Future Use

What does it mean to form an *intention* to use something 'as property'? I regularly use items, and perhaps use them as property, without forming any sort of explicit intention to do so. Take, for example, reading a book. I may be using it, and indeed have formed the relevant intention to do so, but I am unlikely to have overtly intended to use it as property. Rather, barring anybody else's better claim to it, we might simply impute the relevant intention from the fact of my usage. Conversely, I could, upon reading my university library's copy of the same book, form a conscious intention to use it as property. This could mean at least two things. First, I might merely form an awareness that this is an item governed by property rights, but with no concurrent intention that it become mine. Second, I could indeed form an intention that the book becomes mine. Despite this, in the second instance, ownership of the book will not pass to me. I may be in factual possession of the book, but there is no intent on the part of the university that legal title pass to me when I borrow one of their books.[144]

Of course we might think that separated biomaterials are different from books, after all the law considers these to be *res nullius* while attached; in which case perhaps intention may be relevant to the *de novo* creation of property rights in biomaterials. Hardcastle thinks that in most cases the requisite property rights would initially be allocated to the source:

> In most circumstances, A's consent to the removal of biological materials would also be sufficient to constitute the consent necessary for a valid expression of intent to the use of materials as property. By giving consent, a source will usually be aware that biological materials are being removed and will be used as property for various purposes.[145]

---

[144] In Chapter 6, we will return to the distinction between factual and legal possession.

[145] Hardcastle, *Law and the Human Body*, pp. 151–152. Non-consensual removal from living persons is covered by battery and wrongful removal ought not to give rise to property rights according to Hardcastle (pp. 153–154).

Thus the source's intention for the materials to be used as property is transformative.

The difficulty with this is that, contrary to Hardcastle's view, it is unlikely that persons ordinarily form any such intention regarding their separated materials. I have previously argued that, from the point of view of the source, 'if the intention requirement entails "conscious" or "deliberate" intent to create property, then it will falter before it even gets going'.[146] The reason for this is that for an intention to form, individuals need to be aware of the uses that their separated materials might be put to, or indeed that they might be used at all. This is not always going to be the case, especially given the exemptions from the consent requirements contained in the Human Tissue Act 2004.[147] Moreover, guidance from the Medical Research Council (MRC) encourages researchers to obtain generic rather than specific consent.[148] This is to allow for uses or use in research not anticipated at the time of consenting.[149] Yet this creates a difficulty for any purported intention requirement, since the very point of generic consent is that all future uses cannot be specified.

One might argue that knowledge of these possible uses is not necessary. The fact that tissue is being removed for certain purposes (which may include research) is enough for individuals to be aware that they will be used as property. But this will not do. If the starting position is that the source does not own their biomaterials, there is little reason for them to assume (unless explicitly told) that others would come to do so. Indeed, the language of policy documents is not infrequently constructed to convey this lack of ownership. For example, the MRC guidance on the use of human biological materials states that '[d]onated samples are often

---

[146] Quigley, 'Property in human biomaterials', 680.

[147] *Ibid.* See also Chapter 2, Section 3.1.2 of this book.

[148] Medical Research Council, *Human Tissue and Biological Samples for Use in Research: Operational and Ethical Guidelines* (November 2014), p. 6. Available at: www.mrc.ac.uk/publications/browse/human-tissue-and-biological-samples-for-use-in-research/ (accessed 27 November 2017). Previous iterations of the HTA's Code of Practice on Consent also did this, 'it is good practice to request generic consent because this avoids the need to obtain further consent in the future' (Code of Practice 1: Consent (2014), para. 40). However, the most recent version has moderated this, mentioning it as an option rather than the preferred route (Code of Practice A: Consent, paras 41 and 42; Code of Practice E: Research, paras 45 and 46).

[149] Note that there may be human rights implications of obtaining such consent. McHale argues that it could be subject to challenges under the Human Rights Act 1998 and the European Convention on Human Rights; in particular Article 8 (right to privacy). (J. McHale, 'The legal regulation of human tissue' in J. Laing and J. McHale (eds) *Principles of Medical Law* (Oxford: Oxford University Press, 2017), pp. 1005–1047, para. 9.14).

described as "gifts" although it is recognised that donors of samples are not usually regarded as having ownership or property rights in these.'[150] It is also sometimes the case that gifts and donations are referred to *as if* they are not property, *as if* they are an alternative to the property paradigm. We will see in Chapter 9 that, even though it is ordinarily not acknowledged when gifting is discussed in relation to human bio-materials, the law of gifts is an integral part of the law of property. For this reason, donation cannot stand as an alternative to property in the manner in which some seemingly think it does. For now, however, we need simply note that the framing of the consent transaction makes it unlikely that individuals will form any intention about the proprietary status of their biomaterials.

Even if we could agree that intention is sometimes relevant, this would not help us in those situations where no intention is formed (which I surmise for the reasons set out above are more usual). Hardcastle's suggestion is that the requisite rights be allocated by default to the source of the materials.[151] Similar views have been expressed by both Whitty and Price.[152] If this is the relevant position, then it does not hinge on the necessity of having an intention require-ment.[153] Nothing beyond the removal of the biomaterials would be required to create the requisite rights and allocate them to the source, something considered but then set aside by Hardcastle.[154] The reason for putting it to one side is that he did not consider the common law to support such a position. He was, however, writing before the *Yearworth* case. It is submitted that, at the very least, this case has opened the door for mere detachment/separation to be viewed as sufficient in law to generate property rights in biomaterials. We could argue, as I have already mentioned, that the decision would be consistent with the view in *Kelly* that property is created where the materials in question have a *use beyond their mere existence*. This reading is certainly sug-gested by their Lordships' emphasis on the future use of the men's sperm samples.[155]

All the same, caution is needed here regarding how we should understand (the significance of) future use. Since the samples perished when the storage unit malfunctioned, any uses that the sperm could have been put to in the

---

[150] MRC, *Human Tissue and Biological Samples*, p. 6.
[151] Hardcastle, *Law and the Human Body*, p. 155.
[152] Whitty, 'Rights of personality', 224 and Price, *Human Tissue*, pp. 264–267.
[153] Quigley, 'Property in human biomaterials', 681.
[154] Hardcastle, *Law and the Human Body*, pp. 149–150.   [155] *Yearworth* at [5] and [45].

future were notional, not factual. The men may well have intended to use them, but they never did. They could not. And this was of course the root of their case. Additionally, if future use in, and of, itself is relevant to the potential attribution of property rights, then in this context it must necessarily encompass future *non-use*; that is, the liberty to not use the sperm samples at all if they did not wish to do so. Indeed, three of the men had recovered their natural fertility by the time that the case reached the courts,[156] rendering redundant their need to actually use the samples. What is more, regarding the effect of the provisions contained within the HFE Act, the Court explicitly recognised that the men were at liberty to not use the samples: 'the Act assiduously preserves the ability of the men to direct that the sperm be *not* used in a certain way: their negative control over its use remains absolute'.[157] Consequently, neither use in a positive sense nor the intention to use can be viewed as the basis of the decision.

6   Concluding Thoughts: Towards Separation?

The *Yearworth* case demonstrates that there are occasions, such as when damage to samples is caused, that fall entirely outwith the possible purview of a free-floating consent regime. An appeal to property may, therefore, be necessary in order to provide effective and justifiable remedies where wrongs have been done or particular interests have been infringed. A recognition of this is important because the challenges in this respect are not just confined to instances of damage to stored tissue. They may come to the fore where there is a conflict between the interests of different parties regarding the control of biomaterials. This was illustrated by the US cases discussed in the previous chapter and cases such as *JCM* v. *ANA* and *Clark* v. *Macourt* discussed here.

  Yearworth has also been significant in being the first English case to explicitly recognise the source as the proprietor of their sperm. It is also noteworthy in its move away from the work/skill exception as the sole means of bringing about the transformation in legal status from non-property to property. It remains to be seen how the courts will deal with cases involving non-gametic biomaterials and whether or not the scope of *Yearworth* will be extended to include those. Nevertheless, the

---

[156] The effect of this was to limit their claims to damages for psychiatric injury 'between the date when they received news of the loss and the date when they learnt of the recovery of their fertility' (*ibid.* at [10]).
[157] *Ibid.* at [45] [emphasis in the original].

evolution in the legal position is important, if only for opening the door to further property analyses in the future.

Yet, while the case represents an evolution in terms of the jurisprudential reasoning regarding the property status of biomaterials, it also raises numerous (legal) philosophical questions. According to Harmon and Laurie:

> In the end, we are left to wonder at the foundation and appropriateness of the Court's conclusion that the claimants rightly have a property interest in their body products or parts. How is the finding of property conceptually defended? On what moral foundations is the finding of property based?[158]

This is a reasonable criticism, albeit one which cannot be confined to this recent decision. The case law regarding property in biomaterials on the whole is not voluminous and has developed in a fragmented fashion. The consequence of this is that we ought to be wary about going too far with attempts to discover general (and generalisable) principles or any coherent philosophical foundations for *Yearworth* or the other cases.

One conclusion which flows from the discussions in this chapter is that nothing beyond the fact of separation from the person does the normative work of transforming sperm from *res nullius* to *res* capable of being governed by property rights. To those who view property rights in biomaterials as protective of a person's interests therein, this might be an attractive conclusion. Separation becomes both necessary and sufficient to bring about the requisite legal transformation, with the attendant rights being automatically allocated to the source. This is appealing because if mere separation is *not* enough, to both create the legal rights *and* to justify their allocation to the person from whom they came, it leaves open the possibility that the unowned thing can be (unjustifiably) appropriated by parties other than the source. Vesting property rights (at least originally) in the source of the biomaterials would be consistent with the developments in *Yearworth*, and arguably with the purported focus on individual control within both the Human Fertilisation and Embryology Act and the Human Tissue Act 2004.

Yet, despite this seeming benefit of mere separation, whether limited to sperm samples or biomaterials more generally, such a principle would be unsatisfactory. While conceiving of separation as normatively transformative for the purposes of the categorisation of legal rules might be

---

[158] Harmon and Laurie, 'Property, principles, precedents, and paradigms', 486

useful, it cannot stand alone if we are concerned about the *moral justification* for the creation and allocation of property rights in biomaterials. If biomaterials are *res nullius* while attached to us, upon what basis do they become *our* property once separated from us? The problem here is simple. Where the source of the biomaterials is not considered the owner (at least morally speaking) prior to their removal, we have no prima facie reason for thinking that any new property rights (moral or legal) created upon separation should vest in them. More is needed to undergird the allocation of property rights in separated biomaterials to the source if we are to be satisfied that it is a philosophically defensible conclusion. Such a position is justifiable, but we need to look beyond the law for the reasons why this is so. Providing a justification is the principal endeavour of this book, but in order to offer this, we first need a more robust picture of property and property relations, something which is the task of the next two chapters.

PART II

Property and Persons

5

What Is Property? I

Bundles and Things

1 Introduction

'What is property?' is a seemingly simple question. Yet, as we all know, appearances can be deceptive and the answer to this question is not straightforward. The reason for this is twofold. First, property's conceptual, philosophical, and legal terrain is contested. When we talk of property there are difficulties in pinpointing exactly what it consists of. This is essentially a problem of meaning, and there are, thus, divergent understandings of the term 'property'. Honoré's account of ownership, which in the previous chapter we saw received positive treatment in *Yearworth*, is often taken to exemplify the 'bundle of rights' conception of property. And it is the bundle view, partially due to Stephen Munzer's influential work,[1] which lawyers and ethicists who are interested in property in the body and biomaterials will be most familiar. This understanding of property has, however, come under fire in recent times. James Penner, for example, questions the cogency and usefulness of the bundle.[2] He argues that the nature of property cannot be satisfactorily explained by such an analysis, saying that the bundle 'is little more than a slogan' and that 'the Hohfeld–Honoré schema is little more than an association of the views of two legal philosophers'.[3] Henry E. Smith insists that the bundle view 'does not explain the organization and structure of property... [it] could be a partial outlook, but it is not a theory'.[4] There have been wide-ranging and trenchant debates about whether property has a 'definable essence'[5]

---

[1] Munzer, *Theory of Property*.
[2] J.E. Penner, 'The "bundle of rights" picture of property' (1996) 43 *UCLA Law Review* 711.
[3] *Ibid.*, 714.
[4] H.E. Smith, 'Property as the law of things' (2012) 125 *Harvard Law Review* 1693, 1700.
[5] Penner, 'Bundle of rights', 723.

or whether it is a flexible bundle without a core set of necessary characteristics.[6]

Second, the question of what property consists of does not stand alone and, therefore, cannot be addressed in isolation. Simon Douglas notes that '[t]here are a number of basic questions that all systems of property law need to be able to answer. The most important include: what is the content of a property right? how are property rights created? how are property rights transferred? and how are property rights destroyed?'[7] If we want a working account of how the law operates and how the uses of biomaterials can be regulated in that context, then we need to be able to answer these questions. I do not propose to provide answers to all of these in this book. Rather, my overall purpose is to draw on debates regarding property in order to shed light on the more specific issue of property in, and ownership of, human biomaterials. To this end, here, and in the next chapter, I focus on examining issues related to the problem of meaning, as well as the substance of property (rights) and ownership. Principally this involves probing some of the contours of the attendant property doctrines and debates to determine whether or not property has a definable core or unified set of characteristics. The position I reach by the end of the next chapter is that property rights properly conceived are entitlements which carry with them corresponding (and enforceable) obligations on the part of others. The core of these rights is based in our liberties to control the uses of particular objects. Additionally, I defend ownership as being the position of ultimate normative authority which owners enjoy in respect of their things.

In attempting to get to the core of property, however, we need to go beyond the formal application of property law (to the use of biomaterials). Existing legal property doctrine is clearly central to the real-world

---

[6] See, for example, the papers in the special symposium 'Property: A Bundle of Rights?' (2011) *Econ Journal Watch* 8(3).

[7] S. Douglas, 'Property rights in human biological material' in I. Goold, J. Herring, L. Skene, and K. Greasley (eds), *Persons, Parts and Property: How Should we Regulate Human Tissue in the 21st Century?* (Oxford: Hart Publishing, 2014), pp. 89–108, p. 93. Rostill outlines similar questions that he thinks were not captured by the account of ownership given in *Yearworth*. For him, such an account would explain:

> (1)... how and when it is acquired (ie, the conditions that must be satisfied for a person to acquire legal ownership of a particular (type of) thing); (2)... how it is lost (ie, the conditions by which persons who have legal ownership of a particular (type of) thing cease to have that ownership); and (3) explains the legal consequences that attach to it, especially the powers, rights, duties and/or immunities that the law regards as grounded by legal ownership ('The ownership that wasn't meant to be', 16).

practicability of using property law as a framework to deal with biomaterials. However, we also need to be attentive to the philosophical dimensions of property and how this relates to the relevant legal features. Ultimately, therefore, the account given in these two chapters is a philosophical one in which, drawing on the work of James W. Harris, use and control are advanced as central to a general understanding of property, as well as to the significance to persons of having property rights. In arriving at this account, this chapter examines the relationship between property (relations) and things, as well as the commonplace idea that property consists of a bundle of rights and other relations. I conclude that, while the bundle of rights view of property may be a useful metaphor, we should not expect more from it at either a conceptual or normative level. Moreover, the bundle view does not seem to accurately reflect the operation of the law of property, which protects property interests principally by employing exclusion strategies; to wit, duties of non-interference which are imposed on third parties. This will lay the groundwork for the next chapter where I move on to explore other factors. There I outline the core of property, ask what it means to have a property *right*, and examine the relationship between property, possession, and ownership.

2   Property, Persons, and Things

As we are about to see, property is a complex business. In this section I explore this complexity by examining the relationship between property, persons, and things. What we will see is that the multifarious interests and relations involved explain the appeal of bundle views of property. Nevertheless, we will also see that in the end this amounts to a bundle of theoretical and practical problems.

2.1   Things, Objects, and Biomaterials

The idea of property *as* things is sometimes caricatured as the common everyday understanding of property, while property as rights and other relations between persons is said to be the legal understanding of the term.[8] When the person on the street speaks of property they are supposedly referring to a thing; that is a tangible item or material resource. When they

---

[8] See generally Honoré, 'Ownership'; Becker, *Property Rights* Ch. 2; C.B. Macpherson (ed.), *Property: Mainstream and Critical Positions* (Oxford: Basil Blackwell, 1978), Ch. 1; Munzer, *Theory of Property*, Ch. 2; and J. Waldron, *The Right to Private Property* (Oxford: Clarendon Press, 1988), Ch. 2. See also Grubb, 'I, me, mine', 300–302.

say 'this is my property' they are talking of their car, their house, their book, or the clothes they are wearing.[9] However, when the jurist or political theorist or philosopher refers to property they are purportedly speaking of property as 'rights'. When they say 'this is my property' they are referring to a set of rules which govern relations between people with regards to their car, their house, their book, etc. The notion of property as things might make sense in our everyday conversations. When I say to you that 'I own this pen' or 'that car is the next-door neighbour's' there does not usually need to be any further discussion. Nonetheless, problems arise when there is reason to dispute the ontological and normative content of such statements. If you were to disagree with my assertions regarding the pen, and instead claim that it was yours, there would be little point in me replying that the 'pen is property'. The mere statement that something is an item of property is not sufficient to help to resolve the situation as it does not add any information that might lead to a solution. Describing it thus does not tell us the kind of information we would presumably want to know; information about who has proper title to the pen, who possesses it, who can use it and how, who can give it away, etc. Use of the term property in this way is to treat it as a descriptive noun which does not specify its content in a useful manner. To use it in this way is to make a claim about the nature of the thing. It essentially makes property synonymous with objects; it would consider property as the pen, as the car, as the house, and so on. It is to claim that some attribute or group of features that these objects display qualifies them as property or denotes that they are property. If this is the case then the defining attribute or group of features would need to be identified, which is something that cannot be done.

Think about the following example. If I were to speak to you on the phone and talk about my new car you might not know the exact details of the car (colour, make, size, etc) but you would be able to engage with the idea of the car. You can do this because, although there are no features or group of features that are shared by all cars, there is what Ludwig Wittgenstein described as 'a complicated network of similarities over-lapping and criss-crossing'[10] which enables you to identify with the car's

---

[9] The use of possessive pronouns has been argued, by J.W. Harris, to be of merely reflexive significance in respect of oneself and one's body [*Property and Justice* (Oxford: Oxford University Press, 2001) p. 188]. It is, of course, the case that not all uses of 'my' indicate a claim to a proprietary relationship, however, in Chapter 7, I will argue that Harris' contention regarding the self and the body is incorrect.

[10] L. Wittgenstein, *Philosophical Investigations*, trans. G.E.M. Anscombe (Oxford: Basil Blackwell, 1968), p. 32.

car-ness. 'Car' is a descriptive noun of which we would have a general shared understanding. On the other hand, if I were to speak to you on the phone and call something property, in order to understand what I am saying, you would still need to know what that something is; you would need to know what kind of object it is, be it land, a house, or perhaps some jewellery. We cannot talk about the property-ness of property in the same way that we can talk about the car-ness of cars. This is because property does not describe or denote the physical thing; it cannot be defined in this way. Property is not synonymous with objects themselves and it does not make sense outside of ordinary everyday conversations to treat it as if it were. Having said that, the concept of property does not exist devoid of any reference to things or objects;[11] such a position would also not be intelligible or useful. Things are properly considered to be the *objects of property*.[12] They are in effect the items at issue and the role of the institution of property is to determine how these things are to be dealt with.

The notion of a thing is important not only because the very purpose of property law is to govern our use of things, but because we need to know

---

[11] In saying this, I note that intangible intellectual property is commonly treated as a category of property. Simon Douglas and Ben McFarlane, however, express the persuasive view, that intellectual property does not share enough features of property proper to count as such. In particular, they say that if the 'right does not relate to a physical thing, it should not be seen as a core case of a property right, as the right does not correlate to a general duty, prima facie binding on the rest of the world, not to physically interfere, carelessly or deliberately, with a particular thing' ('Defining property rights', p. 239). In this way we might see intellectual property as an unfortunate case of linguistic slippage. See also McFarlane, *Structure of Property Law*, pp. 132–153.

[12] Both Macpherson and Grey offer an interesting historical account of the misconception of property being identified with things (Macpherson, *Property*, and T.C. Grey, 'The disintegration of property' in J.R. Pennock and J.W. Chapman (eds), *Property: Nomos XXII* (New York: New York University Press, 1980), p. 69). In the seventeenth century, property was generally considered to be a 'right in something' (Macpherson, *Property*, p. 7). However, by the time we reach the eighteenth century the everyday sense of the word had changed to mean 'things that are owned by persons' (Grey, 'The disintegration of property', p. 69). At this time most property was in the form of land, but this land came with a great many restrictions on its usage. However, over time these restrictions lessened, giving people greater freedom and rights with respect to the land. This, according to Macpherson, can be explained by the move to the 'full capitalist market economy from the seventeenth century on' (Macpherson, *Property*, p. 7). The growth of the market economy not only brought with it an ever increasing array of rights in land making it more freely marketable, but also a great expansion in the kinds of things that became saleable (pp. 7–8). Eventually this meant that the rights that a person could have regarding the land or the thing increased to such an extent that 'one did not have to look behind the thing to the right. The thing itself became... the property' (p. 8).

whether any particular object is a 'thing' *in the relevant sense*. This is not ordinarily an issue since most items which we deal with on a daily basis are incontrovertibly and uncontroversially items which can be governed within the realm of property (cars, bicycles, pens, houses, and so on). However, managing biomaterials in such a manner is not only ethically contentious (for some), but poses a specific problem for the law. The existing legal framework for biomaterials has been substantively influenced by the no property rule and this historical baggage creates difficulties and gaps regarding 'things' of human origin. When biotechnological advances occur we need to determine how the products of these advances can and ought to be governed. Therefore, crucial to an assessment of the applicability of the law of property to biomaterials is a determination of the thing-ness or thinghood of biomaterials.[13] In this manner, the construction of things within the law becomes normatively significant.

At least in this respect the law is clear. As Donna Dickenson notes, the 'common law posits that something can be either a person or an object – but not both – and that only objects can be regulated by property-holding'.[14] Accordingly, a variety of related criteria have all been suggested as normatively (and descriptively) relevant in delineating property from non-property, including distancing, separability, and detachment. For example, Harris said that '[f]or an entity to be a proprietary subject matter, a human subject must be distanced from it in two ways. It must be something that others could be accused of "taking" and something the subject himself could be seen to control or use as "owner".'[15] Meanwhile, Penner's separability thesis states that '[o]nly those "things" in the world which are contingently associated with any particular owner may be the objects of property. . . "separability" informs our understanding of what things can be property'.[16] Rohan Hardcastle takes a similar line, maintaining:

> [I]t is clear that for a thing to be the subject of property rights it must be distanced from human subjects. For example, the use of an individual's talents is not separable from the individual and therefore not capable of classification as a thing that can be the subject of property rights. Similarly, it is not possible to say that we own 'our entire bodies'.[17]

[13] I borrow 'thinghood' from James Penner. See J.E. Penner, *The Idea of Property in Law* (Oxford: Oxford University Press, 1997), p. 111.

[14] D. Dickenson, *Property in the Body: Feminist Perspectives*, 2nd edn (Cambridge: Cambridge University Press, 2017), p. 5.

[15] Harris, *Property and Justice*, p. 332.   [16] Penner, *Idea of Property*, p. 111.

[17] Hardcastle, *Law and the Human Body*, p. 15.

If we consider the cases examined in the last two chapters we can see that separation is normatively significant (legally speaking) to the property question. There we saw that the application of work or skill is supposedly transformative in respect of human biomaterials. It alters their legal standing, transforming them from *res nullius* to *res* and bringing them into the realm of property. Although *Yearworth* has established an alternative basis for property in biomaterials, one that does not require the application of the work/skill exception, the cases are, nevertheless, unified by the condition of separation. Thus, separation from persons is, as I have noted elsewhere, 'a bright line which must be crossed as a prerequisite for the transformation to *res* to take place... crossing the normative line seems to render human tissue capable of being governed by property considerations'.[18] This position (or some variation thereof) is simply a reflection of the operation of the law more generally. Lord Bingham's comments in *R v. Bentham*,[19] which were cited in *Yearworth*, are illustrative of this. He said, '[o]ne cannot possess something which is not separate and distinct from oneself. An unsevered hand or finger is part of oneself. Therefore, one cannot possess it... What is possessed must under definition be a thing. A person's hand or fingers are not a thing.'[20]

One response to this one might be to point out that in everyday language people do in fact refer to their hands, fingers, and other body parts as 'things'. However, this is not the general sense utilised by those who maintain such positions; instead they are referring to some kind of normative distinction between persons as subjects and things as objects. They take this division to not only be explanatory of the legal landscape, but also part of the justification for it. Given this, the answer to whether biomaterials can properly be considered to be the objects of property is relatively straightforward from a *doctrinal* perspective. As Douglas observes '[w]hen we ask whether a person, A, can hold property rights in human biological material, therefore, we are only concerned with material that is *physically separate* from A.'[21]

---

[18] Quigley, 'Property in human biomaterials', 669.   [19] [2005] UKHL 18.

[20] *Ibid.* at [8]. The specific question at issue in *Bentham*, as articulated by Lord Bingham, was '[c]an a person who has his hand inside a zipped-up jacket, forcing the material out so as to give the impression that he has a gun, be held to have in his possession an imitation firearm within the meaning of s. 17(2) of the Firearms Act 1968?' (at [1]).

[21] Douglas, 'Property rights in human biological material', p. 96 [emphasis added]. A dichotomy between the world of persons and the world of things is intuitively appealing. Moreover, conceiving of the body as a normative boundary is useful in conceptualising how the law is structured to deal with a variety of interests. Nevertheless, this division is not nearly as philosophically neat as the law and the positions outlined suggest. As we

2.2   Rights, Relations, and Metaphors

While things which are separate from persons are properly considered to be the objects of property law, we should not infer from this that the relationship of consequence is that *between* persons and things. Honoré, for example, says that '[t]here can, obviously, be relations between persons and things, not merely between persons and persons.'[22] He concedes that the way in which we protect property rights is by regulating relations with other persons,[23] but he thinks that the purpose of doing this is the 'holder's relation *to* the thing'.[24] It is in this sense that he thinks that there can be relations between persons and things. Even though we can see why he says this, such a characterisation has the potential to confuse discussions. It would seem more accurate to say that persons can stand in relation *to* things, but this is not the same sort of proposition as there being relations *between* persons and things. In this respect it is relations between persons *with regards to* certain objects which are at issue.

Consider Jeremy Waldron's example of Susan and her Porsche. He says that '[t]he layman thinks of this as a two-place relation of ownership between a person and a thing: Susan owns that Porsche. But the lawyer tells us that legal relations cannot exist between people and Porsches, because Porsches cannot have rights or duties or be bound by or recognise rules.'[25] It seems axiomatic that there cannot be relations between persons and things. It makes no logical sense to think of property relations (whatever they may be) as being between an individual and an object. This is because objects or things cannot hold up their end of whatever such a bargain would entail. As Waldron notes, they cannot have rights, duties, liabilities, etc. towards persons, and it makes little sense that persons should have these towards them. It does not take a lawyer to point out that however much Susan might lovingly fill her Porsche up with petrol, or dutifully change its oil, it will never be able to reciprocate. The only logical approach is to conceive of these relations as existing between persons. It is clear that, legal or otherwise, the relations must properly be between persons; 'between Susan and her neighbours, say, or Susan and the police, or Susan and everyone else'.[26] But what do these relations consist of and what is it about them which marks them out as germane to the property question?

---

will see in Chapter 8, drawing a bright line between persons as subjects and everything else as objects is difficult in the biotechnological world.

[22] A.M. Honoré, 'Rights of exclusion and immunities against divesting' (1960) 34 *Tulane Law Review* 453, 463.

[23] *Ibid.*, 464.   [24] *Ibid.*, 465.   [25] Waldron, *Right to Private Property*, p. 27.   [26] *Ibid.*

A cursory consideration of Waldron's example reveals that there are many legal relations that exist, or could potentially exist, between Susan and all manner of other people. She has a variety of 'rights, liberties, duties, and powers' regarding the car.[27] She is at liberty to drive it, but not to drive it without a licence. She has a (claim-)right against others that they refrain from using it. These other persons have correlative duties of non-interference, although Susan has the power to waive these duties and permit others to use the Porsche. She has duties not to use it in a way which disturbs others or damages things that they own. She also has the power to transfer ownership of the car, thereby, changing not only her own rights, liberties, duties, and powers, but also those of the new owner.[28] Taken together, we could describe these as the jural relations which form the disputed property 'bundle'.

On the bundle view the individual elements of the bundle are seen to be collectively sufficient for ownership, but none are individually neces-sary or sufficient.[29] This is important because the law does not simply (or even) protect ownership. A look at any property law textbook reveals there is a diversity of interests which the law must deal with and which it is called upon to regulate. Many of these involve situations where a person's interests and rights are constitutive of something less than full ownership; for example, leases, hire purchase, easements (rights of way), and bailments.

To illustrate, consider the distinction between a tenant and a house owner. Despite having something less than ownership, a tenant has a reasonably extensive set of rights and legal protections regarding the house. This includes immediate rights of possession, along with a certain set of liberties regarding the use of the house and powers to control those uses. This may even include a certain amount of control over the use that they can permit third parties to put the house to. Yet despite having de facto possession of the house whilst residing there as a tenant, they do not have the power to sell or give away the house to another person. A tenant does not have ultimate control over the disposition of the house; this rests with the owner. This is a much simplified example of a situation where different parties have differing (albeit overlapping) legal and other inter-ests with regards to the same object, and where an assemblage of some relevant elements designates one of them as the 'owner'. The reality of property interests in either land or chattels (moveable property) is not nearly as straightforward.

<hr />

[27] *Ibid.*   [28] *Ibid.*   [29] Honoré, 'Ownership', pp. 112–113.

Consider the following extended example from Robert Ellickson. Here, O is the *fee simple* owner (the greatest ownership interest in land recognised by law) of a parcel of land (Whiteacre):

> Through voluntary acts, O might fragment rights in Whiteacre along at least the following five dimensions:
>
> (1) subdivision of Whiteacre into parcels of lesser acreage. O might, for example, divide Whiteacre into two parcels, Blackacre and Redacre, retain ownership of Blackacre, and sell Redacre in fee simple to neighbor N.
>
> (2) decomposition of particular privileges of use. Thereafter O might, for example, sell mineral rights in Blackacre to an oil company, enter into a grazing lease with farmer F, and grant N an easement entitling N to cross Blackacre to access Redacre.
>
> (3) temporal limitations on entitlements. O could limit a transferee's rights to a less-than-infinite period of time, and also create various forms of future interests. For example, O could limit F's lease of grazing rights on Blackacre to a one-year term starting immediately, and simultaneously negotiate with farmer G a follow-on lease whose one-year term would commence as soon as F's lease had come to an end.
>
> (4) concurrent ownership. To make matters yet more complex, O's follow-on grazing lessee might be with not just one farmer (G), but with three (G, H, and I), who would concurrently own undivided interests in the lease.
>
> (5) security interests. O, after entering into all of the above transactions, might grant M a security interest in Blackacre to secure a loan that M had made to O.[30]

Whilst interests in chattels are not as divisible as those in land, they nonetheless display similar features.[31] To illustrate, let us think about Jane's newly acquired laptop:

> Jane has ownership of the laptop. Through voluntary acts she might fragment rights in the laptop in the following ways:
>
> (1) chattel leases: Jane can lease the laptop to Peter for a defined period of time. During this time Peter will acquire certain rights regarding the laptop. At the end of the lease they will revert to Jane.

---

[30] R. Ellickson, 'Two cheers for the bundle-of-sticks metaphor, three cheers for Merrill and Smith' (2011) 8 *Econ Journal Watch* 215, 216–217.

[31] For a general discussion of property rights in chattels see S. Douglas, *Liability for Wrongful Interferences with Chattels* (Oxford: Hart Publishing, 2011), Ch. 3. Note that Douglas maintains that not all of the interests listed in the example below ought to be viewed as property rights because not all can be protected by the chattel torts (mainly trespass, conversion, and negligence).

(2) bailment: For a fee, Jane could put her laptop (perhaps along with other items she owns) into a storage unit (paid bailment). Alternatively, she could loan it to a friend to use or look after (gratuitous bailment).

(3) reversionary interests: While the laptop is leased or bailed out, as the 'true owner', Jane will retain a lesser set of interests in it. The rights held by the lease or bailee will revert to her at the end of the lease or bailment term.

(4) transfer of reversionary interest. Before the term is up, Jane might sell or give her reversionary interest to a third party.

(5) possessory security interests: Jane might take her laptop to the local pawnbroker, leaving it there in return for a loan of £200. If and when she subsequently pays back the money plus any accrued interest, she will be entitled to the return of the laptop (pledge).

Given such complexity and variation, we need something that can capture the different types of property relations and that the 'degrees' of property which can exist. This is no easy feat and, the attempt to account for the complexity and structure of property (law), has spawned a minor academic industry in metaphor creation. Property has variously been described as a bundle of rights (i.e. right to use, manage, possess, etc.),[32] a collection of sticks,[33] a tree with a trunk and branches (representing core and other entitlements),[34] and as being modular (describing the interdependent nature of parts of a complex system).[35] These metaphors supposedly explain and help us to conceptualise this contested concept. Not infrequently, they are also treated as having significant normative force;[36] that is, they can tell us how the law *ought* to treat property holders. However, as we are about to see, while these 'structural metaphors', as Thomas Merrill calls them,[37] offer certain advantages in understanding the complicated property landscape, often their explanatory and normative uses are limited. More than a descriptive metaphor is needed (however seemingly apt) if we are to tell the normative story of

---

[32] Munzer, *Theory of Property*, p. 23.

[33] S. Munzer, 'A bundle theorist holds on to his collection of sticks' (2011) 8 *Econ Journal Watch* 265.

[34] A. di Robilant, 'Property: A bundle of sticks or a tree? (2013) 66 *Vanderbilt Law Review* 869.

[35] H.E. Smith, 'Property as the law of things'. See also Thomas Merrill's comments on this, including some reservations about modularity, T.W. Merrill, 'Property as modularity' (2012) 125 *Harvard Law Review* 151.

[36] See, for example, di Robilant's comments on the advantages of the tree conception ('Property', 876).

[37] Merrill, 'Property as modularity', 152.

property. In particular, we need to know what interests property is intended to facilitate or protect since we cannot know whether or not something counts as a property right in isolation from these.[38]

There is not space here to examine all pertinent aspects of the relevant property debates (or even the different metaphors) which, in any case, can be found elsewhere.[39] I confine myself, therefore, to a brief examination of property as a bundle of rights. I indicate why the bundle looks useful when considering whether or not biomaterials can be regulated by property relations, before briefly highlighting some of the key difficulties that this poses. I focus on the bundle view because it is one of the two most discussed views of property. It is also the one most familiar to those interested in property in biomaterials within bioethics and medical law. The other, largely competing, view is of property as a type of exclusionary interest. This latter understanding will be discussed in Section 4 when I explore how the law protects our use and control of things.

2.3   Constructing Useful Bundles

Munzer notes that 'Hohfeld's conceptions are normative modalities [claim, privilege/liberty, power, and immunity]'. In the more specific form of Honoré's incidents, these are the relations that ostensibly constitute property. Metaphorically, they are the 'sticks' in the bundle called 'property'.[40] Property as a bundle of rights has been the subject of extensive debate over the last twenty years or so. For some, the bundle of rights account is a thoroughgoing theory of property[41] and offers a number of advantages over the old (seemingly absolutist) Blackstonian view of property as an unqualified right to exclude.[42] Conceptualising

---

[38] E. Claeys, 'Bundle-of-sticks notions in legal and economic scholarship' (2011) 8 *Econ Journal Watch* 205, 212.

[39] See, for instance, the papers in the special symposium 'Property: A Bundle of Rights?' (2011) *Econ Journal Watch* 8(3), as well as Munzer, *Theory of Property*, di Robilant, 'Property', Smith, 'Property as the law of things', Merrill, 'Property as modularity', and T. W. Merrill and H.E. Smith, *Property: Principles and Policies*, 3rd edn (Foundation Press, 2012).

[40] Munzer, *Theory of Property*, p.23.

[41] See generally, Munzer, *ibid.* and 'Bundle theorist'.

[42] Blackstone said that ownership is 'that sole and despotic dominion which one man claims and exercises over the external things of the world, in total exclusion of the right of any other individual in the universe' (*Commentaries*, Book II, 2). Although, note that some scholars dispute whether this was really Blackstone's view, despite the frequency with

property as a *bundle* of rights and other (legal) relations (i.e. right to use, manage, possess, etc.), at least at first glance, seems to take account of the sorts of permutations outlined in Ellickson's example above. It ostensibly represents an open and flexible approach.[43] If property is a bundle, then it can be disaggregated into its individual elements.[44] Thus, the bundle view apparently explains how individual rights and other elements can vest in one person, or can be distributed among many different persons or legal entities. Furthermore, it allows that the sticks in the bundle (each of which is sometimes described as a property right in and of itself) can be divided and rearranged to form different clusters of ownership and lesser property interests. We can see, for example, that such divisions and rearrangements seem appropriate to the partition of Whiteacre into Blackacre and Redacre, as well as to the distinction to be drawn between owner and tenant. Additionally, the bundle imagery can be invoked to make sense of transfers. If the tenant in the example in the last section subsequently purchased the house, we could conceptualise this as the transfer of a variety of 'sticks' from the original owner's bundle to hers. The bundle conception seemingly enables us to identify and make a fine-grained analysis of the relevant normative legal relations of which property is comprised.

Jane Baron notes that, importantly, the bundle conception focuses on relations *between* persons: it 'directs attention toward the effects of property rights (powers/privileges/immunities) on other people, be they other owners or nonowners, and this attention enables assessment of whether the relationships property constructs are morally and socially acceptable'.[45] Another advantage of the bundle, according to Baron, is that it is flexible, allowing for progression and development, rather than a

---

which this trope is referred to. Carol M. Rose, for example, says 'perhaps it is the fate of canonical texts to be cited rather than read, because it seems that if property lawyers and scholars have read Blackstone, they have not read *much* Blackstone. If those who quote Blackstone's definition read further, they might come to think that Blackstone posed his definition more as a metaphor than as a literal description – and as a slightly anxiety-provoking metaphor at that' ('Canons of property talk, or, Blackstone's anxiety' (1999) 108 *Yale Law Journal* 601, 602). Rose notes that the 'canonical' statement was merely a departure point for Blackstone to look at 'various argumentative modes that now reappear in modern property scholarship' (*ibid.*).

[43] Quigley, 'Property and the body', 632.

[44] For an in-depth discussion and critique of the disaggregative view of property see Penner, 'Bundle of rights'.

[45] J. Baron, 'Rescuing the bundle of rights metaphor in property law' (2014) 82 *University of Cincinnati Law Review* 57, 85.

fixed view of property.[46] In this respect we might think that it is particularly suited to dealing with the challenges regarding biomaterials.

Goold, for example, has demonstrated that a number of the standard elements of the bundle are commonly held by individuals and institutions in respect of human tissue and that they can even be implied in some of the legal decisions like those discussed in the previous two chapters. For example, in *Kelly* she argues that 'the Royal College's right to possess was tacitly recognised by the finding that Kelly had stolen preserved body parts from its museum'.[47] We may also think that in this case the consequence of the decision was that the Royal College was deemed to have other relevant elements of the bundle; that they were at liberty to use and direct the uses of the body parts as they saw fit, that they could transfer them elsewhere, and so on. Similar analyses could also be applied to a range of other biomaterials. If we think about cell lines, it is manifest that researchers and their institutions hold a number of significant elements of the putative bundle. They possess the lines, they can use them for a variety of purposes, they can destroy the lines when no longer needed, and they regularly transfer them to others, including by way of sale. Likewise, where 'new' materials of human origin are created, we could simply interrogate the incidents in an attempt to ascertain if any particular object is to be governed by property rules. On the face of it, therefore, it looks like the bundle is helpful in thinking about the specific case of property in biomaterials, particularly in light of novel technological developments. But how do we determine if the elements of the putative bundle are proprietary in nature?

Penner, who is critical of the bundle thesis, notes that on one version of the thesis the answer to this question is largely a matter of legal history. What counts as property is merely the combination of rights and other elements which have become associated with each other over the course of time.[48] If the bundle is conceived in such a manner, when trying to determine if a person has property rights we need only discern whether or not they hold the requisite elements; for example, whether they have the rights to possess, use, and manage the item(s) in question. As Penner explains, 'in a particular case the various incidents or indicia of property

---

[46] *Ibid.*, 82–85.

[47] I. Goold, 'Sounds suspiciously like property treatment: Does human tissue fit within the common law concept of property?' (2005) 7 *University of Technology Sydney Law Review* 62, 72.

[48] Penner, 'Bundle of rights', 722. Cf. Alan Brudner, 'The unity of property law' (1991) 4 *Canadian Journal of Law and Jurisprudence* 3.

may add up in some way, or show sufficient resemblance to a paradigm, such that "property" is correctly applied to describe it'.[49]

We could interpret the decision in *Yearworth* in such a manner. If, for example, we examine this case *ex ante*, we might well determine that the rights held by the men resemble the incidents ordinarily associated with ownership. And this is what the Court seemingly did. Recall, their Lordships stated that 'the concept of ownership is no more than a convenient global description of different *collections of rights* held by persons over physical and other things'.[50] On this view, when we need to determine the property status of particular biomaterials we only need ask if the necessary (historically accepted) incidents are present. This would ostensibly tell us if they are capable of being governed by property relations. The Court did this when it cited (positively) Honoré's identification of the 'liberty to use' as 'a cardinal feature of ownership'.[51] Nothing more appears to be going on here than an assessment of whether the sperm 'looks like' property.

In many instances, as Lori Andrews has said, 'the legal treatment of bodies and body parts sounds suspiciously like property treatment'.[52] I agree it often does.[53] But more is needed. When thinking about property as a bundle of rights we need to bear in mind the following point made by Penner. He notes that '[t]here is no canonical formulation of the bundle of rights picture... Therefore to criticize [it] is not to criticize a particular theory; any number of specific explicit theories or approaches to understanding property may appear to flow from it.'[54] Although we might talk as if there is one unified account of what the bundle entails, this is an imprecise depiction. Having said this, there is not space here to deal with all the potential formulations of the disputed bundle,[55] so I confine myself to examining two general ways in which bundle views do not seem to offer an adequate account of property. The first of these relates to the supposed nature of the bundle as a model for identifying and classifying property relations and the second is to do with the actual operation of the law of property.

---

[49] Penner, 'Bundle of rights', 723.   [50] *Yearworth* at [28] [emphasis added].

[51] Honoré, 'Ownership', p. 116. Cited in *Yearworth* at [28].

[52] L. Andrews, 'My body, my property' (1986) 16 *Hastings Center Report* 28, 29.

[53] As does Imogen Goold who titled her article, examining instances which look 'suspiciously like property treatment', after this quotation from Andrews. See Goold, 'Sounds suspiciously like property'.

[54] Penner, 'Bundle of rights', 714.

[55] For a comprehensive account and critique of these see Penner's article generally, *ibid.*

2.4   A Bundle of Problems: Theoretical and Practical Issues

Flexibility is inherent in bundle views and this is seen as a strength by some. Indeed, some time ago I wrote that while all the elements of ownership 'may not be applicable to things we consider to be property, each item within the "group" of property will share similarities and relations with other items in the group'.[56] I imagined, as suggested by Richard Flathman, that Honoré's account of property ownership could be explained by a Wittgensteinian family resemblance analysis:[57]

> Wittgenstein uses the example of games and shows us that there is no single characteristic or group of characteristics that all "games" have in common.'[58] At first glance this is appealing and seemingly explains the observation that 'not all things generally considered to be property share all the same characteristics or sets of characteristics.[59]

I believe that this contention is now in need of revision. It is premised on the assumption that there are no unifying features of property. This is, however, a largely contestable supposition. It is a view which is propounded because the complexity of property relations seems to (a) be explained by a 'flexible and malleable'[60] concept and (b) require such flexibility in order to do any normative work.[61] As much as it might seem desirable, this flexibility may be problematic.

---

[56] *Ibid.*

[57] R. Flathman, 'On the alleged impossibility of an unqualified disjustificatory theory of property rights' in J.R. Pennock and J.W. Chapman (eds), *Property: Nomos XXII* (New York: New York University Press, 1980), pp. 221–243. For a later and more extensive Wittgensteinian analysis of property rights see Penner, Bundle of rights', 783–799.

[58] Quigley, 'Property and the body', 632.   [59] *Ibid.*

[60] B. Hoffmaster, 'Between the sacred and the profane: bodies, property, and patents in the Moore case' (1992) 7 *Intellectual Property Journal* 115, 128.

[61] Penner argues that it is the reliance on, and adherence to, the classical view of concepts, which 'generates a sense that property is to be regarded as something less than a determinate concept' ('Bundle of rights', 774). He demonstrates that a family resemblance model can aid us in getting to the meaning of property, but that on a criterial view of family resemblance there 'is no inherent "flexibility" about a term's meaning; rather, a term applies as broadly or narrowly as its meaning allows, on the basis of different criteria in different circumstances' (797). Thus, it could be argued that my earlier usage of family resemblance to make sense of property fell prey to the classical understanding of concepts, whereas a criterial view leads us to the conclusion that there is a set of criteria which can be applied, albeit in different circumstances, which capture the meaning of the term property. These criteria, however, are not a multitude of disparate sticks which can be bundled together in different ways, but an identifiable core which reflects the meaning

The implication of such flexibility, according to Penner, is that 'the very nature of property is that of an *infinitely divisible composite*, which can be disintegrated into or built up from less extensive rights'.[62] It is this disaggregative character which forms part of his disquiet with bundle views in general. If what is meant by those employing the bundle conception is that property is a collection of 'fundamentally distinct norms' (rights, liberties, powers, etc.),[63] then it is hard to see how this can be of help to us. The reason is that this account lacks specificity. It regards property as a concept with no central features shared by the 'property' designator. It also suggests that there are no real limits on the plasticity and decomposability of the rights and other elements contained in the bundle. It is not just that the individual sticks in the bundle can be traded at will, but that they could also be divided and rearranged to give different rights or clusters of rights. This divisibility can be illustrated if we think about the right to possess. This right, according to Honoré, can be divided into 'the right (claim) to be put in exclusive use of a thing and the right to remain in control'.[64] Each of these could thus be considered as a separate incident. Other elements could be similarly split up or combined to make new (clusters) of rights, with each element in itself being considered a property right.[65]

Disaggregative accounts of property partially reflect the influence of economic views of property where economic actors are at liberty to make consensual agreements amongst themselves regarding the sticks in their bundles. They suggest that that each element or use of the item in question is capable of being the 'subject of a transaction',[66] something that is illustrated by both the land and chattel examples given in Section 2.2. The putative bundles regarding Whiteacre and the computer can be fragmented in a number of ways. Consider also the example of a car given by Penner which further illustrates the potential decomposability of the rights involved. He says, 'my selling you the rights to use my car for a day is regarded as my transferring one of the "sticks" of the bundle that constitutes my ownership, which stick is itself a property right. . . presumably I have 365 such sticks for each year I own it'.[67] Here, I could transfer

---

of the term. In Section 4 and the next chapter, I argue that these are liberties and powers related to our interests in using and controlling particular items.

[62] Penner, *ibid.*, 734 [emphasis added].

[63] *Ibid.*, 741. Here, Penner is not advocating this view; he is merely describing how the term has come to be used in certain quarters.

[64] Honoré, 'Ownership', p. 113.   [65] Penner, 'Bundle of rights', 734.   [66] *Ibid.*

[67] *Ibid.*

you the liberty to use my car on Monday, then on Tuesday, then again on Wednesday, and so on. Presumably, we could even conceive it in smaller temporal slices, where my rights are counted by the hour, if we were so minded. This potential to fragment property (relations) famously prompted Thomas Grey to declare that property had disintegrated. He argued that:

> When a full owner of a thing begins to sell off various rights over it – the right to use for this purpose tomorrow, for that purpose next year, and so on – at what point does he cease to be the owner, and who then owns the thing? You can say that each one of many right holders owns it to the extent of the right, or you can say that no one owns it.[68]

Thus, when taken to the extreme this decomposability seems to descend property (rights) into absurd, and potentially useless, fragmented complexity.

The task identified in the last section of assessing whether or not something 'looks like' property seemed easy enough. It appeared that we could simply enumerate the different legal relations that govern the use of cell lines, tissue collections, or any other biomaterials and declare them to be of a proprietary nature if they measured up. Yet if property is so fragmented, property is no longer an organising idea.[69] There is no touchstone by which we can claim 'this is property' or 'so and so owns this'. All we can do is point to individual rights and entitlements and attempt to tie these individually to particular holders of them. Without a distinct core, the bundle is seemingly rendered too loose to do any solid conceptual or normative work.

For Grey, the disintegration of property means that it 'ceases to be an important category in legal and political philosophy'.[70] This conclusion is too hasty, however. First, we could rescue the bundle by conceiving of the property rights within it, not as an 'infinitely divisible composite', but as discrete bounded packages. In the car example we would not see the bundle as entailing 365 sticks for each year I own the car. Rather, my right to sell the use of my car for a year involves rights which are derived from a set of overarching rights. But if the bundle ought to be represented as

---

[68] Grey, 'The disintegration of property', p. 70.

[69] I take the phrase 'organising idea of property' from Waldron. He argues that the concept of property can be conceived of as an abstract idea, 'something like the idea of a name/object correlation' (*Right to Private Property*, p. 39). This expresses the sense that each object or resource belongs to an individual and is the general or 'organising' idea of property (p. 42).

[70] Grey, 'The disintegration of property', p. 81.

a bounded set of overarching rights, this suggests that we can identify a *core* from which the derivative rights originate. And if this is the case, then the bundle is not a disaggregative collection of sticks, it is something much more concrete. We might still persist in describing property as a 'bundle', but this depiction would be of no more than figurative significance.

Second, Grey's claim is based on taking an economic perspective on the development of property. The view that entitlements can be traded at will (inherent in the disaggregative picture) represents the very nub of market liberalism. Accordingly, Grey reaches his conclusion because he thinks that something like thing-ownership has been replaced by 'a system of economic entitlements'.[71] But, as Munzer contends, '[e]conomic value need not be the only sort of value protected by property law.'[72] I, therefore, submit that there is something more going on than disaggregative views of the bundle would suggest. Specifically, such accounts are neither reflective of the law of property nor of its normative core. This normative core will be discussed in the next chapter. Before that, however, it is instructive to think about the lessons to be gained by interrogating the actual operation of the law of property. This is so, because doing so indicates other limitations to theorising property using a bundle view.

3 Exclusion, Non-interference, and Property Forms

It is the lack of a 'definable essence'[73] engendered by the flexibility and mutability of bundle conceptions of property which is a problem for some. As such, there have been efforts to identify what is distinctive about *property* rights, to rescue property from a problematic metaphor. This usually involves refocusing discussions to emphasise either the centrality of the 'thing' to a conception of property or particular sticks in the putative bundle. For example, Penner argues that 'property is what the average citizen, free of the entanglements of legal philosophy, thinks it is: the right to a thing'.[74] Merrill and Smith have defended the importance of the *right to exclude* from a thing.[75] Merrill says: '[g]ive someone the right to exclude others from a valued resource . . . and you give them property.

[71] *Ibid.*, p. 82.   [72] Munzer, 'Bundle theorist', 269.   [73] Penner, 'Bundle of rights', 723.
[74] Penner, *Idea of Property*, p. 2.
[75] T.W. Merrill, 'Property and the right to exclude' (1998) 77 *Nebraska Law Review* 730; Merrill, 'Property as modularity', 153–154; and H. Smith, 'Exclusion versus governance: Two strategies for delineating property rights' (2002) 31 *Journal of Legal Studies* 453.

Deny someone the exclusion right and they do not have property.'[76] Similar to Merrill and Smith, Simon Douglas and Ben McFarlane also point to the significance of exclusion, but, drawing on case law, they focus specifically on duties of non-interference. They advocate limiting property rights to those rights 'where the rest of the world is under a prima facie duty to [the right-holder] not to deliberately or carelessly interfere with a physical thing'.[77] These views build on the fact that, doctrinally, exclusion and non-interference are important. Exclusion and non-interference are the principal ways in which the law protects property interests.[78] What we will see in the final section of this chapter, and throughout the next chapter, is that exclusion is the mode by which *use and control* regarding things are given effect. In the next chapter I will also delve deeper into how this relates to the idea of rights and interests, but for now I take a brief look at how the law of property operates with respect to exclusion.

3.1   Protecting Property

The law protects proprietary interests by the imposition of duties of non-interference on other parties and provides remedies or sanctions (civil or criminal) for breaches of this duty. F.H. Lawson and Bernard Rudden outline the general rules which can be found in the law regarding the protection of ownership in moveables:

> First, [the owner] is of course protected against anyone who takes it or comes by it without her consent – thieves if stolen, finders if lost. Secondly, she may claim against any transferee from such a person. Thirdly, she may claim against any person who has it with consent if that consent has been lawfully withdrawn... Fourthly, she is protected against anyone who, in good faith, bought and took delivery of the thing from someone who was not the owner but was in possession with the owner's consent.[79]

In addition to the common law, this protection is largely achieved via the provisions of the Theft Act 1968 and the Torts (Interference with Goods) Act 1977. Under the Theft Act a 'person is guilty of theft if he dishonestly appropriates property belonging to another with the intention of

---

[76] Merrill, 'Property and the right to exclude', 730.
[77] Douglas and McFarlane, 'Defining property rights', p. 220.
[78] See Chapter 6, Section 2 for a discussion of the usage of the word 'interests' in this book.
[79] F.H. Lawson and B. Rudden, *The Law of Property* (Oxford: Oxford University Press, 2002), p. 66.

permanently depriving the other of it'.[80] The torts which protect chattels (also referred to as the chattel torts) mainly comprise trespass, conversion, and negligence.[81]

Trespass is concerned with direct interferences with goods.[82] It is both a strict liability wrong (no fault or negligence on the part of the trespasser need be proven[83]) and is actionable per se (no proof of damage to the goods in question is needed[84]). It is the lack of authorisation on the part of the owner (or person in possession) which is determinative.[85] In *Fouldes* v. *Willoughby*,[86] for example, the defendant had removed without permission the plaintiff's horses from a ferry to the quayside. Although the specific question under appeal in this case was whether there had been a conversion (more on this below), the Court was of the opinion that 'simple asportation [movement] of a chattel' could constitute a trespass.[87] Similarly, in *Kirk* v. *Gregory*[88] the defendant had moved pieces of jewellery from one room to a cupboard in another for safekeeping. These items subsequently went missing. The Court accepted the defendant acted in good faith, but nonetheless held that a trespass had been committed. The crux of the matter was that the defendant had not

---

[80] s. 1(1).

[81] See generally, Douglas, *Liability for Wrongful Interferences*. Note that there is some debate over how the torts should be classified and structured, what their requirements are, as well as what the relationship between them is. See S. Green, 'An introduction to wrongful interference actions' in D. Nolan and A. Robertson (eds), *Rights and Private Law* (Oxford: Hart Publishing, 2011), pp. 525–551.

[82] Bridge, *Personal Property Law*, p. 80. Note that Halsbury's talks about 'deliberateness' (*Halsbury's Laws of England* (5th edn, 2015), vol. 97, paras 686 and 689) and Douglas argues that the directness requirement has long since been abandoned in favour of an 'intentional' interference requirement (Douglas, *Liability for Wrongful Interferences*, pp. 104–114). Douglas' position that the chattel torts can now be divided into intentional (trespass and conversion) and non-intentional (negligence) interferences is arguable, however. For a more 'traditional' analysis see J. Steele, *Tort Law: Text, Cases, and Materials* (Oxford: Oxford University Press, 2014), pp. 891–910.

[83] *Wilson* v. *Lombank Ltd* (1963) 1 All ER 740. In this case representatives of defendants, incorrectly believing that the defendants had legal title to the car, took the car from the forecourt of a repair garage. Even though they had no intentions of committing a trespass, it was held that one had been committed.

[84] *Penfolds Wines Pty Ltd* v. *Elliot* (1946) 74 CLR 204 at 214.

[85] *Ibid.*, 'A mere taking or asportation of a chattel may be a trespass without the infliction of any material damage. The handling of a chattel without authority is a trespass.' See also Roch LJ's comments in *Vine* v. *Waltham Forest BC* [2000] 4 All ER 169: 'The act of clamping the wheel of another person's car, even when that car is trespassing, is an act of trespass to that other person's property unless it can be shown that the owner of the car has consented to, or willingly assumed, the risk of his car being clamped' (at 175). See also *Halsbury's Laws*, vol. 97, para. 687.

[86] (1841) 151 ER 1153.   [87] *Ibid.* at 1155.   [88] (1876) 1 Ex D 55.

proven that it was in this particular case reasonable or necessary that the goods be so interfered with.[89] The directness element is met where there is direct physical interference of the chattel which goes beyond that which is 'acceptable in the ordinary conduct of everyday life'.[90] Moreover, the interference needs to be a 'wilful act' and not be involuntary.[91]

Conversion, as noted in relation to the *Moore* case in Chapter 1, occurs when one party deals with the thing in a manner which is inconsistent with the right of another to possess or be put in possession of the thing. The line between trespass and conversion is, according to Sarah Green, the difference 'between acting in relation to another's assets as if they belonged to that other and acting in relation to another's assets as if they were one's own'.[92] Thus if I move your bicycle because it is leaning against the railings where I want to secure my own, I may commit a trespass. But if you give me your bicycle to look after and I subsequently refuse to give it back to you, I may be liable in conversion. I have excluded you from its use and enjoyment and used it to my own ends.[93] In *Fouldes v Willoughby* mentioned earlier, for instance, a conversion was not found, because the defendant never acted as if the horse did not belong to the plaintiff.[94] Also note the difference between the bicycle examples given and moving your bicycle to get to my own which is underneath it. Moving the bicycle in this instance would count as conduct which is acceptable in the course

---

[89] *Ibid.* at 58–59.

[90] *Collins* v. *Wilcock* [1984] 1 WLR 1172 at 1177. Note that this case was actually a case regarding an alleged assault, but this general position with regard to trespass (be it to the person or goods) was endorsed in *White* v. *Withers LLP* [2009] EWCA Civ 1122 at [61].

[91] Bridge, *Personal Property Law*, p. 82. See here *et seq.* for a discussion of the relationship between wilfulness, intentionality, and issues regarding negligence and strict liability.

[92] Green, 'Wrongful interference actions', p. 527. For the elements of conversion see *Kuwait Airways Corporation* v. *Iraqi Airways Company* [2002] UKHL 19 at [39]. Although deliberateness was mentioned in this case, Sarah Green and John Randall argue that this is liable to cause confusion. They say that 'conduct need not be deliberate in the sense that the actor was aware of what its consequences would be; only in the sense that the actor had control over the commission of the act itself' (*The Tort of Conversion* (Oxford: Hart Publishing, 2009), pp. 69–70). Green, drawing on Peter Cane, contends that what is at issue is not that the action be deliberate *per se*, but that it is voluntary. See 'Wrongful interference actions', p. 531 and P. Cane, 'Causing conversion' (2002) 118 *Law Quarterly Review* 544, 544.

[93] McFarlane, *Structure of Property Law*, p. 144.

[94] See Green and Randall, *Tort of Conversion*, pp. 67–68. Note here their comments regarding 'intention': 'Conversion is a tort of strict liability. The intention of the defendant in relation to the claimant is, therefore, of no significance. . . Nevertheless, although the defendant's intention is not a necessary element of the tort, it will often indicate something material about the defendant's interference' (p. 67).

of everyday life.[95] Accidental interferences also would not count as conversion.[96] Like trespass, conversion is actionable per se and liability is strict.[97] The key to conversion is that the interference must be inconsistent with the property rights of the owner or persons with (a right of immediate) possession.[98]

Unlike either trespass or conversion, which require the act to be wilful, actions arising because of the negligent behaviour the tortfeasor do not. As noted by Green, the 'usual elements' are required to succeed in negligence: 'a breach of a duty of care, the existence of actionable damage which is of a type which should have been reasonably foreseeable by the defendant, and a causal link between that breach and the actionable damage suffered'.[99] Most often, actionable damage is taken to be actual damage to the goods themselves. Green, however, points to what she says is one of the more obscure wrongful interference actions, negligent damage to *interests* in goods.[100] Such an action would be appropriate in cases where there is no damage to the chattel itself, but negligence on the part of some third party has interfered with the claimant's use and enjoyment of it.[101]

---

[95] *White* v. *Withers* at [61] drawing on *Collins* v. *Wilcock* at 1177.

[96] *Kuwait Airways* at [39]. For an in-depth analysis of this case see S. Douglas, '*Kuwait Airways Corporation v Iraqi Airways Company* [2002]' in S. Douglas, R. Hickey, and E. Waring (eds), *Landmark Cases in Property Law* (Oxford: Hart Publishing, 2015), pp. 205–226.

[97] *Kuwait Airways* at [129].

[98] As Bridge puts it, the 'interference must be so serious as to amount to a denial of the claimant's title' (*Personal Property*, p. 88).

[99] Green, 'Wrongful interference actions', p. 531.

[100] *Ibid.*, pp. 526 and 531–534. As noted earlier, s. 1 of the 1977 Act provides for actions relating both to damage to goods and damage to *interests* in goods.

[101] Green, 'Wrongful interference actions', pp. 531–534. The remedies recoverable via the chattel torts are variable depending on the facts and circumstances (for example, sometimes recovery of the item itself, sometimes damages – which in turn are sometimes nominal and sometimes more substantive) (Bridge, *Personal Property Law*, pp. 113–124). Generally, those with (an immediate right to) possession are entitled to sue, but who exactly this is determined to be may be dependent on the facts and context of particular cases (pp. 84–86 and 101–102). It may, for example, be the owner or a bailee or indeed both of these parties. In instances where there has been a gratuitous bailment where the owner retains a legal right of possession (even if not factual) they may be able to sue a third party who has converted the goods in question. Conversely, where the bailment is a term bailment and the owner cannot (yet) demand to be put in possession of the item, then only the bailee and not the bailor may be entitled to bring an action against a third party. For reasons of brevity I leave aside issues of double liability (where both the bailor and bailee might sue the wrongdoer) and debates regarding a *ius tertii* defence (where defendant relies on claim that a third party has a better entitlement to the

Together the various elements of the civil law (via the torts) and the criminal law (theft) relating to chattels represent an exclusionary approach, essentially imposing duties on others to 'keep out'.[102] The effect of this is that the law creates a protective boundary around core property interests. Nevertheless, focusing on the exclusionary aspects of property, while a reasonable representation of the day-to-day working of the law, misses crucial parts of the wider picture. Several commentators have observed that non-interference or exclusion is not, and cannot be, the whole story when it comes to property. Anna di Robilant notes, the 'focus on the right to exclude misses the fact that property doctrines are much more varied and complex than merely securing assets through bright-line trespass rules'.[103] Larissa Katz thinks that 'a boundary approach... properly recognizes that there is a concept of ownership at work in law, but it does not account for the phenomenon of ownership: it fails to explain its crucial features'.[104] For her, exclusion-based approaches miss what is normatively distinctive about being an owner (something I will return to in the next chapter). Even some of those who argue that the right to exclude is significant, admit that there is more to the property story. Smith, for example, notes that '[c]auses of action like trespass implement a right to exclude, but the right to exclude is not *why* we have property. Rather, the right to exclude is part of *how* property works. Rights to exclude are a means to an end, and the ends in property relate to people's interests in using things.'[105]

Therefore, while exclusion, or some variation thereof, can explain the approach of the common law to protecting property rights, it does not in itself tell us what is being protected. Trespassory rules qua duties of non-interference can delineate the bounds of our property rights, but they do not tell us much (if anything) about the *content* of the interests which they protect. For this we need to look beyond legal doctrine to the philosophical foundations of property (law). The content of these interests is important (whether property is conceived of

---

goods than the claimant). See, however, Bridge, *Personal Property Law*, pp. 105–109 and Rostill, 'Relative title and deemed ownership', 48–52.

[102] For a discussion of the exclusionary approach of the law see J. Wall, *Being and Owning: The Body, Bodily Material, and the Law* (Oxford: Oxford University Press, 2015), pp. 113–121.

[103] di Robilant, 'Property', 874.

[104] L. Katz, 'Exclusion and exclusivity in property law' (2008) 58 *University of Toronto Law Journal* 275, 277.

[105] Smith, 'Property as the law of things', 1704.

as a social, moral, or legal institution) because it is closely connected to the *why* of property. The why may be multi-stranded and include considerations such as scarcity, stability of possession, conflict resolution, and the problem of allocation. As we will see in the final section of this chapter, however, these matters converge around (and can perhaps be collapsed into) a narrative about the use and control of things in the external world.

3.2   Restricting Property Forms

Before drawing Section 3 to a close we should note that, in working to protect our proprietary interests the law is not nearly as open and flexible as (at least extreme versions of) the bundle picture of property implies. We are not free to make all manner of agreements with others regarding the so-called sticks in our bundle. We cannot split, trade, recombine, and otherwise rearrange our rights as we wish. The law draws a distinction between the operation of property rights and other types of rights. Property rights unlike other rights such as personal rights, as we will in the next chapter, are good against the world. This means that the duties relating to, for example, the bicycle that I own are enforceable against all persons. Your duty of non-interference regarding my bicycle does not arise because of any special arrangement between us, but simply in virtue of my property rights.[106] There is, as elucidated by Rudden, a 'reluctance of the law to recognise new forms of burden on property conferring more than contractual rights'.[107] Merrill and Smith describe this as a matter of the law's approach to the *customisability* of rights.[108] For example, the law of contract 'recognises *no inherent limitations* on the nature or duration of the interests that can be the subject of a legally binding contract'.[109] By contrast, the law of property is much more closed, generally adhering to a standard menu of property

---

[106] See Chapter 6, Section 3.2.
[107] B. Rudden, 'Economic theory versus property law: The *numerus clausus* problem' in J.M. Eeklaar and J. Bell (eds), *Oxford Essays in Jurisprudence* (Oxford: Clarendon Press, 1987) pp. 239–263.
[108] T.W. Merrill and H.E. Smith, 'Optimal standardization in the law of property: the numerus clausus principle' (2000) 110 *Yale Law Journal* 1, 3.
[109] *Ibid.* [emphasis added]. Although they do note that there may be public policy reasons for not allowing certain types of promises (the essence of contract) to be legally enforceable.

interests, resisting the ad hoc creation of new ones (the *numerus clausus* principle).[110]

This principle is more familiar in civil law systems where the relevant civil codes set explicit limitations on property rights: 'the number of absolute rights is limited, their content is restricted and it is laid down in mandatory rules how absolute rights can be created, transferred and extinguished'.[111] However, a number of commentators (most prominently Merrill and Smith) now recognise the existence and operation within common law systems of the *numerous clausus* principle; that is, that property rights comprise a 'closed list' and there are limitations on the creation of new ones. This is most clear in respect of land where legally enforceable property rights are relatively easily identifiable; for example, fee simple ownership, easements, leases, and so on. Correspondingly, it is in cases concerning disputes over land and waterways that we find statements from the courts to this effect.

In *Keppel* v. *Bailey*,[112] for instance, Lord Brougham declared that '[i]t must not be supposed that incidents of a novel kind can be devised and attached to property at the fancy and caprice of any owner.'[113] This was subsequently reinforced in *Hill* v. *Tupper*[114] with Pollock CB noting that:

> A new species of incorporeal hereditament [the potential right at issue in the case] cannot be created at the will and pleasure of the owner of property; but he must be content to accept the estate and the right to dispose of it subject to the law as settled by decisions or controlled by act of parliament.[115]

The particular facts of these cases need not concern us here as we are interested in the broad implications for bundle views of property.[116] The general lesson is that the law does not treat property rights as completely decomposable bundles from which individual incidents or rights can be

---

[110] See Rudden, 'Economic theory'; Merrill and Smith, 'Optimal standardization'; and Swadling, 'Property', pp. 175–177.

[111] S. van Erp, 'A *numerus quasi-clausus* of property rights as a constitutive element of future European property law?' (2003) 7.2 *Electronic Journal of Comparative Law*, 8.

[112] (1834) 39 ER 1042.   [113] *Ibid.* at 1049.   [114] (1863) 159 ER 51.   [115] *Ibid.* at 53.

[116] For an in-depth discussion see B. McFarlane, '*Keppell v Bailey* [1834]; *Hill v Tupper* [1863]: The *numerus clausus* and the common law' in N. Gravells (ed.) *Landmark Cases in Land Law* (Oxford: Hart Publishing, 2013), pp. 1–32.

hived off such that they will still be protected *as* property (in essence a type of right enforceable against all comers).[117]

Although, as Sjef van Erp and Bram Akkermans note, 'it is difficult to find any direct statement of the rule',[118] the law in relation to chattels can also be plausibly thought to employ similar limitations.[119] There is some debate over whether these consist strictly of a *numerus clausus*. The fact that there are constraints on the list of rights which count as property right need not, for example, imply (as in civil systems) that courts cannot and will not add to it in the future.[120] Nonetheless, the essential point is that there are doctrinal limitations on what rights will be recognised and subsequently enforced as *property* rights. Hence, theorising property as a mutable and 'infinitely divisible composite' does not aid us in identifying whether particular collections or bundles of rights 'resemble' the paradigm of property, because the law does not work that way.

4   Beyond Exclusion: Controlling the Uses of Things

As Alison Clarke has stated, '[t]o say that the defining characteristic of my ownership of a [thing] is my right to exclude you from it is an extraordinarily negative, and potentially misleading, way of putting it.'[121] Being able to exclude others from those resources which I own (along with the fact that the law will impose duties of non-interference to protect this) is undeniably part of the story. It is not, however, the whole story. Any interests I have in excluding others do not by themselves speak to the 'definable essence' of property and ownership. To get to this we need to ask what it is we are protecting when we impose duties on third parties with respect to the objects we own. And to this end the answer is remarkably straightforward. The normative core of property and ownership lies in persons' interests in controlling the uses of things.

---

[117] *Ibid.*, pp. 21–22.

[118] S. van Erp and B. Akkermans, *Cases, Materials and Text on Property Law* (Oxford: Hart Publishing, 2012), p. 346.

[119] See generally, Douglas, *Liability for Wrongful Interferences*, Ch. 3.

[120] van Erp, 'A *numerus quasi-clausus*', 10. van Erp makes this observation in relation to the *numerus clausus* and American common law, arguing that what is going on is simply 'standardisation' and that this 'means that a limited number of categories is used for practical reasons, but it does not imply that this number is completely closed' (10). It is reasonable to think, however, that this is also reflective of English common law.

[121] A. Clarke, 'Use, time, and entitlement' (2004) 57 *Current Legal Problems* 239, 241.

We can see this in Jeremy Waldron's characterisation of private property systems. He maintains that the abstract idea of such a system is that 'a rule is laid down that, in the case of each object, the individual person whose name is attached to that object is to determine how that object shall be used and by whom. His decision is to be held up by society as final.'[122] This speaks first to the fact that one of the primary functions of any system of property is to govern the allocation of (rights over) resources.[123] This is achieved through the system of rules that comprise property institutions, such as trespassory ones which impose duties of non-interference or others which govern how the requisite rights are acquired and how they can be transferred. At a societal level it is important that the system as a whole can determine who has the requisite rights (and thus control) regarding resources. This broader function is closely related to the importance of property at an individual level, where it is the power to control how objects shall be used and by whom that is fundamental.

To illustrate both the allocative and use-control aspects, consider some of the reasons offered by Douglas for the utility of property rights. First, property rights are a way of managing scarce resources.[124] Given that everyone who might want access to, or to use, a particular resource cannot do so, some arrangement is required to determine who can do so and when. While it is surely correct, as Harris maintained, that where there is no scarcity there is no allocation problem and thus no need for a system of property rules,[125] we must interpret scarcity quite loosely. It need not necessarily mean scarcity writ large. It may simply mean that a resource is scarce in the sense that exclusive use of it by one party makes it scarce. So, for example, if you and I are walking on a beach which is replete with attractive stones, we might both happen upon and want the same stone. Although there are more than enough other stones for each of us to choose from, the fact that we both want to acquire and use the same one creates scarcity of a sort. Hence even though scarcity may sometimes be more imagined than

---

[122] Waldron, *Right to Private Property*, p. 39. Note that this goes to the question of what the function of a property system is.

[123] Harris noted that, when coupled with contract, property can take on the dual function of 'governing both the use of things and allocating items of social wealth' (*Property and Justice*, p. 26). This is something which we will return to in Chapter 9.

[124] Douglas, 'Property rights in human biological material', pp. 99–100. See also Harris, *Property and Justice*, p. 24, which he draws on.

[125] Harris, *Property and Justice*, p. 24

real, a system of rules is required to govern the allocation of (rights over) resources.

Of course, in the case of a variety of human biomaterials the scarcity is sometimes not merely notional. This can be seen clearly in the *Moore* case. Here, researchers discovered that Mr Moore's splenic tissue displayed some unique characteristics and that they could create valuable cell lines from these. In a very real sense, the splenic cells, along with other biological samples from the plaintiff, were scarce.[126] And this brings us to a second issue. Where there is scarcity, conflicts may ensue.[127]

The resultant court proceedings in *Moore* revolved around the desire of both parties to control the use of the materials. The defendants (researchers) wanted literal possession and control for further research purposes, while the plaintiff wanted compensation for having been non-consensually dispossessed of his rights to control the uses of the samples. In this case, the actions of the defendants meant that Moore's ability to direct the uses to which his tissues could be put was taken away. When property rights are allocated in a particular manner and sets of rules established, the system as a whole can work to either reduce or readily resolve such conflicts. For instance, if there had been established legal recognition that property rights in separated biomaterials initially vest in the source, then researchers would have had a clear normative steer regarding the acquisition of such materials for their own uses. Ambiguities over how to *validly* acquire them would have been reduced.[128] And if the case had still come before the courts, the route to redress for Moore would have been more straightforward.

And so a third, and perhaps predominant, reason in favour of property rights is that without the protection that various rules within a property system give (be they socially, morally, or legally mediated) we risk instability of possession with regards to objects we currently hold. This instability, as Douglas notes, is something which the law tries to avoid.[129] In this respect, he is critical (and rightly so) of the decision in *Moore*, noting that the 'arguments advanced [in the case] against the recognition of property rights do not deal with the vulnerability that a finding of "no

---

[126] Douglas, 'Property rights in human biological material', p. 102.   [127] *Ibid.*, p. 100.
[128] See generally, Chapter 9 on the issue of the legitimate use and transfer of biomaterials.
[129] Douglas, 'Property rights in human biological material', p. 101. For his general discussion of this point see pp. 99–101.

property" creates'.[130] He is particularly concerned about the position of researchers and their institutions of a general lack of established property rights in biomaterials:

> [T]he law tries to protect peaceful possession by allocating property rights in the thing to a particular person. Unless such a right is recognised in a case such as *Moore*, there would be nothing to stop someone, such as a rival researcher, from taking the tissue samples from the defendants with complete impunity.[131]

This is surely correct. However, as the cases in the first part of this book demonstrated, both in practical and legal terms vulnerability to dispossession is less a problem for third parties, such as researchers, than it is for the sources of biomaterials. Moreover, in most of the cases examined in chapters 3 and 4, the issue is not one of a lack of recognition of property rights *tout court*, but of an asymmetry in recognition, and thus protections, between the source and other parties. *Moore* and *Greenberg* are key exemplars of this. Specifically in *Moore*, the Court never explicitly denied property rights to the defendants. Indeed the entire direction and tenor of the decision was such that their rights in this respect were unlikely to have ever been in doubt in the minds of the majority. Our reasons to think this are twofold.

First, the decision considers at length reasons why *Moore himself* (not the defendants) could not own his biomaterials or the subsequent cell line.[132] It was not focused on the issue of property in biomaterials as a wider question or as applied to other parties. And in fact Panelli J, on behalf of the majority, said that 'we do not purport to hold that excised cells can never be property for any purpose whatsoever'.[133] Second, and relatedly, a substantive part of the reasoning was that it was presumed that the property torts (specifically conversion) were 'not necessary to protect *patients' rights*'.[134] Presumably, however, the same need not be said of the rights and interests of researchers and their institutions. This is especially evident given the overriding emphasis throughout the decision on the protection of these actors' rights to use to the materials in question. Broussard J, dissenting, gets to the heart of the matter, saying:

> If, for example, another medical center or drug company had stolen all of the cells in question from the UCLA Medical Center laboratory and had

---

[130] *Ibid.*, p. 103.   [131] *Ibid.*, p. 102.   [132] *Moore*, Supreme Court.   [133] *Ibid.* at 160.
[134] *Ibid.* [emphasis added].

used them for its own benefit, there would be no question but that a cause of action for conversion would properly lie against the thief, and the majority opinion does not suggest otherwise. Thus, the majority's analysis cannot rest on the broad proposition that a removed body part is not property, but rather rests on the proposition that a patient retains no ownership interest in a body part once the body part has been removed from his or her body.[135]

Accordingly, the potential for the researchers to be dispossessed of the biomaterials is small since their property rights are not in question. The same cannot be said for the plaintiff, regardless of whether we view the matter in the manner of Justice Broussard or that of the majority. The asymmetric recognition of property means that there is no stability of possession for those who are excluded from the property paradigm. Instead the tendency to vest property rights in third parties leaves the source susceptible to being dispossessed of their biomaterials.

In saying this, this is not only (or even) about the physical possession of biomaterials. The more basic issue is one of who can *control* this use and possession. Those who are recognised as property rights holders control the uses of the things in question. Those who are not, do not. By denying that Moore had property rights, he was denied control over the uses to which his excised splenic and other tissues could be put. The decision failed to even recognise that he could have such interests and so he was left with an unsatisfactory remedial response. Likewise, it is essentially use and control which is at issue in *Yearworth*. When the samples perished, the men lost their ability to control the uses of their sperm samples. They could not use them for their own reproductive ends, donate them for IVF or research, or order them to be destroyed on their own say-so. The Trust's negligence had removed any control that they might have had in this regard. This is why in that case, taking a property approach was appropriate.

The interests at issue when we talk of property interests are ones which encapsulate the *use* that a person can put objects to and the *control* that they have over those uses. Property, as Clarke notes 'is about the freedom to make use of things, either generally or in a particular way'.[136] Any right to exclude is simply a way of protecting that freedom.[137] Accordingly, if

---

[135] *Ibid.* at 153–154.   [136] Clarke, 'Use, time, and entitlement', 241.
[137] *Ibid.*, 242. Note that, we can view exclusion itself, as distinguished from specific exclusion strategies such as the imposition of legal duties of non-interference, as an element of our wider control over the uses of things.

the imposition of duties of non-interference is the general *how* of property, then the *why* consists of the interests we have in the *use and control of things*. In the next chapter, drawing on Harris, I argue that property comprises a unified conceptual core of use-*privileges* and control-*powers*. This, we will see, reflects the logical structure of systems of property and of what it means to have a property *right* (as distinguished from mere interests).

5   Conclusion

Previously I have defended the view that '[p]roperty can usefully and convincingly be identified as a set of rules governing the relations between persons *with regards to* certain objects and, as such, consists of a bundle of jural relations.'[138] This contention is broadly correct in the sense that property, as we saw earlier, is a set of rules governing our use of things. Indeed, that is arguably the fundamental purpose of property law. However, the bundle imagery ought at best to be invoked in a qualified manner. It is not explanatory because it does not reflect the everyday operation of property law. It also falls short of providing a normative theory of property since it does not aid us in identifying what ought to be considered as falling within the realm of property. Thus, while the bundle may be a useful metaphor which can help us more easily conceptualise complex and difficult terrain, we should not expect more at either a conceptual or normative level.

Although the question of what ought to be subject to property is partly an ethical and policy question,[139] we nonetheless cannot debate the merits of this either way in the absence of a defensible account of property. Merely identifying the presence of particular rights or clusters of rights is not enough to tell us whether the law does or can protect these qua property. The reason is that designating property (or ownership) as a 'global description', be it conceived as a bundle or otherwise, can only be relevant if we know *which* collections of rights are key and whether these rights (once identified) are of a proprietary nature. Therefore, central to any normative endeavour is being able to point to those fundamental features which denote property. In looking for these, however, we should not err by focusing merely or solely on

---

[138] Quigley, 'Property and the body', 667.
[139] Douglas, 'Property rights in human biological material', p. 97.

the exclusionary function of the law. If we do, we risk overlooking important aspects of property interests. In this chapter I have begun to make the case that the normative core of property and ownership is the interests we have in *the use and control of things*. This task continues the next chapter.

6

What Is Property? II

Rights and Interests

1 Introduction

Chapter 5 drew to a close noting that property law is less flexible than bundle views suggest. Property law does not allow the ad hoc creation of new property forms through the trading, splitting, and rearranging of our interests and rights over things. We saw that exclusion is the strategy via which the ends of property are achieved. The law regulates our dealings with each other regarding external objects via sets of trespassory (and other) rules. It imposes duties of non-interference on third parties. This is the 'how' of property, but it is not the 'why'. It is essential that we appreciate both the how and the why if we are to have an account of property which is conceptually coherent, reasonably representative of the position of the law, and speaks to the moral story which underpins and justifies property and ownership. In the final section we began to see that the purpose (and thus core idea) of property is located in the interests that persons have in controlling the uses of resources, be they land, cars, houses, or indeed biomaterials.

In this chapter I build on this, drawing on Harris' account of ownership interests (what I will call 'property' interests) as an open-ended set of use-privileges and control-powers.[1] I then tease out two tricky aspects of property-speak. The first of these relates to property rights. So far in this book I have referred sometimes to rights or interests and sometimes to particular (legal) relations such as the liberty to use or the power to control. However, it bears being more precise about what it means to have a property *right*. This is both for the sake of clarity and because doing so will help shed further light on the structure of *property* relations. The second relates to the relationship between property, possession, and ownership. In considering this I focus in particular on ownership as a normative concept which operates as a background philosophical idea in legal discussions regarding property.

---

[1] Harris, *Property and Justice*, pp. 26, 30, and 130.

2   Property Interests

As we are about to see, the structure of property is best viewed as comprising a *core* and *periphery*. This organisation of elements is suggested by the logical priority of particular features over others. Property systems are built around an elaborate structure of rules, including those which govern the acquisition (appropriation) and loss or transfer (expropriation) of objects of property, as well as those which regulate the behaviour of third parties who might infringe our property-based interests (trespassory).[2] Each of these categories governs distinct aspects of our use of things. More specifically these rules govern how we protect, acquire, and divest ourselves of our *interests* and *rights* (and any attendant duties) regarding particular objects. Such rules may be enforced 'by informal social pressure, or by legal sanctions (civil or criminal)'.[3] Yet regardless of whether they are formal or informal, the rules themselves do not make sense if we do not know which interests and rights we are acquiring, ridding ourselves of, or protecting. A core concept of property (interests) is first needed.

Thinking about the function of different elements within a system of property will begin to illustrate property's core-periphery structure. Consider trespassory rules. These are stipulative. They demand that others 'stay out' or 'do not steal'.[4] They are essential components of any system of property since they entail a duty on others to not interfere with our proprietary interests. Coupled with remedial actions they provide a means for redress should an infringement take place. However, trespassory rules would not be coherent without a pre-existing conception of what those interests consist of. This is so because the duty to 'keep out' is not free-floating. It is a duty *in respect of something*; that something being our core property interests. If property is just a bundle of norms – rights, liberties, powers, and so on – then we cannot identify any such core interests. As we saw in the previous chapter, the rights and other elements of the putative bundle are too mutable. But identifying some set of core interests is necessary. We can see this, for example, with theft. Without some conception of property interests the very idea of theft is rendered unintelligible. We can imagine a society where theft does not exist, not because its citizens are all upstanding members of the community, but because nobody owns anything. No member of this society (or grouping within that society) has any normative claim over any object such that

---

[2] *Ibid.*, pp. 23–41.   [3] *Ibid.*, p. 25.   [4] *Ibid.*

they can exclusively direct its use; neither can they exclude others from its enjoyment. As such, no infringement amounting to theft is made when one member of this society takes an item to use for themselves since no-one else had any prior property claim to it.[5]

Like trespassory rules, other categories of rules also presuppose core property interests. Rules governing the acquisition of items are needed, say, to discourage or resolve (potential) conflicts regarding the control of particular objects. Thus, we might have an appropriation rule requiring that any transfer of objects between parties must be consensual. Such a rule takes as read that there are pre-existing interests which different parties might have in the object and that these interests need to be appropriately delimited. Together the various rules and elements which are built around core property interests delineate the scope and boundaries of those interests (something we will see further in Section 3).[6] This is important because, even though certain elements are analytically separable and do not constitute an intrinsic part of the concept of property itself, they are nonetheless crucial to the smooth running of the wider institution of property. They determine, for instance, when and under what circumstances the person can acquire or give up their rights over the object. Nevertheless, such rules are silent on the *content* of the interests which they support, protect, or alter.[7] Yet it is these interests which are essential to any understanding of property and represent its normative foundations. The normative core, as identified in Chapter 5, centres on *use and control*.

The centrality of use and control for property and ownership is widely recognised. For instance, John Christman gives an account of 'control ownership' as comprising 'rights to possess, use, manage, modify, alienate, and destroy one's property. These rights, liberties, and powers all

---

[5] Harris maintained that '[n]othing could be owned if nothing could be stolen (or otherwise wrongfully interfered with)' (*ibid.*). It is not wholly clear what he meant by this. If it is a conceptual claim, then on a literal reading one might charge that it risks getting things backwards since it suggests that the idea of ownership must be premised on that of theft. His purpose, however, may simply have been to draw attention to the importance of non-interference for property and ownership. Saying that I own something would be little more than a platitude if there were no restrictions on the interferences that third parties could subject my use and enjoyment of that thing to. In this case the logical priority of theft or interference could be acknowledged. As L.W. Sumner notes, '[s]ince in the absence of all rule systems everything would be (implicitly) permitted, the primary function of such systems is to impose constraints on this condition of unlimited permissiveness. It is therefore natural to treat restrictions as pragmatically prior to permissions' (*The Moral Foundation of Rights* (Oxford: Clarendon Press, 1989), p. 23).
[6] See generally Harris, *Property and Justice*, pp. 32–39.   [7] *Ibid.*, p. 64.

concern interests of owners to *control* the goods in question.'[8] Similarly, Robert S. Taylor talks of 'control incidents' or 'control rights': 'the rights of use and exclusion, the power of transfer, and an immunity from expropriation'.[9] These are, however, simply amended bundles. They are attempts to 're-aggregate' the bundle around the 'sticks' related to use and control. While this is necessary due to the problems with the disaggregative nature of bundle theses, it nonetheless runs the risk of falling prey to the self-same theoretical and practical problems. There is also a danger with amended bundles that they include elements which are more properly seen as part of wider property *systems* rather than its conceptual and normative core.[10] Like the no-theft-without-property point, immunity from expropriation, for example, must be immunity in respect of pre-existing or logically prior interests.

As such, we can conceptualise property (interests) as an overarching set of use-*privileges* and control-*powers* which persons hold in relation to particular objects.[11] This dual core encapsulates the *why* of property; that is, persons' multifarious interests in controlling the uses of things. In this manner it operates as a unifying conception. It represents a more abstract conceptual and normative idea under which a number of potential interests and rights are subsumed (or from which they can be derived). Additionally, it identifies and incorporates the operative normative relations: privileges (liberties) and powers.

Consider, for example, my ownership of a book. Although my property rights in my book pertain to my actual possession and use of it, this is not all that is entailed by my rights over it. My liberty to use my book is not merely about my physical use (or not) of the book. Fundamentally, it is about the exercise or not of the *liberty* itself. Equally, the power to manage is exactly that: a *power*. It is rightly seen as a type of control over use and possession, but it is not just about control of the object itself. Importantly, it concerns a person's sphere of action regarding their property rights. Hence, the power to manage the uses regarding my book includes, for example, my power to waive your duty to not use it or my power to transfer it to you. This is important since, as we will see in

---

[8] J. Christman, *The Myth of Property: Toward an Egalitarian Theory of Ownership* (Oxford: Oxford University Press, 1994), p. 128.

[9] R.S. Taylor, 'Self-ownership and the limits of libertarianism' (2005) 31 *Social Theory and Practice* 465, 466–467.

[10] Such was Harris' observation about some elements of Honoré's incidents of ownership (*Property and Justice*, p. 126).

[11] *Ibid.*, p. 130.

the next section, these liberties and powers are crucial to our under-standing of the structure of property *rights*.

Viewing property interests as a set of use-*privileges* and control-*powers* in relation to things has a variety of advantages. First, it allows us to conceive, as Harris did, of property relationships as falling along a spectrum.[12] This extends from more circumscribed ones where, for example, there is no power to transfer[13] to 'full-blooded ownership', where persons have *'prima facie*, unlimited privileges of use or abuse over the thing'.[14] Conceptualising property interests in this manner encompasses and takes account of the variety of property relations which might exist. It recognises that property is not an all or nothing idea. There are different degrees to which a person might be the holder of property rights; thus indicating and reflecting the differing degrees of use and control that an individual might have over certain objects. This we saw in the last chapter, for example, where I distinguished between a tenant and a house owner and between someone who is a bailee of a computer as opposed to its owner.

Note that Harris termed the relevant interests as 'ownership' not property interests. However, I prefer to use the term property (or pro-prietary) interests. I do this because property is a wider concept than ownership per se. This, Harris himself accepts when he says on the first page of his book that '[p]roperty is a legal and social institution governing the use of most things and the allocation of some items of social wealth.'[15] Although this describes the *institution* of property, it is reasonable to align our terminology when talking of interests or rights. We commonly refer to property rights rather than ownership rights and the common-sense analogue to a property right is a property interest (something which one must have if one is to have a property right, as we will see in the next section). In addition, the purpose of my analysis is not confined to the strictly juridical, but is concerned with the conceptual and philosophical. Hence, as we will see in Section 5, I reserve the term ownership to denote a position of *ultimate normative authority*. Because there are interests

---

[12] *Ibid.*, p. 64.   [13] Termed 'mere property' by Harris (*ibid.*, pp. 28–29).
[14] I*ibid.*, p. 30.
[15] *Ibid.*, p. 3. This is to be differentiated from the narrower legal answer he gave later in the book: '"property" [legally speaking] comprises (1) ownership and quasi-ownership inter-ests in things (tangible or ideational); (2) other rights over such things which are enforce-able against all-comers (non-ownership proprietary interests); (3) money; and (4) cashable rights' (p. 139). And this in turn must be separated from seven usages of 'property right' where he sought to distinguish between different legal and extra-legal uses of the term (p. 169).

and rights which persons might have in virtue of being owners, but which non-owners may also hold, I use the wider terminology of property interests and rights.

A second reason to conceive of property interests as an overarching set of use-privileges and control-powers is that this conception of property interests can accommodate both open-ended and non-open-ended content with respect to the interests at issue. It includes, in Harris' terminology, both ownership interests and non-ownership proprietary interests.[16] The former are open-ended with respect to the exact content of the interests they encompass: 'One cannot produce a definitive catalogue of the uses that a person may make of a thing, or of the control-powers he may exercise in respect of it.'[17] For example, if I own a book, I may read it, write in it, use it to prop up the leg of a table, loan it to a friend, give it away, burn it, and so on. To a certain extent, the uses to which I may put my book are unrestricted and bounded only by the limits of my imagination. This is not a claim about the conceptual divisibility of the constituent privileges and powers (as is entailed in the bundle views examined in the previous chapter). It does not entail an unbounded infinite set of property interests (or rights) regarding the book, such that each use I can put my book to needs to correspond to a similarly named right for practical purposes. Although it may be difficult to enumerate exactly what such uses may be, they are nonetheless encompassed, constrained, and bounded by some overarching notion of use and control.[18] This does not entail absolute free rein over the uses of my book. For reasons external to the conception and institution of property, constraints can be (and indeed are) put on the exercise of the requisite privileges and powers. I cannot beat you around the head with it nor can I burn it in a manner which would cause public harm or nuisance.[19]

By including both open-ended and non-open-ended interests, I again depart from Harris. His ownership spectrum included only open-ended interests. However, my broader view of a property spectrum which encompasses varying (degrees of) property interests, allows the admission

---

[16] *Ibid.*, pp. 55–58.   [17] *Ibid.*, p. 31.

[18] This could be viewed as analogous to set theory where there may be a bounded set, but still infinitely many elements within that set. For example, the set of all cars may potentially have infinitely many varieties, but they ultimately all share the overarching theme of being a car. Notwithstanding the potential for things like cars and property rights to be fuzzy sets, the boundary is still reasonably well demarcated.

[19] Harris, *Property and Justice*, p. 333. Also, it is open-ended in a way in which my scope of action in relation to someone else's book is not. I am, for instance, subject to the restrictions noted in the main text, more at liberty to burn my own book than I am my neighbour's. Thank you to Daithí Mac Síthigh for this point.

of non-open-ended interests as well. Admitting non-open-ended interests encapsulates our ordinary usage of the terms property and property rights, which we often marshal to encompass situations from ownership to leases to lesser interests such as rights of way. It thus takes into account property interests such as easements, which are not open-ended in their content.[20] While an easement grants a right to pass over another's land, those granted such uses do not have open-ended privileges and powers with respect to the parcel of land in question.

Finally, envisaging property interests as a set of use-privileges and control-powers can account for the differing ways in which (legal) philosophers and property lawyers sometimes employ the term 'interests'. The former group tend to utilise interest and interests in a wider sense than the latter group. For instance, Joel Feinberg considered having an interest in something as being akin to having a *stake* in that thing.[21] Joseph Raz, on the other hand, sees a person's interests as being aspects of their well-being.[22] These conceptions reflect the dual way in which we sometimes talk of interests; that is, the idea of persons *having interests in* particular states of affairs, as well as something *being in their interests* (being to their advantage or benefit, or promoting/supporting their well-being). By contrast, property lawyers commonly talk about interests *as* particular forms of property. Thus we find ownership, leases, easements, and so on all being referred to as ownership or property interests. In this manner each 'interest' actually refers to a specified range of rights and other elements. Indeed, Bridge, reflecting this way of talking about them, states that '[p]roprietary interests in chattels are defined as possession and ownership'.[23] The conception of property interests set out in this section, however, admits both the philosophical and legal usages of the term.

3   What Does It Mean to Have a *Property Right*?

The next challenge is twofold: to identify, first, when something counts as a property *right* as opposed to a property *interest* and, second, what

---

[20] Harris, *Property and Justice* p. 56.

[21] J. Feinberg, *The Moral Limits of the Criminal Law: Harm to Others* (Oxford: Oxford University Press, 1984), pp. 33–45.

[22] J. Raz, 'On the nature of rights' (1984) XCIII *Mind* 194, 195.

[23] Bridge, *Personal Property Law*, p. 30. Mirroring this in relation to rights, he also says that '[p]ossession and ownership together [exhaust] the category of legal property rights in a chattel' (p. 46).

features of those rights (in addition to encompassing use-privileges and control-powers) mark them out as being proprietary in nature.

3.1   Rights as Structurally Complex

When we claim that we are entitled as a matter of *right* to have or to do something, we are making a stronger statement than the expression of a mere desire or want; be this about what we have a right to (not) do or what we have a right that *others* (not) do.[24] When I say, for instance, that I have a right to ride my bicycle, there is (usually) more going on than the assertion of my bare liberty to ride said bicycle. The term right, though, can be ambiguous, both in everyday usage and in the academic literature. Thus unpicking uses of 'right' and distinguishing between different types of normative relations is necessary if we are to get at the idea of a *property* right. What we are about to see is that no single configuration of incidents (claim, liberty, immunity, power) describes a right. Different ones may count as rights. Moreover, rights are often (although not always) structurally complex.[25]

More than a century ago, Hohfeld argued that 'the term "rights" tends to be used indiscriminately to cover what in a given case might be a privilege, a power, or an immunity rather than a right in the strictest sense'.[26] He wanted to reserve the term 'claim' for what we call a right; in particular, seeking to differentiate claims from privileges (liberties).[27] Claims are defined in terms of the correlative duty which they entail.

---

[24] L. Wenar, 'The nature of rights' (2005) 33 *Philosophy and Public Affairs* 223, 225. See also L. Wenar, 'Rights' in E.N. Zalta (ed.), *The Stanford Encyclopedia of Philosophy* (Fall 2011 edn). Available at http://plato.stanford.edu/archives/fall2011/entries/rights/ (accessed 27 November 2017).

[25] There is a vast literature on interests and rights in both law and philosophy (and other disciplines). The discussions here necessarily only touch on some of this. For an interesting analysis which differentiates 'ideal type' rights from other types of rights (that is, those which are constrained either by other rights considerations or by considerations external to the concept of rights themselves) see H. Breakey, 'Who's afraid of property rights? Rights as core concepts, coherent, prima facie, situated and specified' (2014) 33 *Law and Philosophy* 573.

[26] Hohfeld, *Fundamental Legal Conceptions*, p. 36. I will not be discussing the specifics of Hohfeld in-depth here. Instead I draw on him in order to shed some light on confusions and ambiguities regarding 'rights'. Hohfeld thought that privilege is more precise (although I use them interchangeably in this book). He thought this in no small part because 'privilege' is correlated accurately with the 'no-right' position; that is, if you have a privilege to do something, third parties have no right that you not do it (pp. 42–45 and 48–49).

[27] *Ibid.*, p. 39.

They are a claim against some party for the performance of some duty or other. This duty might be positive (to do something) or negative (to refrain from doing something) in nature. Liberties on the other hand entail the lack of a duty on the part of the liberty-holder. For instance, to assert that I have a liberty (privilege) regarding my bicycle is merely to say that I am *not* under a duty to refrain from riding it. I can ride it or not as I see fit.[28] Third parties have 'no right' that I either ride or not ride my bicycle.[29] The distinction between these two categories, which in contemporary discourse tend to get called claim-rights and liberty-rights, represents the two main types of rights-assertions: other-focused rights and self-focused rights. From the first person perspective the former are assertions about what I have a right that *you* do and the latter about what *I* have a right *to* do.[30]

The beginning of understanding with respect to rights lies in the realisation that claims, liberties, and other elements often operate jointly. A right is structurally more complex than simply being a bare liberty, claim, power, or immunity. Although their 'structure will be resolvable into combinations of the four "atomic" [Hohfeldian] incidents', rights are 'molecular' in form.[31] For example, my right to ride my bicycle could be described as entailing the following elements: I am at *liberty* to ride it (not under a duty to refrain from doing so); you are under a *duty* not to prevent me from riding it (I have a *claim* against you in this respect); I have the *power* to waive your duty and allow you to ride it instead of me; and I have an *immunity* against you if you *lack* the power to prevent me from riding my bicycle (if you were, for example, a member of the police force I may not have such an immunity as you could exercise your lawful authority to prevent me from cycling in certain circumstances).[32] Exactly

---

[28] Sumner terms each of these components a 'half liberty'. Together the liberty to do and not do something creates a 'full liberty'. He says, '[u]nlike half liberties, full liberties ensure a normatively unencumbered choice between options' (*Moral Foundation of Rights*, p. 27).

[29] Hohfeld organised his jural relations into opposites (right:no-right, privilege:duty, power:disability, immunity:liability) and correlatives (right:duty, privilege:no-right, power:liability, immunity:disability) (*Fundamental Legal Conceptions*, p. 36). I do not go into these fully here, but for in-depth discussions of these see Sumner, *Moral Foundation of Rights*, pp. 18–39; P. Jones, *Rights* (Basingstoke and London: MacMillan Press, 1994), pp. 12–25; and Wenar, 'Nature of rights', 224–237.

[30] Wenar, 'Nature of rights', 225. As Sumner notes, 'I cannot have claims *to do*, only claims *that others do*' and 'I cannot have liberties *that others do*, only liberties *to do*' (*Moral Foundation of Rights*, pp. 25 and 26).

[31] Wenar, 'Nature of rights', 225; Sumner, *Moral Foundation of Rights*, p. 19.

[32] For more on the structure of rights and the individual incidents see generally Wenar, 'Nature of rights', 224–237.

what the elements of any individual right consists of will depend on the particulars of the case at hand. But the example just given illustrates the fact that there may be a cluster of things going on when we assert that we have a *right* to ride our bicycles, something which holds whether we are talking about rights regarding bicycles, bodily integrity, freedom of expression, biomaterials, or whatever it may be.

From the bicycle example we can also note two things about the structure of rights. First, powers and immunities differ from liberties and claims. They do so because they involve either (a) *altering* the normative position of the rights-holder and/or third parties with respect to the right (powers) or (b) protecting that position from alteration by others (immunities). This division is ordinarily represented as first-order (liberties and claims) and second-order incidents (powers and immunities), where second order incidents alter first-order ones. Accordingly, I can exercise my powers in relation to my (rights over my) bicycle by allowing you to borrow it. In so doing I alter our respective normative positions. These normative positions are cashed out minimally in terms of our respective liberties and claims. You will be at liberty to ride the bicycle. I will no longer have a claim against you that you not ride it. Consequently, you will no longer be under an immediate duty of non-interference with respect to the bicycle. Second, we can conceive of the relations between the incidents as being constituted of a core and a periphery.[33] The core of a right describes the determinative content of that particular right, while the periphery protects or alters this core (and as a consequence the duties of others with respect to the core).[34] So in our current example, my liberty to ride the bicycle is the core content of the right. The duty entailed by the claim protects my liberty to do so, while powers and immunities alter this core liberty.

This is not to say that all rights have (just) liberty at their core. Some rights may have claims (and other incidents) as their central component. My right to an education is best taken as a claim against the state (or society) for the provision of the requisite resources. It clearly must entail a range of liberties in order to pursue any education provided (being free to attend school, etc.); however, in this case those liberties are not the purpose driving the assertion of the right. Other rights with claims at their core, such as the right to bodily integrity, may be negative in nature.

---

[33] C. Wellman, *A Theory of Rights: Persons Under Laws, Institutions, and Morals* (Totowa: Rowman and Allanheld, 1985), pp. 81–95.
[34] Sumner, *Moral Foundation of Rights*, p. 48.

My right in this regard can be viewed at its most basic as a claim against others' interference with regards to my body.[35]

The lesson here is that, in many cases, our rights-assertions are not simply reducible to individual (bare) Hohfeldian incidents if they are to have the normative force that we ordinarily think rights to have. This is not to say that we cannot analyse the components of the right in terms of those incidents (we can), but that a right is more than its bare central element. Adjuncts to the core interest involved are necessary to give the right the requisite force. In our ongoing example, without other elements my liberty to ride my bicycle is just a bare liberty lacking in protection. It is other elements which form what Herbert Hart termed a 'protective perimeter' around that liberty.[36] He conceived of this perimeter not as including duties which are directly correlative to the liberty itself, but as ones which arise at a more general level. As such, my liberty to ride my bicycle may be protected by general duties of non-interference which other persons have towards me and items in my possession. Similarly, Sumner conceptualises rights with liberty at their core as comprising a liberty which is protected by a 'protective perimeter of claims, powers over both the core liberty and these protective claims, immunities against the like powers of others, and so on'.[37]

We might think, by contrast, that rights with claims at their core are different; perhaps because claims can be viewed as already intrinsically containing a protective stipulation in the form of the duty which they entail. Recall that Hohfeld essentially described claims in terms of their correlative duties. We might interpret this as meaning that bare claims can be rights, but this only holds on a definitional tautology: all claim-rights are rights. I take a bare claim to be exactly that: bare. It is simply an appeal to others that they do or not do something or other. Without a correlative duty, a claim is all that it is; a request for performance rather than a demand for it. Besides, most rights with claims at their core will, as Sumner puts it, also be 'structurally complex'.[38]

Coming to an understanding of what a right is, requires us to pay some attention to the function of rights, as well as their form and content.

---

[35] This is so notwithstanding the fact that this right may be intimately connected to (or even necessarily dependent on) other more positive rights, without which it may be on extremely shaky grounds. For instance, it is conceivable that any so-called right to bodily integrity is rendered substantively moot if our basic needs such as adequate food, shelter, and health are not met.

[36] H.L.A. Hart, *Essays on Bentham: Studies in Jurisprudence and Political Theory* (Oxford: Clarendon Press, 1982), p. 171. See also Sumner, *Moral Foundation of Rights*, pp. 48–49.

[37] Sumner, *Moral Foundation of Rights*, p. 48.   [38] *Ibid.*

Questions of the exact function of rights have been the subject of long-standing debate amongst rights theorists. Much of this has centred on a stand-off between those who favour a control analysis (will theory) and those who argue for a benefit analysis (interest theory) of rights. The will theory of rights takes as key the control that a person has over their right, in particular, the power to alter the duties that others have in respect of one's right.[39] Rights on this view are protected choices. Conversely, on interest theory, rights function to confer a benefit on the rights-holder or to promote their well-being. Here rights are seen as protected interests.[40] In holding, as I did in the previous section, that use and control are the central components of property, we might think that the notion of a property *right* is more closely aligned with the will theory of rights; the function of the right being to protect a person's interests in using and *controlling* the uses of things. Yet such an account is not incompatible with interest theory. A compatible interest theory analysis would view the use and control we have (or want) in particular items to be the basic interests at issue. These could then be held to be sufficient to generate (property) rights in respect of those interests.[41]

Despite this seeming compatibility with either of the main rights theories, single function theories may unnecessarily narrow down our understanding of the purpose of rights,[42] which as we have already seen can be complex. For this reason I follow Leif Wenar who proposes a 'several function' theory of rights. He argues that 'there is no one thing that rights do for rightholders. Rights have no fundamental normative purpose in this sense.'[43] This is not to say they have *no* normative purpose, merely that the functions may be manifold. On his view, the Hohfeldian incidents under discussion can be rights 'so long as they mark exemption, or discretion, or authorization, or entitle their holders to protection, provision, or performance'.[44] In other words, they can be rights, if they are *entitlements* to do or have something (or not to do or have that thing). The language of entitlements (unlike mere claims or liberties, etc.) suggests that the performance of a duty is demanded. Thus, according to Wenar, rights are

---

[39] See H.L.A. Hart, 'Are there any natural rights?' (1955) 64 *Philosophical Review* LXIV 175, 178–180; Hart, *Essays on Bentham*, pp. 162–193 and 183–184; and Sumner, *Moral Foundation of Rights*, p. 46.

[40] J. Raz, 'On the nature of rights'. See also M. Kramer, 'Rights without trimmings' in M. Kramer, N.E. Simmonds, and H. Steiner (eds), *A Debate over Rights: Philosophical Enquiries* (Oxford: Oxford University Press, 1998, reprinted 2002), pp. 60–101.

[41] According to Raz, the interest must be 'a sufficient reason for holding some other person(s) to be under a duty' ('On the nature of rights', 195).

[42] Wenar, 'Nature of rights', 237.   [43] *Ibid.*, 248.   [44] *Ibid.*, 252.

'entitlements (not) to perform certain actions, or (not) to be in certain states; or entitlements that others (not) perform certain actions or (not) be in certain states'.[45] This is appealing because it captures an important feature of rights-assertions; that is, that others, by dint of social, moral, or legal force, are compelled to act or refrain from acting in a particular manner. The obligation created by the third-party duty is what gives teeth to my assertion that I have a *right* (as opposed to some other contention) to ride my bicycle. Simply being at liberty to do this, or to any manner of things, tells us nothing, and on its own demands nothing, of others in the world.

3.2   From Property Interests to Property Rights

The structure of property rights reflects the general molecular form of rights and the conceptualisation of them as comprising a core and a periphery. As already noted in Section 2, we can conceive of property interests as consisting of a dual core of use-privileges and control-powers. In this way our property interests encompass a combination of first-order (liberties/privileges) and second-order (powers) Hohfeldian elements. However, while this dual core encompasses our property interests, as we have just seen, we ought only to view them as *rights* when they are entitlements – that is, when they are supplemented by a duty imposed on third parties to refrain from interfering with those interests (often characterised by not interfering with the thing itself). Consequently, when the dual core of property interests is protected by a perimeter of trespassory rules which impose duties on others, we might properly say that we have a property right. The trespassory rules form the *boundary* which dictates the uses and control that others can exercise over a resource. In the case of full-blooded ownership, such a boundary might mean the complete exclusion of third parties from a particular resource. In this manner, property interests and trespassory rules provide the foundation around which property institutions, and other concomitant rules are built; the 'twin pillars' as Harris put it.[46] Without trespassory rules (minimally a duty to exclude or of non-interference), then property claims have no bite. This is important in the context of property because, as Macpherson notes, '[w]hat distinguishes property from mere momentary possession is that property is a

---

[45] Wenar, 'Rights'.   [46] Harris, *Property and Justice*, p. 6.

claim that will be *enforced* by society or the state, by custom or convention or law'.[47]

Property rights (like other species of rights) then are structurally complex. They contain 'nested layers of components',[48] with different incidents functioning to support or alter a person's core liberties and powers. These different incidents may fall into other categories of rules, such as expropriation and appropriation, described earlier in the chapter. But despite this and despite my contention that property rights must come bundled with a set of exclusionary duties, it is worth reminding ourselves that certain elements ordinarily associated with property are analytically presupposed by other more fundamental elements. Specifically, the existence of property interests (use-privileges and control-powers) are taken as read by the rules which surround them. This includes any claims and their correlative duties. As explicated by Harris:

> Any 'claim-rights' (in Hohfeld's sense) which accompany ownership interests have the same content as the duties which trespassory rules impose. . . The crime of theft and the tort of conversion would be meaningless unless it were presupposed that there was someone, the owner, who has special privileged relations to chattels.[49]

Accordingly, when we assert our property rights we are in fact making a collection of normative assertions. These comprise a number of interrelated elements which together we can say constitutes the right.

Persons, however, have all sorts of rights which are not proprietary in nature (at least as far as the law is concerned). How, therefore, are we to distinguish between rights which can be said to pertain to property and those which cannot? To (partially) answer this we need to examine the relationship between the holder of the rights and those parties who are under a duty consequent on the right. Consider the following example from Hohfeld. He asks us to 'Suppose that A is the owner of Blackacre and X is the owner of Whiteacre. Let it be assumed, further, that, in consideration of $100 actually paid by A to B, the latter agrees with A never to enter on X's land, Whiteacre.'[50] What types of rights exist

---

[47] Macpherson, *Property*, p. 3 [emphasis added]. Note the different levels at which property operates: some legal, some extra-legal. Thus, while the explicit trespassory rules within any given legal system create sets of duties, there are also moral analogues of these; for example, moral duties of non-interference.

[48] Sumner says this in relation to rights generally (*Moral Foundation of Rights*, pp. 48–49).

[49] Harris, *Property and Justice*, p. 126.

[50] Hohfeld, *Fundamental Legal Conceptions*, p. 77.

between the parties in this scenario? What duties do they have and to whom are they owed?

Despite the fact that we oftentimes make agreements regarding items which in ordinary parlance we call property (our land, cars, books, houses, etc.), not all rights in respect of such things are *property* rights. The agreement between A and B (let us call them Jack and Jill) exists in respect of a parcel of land: Whiteacre. This parcel of land is something which can uncontrovertibly (and uncontroversially) be subject to property rights. Nevertheless, the right that Jack has against Jill with regards to Whiteacre (of which X – let us call her Joanna – is the owner) is not a *property* right. Jack 'has no similar and separate rights concerning Whiteacre availing respectively against other persons in general'.[51] His right is a right *in personam*.[52] It exists only in virtue of the specific agreement between himself and Jill regarding the land; no-one else is bound by the duty arising. This is the essence of contractual rights.

The terms of such an agreement notwithstanding, Jill already has general duties with regards to Whiteacre; as indeed she does in respect of Blackacre or any other parcel of land. These are consequent on the general rights of the owners that she and other persons not trespass on their land. Hohfeld conceptualised these rights as availing 'against persons constituting a very large and indefinite class of people'.[53] Commonly, however, these *in rem* rights are referred to as being exigible *against all persons*. Although there may be persons or classes of persons not bound by the duty (the police undertaking an investigation, for instance), it is useful shorthand to think of them in this manner. It conveys the message that persons generally (including Jill) have a *duty* not to trespass on either Jack or Joanna's land. That duty holds unless an

---

[51] *Ibid.* The purpose of the section from which I have extracted this quotation from Hohfeld is not to distinguish property rights from other types of rights. At this point he is making the argument that we ought not to make the mistake of characterising *in rem* rights as rights *against* things simply because *in personam* rights are rights against persons. They also avail against persons; the difference merely being the number or classes of persons (p. 77). In this book, I have never presented rights (or indeed other normative relations) as being anything other than relations between persons.

[52] *Ibid.*, p. 72. He characterises it as a paucital right: 'either a unique right residing in a person (or group of persons) and availing against a single person (or single group of persons); or else it is one of a *few* fundamentally similar, yet separate, rights availing respectively against a few definite persons'.

[53] *Ibid.* These are multital rights: 'one of a large *class of fundamentally similar* yet separate rights, actual and potential, residing in a *single* person (or single group of persons) but availing *respectively* against persons constituting a very large and indefinite class of people'.

exemption is granted, say in the form of permission to enter. No special agreement needs to be in place for the right and the ensuing duties to exist. If I am a would-be trespasser, it does not matter that I do not personally know or cannot even identify the owner(s) of the land in question. It is enough that some person holds legal title to this land, that this person is not me, and that I have not been granted any sort of exemption which permits me to cross over the land. The consequence of this is that, for all intents and purposes, it is normatively immaterial (to me) when ownership of, let us say, Blackacre changes hands.[54] True, I no longer owe any duties to Blackacre's original owner, but instead owe them to the new one. However, all that I need to know in order to understand my duties is that the new owner is *not* me.

The situation regarding moveables is no different. To borrow an example from Francisco Morales: when trespasser-George walks past an unattended computer in the library it does not matter that he does not know who the owner is. There is a presumption that there is an owner and this is enough for George to know that he is under a duty not to walk off with the computer.[55] Furthermore, it is not just George who is under this duty, but anyone else who might walk past and be tempted to appropriate or otherwise interfere with (the owner's rights regarding) the laptop.

From this we might be tempted to say that all *in rem* rights are property rights. The rights that each of us has with regards to our bodies are principal examples of *in rem* rights. My right not to be caused bodily harm avails not only against you, but against all other persons in the

---

[54] A similar point is made by Penner when he argues that the 'duty not to interfere with the property of others is not owner-specific. We do not need to identify the owner in order to understand the content of that duty' (*Idea of Property*, p. 23). He does, however, come at this from a slightly different position. He asks us to consider what the situation might be if ownership of Blackacre were to be transferred to another person. He contends that it is incumbent on the Hohfeldian model that every time the piece of land changes hands that the duties of all persons within the set of 'indefinite and large number of people' also change. If the land is transferred from A to B, then all those who owed a duty of non-interference to A now owe one to B. For him, a better conception of the duties involved is one where only A's and B's rights and duties have changed. This contention notwithstanding, although the *content* of *my* duty does not change when Blackacre transfers from A to B, the recipient of the duty has changed. So while most of the time it is, as I noted in the main text, normatively immaterial to me that ownership has changed hands, this change will make a difference if I breach my duty not to trespass. Again, however, the normative change is not the content of the duty, but the recipient of it.

[55] F.J. Morales, 'The property matrix: An analytical tool to answer the question, "is this property'?" (2013) 161 *University of Pennsylvania Law Review* 1125, 1126.

world. Can we, therefore, call these property rights? The property lawyer would deny that this could be the case. They would point out that the law, as we saw in Chapter 5, requires that objects governed by property rights must be things in the relevant sense – they must be separate and distinct from the holder of the property rights. Hence, although we hold rights with regards to our bodies which are exigible against all persons, the body is not an extra-personal object and so we cannot have legal property rights in respect of it.[56] Nevertheless, whilst we can readily admit that this is how the *law* categorises particular types of rights, as we will see in Chapter 8, the boundary between subject and object (and thus the types of rights which such a distinction creates) is not nearly as philosophically neat.[57]

4   Property and Sperm Revisited

If the relevant duties entailed by the right must in essence be good against all-comers to count as a *property* right, how does this sit with the decision in *Yearworth*? Does that decision recognise or impose duties binding on the rest of the world in relation to the sperm samples? As we saw in Chapter 3, Rostill says that:

> [T]he conclusion that the men had 'ownership' for the purposes of their claims against the defendant was not a deduction from or an incident of the more general statement that they had legal ownership or possessory title for the purposes of a claim in negligence. Rather, the conclusion was confined to those particular purposes, to those specific claims.[58]

---

[56] I take the phrase 'extra-personal objects' from Eric Mack's work. See E. Mack, 'Self-ownership and the right of property' (1990) 73 *The Monist* 519.

[57] This should not be interpreted as falling foul of Nicholas McBride's reductionist critique. He says: 'Many people believe: 1. All rights that are "good against the world" are "rights in rem". Other people believe that: 2. All "rights in rem" are based on the right-holder having a proprietary interest in some thing. I think it is perfectly legitimate to believe that either 1. or 2. is true. . . But what you cannot – must not – do is believe that both 1. and 2. are true. If you do, you will end up believing: 3. All rights that are "good against the world" are based on the right-holder having a proprietary interest in some thing' (N.J. McBride, 'Rights and the basis of tort law' in D. Nolan and A. Robertson (eds), *Rights and Private Law* (Oxford: Hart Publishing, 2012), pp. 331–365, p. 348). For the avoidance of doubt, I do not think that all *in rem* rights arise out of *legal* proprietary interests. However, as we will see in Chapter 8, I do think that self-ownership, which is a property concept (albeit extra-legal), offers the best justification for why we ought to recognise property in separated biomaterials (legally speaking); particularly if we want to allocate the rights involved to the source of those materials.

[58] Rostill, 'The ownership that wasn't meant to be', 16.

If he is correct about the narrowness of the scope of the decision, then the ownership at issue in the case was not ownership qua a legal property right, but something else. In this vein, Rostill contends that what was at issue was a philosophical or conceptual view of ownership and not the particular rights or entitlements which are the concern of property law. If this is the case, then the significance attributed to this case by some of us in terms of the property in the body debate is misplaced.

Why then does he think that the duties at issue were not *in rem*? The reason is that he places particular emphasis on the role 'context' played in the decision, arguing that 'the court decided that the men had "owner-ship" (for the purposes of the tort of negligence) *against the trust*; that the men's "ownerships" grounded duties of a certain kind *on the trust*'.[59] In support of this point he summarises, as follows, a couple of the key conclusions reached by the Court:

> The licence-holder has duties, but 'no person other than each man had any rights in relation to the sample he had produced'... There was a 'precise correlation' between, on the one hand, 'the primary, if circum-scribed, rights of the men in relation to the use of the sperm', and, on the other, 'the consequence of the trust's breach of duty, namely the preclu-sion of its use'.[60]

On this basis he does not see the decision as binding on anyone else and, therefore, denies that the decision recognised a property interest in the sperm samples.

While this is a provocative interpretation of the decision, it is not apparent that their Lordships intended for the scope of the requisite duties to be confined only to the Trust. True, they had to decide the case on the facts in front of them. In this respect it is clear that their attention had to be on the Trust and any breach of duties on its part. After all it was the purported negligence on the part of the Trust which was at issue. Nevertheless, this focus does not entail the conclusion that no one else was, or could have been, under a duty to the men regarding their sperm. To draw this conclusion is to read too much into it.

First, taking the decision as a whole, there is no indication that their Lordships viewed themselves as deciding the matter on anything other than the usual run of property law (albeit a novel extension of it). This much is obvious not in the least through their use of standard property law cases throughout the judgment. In particular their treatment of *Leigh*

---

[59] *Ibid.*, 17 [emphasis added].
[60] *Ibid.*, 15. References individually removed, but generally citing *Yearworth* at [45].

and Sillavan Ltd v. *Aliakmon Shipping Co. Ltd*[61] goes a long way to supporting the view that they were indeed interested in *legal ownership*. A key question in this case, which was about damage to goods badly stowed in a ship, was whether the plaintiffs who had contracted to buy the goods could bring an action in negligence. Lord Brandon's answer was no, because 'in order to enable a person to claim in negligence for loss caused to him by reason of loss of or damage to property, he must have had either the legal ownership of or a possessory title to the property concerned at the time when the loss or damage occurred'.[62] This is then cited positively in *Yearworth*, with Lord Judge CJ saying, '[i]n what follows we will, albeit only for convenience, elide the concepts of legal ownership and possessory title into the word "ownership"'.[63] On its own this could be interpreted as merely rolling the men's possessory title over the sperm into ownership. However, what actually follows is a thorough-going discussion of *ownership* as applied to the human body and parts.[64]

Rostill criticises this part of the judgment, insisting that 'at no point in its judgment [are two key questions] expressly identified'.[65] These questions are 'were the men capable of "owning" the sperm?' and '[d]id each of the men have "ownership" of the sperm he had produced at the time of the defendant's negligence?'[66] According to Rostill, these are the questions which needed to be asked and answered so as to determine whether the claimants 'satisfied the requirements of the rule stated by Lord Brandon'.[67] The problem with this contention is that, while we might accept that the Court never explicitly asked these particular questions, it most certainly answered them. The conclusions drawn following the discussion of ownership unambiguously declares that '[b]y their bodies, they alone generated and ejaculated the sperm'[68] and that 'the men had ownership of the sperm for the purposes of their present claims'.[69] Although we can raise issues with this reasoning, as I indicated in Chapter 4, the answers to the questions posed are clear: yes the men were capable of owning their sperm and yes they did indeed have ownership at the time of the defendant's negligence.[70]

The main reason Rostill denies that the Court was concerned with *legal* ownership is that he denies that the duties at issue were ones that could be said to be exigible against the rest of the world: 'If the court thought that

---

[61] [1986] AC 785.   [62] *Ibid.* at 809.   [63] *Yearworth* at [25].   [64] *Ibid.* at [26]–[44].
[65] Rostill, 'The ownership that wasn't meant to be', 15.   [66] *Ibid.*   [67] *Ibid.*
[68] *Yearworth* at [45(f)(i)].   [69] *Ibid.* at [45(f)(v)].
[70] Chapter 4, sections 2 and 5. I will return to what is essentially 'fruit-of-the-labour' reasoning in Chapter 8.

the men had "ownership" against the trust only, we may infer that the court did not regard the men's "ownerships" as (prima facie) sufficient reason for holding all persons to owe the men certain duties.[71] There is, I suggest, little evidence that their Lordships did indeed regard the duties owed in this manner. Again, Lord Judge CJ's own comments on this indicate that they viewed their decision as operating within the ordinary limits of property law:

> Had we reached the conclusion that the law in respect of parts or products of a living human body precluded our holding that the men had owner-ship of sperm for the purposes of their claims in the tort of negligence, it would clearly have been important for us to proceed to enquire whether nevertheless they had such lesser rights in relation to it as would render them capable of having been bailors of it. Our conclusion that the men had ownership of it for the purposes of their claims in tort obviates the need for that particular enquiry: for from that conclusion it follows a fortiori that the men had sufficient rights in relation to it as to render them capable of having been bailors of it.[72]

This passage, perhaps even more than the comments regarding *Aliakmon*, demonstrates not only were their Lordships were talking about legal own-ership, but that they were concerned about property rights more generally. First, it emphasises the determination that the men had ownership. Second, even if we leave aside the question of ownership per se, the fact that there was a bailment (even if it entailed lesser possessory rights) points us towards a property analysis.

Bailment is a bit of an oddity as it stands at the property–contract interface. As explained by Christopher Newman, it 'looks like "property law" because it governs certain rights and obligations that people have with respect to an identified object of ownership. It looks like "contract law" because, broadly speaking, the parties choose whether to enter into the relationship and how to define the scope of the attendant duties'.[73] As such, if we view the relationship, and duty of care which arose in *Yearworth*, as sitting on the contractual end of this, then we may deny (as Rostill has) that the rights involved are *in rem*; instead, viewing them as arising purely *in personam*. However, I do not think that this is how the Court saw it. Liability lay not only because of an *in personam* relationship between the men and the unit, but also because of an *in rem* one

---

[71] Rostill, 'The ownership that wasn't meant to be', 18.   [72] *Yearworth* at [47].

[73] C.M. Newman, 'Bailment and the property/contract interface' (2015) George Mason Legal Studies Research Paper No. LS 15–12, 1. Available at SSRN: https://ssrn.com/abstract=2654988 (accessed 27 November 2017).

consequent on the men's property rights over the sperm. This is clear from the fact that they say that liability also lay in tort; specifically, negligence consequent on damage to chattels, which in this case were the sperm samples.[74] The bailment aspect of the decision was more to do with the measure of damages. And even though the Court said that these 'may be more akin to that referable to breach of contract than to tort',[75] they are explicit that the bailment in this case was not in itself contractual (it could not be since it was gratuitous).[76]

If the decision in *Yearworth* did, as Rostill argues, run contrary to the view that the men had *in rem* rights regarding their sperm, then this would have some troubling implications. What, for instance, should the Court have done if there had been a break-in at the fertility unit and the men's samples were taken. Are we to presume here that the men have no rights against the 'thieves' that they not interfere with their samples? On Rostill's reasoning, the duty that was breached only existed because of the particular circumstances that entailed between the men and the fertility unit. Hence, they could have no cause for complaint against anyone else for infringements or damage done, since no one else is under any relevant duty. Similarly, what of a situation where an engineer from an outside company accidentally unplugs the freezer in which the men's samples are stored? Ought the company to escape liability on the basis that only the fertility unit is under a duty to the men? I suggest that it is unlikely that the Court would have viewed the duties as so narrowly confined. As Newman argues regarding bailment in general, '*in rem* norms do not cease to become relevant and applicable the moment we enter into *in personam* transactions. Rather, they continue by default to govern every aspect of the interaction not specifically altered by contract or license.'[77] Of course we cannot know what their Lordships would actually say since we can only read the decision as given. It is for future cases to reveal the scope of the ownership involved. Nevertheless, the attention given by the Court to the Trust's specific duties (and thus negligent breach of those) in *Yearworth* is more plausibly interpreted as an appropriate focus to resolving the case given the facts as they stood.

5   Property, Possession, and Ownership

Thus far I have argued that use-privileges and control-powers are the foundation of what it is to have a property interest. When a person's

---

[74] See discussion generally, *Yearworth* at [46]–[50].   [75] *Ibid.* at [50].
[76] *Ibid.* at [48(h)].   [77] Newman, 'Bailment and the property/contract interface', 5.

property interests are protected by a perimeter of trespassory rules, and where the duty entailed by these is generally exigible against all other persons, we can claim that they have a *property right* (properly so-called). In saying this, however, we need to be attentive to the distinction between ownership and other forms of property (rights). We might, for example, describe tenants as having property rights even though they are not the owner of their residence. What is it, however, which marks out owners from non-owners?

5.1   Better Rights of Possession

Let me start by noting that it is sometimes said that English law protects possession not ownership. Swadling, for example, says, 'despite what a layperson might think, English law has no notion of "ownership"'.[78] Similarly, Wall contends that ownership is not a *legal* relationship.[79] He says, 'the law does not protect "ownership" per se, it protects proprietary rights, statutory rights, rights of privacy and bodily integrity and relationships of trust and confidence. Ownership is protected through the vindication of these rights'.[80] Much of the law in this respect centres on possession, which is protected on the basis of *relative title*; that is, the person with the better right to possession. In *Yearworth*, the mere fact that the unit had been put in *possession* of the samples would be enough to generate rights vesting in the unit relating to the sperm samples. Both bailors (the men) and bailees (the unit) have rights of possession in law; they each have 'title' to it.[81] The former have legal title and the latter possessory title. The unit's title is good against all except the men as the 'true owners'. Thus, we might say that, for all intents and purposes, the men had *relatively better* rights over the samples than anyone else, including the unit. Although the men did not have de facto possession of the samples, they could have been said to hold legal title to them.[82] In this manner, even if we deny that English law protects ownership in and of itself, we might accept that relatively speaking, the men held both

---

[78] W.J. Swadling, 'Ignorance and unjust enrichment: The problem of title' (2008) 28 *Oxford Journal of Legal Studies* 627, 640.

[79] J. Wall, 'The trespasses of property' (2014) 40 *Journal of Medical Ethics* 19, 19.

[80] *Ibid.*, 20.

[81] D. Sheehan, *The Principles of Personal Property Law* (Oxford: Hart Publishing, 2011), p. 12.

[82] For a discussion on types of possession and the relationship of this to legal title see *ibid.*, pp. 7–24.

better rights to possession and better title regarding the samples. All the same, it is less than satisfactory to claim that there is *no* concept of ownership at work, even if this is an extra-legal one. Without a background concept of ownership, we have no touchstone against which to measure better rights of possession or better title.

Duncan Sheehan, in response to Swadling's claim of no ownership, considers the status of previously unowned items where there are no competing interests. He says that:

> Relativity of title implies merely that there are two titles. I cannot say that my title is better than yours if nobody but myself has rights over the asset. If therefore I take possession of a wild animal, there are no other interests in the animal and even in English law I can be said to own it.'[83]

But even when there are other competing interests in a chattel, and even though the system works largely through the protection of possessory rights, we could still reasonably claim that there is some notion of ownership in operation.

It is not unusual for the person with the best rights regarding the thing to be considered to be the owner.[84] This is certainly the view of some commentators. Bridge, for example, notes that 'ownership is largely expressed in terms of the vocabulary of possession since, in the words of Pollock and Wright, "possession is in a normal state of things the outward sign of ownership"... [O]wnership amounts to the best available possessory right.'[85] Here the relationship *between* ownership and possession is often significant when it comes to moveables, since determining possession may often answer the question of who is the owner of a thing. As Lawson and Rudden point out, 'all the law can do is to start by assuming that if we have something in our possession then it is ours'.[86] Here they intend 'ours' to signify a claim to something qua owner. At the level of starting principle this seems appropriate. Rostill says that 'in a society in which most people generally abide by the law, and in which it is typical for owners to be in possession of the things they own, it might be reasonably safe to presume, *in the first instance at least*, that a person in

---

[83] *Ibid.*, pp. 13–14. Unlike, for instance, the laptop example from earlier, wild animals are not the sorts of things which are ordinarily presumed to have owners.

[84] Bridge, *Personal Property Law*, p. 44; McFarlane, *Structure of Property Law*, p. 146 (although note he disagrees with such an analysis).

[85] Bridge, *Personal Property Law*, p. 30, quoting F. Pollock and R. Wright, *An Essay on Possession in the Common Law* (Oxford: Oxford University Press, 1888), p. 4.

[86] Lawson and Rudden, *Law of Property*, p. 64.

possession of a chattel has ownership of it'.[87] Nevertheless, it is not always straightforward and we ought to note a couple of interrelated issues.

The first is that all instances of possession are not instances of ownership. Tenants, for example, are in de facto possession of the residences in which they are living, but they are not the owners. Moreover, many cases of apparent possession do not amount to legal possession. To appropriate an example from Sheehan: guests at your dinner party do not acquire a legally protected right to possess your cutlery merely because they hold some of it to eat their dinner. This is because, even though they may currently be in factual possession of the knife and fork, you as the owner lack any relevant intention that *legal* possession or ownership should pass to them.[88] The second point is that non-owners can avail themselves of property-based torts such as conversion or trespass to goods, and so on. This is part of why some claim that English law is more about possession rather than ownership; the law explicitly protects rights of *possession*.

Take, for instance, the fertility unit in *Yearworth*. Upon taking receipt of the sperm, the unit takes on the position of bailee, along with the corresponding duty of care which this entails. Earlier I proffered the example of a visiting engineer who had unplugged the storage unit, the result being that the samples perished. The damage to sperm, therefore, had not been caused by the fertility unit's negligence. I suggested that it would be unlikely that the engineer (or his company) could escape liability in such a situation. One of the reasons is that the fertility unit could bring an action for negligent damage of property against the engineer. Why could they do this? After all they were not the owners, they were simply storing the samples on behalf of the men.

The right of bailees to sue is in little doubt, deriving as it does from the general ability of those in possession of goods to bring actions under the chattel torts. As stated by Collins MR in *The Winkfield*,[89] 'possession is good against a wrongdoer and... a long series of authorities establishes this in actions of trover and trespass at the suit of a possessor'.[90] As Rostill notes, the rights of bailees do not 'rest on the ground that the bailee *is liable to the bailor* for the loss of the goods converted or destroyed'.[91] This much can be understood from Collins MR's treatment (in *The Winkfield*) of the earlier case of *Armory* v. *Delamirie*.[92] In this case, involving the finding of a jewel by a chimney sweep, it was held that finders acquire

---

[87] Rostill, 'Relative title and deemed ownership', 48 [emphasis added].
[88] Sheehan, *Personal Property*, pp. 9 and 11–12.   [89] [1902] P 42 (CA).   [90] *Ibid.* at 54.
[91] Rostill, 'Relative title and deemed ownership', 42 [emphasis added].
[92] (1721) 93 ER 664, (1722) 1 Stra 505.

property rights, which can be defended against 'all but the rightful owner'.[93] The Master of the Rolls in the later case took this as a strong indication that the rights of bailees to bring an action arise independently of the interests of the bailor.[94]

One explanation for this is that the law is configured around rights of possession and, therefore, it does not really matter whether it is the possession of owners or non-owners which is subject to interference. The engineer through his negligence can be said to have interfered with the fertility unit's peaceable possession of the samples. However, in cases, for example, where the bailee has the object at issue for safekeeping, and suffers no material loss themselves, it does not seem satisfactory to say that the law is merely (or only) interested in possession. Why should it be particularly bothered about possession on such occasions? An alternative explanation has recently been defended by Rostill. He argues that English law contains a doctrine of *deemed ownership*. By this he means that 'in certain circumstances, a person is to be deemed to be the owner of a tangible chattel';[95] that is, the law treats such a person *as if* they have 'the rights, powers etc. that he would have if he were the owner'.[96] This conclusion echoes Lawson and Rudden's comments regarding the starting assumption which the law must make when it comes to chattels.[97]

What then does it means to have 'ownership' rights or to be an owner in the first place?

5.2   Being 'the Owner'

McFarlane makes a distinction between 'ownership' and 'Ownership': the former being an abstract concept and the latter being a specific legal property right.[98] He says that '[i]t is very difficult, and generally impossible, to list *all* the rights of use inherent in Ownership'.[99] Although he follows Harris in conceiving of these uses as open-ended, he argues that, in effect, a person has Ownership when they have the right to immediate exclusive control of the thing in question,[100] and this is a property right when, as we saw in the last section, it imposes a duty of non-interference on all-comers.[101] On this account, it is plausible to think that the men in *Yearworth* did indeed have Ownership qua a specific legal property right

---

[93] *Ibid.*   [94] *The Winkfield* at 55.
[95] Rostill, 'Relative title and deemed ownership', 31.   [96] *Ibid.*, 37.
[97] See accompanying text at note 86 above.
[98] McFarlane, *Structure of Property Law*, p. 140.   [99] *Ibid.*   [100] *Ibid.*, pp. 140–141.
[101] *Ibid.*, pp. 142–143 and 153.

in their sperm. They could reasonably be thought to have had a right of immediate exclusive control in the samples, since they could have directed the unit to destroy them. 'Immediate' here need not necessarily be interpreted in a literal temporal sense, but as an indication of the power of the men to alter the normative position of the unit with regards to the samples held. On the say so of the men, the unit would have lacked the liberty to continue to store and possess the samples. This would have been the case regardless of whether the samples were, in practical terms, able to be immediately disposed of.

That this is so is obvious if we consider other items that the law could be said to protect qua Ownership. The fact that I am away on holiday when the book I ordered online is posted through my letterbox does not negate the Ownership I have just acquired in it, even though I am not physically there to take exclusive control of it.[102] Nevertheless, taking Ownership to be a *particular* legal property right and speaking of this in shorthand as a right to immediate exclusive control raises two interrelated questions. First, how do we know that the right of exclusive control appropriately captures the core of what it is to be an owner? Second, what is the connection between Ownership and ownership?

McFarlane might respond to these questions by drawing our attention, as he does in his book, to the difference between being '*an* owner' and being '*the* owner'.[103] The latter is the person capable of asserting the *best* right relatively speaking regarding any particular item, while the former accounts for the fact that the law can recognise multiple parties as having a right to exclusive control exigible against the rest of the world. Consider McFarlane's example, along with his reasoning.

> Peter has Ownership of a bike, Jane steals Peter's bike, by taking physical control of it without Peter's consent or other lawful authority. Timmy, acting without the consent of Peter or Jane or other lawful authority, takes the bike from Jane.[104]
>   ... It is true that each of Peter and Jane has *acquired* [their] property right in a different way: Peter, perhaps, by buying the bike from a retailer; Jane by taking physical control of the bike. Nonetheless, the *content* of the two rights is indistinguishable:

---

[102] See, for example, *White* v. *Withers LLP* where the claimant was essentially deemed to have title to letters which had been posted to him even though he had never been in factual possession of them. In the situation where letters are posted through the letterbox, actual delivery has taken place.

[103] McFarlane, *Structure of Property Law*, p. 146.

[104] *Ibid.*, p. 144. In McFarlane's example, I have taken the liberty of substituting the letters used in the original with names.

1. The rest of the world is under a prima facie duty to Peter not to interfere with Peter's use of the bike. So (i) when Timmy takes the bike, Timmy commits a wrong against Peter; and (ii) when Jane takes the bike, Jane commits a wrong against Peter.
2. The rest of the world is under a prima facie duty to Jane not to interfere with Jane's use of the bike. So: (i) when Timmy takes the bike, Timmy commits a wrong against Jane.[105]

We might be tempted to call Peter's right Ownership and Jane's right Possession, but McFarlane asks why we should do this since, as far as the law is concerned, the *content* of rights is the same.

Support for the parity of the content of the right is to be found in the law of finders. Finders (even if they are wrongdoers such as thieves) can assert rights against the rest of the world. Such rights, however, while good against everyone else, are not good against the original owner.[106] Thus, Peter can assert his relatively better claim to the bicycle against both Jane and Timmy.[107] Despite this, McFarlane argues that if the content of the rights are the same, then we ought to give them equivalent labels.[108] Hence, he thinks we should call the right Ownership, whosoever is asserting it. This he confesses is counter-intuitive, especially in case of wrongdoers.[109] I agree, it is; so much so that we should be wary of taking this approach to possession and ownership.

We might at this point ask ourselves why we should call this Ownership. Indeed McFarlane acknowledges that the property right at issue could be renamed 'Exclusive Control Forever' or 'The Core Property Right'.[110] He resists this move, saying that it 'would come at a cost: we would no longer be able to refer to anyone as *an* owner of a thing'.[111] I am not convinced that this is a cost, however. Or, if it is, then it is one that I would willingly accept in exchange for the benefit of conceptual clarity. It is not obvious to me that we need to be able to call just anyone *an owner*. Insofar as the law sometimes assumes that certain persons are owners or treats them *as if* they are (as we saw in previous section), then it does this for a purpose. In the first instance it assumes

---

[105] *Ibid.*, p. 145.
[106] *Armory* v. *Delamirie* (1722) 1 Stra 505; *Costello* v. *Chief Constable of Derbyshire* [2001] 1 WLR 1437.
[107] Note that only Peter can do this. It will not be accepted as a defence by Timmy against Jane that Peter is the true owner.
[108] McFarlane, *Structure of Property Law*, p. 145.   [109] *Ibid.*   [110] *Ibid.*, p. 146.
[111] *Ibid.*

that they are *the* owner, unless and until it might be proven otherwise.[112] Evidence that the bicycle is in fact Peter's and not Jane's or Timmy's, establishes that Peter is the owner. Perhaps, for example, he can produce a receipt from the bicycle shop in which he bought it. If for a time the law protected Jane *as if* she were the owner, this is merely a reflection of its baseline presumptions about the normative position of owners (relative or not) and the content of ownership.[113]

McFarlane would not agree. He thinks that a pre-existing property right vesting in another party is not enough for us to say that, for example, Jane's right is materially different from Peter's. But all this really means is that there are occasions where we do not have adequate contextual knowledge about the rights to say whether or not they are different. To focus exclusively on content is to miss what is normatively important about *context*. When this is taken into account, the idea of relativity does indeed make all the difference, normatively-speaking.

In spite of McFarlane's caution that he does not deal with ownership as an abstract concept, we might wonder how his (or any) idea of Ownership can avoid it. What I suggest, therefore, is that we need a background philosophical (possibly extra-legal) concept of ownership (small 'o') against which the requisite legal rights can be assessed. Indeed, it is only by having a

---

[112] My thanks to Luke Rostill for his insights regarding this point. For him, 'title is about proof, not about rights. . . One could say that there is a rebuttable presumption that the possessor is the owner' (personal communication, 4 April 2014).

[113] In other cases, such as bailments or loans, when the law treats persons as if they have the rights ordinarily associated with ownership, this does not mean that they actually are owners. Yet there are good reasons why current possessors can avail themselves of the same property-based remedies, not in the least because doing so 'serves the common interest by discouraging interferences with the possession of goods and securing social harmony and public order' (Rostill, 'Relative title and deemed ownership', 48). Like in Chapter 5, I leave aside any potential debates regarding *ius tertti* defences. For what it is worth, Rostill thinks that s. 8(1) of the Torts Interference with Goods Act 1977 supports a deemed ownership thesis. This section states:

> The defendant in an action for wrongful interference shall be entitled to show, in accordance with rules of court, that a third party has a better right than the plaintiff as respects all or any part of the interest claimed by the plaintiff, or in right of which he sues, and any rule of law (sometimes called jus tertii) to the contrary is abolished.'

For Rostill, where a defendant bringing, for example, an action in conversion has shown that a third party has better right to possession as against the claimant, then the claimant's '"ownership" has been exposed for what it is: a fiction; and he has been exposed as someone who did not have, at the relevant time, a property right in the thing – and, thus, as someone who, as we now know, was not wronged' (52).

background account of ownership can we make sense of much of the legal landscape. This is so, even if we think that the day-to-day doctrinal operation of the law is based in possession rather than ownership.

5.3   Ownership as Normative Authority

Ownership, according to Katz, 'is an exclusive position that does not depend for its exclusivity on the right to exclude others from the object of the right. What it means for ownership to be exclusive is just that owners are in a special position to set the agenda for a resource'.[114] In directing our attention to the agenda-setting feature of ownership, Katz reminds us that it is the relative difference in the *normative positions* of owners and non-owners which is the key to understanding ownership. Owners are in a 'special position'[115] with respect to non-owners. Notably this is something which is not captured fully by focusing on rights of exclusion or non-interference,[116] or even rights of exclusive control (since non-owners may have exclusive control in certain circumstances). Consider once again the example of the tenant.

A tenant can be said to hold a number of rights and legal protections. For instance, they have immediate rights of possession regarding the house in question. They also have a reasonable set of liberties and powers regarding the use of the house. These are, in the sense outlined in Section 2 above, open-ended. The tenant can come and go as they please. They can use the house for any number of activities so long as these are not prohibited either by some general rule (say using the house as an illicit drugs den) or by a specific rule as laid out in the tenancy agreement (perhaps 'no parties allowed'). They can use the house for reading, sleeping, cooking, exercising, and so on; the list of these activities is not definitive. Their interests in these respects are also protected by legal trespassory rules. Even the owner of the house has a duty of non-interference in this respect. The owner may not simply drop around to the house on a whim; they cannot enter without giving notice and or at unreasonable times.[117] Yet, despite having de facto possession of the house and having recognisable (and recognised) property rights, there is a crucial normative disparity between their position and that of the owner. Tenants do not, for example, have the power to give away or sell the house to another person.[118] Neither can they deliberately damage it

---

[114] Katz, 'Exclusion and exclusivity', 277–278   [115] *Ibid.*, 281.   [116] *Ibid.*

[117] See, for example, Landlord and Tenant Act 1985, s. 11(6).

[118] Although we will see later in the book that the power to sell is not an analytical part of property.

or, without permission, redecorate it. They have a lack of ultimate control over the disposition of the house. And it is this which sets them apart in a normatively relevant sense from the owner.

Harris explained that '[w]ithin parameters. . . it is taken as obvious that an owner is entitled to suit himself. Whether his reasons for exercising use-privileges, control-powers, or powers of transmission are cogent or not, it is enough that they are his reasons.'[119] Non-owners, including tenants, are plainly not entitled to suit themselves. Dan Fuller puts his finger on it when he describes ownership as a position of *normative authority*:

> The owner occupies a position that allows them to direct the path the thing takes through the world, the rights that surround it and the relations of others with respect to it. They are not necessarily the person with practical control over the thing at a given time. They are the normative anchor of the network of relations that attend it.[120]

This suggests that it is the extent of the powers to alter the normative position of others that is the key. The owner is the person with the ultimate power to control the disposition of the object in question. We can see that this relates back to the proposition that the core of property is use-privileges and control-powers with respect to particular resources. Harris thought that a person has 'full-blooded ownership' where they have '*prima facie*, unlimited privileges of use or abuse over the thing, and, *prima facie*, unlimited powers of control and transmission, so far as such use or exercise of power does not infringe some property-independent prohibition'.[121]

Full-blooded ownership is the paradigm model of ownership, but it is just that: a model. It functions as an archetypal touchstone for our concept of ownership. Practically speaking, ownership need not entail that persons are always full-blooded owners. Given the restrictions imposed by law (for policy and other reasons), it is doubtful that any of us have full-blooded ownership over items in Harris' sense. It serves, nonetheless, to remind us of the centrality of use and control to property and ownership (even if it is not full-blooded).

The value of control is captured in Katz's characterisation of ownership: that it is not so much the right to exclude, but the agenda-setting authority of the owner which is significant: 'Ownership requires not that

---

[119] Harris, *Property and Justice*, p. 65.
[120] D. Fuller, 'Ownership as authority' (2014) 5 *King's Student Law Review* 16, 18.
[121] Harris, *Property and Justice*, p. 30.

others keep out so much as that they fall in line with the agenda the owner has set.'[122] It is, thus, the power of the right-holder to alter the normative position of third parties which is crucial. Owners are the ones with the normative authority to exercise (or not) the use and control. It is their interests which are at issue and they are the holders of the requisite rights. They can thus be said have ownership when their rights with regards to the thing are better than all others *and* when they are the one with the power to authorise a change in the normative baseline.

If we think again about *Yearworth*, conceiving of ownership as a position of normative authority would fit with the decision in that case. It was the negative control the men had, consequent on the provisions of the HFE Act, which was seen as indicative of the men's ownership.[123] Certainly their use of the sperm was limited by the Act. But the fertility unit's use and control over the samples was even more limited. If, for example, the men decided they no longer wanted their samples, the fertility unit would not have been at liberty, without consent, to use them for their own purposes. In addition, the men could, at any point, have instructed the fertility unit to destroy their samples. The unit could not lawfully have continued to store the sperm if such a direction had been issued. Jan Narveson says that 'for person A to "own" item x, is for A to have the *right* to determine the disposition/use of x as A sees fit – A has a veto over anyone else's use of it'.[124] Despite the statutory limitations placed on the use of the sperm samples, there is no doubt that the men (indeed all gamete providers) have the requisite veto. Conceptually being an owner entails having a degree of control over how others can use a resource that those with fewer rights or entitlements do not have.

One response to this might be to claim that the necessary normative authority rests not with gamete providers, but in fact with the state. The reason for this is that the storage of gametes in licenced units is limited by statue to a ten-year period. Although individuals can apply to have this extended on occasion, ordinarily the ten-year time limit applies, after which time any samples held must be destroyed by the unit in which they are held. Nevertheless, this has nothing to do with the property rights (or otherwise) of the gamete providers. It is a matter of policy based on considerations which are independent of property. Specifically, this position is based on concerns regarding the safety of using gametes for IVF

---

[122] Katz, 'Exclusion and exclusivity', 278.   [123] See Chapter 4, sections 2.1 and 5.2.
[124] J. Narveson, 'Libertarianism vs. Marxism: Reflections on G.A. Cohen's *Self-Ownership, Freedom and Equality*' (1998) 2 *Journal of Ethics* 1, 7.

after prolonged storage. As such, it is a position which is subject to revision as our scientific understanding of the relevant storage processes and IVF techniques advances.

In many ways this is no different from the treatment in law of any other item which may be deemed to fall within a proprietary framework. For example, think about an owner (or leasee) of a car which has failed its annual vehicle safety test. In such cases, the permitted sphere of action regarding the car is severely curtailed. If the car is reparable, then this may only be a temporary state of affairs. Alternatively, if the car is beyond repair, then the owner's liberties and powers with respect to it are permanently limited. Regardless, we would not usually claim in such instances that the state was the actual owner. We would not claim that the state was the 'normative anchor of the network of relations' that attend the car. Equally, in relation to the sperm samples at issue in *Yearworth*, it was the men and not the state who occupied the relevant position of normative authority. If anyone could have been deemed to have owner-ship of the samples, it could only have been them.

6 Concluding Remarks

At the beginning of the previous chapter I noted that the question 'what is property?' seems simple; yet, giving an adequate answer, as we have seen, is not straightforward. Over the course of that chapter and this one, I have given an account of property and ownership which emphasises six aspects. First, property law is the law of things.[125] It is the mode by which our use of things in the external world is governed *by the law*. This is not to say, however, that property *is* things. The second significant aspect of property is that it is appropriately conceptualised as relations (legal or moral) *between* persons *in respect of* things. What is important about these 'things' is the use and control we have of them. This is the third factor: the *use* that a person can put objects to and the *control* that they have over those uses are in essence the moral story of property. In the remaining chapters of the book we will see that this is crucial in terms of the (self-ownership) interests that persons have in their embodied selves, as well as the property interests they have regarding separated biomaterials.

The fourth element which I drew attention to, is the distinction between the core philosophical idea of property and the manner in

---

[125] See, in particular, Smith, 'Property as the law of things'.

which our property interests are protected. While the core of property is to be located in our liberties to control the uses of particular objects, these are protected via duties of non-interference imposed on third parties (practically this is mediated via the law). In this respect, property *rights* properly conceived are entitlements that carry with them corresponding (and enforceable) obligations on the part of others. This brings us to the fifth point, which centred on the identity of who these 'others' are. Here we saw that property rights are rights *in rem*. The duty to refrain from interfering another person's property (rights) does not arise because of any special arrangement between persons, but is an obligation that is held against a large and indefinite class of persons (in shorthand, it is 'good against the world'). Finally, we saw that the precise relationship between property, possession, and ownership is difficult to capture. Whether or not English law contains a concept of ownership per se is particularly contentious. Nevertheless, I concluded that some (philosophical) notion of ownership must be running in the background if we are to make sense of (a) the powers that owners have to alter the normative status of others, and (b) the protections offered by the law in this respect. Lawson and Rudden sum it up saying: 'the possessor of a thing is protected because he or she has possession; the owner is protected because he or she ought to have possession'.[126]

This comment from Lawson and Rudden also indicates an important distinction to be borne in mind when we talk of property and ownership. On the one hand there is the philosophical basis for recognising different kinds of property rights and, on the other hand, the particular way in which the law of property gives, or does not give, effect to this. The first of these provides the normative background against which we can sketch out general concepts and arguments regarding property, along with their justifications. We can also identify incoherencies and flaws within the approach of the law to dealing with (specific packets of) property. When considering the second aspect, however, we are interested in the *structure* of property law;[127] that is, the various ways in which it protects (or not) property-holders via its particular rules and institutions. The arguments in this book, while they touch on the second aspect, are more concerned with the first. In this respect, the focus use and control presented in this chapter is unselfconsciously

---

[126] Lawson and Rudden, *Law of Property*, p. 65.
[127] For an in-depth and comprehensive examination of this structure see McFarlane, *Structure of Property Law*.

presupposed by certain normative commitments. In particular, it is connected to a liberal conception of autonomy. This conception will be outlined and defended in the next chapter, where I sketch an account of self-ownership interests as the interests that persons have regarding themselves and their bodies.

7

The Scope and Bounds of Self-ownership

1 Introduction

Put simply, self-ownership is the idea that persons, morally speaking, can (and do) own themselves.[1] The conception of the person as self-owner, as having property in their own person, sees the locus of control over that person's actions and life as lying substantively within their own domain. Moreover, it is to see this as grounding entitlements which provide moral reasons for others to refrain from interfering, without justification, in that domain. In this chapter we will see that the core of self-ownership can be captured and described in a manner that mirrors (morally speaking) the discussion on ownership in the previous chapter. Thus, the claim that a person is a self-owner is best seen as the claim that they have a prima facie set of use-privileges and control-powers with regards to their embodied self. Persons are the ones in a position of ultimate normative authority with regards to themselves, their bodies, and their lives. They can, in this way, be viewed as self-owners.

In this chapter, I defend this account of self-ownership as one which is rooted in considerations of the autonomy of persons. My claim is that self-ownership describes the position of normative authority that persons have with respect to their embodied selves. It is both *justified by* and the *logical entailment of* considerations of autonomy. It can also be re-constituted in terms of rights and is a useful way of conceiving of the rights of persons. These rights (when recognised and enforced) are autonomy-protecting. Self-ownership, we will see, need not imply an excessive individualism. While a conception of personal autonomy is central to self-ownership, persons are also required to be morally autonomous and take other agents into account in their moral deliberations.

---

[1] See, for example, G.A. Cohen, *Self-Ownership, Freedom, and Equality* (Cambridge: Cambridge University Press, 1995), p. 68.

2   Embodied Persons as Self-owners

Despite the seeming simplicity and appeal of the idea of self-ownership, it provokes extensive debate and controversy, both as a concept and a thesis (moral, legal, or political). For some, the *concept* of self-ownership is not wholly intelligible. This is understandable. The language employed when attempting to discuss ownership and property makes applying it to the body and self a somewhat counter-intuitive task. Words such as 'thing', 'object', 'material resource', and 'entity' portray an otherness regarding what ought to be considered as the objects of property-speak. Honoré notes that the reason we say that a person cannot own themselves may merely be a deficiency in legal linguistics consequent on the fact that bodies are not 'external material objects'.[2] Linguistic difficulties also run in the other direction. We often talk of 'myself', 'my body', your hand', 'her foot', 'his heart', and so on. Yet one might object, as Patrick Day did, that the concept of self-ownership misconstrues or misunderstands the meaning of these possessive pronouns.[3] Similarly, Harris argued that the 'fact that people deploy possessive pronouns in relation to their bodies is, in itself, no indication of ownership assumptions. . . such pronouns may signify a host of relationships which have nothing to do with owning'.[4]

He was, of course, correct in this observation, but the reverse is also true. The mere fact that there is a range of functions of possessive pronouns does not exclude the possibility that some of these are intended to denote ownership and property relations, even with respect to one's body and self. In this respect, G.A. Cohen explained that 'the term "self" in the name of the thesis of self-ownership has purely reflexive significance. It signifies that what owns and what is owned are one and the same, namely, the whole person'.[5] We are (or our bodies are) as Hillel Steiner maintains, 'owner-occupied'.[6] Some may object to such characterisations, as indeed Ngaire Naffine does. She thinks that self-ownership 'relies on a form of Cartesian dualism';[7] that implicit in the concept is a problematic separa-tion of mind and body. But we do not need a dichotomised view of the

---

[2] Honoré, 'Ownership', p. 130.

[3] P. Day, 'Locke on property' (1966) 16 *The Philosophical Quarterly* 207, 212–213.

[4] Harris, *Property and Justice*, p. 188; Daniel Attas points to seven different uses of possessive forms of grammar in *Liberty, Property, and Markets* (Aldershot: Ashgate Publishing Ltd, 2005), pp. 67–68.

[5] Cohen, *Self-Ownership*, p. 69. See also p. 211.

[6] H. Steiner, *An Essay on Rights* (Oxford: Blackwell, 1994), p. 232.

[7] N. Naffine, 'The legal structure of self-ownership: Or the self-possessed man and the woman possessed' (1998) 25 *Journal of Law and Society* 193, 202.

mind and body in order to make sense of the notion of self-ownership. Instead, we can simply view ourselves as embodied persons.[8]

To say this is to recognise that our bodies are the site of interaction with the world: we 'live *through* our bodies not just in them'.[9] All of our experiences are mediated through them (for better or worse). The minds and bodies of embodied selves are intimately related and, at least presently, inseparable for practical purposes. As Maurice Merleau-Ponty put it, 'the distinction between subject and object is blurred in my body'.[10] Persons can thus be seen, according to Eric Matthews, 'not [as] an amalgam of two things, a body and a subjectivity, or mind: they are "body-subjects" or "embodied subjectivities"'.[11] Embodiment, therefore, encapsulates well the self-referential aspect of self-ownership.[12]

---

[8] The literature on embodiment is large with a long intellectual history which can be found, in particular, in phenomenology, sociology, and feminist theory. It is also a diverse literature with a rich variety of views, accounts, applications, and insights. It would be difficult to even give a flavour of that here, but for a small selection see M. Merleau-Ponty, *Phenomenology of Perception* (London: Routledge and Kegan Paul, 1962); M. Merleau-Ponty, *Signs*, trans. R. McCleary (Evanston: Northwestern University Press, 1964); K. Conboy, N. Medina, and S. Stanbury (eds), *Writing on the Body: Female Embodiment and Feminist Theory* (New York: Columbia University Press, 1999); G. Weiss, *Body Images: Embodiment as Intercorporeality* (New York: Routledge, 1999); J. Leach Scully, *Disability Bioethics: Moral Bodies, Moral Difference* (Plymouth: Rowman and Littlefield Publishers, Inc., 2008); R. Fletcher, M. Fox, and J. McCandless, 'Legal embodiment: Analysing the body in healthcare law' (2008) 16 *Medical Law Review* 321; M. Shildrick, 'Contesting normative embodiment: Some reflections on the psycho-social significance of heart transplant surgery' (2008) 1 *Perspectives: International Postgraduate Journal of Philosophy* 12; J. Kent, *Regenerating Bodies: Tissue and Cell Therapies in the Twenty-First Century* (London and New York: Routledge, 2012); and K. Lennon, 'Feminist perspectives on the body' in E.N. Zalta (ed.), *The Stanford Encyclopedia of Philosophy* (Fall 2014 edn).

[9] Shildrick, 'Contesting normative embodiment', 15. For good overviews of aspects relating to embodied minds see Leach Scully, *Disability Bioethics*, pp. 84–93 and H. Carel, *Phenomenology of Illness* (Oxford: Oxford University Press, 2016), pp. 24–31.

[10] M. Merleau-Ponty, *Signs*, p. 167. For him, this blurring occurs not only in our bodies, but can occur with external objects. His famous example is that of a blind person's walking stick (Merleau-Ponty, *Phenomenology of Perception*, 165). As Shildrick explains, the stick becomes 'an extension of his self-embodiment – and shows that the lived body is not identical with the material entity bounded by the skin' (M. Shildrick, '"Why should our bodies end at the skin?": Embodiment, boundaries, and somatechnics' (2015) 30 *Hypatia* 13, 14–15).

[11] E.H. Matthews, 'Merleau-Ponty's body-subject and psychiatry' (2004) 16 *International Review of Psychiatry* 190, 194.

[12] Embodiment is not commonly discussed in relation to self-ownership, but see D. Russell, 'Embodiment and self-ownership' (2010) 27 *Social Philosophy and Policy* 135. See also Wall, *Being and Owning*, pp. 56–66. Cf. M. Davies, 'Queer property, queer persons: Self-ownership and beyond' (1999) 8 *Social and Legal Studies* 327. Davies draws our attention to the gendered aspects of self-ownership (and property) even in claims regarding its self-referential nature.

While the *concept* of self-ownership simply refers to the idea that persons can own themselves, the *thesis* refers to the claim that self-ownership is both valid and morally acceptable. As such, the thesis involves a wider exposition about the normative implications of accepting self-ownership, and involves arguments relating to the consequences and scope of this ownership.[13] In this way, one could acknowledge that the idea of self-ownership makes sense (in the way that the phrase 'green number' does not),[14] while rejecting the claim that it is an acceptable (moral or political) position to endorse.[15]

To understand much of what is contentious about self-ownership as a *thesis* we need to appreciate that support for it is often located within the libertarian strand of political philosophical thought. Broadly, libertarians are concerned with individual freedom and autonomy, and the position taken is that all persons are, at least originally, self-owners.[16] Proponents have been influenced by the historical writings of a number of philosophers, but John Locke's Labour Theory of Property Acquisition has been particularly influential.[17] As we saw in Chapter 3, he said that:

> [E]very Man has a *Property* in his own *Person*. This no Body has any Right to but himself. The *Labour* of his Body, and the *Work* of his hands, we may say, are properly his. Whatsoever then he removes out of the state that Nature hath provided, and left it in, he hath mixed his *Labour* with, and joyned to it something that is his own, and thereby makes it his *Property*. It being by him removed from the common state Nature placed it in, it hath by this *labour* something annexed to it, that excludes the common right of other Men. For this Labour being the unquestionable Property of the Labourer, no Man but he can have a right to what is once joyned to, at least where there is enough, and as good left in common for others.[18]

---

[13] That this is something akin to Cohen's intended distinction receives some support from the interpretation given by George Brenkert in a critique of Cohen's book. See G.G. Brenkert, 'Self-ownership, freedom, and autonomy' (1998) 2 *Journal of Ethics* 27, 30.

[14] Cohen, *Self-Ownership*, p. 210.   [15] *Ibid.*, Chs 9 and 10.

[16] For example, see Steiner, *Essay on Rights*, p. 233; J. Narveson, *The Libertarian Idea* (Philadelphia: Temple University Press, 1988), pp. 66–68; J. Grunebaum, *Private Ownership* (London: Routledge and Keegan Paul, 1987), pp. 171–172 (Grunebaum refers to the autonomous ownership of self and labour rather than self-ownership); and M. Otsuka, *Libertarianism without Inequality* (Oxford: Oxford University Press, 2003), p. 12.

[17] See Locke, *Two Treatises*, Ch. V. See also H. Grotius, *The Rights of War and Peace*, ed. and trans. A.C. Campbell (London: Hyperion Reprint Edition, 1979) (in particular Book II, Ch. 2 'The general rights of things'); and S. Pufendorf, *The Political Writings of Samuel Pufendorf*, ed. C.L. Carr, trans. M.J. Seidles (Oxford: Oxford University Press, 1994) (in particular, 'On the law of nature and of nations').

[18] Locke, *Two Treatises*, pp. 287–288.

Here we can see that Locke specifically talked of having property in one's own person. This is commonly taken to be equivalent to self-ownership.[19]

There is an extensive literature focusing on the different shades of libertarianism. These range from the far economic right, which advocates maximal market freedom and minimal state interference,[20] to more left-leaning outlooks, which are more concerned with considerations of equality.[21] Generally, both right- and left-libertarians consider self-ownership to be a matter of moral right. The rights secured under a thesis of self-ownership are viewed as important in the protection of a person's interests. Thereafter, however, they diverge. In particular they hold fundamentally different views about the ownership of resources in the external world.

For right-libertarians the idea that persons are self-owners functions as the baseline justification for ownership of everything else in the world at large (sometimes referred to as world-ownership). Persons can legitimately acquire external resources which are thought to be, at least initially, unowned. It is the property in one's own person in addition to some principle of first acquisition or labour mixing which gives one title to resources in the external world. Furthermore, it is not permissible for these resources to be redistributed through taxation or otherwise, even in the aid of third parties. Where the initial acquisition and subsequent transfers are just, the resulting end-state distribution is also seen as just.[22] Thus, as Price has noted, self-ownership is viewed as 'the means to acquiring private ownership of the commons'.[23] On the other hand, left-libertarians, while still adhering to the position that persons are

---

[19] Although note, for example Donna Dickenson's argument that the equivalence of self-ownership with property in the person is a misinterpretation of Locke (Dickenson, *Property in the Body* 2nd edn, pp. 34–35). See also Christman who says, '[i]t is debatable whether Locke himself held the Lockean view of self-ownership' (*Myth of Property*, p. 149). Here I am interested in contemporary versions of self-ownership and only refer to Locke either to give context or where other commentators draw on particular Lockean positions.

[20] See, for example, Nozick, *Anarchy, State, and Utopia*; Rothbard, *For a New Liberty*; Narveson, *The Libertarian Idea*; and Grunebaum, *Private Ownership*.

[21] See, for example, Steiner, *Essay on Rights*; Otsuka, *Libertarianism without Inequality*; A.J. Simmons, *The Lockean Theory of Rights* (Princeton: Princeton University Press, 1992). Vallentyne and van der Vossen offer a concise overview of the different kinds of libertarian arguments with regards to resources, including Lockean and Nozickean libertarianism, sufficientarian (centrist) libertarianism, and equal share and equal opportunity left-libertarianism. See P. Vallentyne and B. van der Vossen, 'Libertarianism' in E.N. Zalta (ed.), *The Stanford Encyclopedia of Philosophy* (Fall 2014 edn). Available at: https://plato.stanford.edu/archives/fall2014/entries/libertarianism/ (accessed 27 November 2017).

[22] Nozick, *Anarchy, State, and Utopia*, pp. 150–155.   [23] Price, *Human Tissue*, p. 236.

originally self-owners, are committed to some variation on the view that external resources are initially owned in some egalitarian manner and that persons can only come to own these with the consent of others or by compensating others for their loss in respect of these.[24]

Given this, much of the relevant political philosophical debate, rather than contending with the challenges of self-ownership per se, revolves around these issues and focuses on the question of how we come to own anything at all. An examination of the various arguments regarding world-ownership is outside the scope of this book. For my purposes, it is the arguments for self-ownership itself that are the focus.[25] Although my arguments may hint at some of the problems with the justification of external holdings, in the main I examine the arguments disentangled from their association with the move to world-ownership. Where I do focus on ownership of objects in the external world, it is because they have a bearing on the arguments relating to ownership of separated biomaterials. My focus is on discussing the normative aspects of self-ownership on their own merits; that is to look at self-ownership simply as *self-ownership*.

My contention, noted in the introduction, is that persons have a prima facie set of use-privileges and control-powers with regards to their embodied self. They are the ones in a position of ultimate normative authority with regards to themselves, their bodies, and their lives. They can, thus, be considered to be self-owners. In this way, being a self-owner has parallels with being an owner more generally. What is special about being an owner is their normative standing. This we saw in the previous chapter. Owners and non-owners occupy different normative spaces relatively speaking. Owners are in a position of normative authority. As such, they (and often only they) have the power to alter the normative position of others. The owner is the person with the ultimate power to control the disposition of the object in question.

In all save exceptional circumstances, we do not question the normative authority of competent persons to the use and control of their own bodies. Price has fittingly said that 'our bodies are the most intimate, sometimes the only, "possession" we have and our ability to sanction

---

[24] See, for example, P. Vallentyne, 'Left-libertarianism and liberty' in T. Christiano and J. Christman (eds), *Contemporary Debates in Political Philosophy* (Oxford: Blackwell Publishers, 2009), pp. 137–151.

[25] As Attas has noted, '[a]lthough the principle of self-ownership is pivotal in libertarian political morality it is rarely argued for' (*Liberty, Property, and Markets*, p. 53). Although see M. Gorr, 'Justice, self-ownership, and natural assets' (1995) 12 *Social Philosophy and Policy* 267.

their use is usually beyond dispute except where the outweighing collective interest is overwhelming'.[26] The bodily boundary is viewed as so significant that the law of battery prevents unauthorised touchings. No damage, injury, or harm need ensue; all that is required is that the contact was intentional and not consensual. Consent, however, alters the normative landscape of the act. Generally, there is no battery where there is consent.[27] The person who consents to contact by another (be it a friend, lover, or healthcare professional) alters the normative baseline of that third party action.[28] By consenting, they waive their right not to be touched. Importantly, it is the person themselves, and only that person, who has the power to do so. In being the nexus of normative control, the person can thus be viewed as a self-owner.

John Christman says, 'self-ownership itself should be understood as a manifestation of control ownership (of oneself)'.[29] Like the ownership interests which we have in other resources and objects, self-ownership interests are open-ended. They are those interests which persons have regarding themselves and their bodies. We can sketch instances of these interests, such as our interests in the disposition of our bodies and having general liberty and control over the direction of our lives and our vital life decisions, but we cannot definitively enumerate them. What unifies our interests is an overarching notion of use and control. When these use-privileges and control-powers are accompanied by corresponding and enforceable duties on the part of others, we can view them as the rights which comprise self-ownership. As a rights-based conception, self-ownership is neither the base justification for action nor the conclusion of our moral reasoning, but functions as an intermediary in the nexus of

---

[26] Price, 'The Human Tissue Act', 821.

[27] Brazier and Cave, *Medicine, Patients, and the Law*, p. 124. The situation with regards to the *criminal* law is somewhat different. For example, in *R* v. *Brown* [1994] 1 AC 212 it was held that consent cannot be a defence to assault occasioning bodily harm and unlawful wounding. The decision was subsequently upheld by the European Court of Human Rights (*Laskey, Jaggard, and Brown* v. *United Kingdom* [1997] 24 EHRR 39). Whether or not this ought to be the view of the criminal law is debatable, something which came across in Lord Mustill and Lord Slynn's dissenting judgments (*Brown* at 256–283). This case was specifically about harm inflicted in the course of sadomasochistic sexual practices. As such, we are left to wonder whether the outcome would have been different outwith such a context, which arguably invited moralising about sexual activity on the part of the Court.

[28] See Chapter 9, Section 2.

[29] Christman, *Myth of Property*, pp. 148–149. Taylor advocates a similar position, 'Self-ownership' (2005).

relevant moral arguments.[30] Being recognised as a self-owner confers certain normative advantages: protections in the use and control of one's self, and protections against infringements, either from others or the state on the exercise of related freedoms.

Although self-ownership has a strong connection to different shades of libertarianism, the account given here should not be construed as such. There may be some parallels in particular with left-leaning libertarianism, but I do not intend any conclusions to be drawn regarding the usual political commitments of libertarians (some of which were indicated above). To the extent that any such commitments either flow from or impact on the conception offered they tend towards a kind of liberal egalitarianism. This much will become obvious during the discussion of self-owners as moral equals in Section 3 of this chapter. Having said that, however, I do note Peter Vallentyne's comment that left-libertarianism is 'a plausible version of liberal egalitarianism because it is suitably sensitive to considerations of liberty, security, and equality'.[31] Whether or not this is so, however, need not bother us for the purposes of this book.

3   Self-ownership Interests and Autonomy

Viewing the person as the source of normative authority with regards to their own bodies and lives is strongly connected to considerations of liberty and autonomy. If taken seriously, such considerations give a certain degree of moral force to invocations of self-ownership. This section, therefore, outlines the relationship between autonomy and self-ownership.

3.1   Liberty and Non-Interference

When we assert that we are self-owners we are drawing a boundary which we think of as normatively weighty. We are asserting that we have particular rights, liberties, privileges, and so on, which are worthy of moral respect in our dealings with others. These will include self-ownership rights pertaining to aspects of our lives such as the disposition of one's body, one's vital life decisions, and probably aspects of individual privacy.[32] They can be seen as forming a perimeter of normative

---

[30] Raz, 'On the nature of rights', 208.   [31] Vallentyne, 'Left-libertarianism', p. 137.

[32] I do not offer a defence of this claim regarding privacy, but on the face of it the rights entailed would seem to be compatible with self-ownership as set out here. Consider, for example, Laurie's definition of privacy as 'a state of separateness from others that primarily protects two kinds of interests: informational privacy and spatial privacy'

protection with regards to an individual's autonomy and liberty. Construing self-ownership in this manner could be seen as falling into the broad category of self-ownership as non-interference. Christman explains that this understanding positions self-ownership as a 'negative barrier' which protects 'in particular against invasions by the state into the private and personal aspects of one's life'.[33] The non-interference view of self-ownership closely parallels Millian accounts of liberty.[34] John Stuart Mill saw self-protection as the only justification for interfering in the 'liberty of action' of others.[35] For Millians, it is not for individuals to explain and justify their reasons and motivations for acting in a particular manner; rather the presumption is in favour of their liberty to do this (unless their actions will cause harm to others). Justification for action falls on those who would interfere with the lives of others.

In this tradition Isaiah Berlin famously asked, '[w]hat is the area within which the subject. . . is or should be left to do or be what he is able to do or be, without interference by other persons?'[36] The general answer, for liberals, is that there should be a presumption of non-interference in all areas where one's actions *only* affect oneself, where others are not being harmed.[37] Self-ownership as non-interference suggests that what is important is a person's sphere of negative liberty; that is, the domain within which they are *free from* the intrusion of others.

(Laurie, *Genetic Privacy*, p. 84). He also says that 'privacy should be taken to refer to a state in which an individual is apart from others, either in a bodily or psychological sense or by reference to the inaccessibility of certain intimate adjuncts to their individuality, such as personal information' (p. 6).

[33] Christman, *Myth of Property*, p. 149.

[34] Note that Christman brackets the non-interference view as Lockean, albeit he notes that it is unlikely that Locke held such view on self-ownership. He does this because he contrasts it with an account of self-ownership which derives from Hegel's arguments regarding property and ownership (*ibid.*, p. 149). For Hegel, property acquisition is key to a person's moral and self-development. See G.W.F. Hegel, *Outlines of the Philosophy of Right*, trans. T.M. Knox, (Oxford: Oxford University Press, 2008), pp. 53–83.

[35] J.S. Mill, *On Liberty and Other Essays*, ed. J. Gray (Oxford: Oxford University Press, 1991), p. 14. Mill himself does not talk of the 'autonomy' of individuals. Instead he is concerned with individual liberty and the limits of state interference in the lives of its citizens.

[36] I. Berlin, 'Two concepts of liberty' in H.E. Hardy (ed.), *Liberty, Incorporating 'Four Essays on Liberty'* (Oxford: Oxford University Press, 2002), pp. 166–217, p. 169. Note that he uses the words 'liberty' and 'freedom' interchangeably.

[37] This may, of course, be overly broad. It is questionable whether there are many, or indeed any, circumstances in civil and social society where one's actions can be seen as purely self-regarding. Mill was aware of this, commenting that an individual's actions can indirectly affect others: 'for whatever affects himself, may affect others through himself'. (Mill, *On Liberty*, p. 16). Mill was also clear that the sphere of a person's harmful other-regarding actions also includes their failure to act (p. 15).

But duties of non-interference are the *how* not the *why* of liberty (and self-ownership); they are merely the mode by which more fundamental interests are protected. This we saw in the previous chapter in relation to the protection of core property interests. Hence, negative liberty can be distinguished from more positive formulations which emphasise *freedoms to* do or be, or pursue one's goals and life plans. These two understandings of liberty are obviously related since carving out a sphere of non-interference makes it more likely that persons will be able to pursue their own goals and courses of action.[38] This is part of why, as we saw in Part I of the book and will see again in the next chapter, it is important to re-examine issues of property in the body and biomaterials. Where source interests are not protected, their sphere of liberty can be interfered with in a manner not in line with their life goals and actions.

It is our interests in this wider domain of liberty which justify any protections offered. To wit, they are the interests we have as autonomous persons. This is because the extent to which our (self-ownership) interests are advanced or thwarted is significant in any assessment of whether or not we can be said to be leading autonomous lives. Nevertheless, in making such an assessment, we do not need to have a determinate list of the relevant interests. If we are committed to principles and protections which are equally liberty-preserving for all, then it leaves it open to each individual to decide for themselves what their interests consist of.[39] Of course, this approach entails a certain element of subjectivism, since different interests will contain different value(s) for each person. Nevertheless, it does not deny that particular interests might be foundational to having *any interests at all*.

Feinberg argued that some interests are 'necessary but *grossly insufficient* for a good life'.[40] Although some combination of such goods is minimally required in order to live our lives in a meaningful manner, our interests in them do not represent our higher interests or goals. For example, at least a minimal level of health might be necessary in order to realise the wants, desires, and goals which contribute to a person's

---

[38] Although it does not ensure that this will happen. Many factors may impact on a person's ability to pursue particular courses of action, including a lack of a resources (be they educational, informational, health-related, etc.).

[39] Here 'equally' is meant in the Dworkinian sense of equal concern and respect rather than base equality. See R. Dworkin, *Taking Rights Seriously* (London: Duckworth, 1977), pp. 272–278.

[40] Feinberg, *Harm to Others*, p. 37 [emphasis added].

other interests.[41] For that reason, it may be essential that our health-related interests are protected if we are to achieve a range of other life goals, but such interests are not necessarily ends in themselves. These ends might consist of the things we can be and do while in good health, such as the activities we take part in or the career we choose (e.g. 'producing good novels or works of art').[42] The realisation of these interests requires us to go beyond mere non-interference. While the restraint of third parties in this respect is crucial to the liberty of persons, autonomy obliges us to think about considerations of persons themselves.

3.2   Beyond Non-interference: Being the Source of Normative Authority

Autonomy is a contested concept. Even the most perfunctory examination of the relevant literature demonstrates why this is so. It is a term with numerous uses and a multiplicity of meanings, which are sometimes applied synonymously and sometimes finely distinguished. These include:

> Liberty (positive or negative)... dignity, integrity, individuality, independence, responsibility and self-knowledge... self-assertion... critical reflection... freedom from obligation... absence of external causation... and knowledge of one's own interests.[43]

Moreover, as set out by Feinberg, when we talk of autonomy we may be referring to autonomy as a *capacity*, an *ideal of character*, or an indication of our *sovereign authority* as persons.[44] The picture appears even more complex when we recognise that, within liberal society, autonomous persons are situated in a variety of contexts in which they can exercise their autonomy: political, moral, legal, social, and so on.[45] Yet despite this apparent diversity of understandings, we can point to a general characterisation of the abstract idea of autonomy.[46]

---

[41] See *ibid.*, pp. 38–45 for the relationship between wants, desires, goals, and interests.

[42] *Ibid.*

[43] G. Dworkin, *The Theory and Practice of Autonomy* (Cambridge: Cambridge University Press, 1988, reprinted 1991), p. 6.

[44] Feinberg, *Harm to Others*, p. 28.

[45] R. Forst, 'Political liberty: Integrating five conceptions of autonomy' in J. Christman and J. Anderson (eds), *Autonomy and the Challenges to Liberalism* (Cambridge: Cambridge University Press, 2005), p. 229.

[46] Both Dworkin and Lindley draw a distinction between the concept and conceptions of autonomy. Autonomy as some sort of overarching concept represents the general

This organising idea is best captured by Feinberg's description of autonomy as a 'political metaphor',[47] meaning something like 'self-rule, self-determination, self-government, and independence'.[48] In principle, individuals can be said to be autonomous to the extent that they govern or control their own lives. The broad character of the liberal conception of autonomy is captured by Berlin's positive formulation of liberty. He said:

> I wish my life and decisions to depend on myself, not on external forces of whatever kind. I wish to be the instrument of my own, not of other men's acts of will. I wish to be a subject, not an object; to be moved by reasons, by conscious purposes which are my own, not by causes which affect me, as it were, from outside. I wish to be somebody, not nobody; a doer – deciding, not being decided for, self-directed and not acted upon by external nature or by other men as if I were a thing, or an animal, or a slave incapable of playing a human role, that is, of conceiving goals and policies of my own and realising them. This is at least part of what I mean when I say that I am rational, and that it is my reason that distinguishes me as a human being from the rest of the world. I wish, above all, to be conscious of myself as a thinking, willing, active being, bearing responsibility for his choices and able to explain them by reference to his own ideas and purposes. I feel free to the degree that I believe this to be true, and enslaved to the degree that I am made to realise that it is not.[49]

On this account we can see that the autonomous person is a rational one who both has the capacity for reason and exercises it; in the decisions they take, and the manner in which they live their lives, this reason is their own and not another's; they do not live under circumstances which constrain or unduly influence them; and they are also active bearers of the responsibility for the choices they make as a result of their reasoning.

Notably, an important aspect of autonomy lies with the ability to exercise control over one's actions and one's life. As such, it is co-extensive with the view of persons as self-owners. To say that someone is a self-

---

characterisation of an abstract idea, whereas different conceptions of the general concept correspond to the diverse specifications of the content of an abstract notion. In this way commentators, when talking about autonomy, may be invoking similar notions in the abstract, but, within that, enumerate distinct ways in which it ought to play out in practice. See Dworkin, *Theory and Practice*, pp. 6 and 9–10 and R. Lindley, *Autonomy* (London: MacMillan Education Ltd, 1986), pp. 3–4. Dworkin draws on Hart's famous exposition in 'Definition and theory in jurisprudence' (1954) 70 *Law Quarterly Review* 37. Both draw on J. Rawls, *A Theory of Justice* (Oxford: Oxford University Press, 1971, revised 1999), Ch. 1.

[47] J. Feinberg, *The Moral Limits of the Criminal Law: Harm to Self* (Oxford: Oxford University Press, 1986), p. 28.

[48] *Ibid.*, p. 27.   [49] Berlin, 'Two concepts of liberty', p. 178.

owner is to see the locus of control over that person's actions and life as lying substantively within their own domain. Broadly speaking, an individual's personal domain 'consists of [their] body, privacy, landed and chattel property, and at least the *vital* life-decisions'.[50] This is part of Feinberg's notion of personal sovereignty: the 'sovereign grants auton-omy freely at his pleasure and withdraws it at his will... sovereignty is basic and underivative. Sovereignty is, in a sense, an *ultimate source of authority*.'[51] Although Feinberg does not speak in terms of self-ownership, the idea of sovereign authority and personal domain located in one's own person is a good descriptor for what is at issue. Self-ownership emphasises the person themselves as the *source* of the control over their personal territory; they have dominion over themselves (this is the core of their personal domain).

This construction accords with Christman's account of self-ownership as self-control.[52] It is a positive understanding of self-ownership where the emphasis is on the particular conditions for autonomy: authenticity, competence, self-control, and so on.[53] Here self-ownership 'is an expres-sion of the person's embodiment in her own body and talents, and is valuable because it is necessary for the self-expression that is constitutive of a truly human life'.[54] As such, an individual is to be considered *personally* autonomous to the extent that they are, at least in some minimal sense, the *source* of the control which determines how they are to think, act, and conduct their life. In liberal society this means that it is open to individuals to decide for themselves what their interests consist of and what they are said to have a stake in with regards to their own lives. This contributes to the formulation and realisation of their interests. This is the essence of being a self-owner.

Despite this formulation, we ought not to take the connection between self-ownership and *personal* autonomy as endorsing any sort of excessive individualism.[55] Self-owners can only be considered *morally*

---

[50] Feinberg, *Harm to Self*, p. 55. In this book I make no claims about a person's landed or chattel property, except where separated biomaterials might be seen as being part of the latter category.

[51] *Ibid.* [emphasis added].

[52] He says, '[w]hat matters in self-ownership... is individual rights to control oneself – to no intervention in use (of one's talents). The specific motivation behind self-ownership involves the strong interest that I have in running my own life.' J. Christman, 'Self-ownership, equality, and the structure of property rights' (1991) 19 *Political Theory* 28, 39.

[53] Christman, *Myth of Property*, pp. 151–152.   [54] *Ibid.*

[55] Cf. Jennifer Nedelsky's argument in 'Property in potential life? A relational approach to choosing legal categories' (1993) VI *Canadian Journal of Law and Jurisprudence* 343.

autonomous when they take other moral agents into account in their deliberations in a manner which is subject to the requirements of public reason. Such a constraint is essential for a liberalism which takes seriously the equality of agents within moral and political communities. As will become evident, different conceptions of autonomy (moral and personal) need not be considered in isolation or independent from each other; instead they are interrelated and overlapping, and in some ways predicated upon each other.

3.3   Liberty, Moral Autonomy, and Public Reason

As we have already seen, accounts of individual or personal autonomy are generally related to Millian accounts of liberty. Moral autonomy, on the other hand, is more often associated with Kantian or neo-Kantian interpretations of autonomy. For Kant, there was one supreme moral principle: the principle of autonomy. Autonomy, in the Kantian sense, refers to *internal moral law*. A person acts autonomously when they act in accordance with moral law which is arrived at through exercising *reason* alone.[56] This is to be contrasted with *heter*onomy, where inauthentic principles are derived from influences external to the self.[57] All other principles derive from the principle of autonomy and are subordinate to it. Through the exercise of reason a person can derive principles which will help them to know what right action consists of. The overarching a priori principle, that the exercise of reason arrives at, takes the form of the categorical imperative (or law of morality) which states: 'act only in accordance with that maxim through which you can at the same time will it become a universal law'.[58]

Contemporary Kantians draw on this understanding of autonomy as moral law. Onora O' Neill's account of autonomy, for example, is premised on a conception of autonomy as 'principled autonomy'.[59] A person acts with autonomy when they act from principles which could be adopted by other persons qua ordinary agents.[60] O' Neill argues that

---

[56] I. Kant, *Groundwork of the Metaphysics of Morals*, trans. M. Gregor (Cambridge: Cambridge University Press, 1997), p. 31 (GW 4:421).

[57] *Ibid.*, p. 47 (GW 4:441).

[58] *Ibid.*, p. 31 (GW 4:421). Kant gave different formulations of the categorical imperative. These formulae properly understood represent not different moral laws, but each express the same law of morality in a different manner. See I. Kant, *Grounding for the Metaphysics of Morals*, trans. J. Ellington (Indianapolis and Cambridge: Hackett Publishing Company Inc., 1993), p. vi.

[59] O' Neill, *Autonomy and Trust*, Ch. 4.   [60] *Ibid.*, p. 85.

the reason we should take seriously the idea of principled autonomy, and the moral principles that flow from it, is that it represents a 'non-derivative, fundamental requirement on thought and action'.[61] By this she means it does not require any appeal to antecedent reasons for action; in other words, we do not have to look behind the principle itself in order to have good reason to think or act. Appeals to antecedent moral or practical reasons are problematic since ultimately they end in appeals to some kind of authority.[62]

Why then should we accept as reasoned any particular mode of thinking or acting?[63] O' Neill's answer is that our thoughts or actions are reasoned when they are conducted in a manner in which they are *accessible to others who are to be the audience for that reasoning*.[64] She says:

> Autonomy in thinking is no more – but also no less – than the attempt to conduct thinking (speaking, writing) on principles which all others whom we address could also conduct their thinking (speaking, writing). Autonomy in action is no more – but also no less – than the attempt to act on principles on which all others could act.[65]

Even if we do not want to subscribe to the Kantian universalisability requirement, there is an important lesson in this conception. Her view of autonomy is based in practical reason which is part of *public* morality. This conception supposes that these 'others' to whom our reasoning is addressed are rational actors. Reasons to act or refrain from acting must be visible and intelligible to rational agents if we are to make claims upon such persons.[66] It is the requirement to take into account, not just our own goals and preferences, but wider moral considerations, which is pivotal for accounts of *moral* as opposed to *personal* autonomy.[67] The connection to Kantian thought is brought out through the emphasis on the public nature of practical reason.

Discussions often, explicitly or otherwise, suggest a distance or incompatibility between personal autonomy and moral autonomy. Consider, for example, the comments of Raz who says that '[p]ersonal autonomy, which is a particular ideal of individual well-being should not be

---

[61] *Ibid.*, p. 95.   [62] *Ibid.*, p. 91.   [63] *Ibid.*   [64] *Ibid.* [emphasis in original].
[65] *Ibid.*, p. 94.
[66] See G.F. Gaus, 'The place of autonomy within liberalism' in J. Christman and J. Anderson (eds), *Autonomy and the Challenges to Liberalism* (Cambridge: Cambridge University Press, 2005), p. 288. For the broader discussion regarding liberalism see J. Quong, *Liberalism without Perfection* (Oxford: Oxford University Press, 2010), especially Ch. 1.
[67] Gaus, 'The place of autonomy', pp. 291 and 297.

confused with the only very indirectly related notion of moral autonomy'.[68] The primacy that is given to individual liberty in contemporary
political theory might indicate one of the reasons why there is a tendency
to emphasise personal or individual autonomy rather than moral autonomy. It might be the case that (Kantian) accounts of moral autonomy are
seen as incompatible, on a certain level, with liberty and liberal theories;
that they constrain rather than free individuals. Yet conceptions of moral
autonomy cannot be considered as sitting wholly apart from accounts of
autonomy qua personal autonomy.

We could conceive of personal autonomy as not containing the
requirement of public reason; that, in the exercise of autonomy in this
sense, our reasons for action need not be in any way public, constituting
a sphere of private reasoning placed apart from considerations of public
morality. However, such a sharp distinction between the requirements
of moral and personal autonomy would be a mistake.[69] This is because
the individual does not live their life in a social, political, or moral
vacuum. There are justified limitations on liberty and even occasions
where coercion could legitimately be used to constrain individual
actions. And herein lies the connection to *moral* autonomy. To the
extent that we act on our own goals, desires, and preferences we can
be said to be personally autonomous. Equally, to the extent that we can
exercise our reason and factor other persons into our deliberations, set
apart from our own concerns, we can be said to be morally autonomous.
This requires us to take account of other moral agents and considerations and to do so in a manner which is visible and intelligible to persons
qua rational agents. If we recognise that there will be few, if any,
occurrences where an individual's actions will be purely self-regarding,
then we can see that we cannot draw a bright line between personal and
moral autonomy.[70] Our decisions and actions are continually required

[68] J. Raz, *The Morality of Freedom* (Oxford: Clarendon Press, 1986), p. 370, note 2.
[69] For arguments regarding the lack of separation between the two conceptions see, for
example, J. Waldron, 'Moral autonomy and personal autonomy' in J. Christman and
J. Anderson (eds), *Autonomy and the Challenges to Liberalism* (Cambridge: Cambridge
University Press, 2005). See also Gerald Gaus who sees personal autonomy as a derivative
of moral autonomy ('The place of autonomy').
[70] Note that the interrelationship between personal and moral autonomy is likely not the end
of the story for the self-owner. Differing conceptions of autonomy operate in different
contexts and spheres of life and, accordingly, each has a role to play where individuals live as
part of social, political, and moral society. In his discussion of political liberty, for instance
Rainer Forst identifies five conceptions of autonomy which he maintains that 'persons of a
law-governed political community must reciprocally and generally grant and guarantee

to take account of others and, therefore, be subject to the requirements of public reason. The focus of autonomy can rarely, if ever, be solely the individual person in isolation.[71]

4 Self-ownership, Autonomy, and Equality

Cohen gave the following description of self-ownership:

> [E]ach person is the morally rightful owner of himself. He possesses over himself, as a matter of moral right, all those rights that a slaveholder has over a complete chattel slave as a matter of legal right, and he is entitled, morally speaking, to dispose over himself in the way such a slaveholder is entitled, legally speaking, to dispose over his slave.[72]

Although he thought that the concept of self-ownership is not incoherent ('the term "self" in the name of the thesis of self-ownership has purely reflexive significance')[73], he maintained that as a (moral or political) thesis it is unappealing. One of the principal reasons why he thought this is because he supposed self-ownership to be 'hostile to autonomy'.[74] If indeed it is hostile to autonomy, then the argument that a person's

---

each other' (Forst, 'Political liberty', p. 229). These different conceptions are: moral, ethical, legal, political, and social autonomy. It is useful to think of this as indicating different contexts and spheres in which autonomy operates rather than thinking in terms of different 'autonomies'. For an in-depth discussion of these see pp. 229–238.

[71] See, for instance, James Grunebaum's 'autonomy principle'. He says that 'everyone ought to act so as to respect each person's equal right to decide for himself what his own good is, how to pursue it, and to promote where possible but never violate each person's fundamental well-being' (*Private Ownership*, p. 143).

[72] Cohen, *Self-Ownership*, p. 68. This proposition is not to be confused with what Harris (incorrectly) claimed is the 'spectacular non sequitur' upon which self-ownership is based (*Property and Justice*, pp. 196 and 229). He said that some versions of self-ownership are based on the assertion that '(1) If I am not a slave, nobody else owns my body. Therefore, (2) I must own myself' (p. 191). He then claimed that '[f]rom the fact that I am not a slave it does not follow that I own myself. No-one owns me' (p. 357). It is not clear who, if anyone, actually makes such an argument about self-ownership. Locke, whom a number of libertarians (right and left) take as their starting point certainly does not. The slavery metaphor (which is unfortunate to the extent that it diminishes the wrong of slavery) is a way of explaining the extent of a self-owner's rights (Cohen, *Self-ownership*, p. 68). When authors such as Murray Rothbard claim that 'taxation is a form of involuntary servitude', they are claiming (rightly or wrongly) that systems of taxation infringe self-ownership not that people are self-owners because they are not slaves (*For a New Liberty: The Libertarian Manifesto*, rev. edn (New York: Libertarian Review Foundation, 1978), p. 85).

[73] Cohen, *Self-Ownership*, p. 69. See also p. 211.

[74] *Ibid.*, p. 237. Attracta Ingram is also critical of self-ownership's relationship to autonomy and indeed of self-ownership in general. See *A Political Theory of Rights* (Oxford: Clarendon Press, 1994), in particular, Chs 2 and 5.

rights of self-ownership are protective of autonomy should be seen as naïve at best and seriously flawed at worst. Here I suggest that, for a liberal conception of self-ownership, the autonomy-protecting position is neither naïve nor flawed (logically or otherwise).

Making this argument has implications for how the related argument (given in the next chapter) can proceed in relation to separated biomaterials. This is because if the property rights we have in these are normatively contiguous and co-extensive with those we have in virtue of our self-ownership – which I will argue they are – then tackling the normative foundations of self-ownership is crucial.

4.1   Rights Restrictions and Autonomy Maximisation

In arguing that self-ownership is hostile to autonomy, Cohen presumed the libertarian position to involve the claim that self-ownership yields *more* autonomy than any other arrangement (the autonomy-maximisation claim).[75] Contrary to this, he contended that '[t]here are many scenarios where some, or even all, have less autonomy than some, or all, would have with some restrictions on self-ownership'.[76] Self-ownership is to be viewed as hostile to autonomy where the consequences of 'universal complete self-ownership'[77] lead to an aggregate reduction in autonomy (where 'aggregate' autonomy is to be read as the sum of the autonomy of individuals).[78] If this is correct then, '[w]e can all benefit in terms of autonomy if none of us has the right to do certain things' (the rights-restriction claim).[79] Cohen's aim in making this argument was to reduce the appeal of self-ownership by demonstrating that it does not do for autonomy what its proponents think it does (i.e. maximisation).

The first thing to note is that libertarians, even with their general concern regarding liberty and autonomy, do not necessarily aim at maximisation.[80] This is especially so given the spectrum of positions and the divergence between right and left-leaning views. Peter Vallentyne, for example, articulates a typical left-libertarian position, saying that '[f]ull self-ownership is sometimes thought to guarantee that the agent has certain basic liberty of action, but this is not so... The protection that self-ownership affords is a basic protection against others doing certain things to me, but not a

---

[75] Cohen, *Self-ownership*, p. 237.   [76] *Ibid.*   [77] *Ibid.*

[78] G.A. Cohen, 'Once more into the breach of self-ownership: Reply to Narveson and Brenkert' (1998) 2 *Journal of Ethics* 57, 85.

[79] Cohen, *Self-Ownership*, p. 237.

[80] Brenkert, 'Self-ownership, freedom, and autonomy', 40.

guarantee of liberty.'[81] Other libertarians think that recognising persons as the holders of self-ownership rights is desirable if it is mutually advantageous.[82] Even Nozick's particular theory, against which Cohen's objections are primarily aimed, is not necessarily underpinned by autonomy – or even liberty – maximisation.

As Will Kymlicka explains, Nozick takes 'the principle of "self-ownership" as an interpretation of the principle of treating people as "ends in themselves"'.[83] For him, 'constraints upon action reflect the Kantian underlying principle that individuals are ends and not merely means; that they may not be sacrificed or used for the achieving of other ends without their consent'.[84] The starting point is respect for persons. For this reason, Kymlicka maintains that Nozick's theory is not a theory of *liberty*, but instead an egalitarian one 'in the sense of being premised on moral equality'.[85] This is not the same sort of proposition as claiming that self-ownership *maximises* autonomy.

Cohen, however, was explicit that he was not addressing all versions of self-ownership, or even all understandings of Nozickean self-ownership. His critique was aimed at just 'one possible interpretation of [Nozick]'.[86] Perhaps he had in mind philosophers such as Jan Narveson.[87] Narveson contends that, for libertarians, 'property rights... *are* liberty rights'.[88] Further, he maintains that they 'are the *only* fundamental rights we have'.[89] For Narveson, self-ownership *is* 'the general thesis of liberty'.[90]

---

[81] Vallentyne and van der Vossen, 'Libertarianism'.

[82] Although not his own position, for a discussion of this see W. Kymlicka, *Contemporary Political Philosophy*, 2nd edn (Oxford: Oxford University Press, 2002), pp. 128–138.

[83] *Ibid.*, p. 107.

[84] Nozick, *Anarchy, State, and Utopia*, pp. 30–31. Although, as noted by Attas, it is somewhat 'ironic that Kant's spirit has been summoned to support the thesis of self-ownership, for Kant himself thought the concept incoherent' (Attas, *Liberty, Property, and Markets*, p. 62). Kant said: 'He is not his own property – that would be a contradiction... He is, however, a person, who is not property, so he cannot be a thing such as he might own; for it is impossible, of course, to be at once a thing and a person, a proprietor and a property at the same time' (I. Kant, *Lectures on Ethics: The Cambridge Edition of the Works of Immanuel Kant in Translation*, trans. P. Heath (Cambridge: Cambridge University Press, 1997), p. 157 (LE 27:386)).

[85] Kymlicka, *Contemporary Political Philosophy*, p. 139. For a discussion of some difficulties with Nozikean self-ownership in the wider context of his historical entitlement theory see pp. 110–127. See also O. O' Neill, 'Nozick's entitlements' (1976) 19 *Inquiry* 468; and L. Davis, 'Comments on Nozick's entitlement theory' (1976) 73 *Journal of Philosophy* 836.

[86] Cohen, 'Once more into the breach', 87.

[87] Cohen did not say who, but insisted that 'some libertarians undoubtedly are concerned about autonomy in the sense of the term [he] identified' (*ibid.*, 87).

[88] Narveson, 'Libertarianism vs. Marxism', 7.   [89] *Ibid.*   [90] *Ibid.*, 9.

It is simply 'liberty of the person'.[91] Yet to claim that self-ownership leads to more autonomy qua liberty would be, in this case, only to make a definitional claim. The reason is because if self-ownership is equivalent to liberty of the person as Narveson asserts, then it will always be true that more self-ownership is equal to more liberty. Contrariwise, a restriction on self-ownership rights would also lead to a restriction on liberty.

Yet liberty is not equivalent to autonomy in a broader sense. Nor, indeed, is it even equivalent to autonomy for the purposes of Cohen's own argument. He was specifically concerned about the *range of choices* open to a person; he said: '[a]utonomy, here, denotes the range of a person's choice'.[92] Presumably, the purported libertarian position is, therefore, that the distribution of rights under libertarian self-ownership would bring about a greater range of choices for each person. As such, Cohen's own counterclaim would be that restricting the rights associated with self-ownership would result in each person enjoying a reasonable range of autonomy qua (effective) choices. Autonomy as a range of choices is, of course, a much narrower version of autonomy than the one offered in this chapter (and perhaps even than libertarians are concerned about).[93] But even on a wider version of autonomy, the position that self-ownership is hostile to autonomy is only tenable if the rights of self-ownership are *not* the logical entailment of autonomy; that is, if they do not flow directly from, and as a result of, autonomy.

Nevertheless, recall that Cohen was making an argument against a particular type of libertarian self-ownership (against one possible interpretation of Nozick). Claims of autonomy-maximisation aside, it is worth coming back to this in order to fully appreciate why he said that '[w]e can all benefit in terms of autonomy if none of us has the right to do certain things'.[94] If self-ownership entails not only rights over our embodied selves, but rights to the acquisition of goods in the external world, then this may have implications, not only for the distribution of resources in society, but with the consequent ability of the members of that society to live autonomous lives.

---

[91] *Ibid.*   [92] Cohen, *Self-Ownership*, p. 236.

[93] George Brenkert argues that Cohen and libertarians such as Nozick are simply using different senses of autonomy. Cohen, according to Brenkert, 'means that individuals have self-control in the sense of an effective (and acceptable) range of choices', while Nozick 'means one's self-control as captured in various rights of self-control' (Brenkert, 'Self-ownership, freedom, and autonomy', 42).

[94] Cohen, *Self-Ownership*, p. 237.

Right-libertarians, as we saw earlier, do couple claims regarding self-ownership with wider commitments regarding external resources. Some argue that self-ownership entails the right to the fruits of one's labour and that any non-contractual interference with this, in the form of taxation for example, is morally objectionable.[95] Yet a state which does not collect taxes to adequately fund collective goods such as social welfare, education, and health care, has unpalatable consequences for the less well-off members of society. It will be lacking in the conditions which enable persons to be as autonomous as they can be. Such conditions include a minimally decent state infrastructure in terms of things like education, health, and employment opportunities. It is for reasons akin to this that Cohen said that restrictions on self-ownership (qua rights) are necessary *if* everyone is to enjoy a 'reasonable degree of autonomy'.[96] This, as we are about to see, is essentially (and rightly) an equality requirement and, as a general claim regarding the permitted scope of action of persons, is entirely reasonable.

4.2   Self-owners as Moral Equals

Since the autonomy argument, for Cohen, is one about a person's range of choices (which I take to mean *effective* range of choices), freedom is necessarily implicated. The range of choices available to individuals flows directly from their de facto freedom of action and freedom of choice, something which may be mediated through or affected by their rights and the rights of others.[97] Feinberg describes de facto freedom of action as the 'absence of effective constraints from any external personal source to actual

---

[95] Nozick claimed that 'Seizing the results of someone's labor is equivalent to seizing hours from him and directing him to carry on various activities. If people force you to do certain work, or unrewarded work, for a certain period of time, they decide what you are to do and what purposes your work is to serve apart from your decisions. This process whereby they take this decision from you makes them part-owner of you; it gives them a property right in you' (*Anarchy, State, and Utopia*, p. 172). Rothbard makes a similar claim saying that 'the entire system of taxation is a form of involuntary servitude. . . part of the essence of slavery, after all, is being forced to work for someone at little of no pay' (*For a New Liberty*, p. 85). It is interesting to note that the common law in England does not enforce specific performance in cases of breach of contract for personal services (see *Halsbury's Laws of England* (5th edn, 2013), vol. 95, para. 307).

[96] Cohen, *Self-Ownership*, p. 237.

[97] Cohen viewed a person's choice-set as a function of their own rights, as well as the rights of others (presumably to the extent that these third party rights impact on that person) (*Ibid.*, p. 237).

or possible choices to act'.[98] Similarly, de facto freedom of choice is the 'absence of effective constraints from any internal source to actual or possible desires to choose to act'.[99] Thus, the range of choices available to any one person depends on freedom from internal and external constraints.

Under this construction, we can take Cohen's argument to be about the effect of rights of self-ownership on external rather than internal constraints. Presumably, the libertarian would contend that the presence of enforceable self-ownership rights reduces these external limitations by holding all others to be under a duty of non-interference regarding a person's scope of action. If this is the case, then Cohen's counterposition would be that restrictions on self-ownership decrease the number of effective external factors that constrain individual choice. To make this claim, however, is really only to say that everyone will enjoy a 'reasonable degree of freedom (of action)' where the distribution of rights does not privilege some over others. In other words, it is an equality constraint such that each person's rights are necessarily restricted by those self-same rights in others. Absent simultaneous moral or political commitments regarding the acquisition of external resources and there is nothing particularly antithetical to (a *liberal* conception of) self-ownership in this.

The liberal account of self-ownership captures the moral idea that a person has the right to determine the disposition and use of their lives and bodies as they see fit. This right to determine – to wit, a person's normative authority – is crucial and is encapsulated by the idea of an overarching set of use-privileges control-powers as set out earlier. The distinction between libertarian and liberal versions of self-ownership is, as Taylor notes, that control self-ownership 'constitutes the *core* of libertarian self-ownership and the *whole* of liberal self-ownership'.[100] The liberal conception of self-ownership can be seen as stopping at the boundary of the person and, thus, is limited to the use and control that an individual has over themselves, their bodies, and their lives. Moreover, this right of determination which persons have in this respect can only ever be prima facie. There are moral constraints on all owners regarding their ownership, including their self-ownership. To support a self-ownership where the person's rights are not (justifiably) circumscribed is to be blind to other moral agents and considerations in the world at large.

What does it mean, however, to say that self-owners cannot be blind to other moral agents and to considerations in the world at large? Broadly it means that self-owners are subject to moral constraints which may

---

[98] Feinberg, *Harm to Self*, p. 65.   [99] *Ibid.*   [100] Taylor, 'Self-ownership', 475.

legitimately restrict the scope of their self-ownership rights.[101] It is to acknowledge that there is more to our moral reasons and reasoning than self-ownership, that self-ownership provides only a prima facie starting point for analysis. There may be other moral considerations at play which are more fundamental doing the operative normative work (although these can also be framed in relation to a person's status as a self-owner where appropriate). Such rules are best thought of as 'general constraints on action'.[102] As Cohen put it, 'universal maximal self-ownership ensures that my right to use my fist stops at the tip of your nose, *because of* your rights, under universal maximal self-ownership, over your nose'.[103] This obligation to take other self-owners into consideration in our plans and moral deliberations casts them as moral equals.[104] Consequently, the relevant obligations and prohibitions function as a source of legitimate moral constraints on a person's rights of self-ownership; these impact on

---

[101] Brenkert argues that self-ownership paints 'an implausibly abstract view of humans and their moral relations' (Brenkert, 'Self-ownership, freedom, and autonomy', 47). He claims that 'one's ownership is abstracted from history. Thus, even though the state of one's powers, the development of one's body, and the keenness of one's intellect are all the product (to varying degrees) of the many people who have played a role in one's development, one has sole dominion over this realm... The implication is that either we are not subject to any duties of gratitude, honor, or support for those who have formed us, or these duties have simply been erased from our account' (47). While this might be correct on certain libertarian conceptions of self-ownership, this is not the picture that I have tried to paint here.

[102] Waldron, *Right to Private Property*, p. 32. We saw in Chapter 6 that we can separate out rights and other elements which do not form analytically intrinsic elements of property or ownership interests. For example, my property interests in my bicycle can be analytically divorced from rules prohibiting the theft of my bicycle. There are other sets of rules, however, where the stipulations contained therein have nothing to do with whether or not property rights are at play. They are independent moral (or legal) considerations. As Harris puts it, one cannot utilise 'one's chattels as the instruments of aggression or destruction'. (*Property and Justice*, p. 136).

[103] Cohen, *Self-Ownership*, p. 215 [emphasis added].

[104] This all raises questions about how far our constraints and obligations stemming from equality stretch. Do our moral obligations regarding self-owners extend not merely to prohibitions, but to positive obligations? To the extent that there are still other persons in the world worse off than I am, am I under an obligation to continually redistribute items that I own in order to achieve some sort of equality of welfare or of resources? A thoroughgoing examination of these matters is outwith the scope of this book, but I raise the questions to indicate that moral reasoning independent of property may be relevant. Consideration as moral equals may entail going beyond the immediate rights which comprise self-ownership. For a discussion on whether equality ought to entail equality of resources or of welfare see R. Dworkin, 'What is equality? Part 1: Equality of welfare' (1981) 10 *Philosophy and Public Affairs* 185 and 'What is equality? Part 2: Equality of resources' (1981) 10 *Philosophy and Public Affairs* 283.

our use and control of the items that we own, including ourselves. Nevertheless, despite the fact that there might be overriding moral considerations which trump putative claims based in self-ownership, there ought to be a presumption in favour of these rights. Such a presumption, at the very least, gives us pause to think carefully about whether infringements are truly justified. Indeed it is exactly this baseline premise which needs to be more explicitly recognised in relation to separated biomaterials. It is not to claim that other factors will never take precedence over or trump the source's property rights in this respect, but it is where we must *start* if the current gaps and asymmetries within the law are to be addressed.

In tying self-ownership closely to personal and moral conceptions of autonomy we can see that self-ownership cannot function in an abstracted manner. If self-ownership is intimately connected to, and derivative from, considerations of persons as autonomous beings it can be seen as promoting equality, but also bounded by the constraints of equality. In recognising the rights that persons have in virtue of their autonomy, it casts them as moral equals. Each person's rights are limited by those self-same rights in other persons making them subject to the constraints of equality.[105] If this is correct then to claim that self-ownership is hostile to autonomy is trivially true when thought of as an *inter*-personal rather than *intra*-personal claim. This is because an individual's sphere of autonomy, and their consequent rights of self-ownership, must be constrained by the autonomy and self-ownership of everyone else. These restrictions must operate if we are to accord equal respect to each person's autonomy and self-ownership, giving each of them a chance to exercise that autonomy. Thus, to a large degree, a person's autonomy and their rights of self-ownership are contingent matters.

In highlighting this, I am particularly mindful of feminist critiques of overly individualistic conceptions of autonomy. Such critiques emphasise the relational aspects of the lives of persons, situating them in broader social and cultural landscapes. As Widdows puts it, these critiques 'reject the notion of a separated and isolated individual and argue for a socially integrated and interconnected conception of the self'.[106] Although there is not space to discuss the details of the relevant accounts

---

[105] Otsuka, *Libertarianism without Inequality*, p. 12.
[106] H. Widdows, *The Connected Self: The Ethics and Governance of the Genetic Individual* (Cambridge: Cambridge University Press, 2013), p. 8. See also Nedelsky who argues that the bounded self prevalent in much autonomy – and property – discourse is problematic ('Law, boundaries, and the bounded self' (1990) 30 *Representations* 162).

and arguments here (i.e. 'relational autonomy'),[107] my conception of self-ownership (and autonomy) ought not to be viewed as implying an excessive individualism. Principally and pragmatically speaking, accounts which are too abstracted from real-world matters, and from the contextualised and embedded nature of peoples' lives, are neither justified nor sufficiently action-guiding to be of much use. As such, by taking into account considerations of moral autonomy, including considerations relating to other moral agents and the world at large, we at least begin with justified underpinnings. As noted elsewhere in this book, moral or policy considerations external to the concept of self-ownership and the institution of property may alter or limit their scope and application. The normative battle that, therefore, must be fought is to decide to what *extent* each individual's rights can be constrained or overridden; that is, how much their autonomy can be restricted. There is not the space to examine this much broader issue here. Nevertheless, the general point is that it cannot be correct to suppose that each particular person's rights of self-ownership are not protective of that individual's autonomy. This is because those rights flow from, and are consequent on, that autonomy.

5   Conceptual and Normative Issues

When the language of self-ownership is invoked we can be seen as making not only a conceptual claim which is descriptive of the interests that persons have regarding themselves and their bodies, but also a normative statement about the moral force of those interests. The appeal of self-ownership lies in the fact that being acknowledged as a self-owner is to be recognised as having freedoms in the use and control of one's self which are worthy of protection against infringements. Further, it is to consider these to be of sufficient moral force to hold other persons or the state under a duty to refrain from interfering with one's exercise of these freedoms. As such, it can be seen as a means of delineating and protecting the individual's sphere of control. We can see why self-ownership thus characterised is an attractive proposition. It is worth, however, examining some concerns and objections to self-ownership which have been raised by various commentators. Doing this enables us to probe further the scope, bounds, and implications of self-ownership. Three main

---

[107] For relational autonomy accounts see, for example, the essays in C. Mackenzie and N. Stoljar (eds), *Relational Autonomy: Feminist Perspectives on Autonomy, Agency, and the Social Self* (Oxford: Oxford University Press, 2000). See also Nedelsky, 'Law, boundaries, and the bounded self'.

objections are dealt with: (1) self-ownership rights are too indeterminate, (2) self-ownership is neither necessary nor desirable, and (3) recognising persons as self-owners is to treat then as things and opens the door for third parties to own them.

5.1 The Indeterminacy of Self-ownership Rights?

One objection made to the idea of self-ownership is that the rights which supposedly comprise self-ownership are too indeterminate to do the work asked of them. Cohen, for example, set out a version of the indeterminacy critique, which he attributed to Ronald Dworkin:

> [T]o own something is to enjoy some or other set of rights with respect to that thing. But one might envisage a number of importantly different sets of rights over themselves and over their own powers in virtue of which we could say of people that they are self-owners. The principle of self-ownership, therefore, lacks determinate content.[108]

This is reminiscent of the types of objections we met in Chapter 5 regarding the bundle of rights views of property. There we saw that it was both the flexible and disaggregative character of the putative property bundle which is the cause of concern for some. Where we consider property to be a flexible concept with different aggregations of rights constituting property, then it is left devoid of 'any necessary defining features'.[109] In other words, if elements of ownership can be divided, rearranged, and recombined in a manner which gives rise to varied sets of rights, then different bundles can constitute property in different contexts. If, therefore, self-ownership is to be considered a bundle of rights in a manner akin to bundle views of property and ownership more generally, then it ought rightly to be seen as problematic. It would, as Dworkin supposedly thought, be lacking in a determinate content.[110] We should, however, reject such a characterisation of self-ownership rights.

---

[108] Cohen, *Self-Ownership*, p. 213. Here Cohen attributes this objection to Ronald Dworkin. A related critique is offered by Barbara H. Fried who says that proponents of self-ownership lack awareness of the 'Legal Realist revolution [and] the resulting "disintegration of property"' ('Left-libertarianism: A review essay' (2004) 32 *Philosophy and Public Affairs* 66, 71–72). Her comments are specifically aimed at libertarians, but could be applied to any rights-based conception of self-ownership. The main problem with this is that such arguments will not appeal to those who do not grant the legal realist assumption that property and ownership have disintegrated.

[109] Penner, 'Bundle of rights', 724.

[110] One response offered by Cohen to this argument is that if indeterminacy is a problem, self-ownership 'is no less determinate than... ownership of other resources'. The

Where we see ownership as displaying core features then we need not worry about its fragmentation. Our core self-ownership interests can be said to consist of a set of liberties and powers that persons have in the use and control of themselves, their bodies, and their lives. These are properly considered to be rights when they entail duties on all others to refrain from interfering with those interests. This set of rights, like our ownership rights in external things, is (subject to justified moral constraints) open-ended. Whilst there might be a degree of indeterminacy within those privileges and powers in virtue of their open-endedness, there are determinate boundaries to the scope of those rights. The rights can be seen as discrete packages which are bounded. They are bounded because even though they could be described in terms of different sets (as Cohen's reportage of Dworkin suggests) they are unified by (and derivative from) an overarching notion of use and control. By locating the normative core of self-ownership in these liberties and powers, the associated rights do have a reasonable degree of determinacy. Seeing it in these terms relies on the recognition that each person's rights must be compatible with those of all other self-owners. None has a more extensive set of rights than any other. Such boundaries give the rights a certain degree of prima facie normative force.

5.2   Neither Necessary nor Desirable?

Two objections, articulated by Harris, are that appeals to self-ownership are neither necessary nor desirable. They are not *necessary*, according to him, since our relevant interests (in use and control of ourselves and our bodies) are covered by the 'bodily-use freedom' principle.[111] And they are not desirable because, if taken literally, they 'would prove too much'.[112]

---

implicit suggestion is that those who think that self-ownership presents a conceptual problem qua determinacy appear not to be concerned on this front regarding ownership of extra-personal objects (*Self-Ownership*, p. 214). It should also be noted that commentators deploy the charge of indeterminacy because they want to argue against self-ownership. However, in doing so, they seemingly ignore the fact that many moral concepts are indeterminate in the manner that they set out.

[111] Cohen, *ibid.*, p. 185.

[112] Harris, *Property and Justice*, p. 184 [footnote omitted]. Although he does so within the wider discussion of self-ownership, Harris mostly talks of body-ownership. He does this, I think, to distinguish the broader libertarian self-ownership claims regarding labour and world ownership from considerations limited to the use and control of one's own person and body. I, therefore, take his comments regarding body-ownership to be relevant to self-ownership in the context of this discussion.

For Harris, bodily-use freedom is the principle that 'a person is free to use his body as he pleases, and, at his say-so, to permit or refuse bodily. . . contacts with others'.[113] It covers the open-ended set of use-privileges and control-powers which persons have over their bodies (something which Harris conceded that they do have).[114] The difficulty is that it is not obvious how this is relevantly different to anything covered by self-ownership which allows (indeed insists) that persons have such privileges and powers with regards to their embodied selves. Perhaps we could claim that bodily-use freedom is a sub-set of the powers and privileges covered by self-ownership, since the latter concept covers more than what we might designate as 'body' (whatever that might mean).[115] Nevertheless, both bodily-use freedom and self-ownership view the person as the source of normative authority in the use of their bodies and the direction of their lives. As such, bodily-use freedom and self-ownership would seem to be much the same thing.

One difference might be that bodily-use freedom has more legal connotations, while self-ownership operates more as a background philosophical idea. Douglas, for instance, interprets Harris as saying that 'the notion that a right-holder, A, has "property rights" in his own body would be superfluous. We do not need to say A has property rights in his body in order to protect him from unlawful interferences with his person. Strict liability torts such as assault, battery, and false imprisonment already protect us against bodily interferences.'[116] There are two problems with this. First, it is not clear why we should call this cluster of legal rights bodily-use freedom rather than self-ownership. Neither is a legal term in itself (although arguably they echo different facets of legal concepts and debate). Second, even if bodily-use freedom is what the law protects in these ways, this does not mean there is not a broader philosophical notion, such as self-ownership, from which the requisite rights flow or can be justified against. Consequently, if I am right and bodily-use freedom and self-ownership amount to much the same thing, then if (per Harris) self-ownership proves too much, the bodily-use freedom principle also proves too much. These ideas stand or fall together. Even so, we need not be overly concerned about this prospect since it is relatively

---

[113] Harris, *Ibid.*, p. 185.   [114] *Ibid.*, p. 185.

[115] See Chapter 8, Section 3, for some reasons we might have to be careful in our treatment of the idea of the 'body'. For an interesting discussion in this regard see Hoeyer, *Rethinking Bodies*, Ch. 3. For a discussion which examines conceptions of the body and how biotechnology 'remakes' the body and self see Kent, *Regenerating Bodies*, Ch. 6.

[116] Douglas, 'Property rights in bodily material', p. 96.

simple to demonstrate that self-ownership does not actually prove too much. Let us consider two examples given by Harris: children and pregnant women.

In the first of these, Harris tells of a line on a children's cassette where the narrator is trying to educate children about a variety of dangers and says: 'Remember your body is your own private property. Your body's nobody's but your own.'[117] He thought this to be an example of property rhetoric and offered it as an example of where appeals to self-ownership are neither suitable nor needed. The purpose of the line from the cassette was to warn young children about a variety of dangers, including inappropriate sexual touching from adults. Harris presumed that if we took too seriously the idea of self-ownership that would mean that 'children could accord sexual favours to adults if they please'.[118] He asks us to imagine a young girl, Samantha, claiming that Uncle Joe could do things to her because her body is her own private property (i.e. self-ownership thus proves too much). This conclusion, however, does not follow from the proposition that persons are self-owners.

The principal problem with Harris' example is that it focuses on individuals who may not yet be full self-owners.[119] Self-ownership, and indeed any ownership, requires that the owner holds the requisite capacities to exercise that ownership. A certain level of capacity is necessary in order to be (considered) autonomous either in thought or action. This is a prerequisite for exercising autonomy or achieving autonomy in the different spheres of one's life, whether moral, personal, political, or any other realm. Where the capacity to exercise rights is not present, and the person is not even minimally autonomous, the idea of self-ownership rights is left devoid of its justification and, thus, any normative force. The justification for being attributed any rights of ownership over oneself is connected to a person's condition as an autonomous being and to their interests in being the source of control within their own lives. The implication of this is that we ought not to conceive of non-autonomous individuals as self-owners.[120]

---

[117] Harris, *Property and Justice*, p. 184 [footnote omitted].   [118] *Ibid.*, p. 185.

[119] Making such a statement may simply raise the question of who is the owner (if indeed there is one). I do not propose to answer that in this book, but see Chapter 8, Section 4, note 83 regarding the paradox of universal self-ownership.

[120] Although on certain views of the interest theory of rights, being autonomous would not be necessary. Thus, if one derived one's conception of self-ownership rights from that particular conception of rights, one could maintain the position that there can be non-autonomous self-owners. However, since my conception of self-ownership is justified by its intimate connection to autonomy, such a view could not be supported here.

Even bare non-interference requires a level of capacity and control on the part of the individual, even if this is just the ability to waive (or not) the duty that others have to refrain from interfering. The rights associated with ownership must, therefore, be *exercisable*.[121] If they were not exercisable, they would be lacking in control which is a central component of both property and rights. As such, they would be rather ineffective rights from the point of view of the rights-holder.[122] The normative authority which attends being a self-owner, like that of owners writ large, entails having the ability (and therefore capacity and capability) to modify or waive the duties that *others* have *towards* them in virtue of their ownership interests. If this is correct, then it poses a problem for those, like Harris, who would use the example of children to try and show why self-ownership is not generally appealing.

Children develop their capacities in terms of autonomy as they grow up and would not be deemed to have an *open-ended* set of use-privileges and control-powers over themselves or their bodies. When they are older, and have developed the requisite capacities, the set of use-privileges and control-powers that they possess will have expanded. Samantha the child could not be said to have the same capacities as Samantha the adult. In this respect, it is not obvious that she ought not to grant sexual favours to whosoever she pleases once she reaches an age where she is competent, in the relevant sense, to do so.

There are, of course, many reasons why children (and even adults) ought to be protected from predatory adults, and not be put in situations such as that described. However, the point is that self-ownership does not entail that children could grant sexual favours if they please, because it is simply not relevant to our immediate moral assessments of such situations. For this reason, it does not tell against self-ownership more generally. Neither does this mean that children (or indeed other non-self-owners) fall outwith the scope of our moral concern, it is merely that other moral reasoning is more appropriate in this sphere. Prohibitions against harming children are morally justified on grounds other than self-ownership

---

[121] Steiner, *Essay on Rights*, p. 57. Elsewhere Steiner has said that '[t]he set of persons who can be right-holders consists entirely, and only, of the subset of persons who count as moral agents: that is, those persons who are capable of exercising Hohfeldian powers, which is what is meant by exercising rights. Only right-exercisers can be right-holders' (H. Steiner, 'Universal self-ownership and the fruits of one's labour: A reply to Churchin' (2008) 16 *Journal of Political Philosophy* 350, 354). This is not to say that duties are not owed to non-rights holders, merely that these are non-correlative duties; that is, not consequent on the existence of a right, but on other moral reasoning.

[122] See Chapter 6, Section 3.1.

rights.[123] The mere fact that they have interests that can be harmed may be enough, even if those interests do not (yet) amount to self-ownership.

Another example which Harris marshalled is that of termination of pregnancy. Here he claimed that certain authors wish to appeal to property arguments to strengthen claims regarding a woman's right to have a termination.[124] In particular he was referring to Jeffrey Goldberg's argument which concludes that 'if a woman has property rights in her body, then the property right at issue in the context of an unwanted pregnancy is the woman's power to exclude the embryo/fetus from her body'.[125] Here the notion of self-ownership is used to highlight the control that women ought to be recognised as having in and over their bodies. I do not intend to rehearse well-trodden ground regarding the morality of abortion here. Considerations of self-ownership may well strengthen the case for the presumption of choice in this arena, but my interest lies in how Harris subsequently uses this to reject self-ownership. His quibble was not with claims about pregnancy per se, but with extensions which he supposed followed from a property analysis. He said that those who argue that 'a woman's body is her own property... may not wish to commit themselves to the view that women are also morally free to sell their bodies for any use, however, demeaning or life-threatening'.[126] Here he was likely thinking of activities such as prostitution and surrogacy, which are discussed in Goldberg's paper.[127]

The first thing to note here is that those who argue for self-ownership may not shy away from such a position. They might think that women should be free to do what they like with their bodies, where doing so does not run afoul of some other moral consideration, such as causing harm to others. They might even think that this is the case where the woman does so because of a particular sub-optimal set of circumstances, such that she would not have made that choice if other more preferable options were available to her.[128]

---

[123] Although we might think that their *future* self-ownership might be relevant to such an assessment.

[124] Harris, *Property and Justice*, 186.

[125] J.D. Goldberg, 'Involuntary servitudes: A property-based notion of abortion' (1991) 38 *University of California Los Angeles Law Review* 1597, 1599 [footnote omitted]. On this see also M. Ford, 'A property model of pregnancy' (2005) 1 *International Journal of Law in Context* 261. Cf. Nedelsky, 'Property in potential life?'.

[126] Harris, *Property and Justice*, p. 186.

[127] Goldberg, 'Involuntary servitudes', pp. 1649–1651.

[128] See, however, Debra Satz's powerful critique of prostitution where she argues that it 'is wrong by virtue of its contributions to perpetuating a pervasive form of inequality: status inequality between men and women' (*Why Some Things Should Not Be for Sale: The*

Yet whatever the general arguments for or against such activities, self-ownership in and of itself does not commit us to endorsing them.

Goldberg's own comments, which Harris did not engage with, suggest one reason why this is so. He says that the law 'treats the power to exclude far more favourably than the power to transfer for maximum value'.[129] He, therefore, thinks that a case can be made for drawing a line between rights to terminate on the one hand and surrogacy arrangements on the other.[130] We can go farther than this, however. Whilst the power to transfer is rightly conceived of as part of our overarching rights of use and control, as I will argue in Chapter 9, this is analytically separable from any rights to income consequent on such transfers. Our core property rights do not include the power to transfer for value. This point aside, there is a broader and more straightforward argument that can be made here. Even if, all things considered, prostitution and commercial surrogacy are not morally permissible, this would not show that self-ownership per se is a non-starter. Without more, all that this would commit us to is the recognition that there are moral constraints (or perhaps merely justified policy limits) on the scope and bounds of our self-ownership.[131]

5.3   Persons as Property?

Finally, in this chapter, there are two interrelated objections to self-ownership which I want to briefly examine. The first is that considering persons as self-owners is to treat them as things, something which is claimed to be prima facie morally impermissible. The second is that if we allow that persons own themselves, then it would be possible for third parties to own them too. My position is that neither of these arguments

---

Moral Limits of Markets (Oxford: Oxford University Press, 2010), p. 153). See generally pp. 135–153. She distinguishes between the moral wrong of prostitution and the appropriate legal response to it.

[129] Goldberg, 'Involuntary servitudes', 1631, note 120.

[130] He argues that 'the state is deemed to have taken the property of a woman pregnant against her will when it prohibits abortion... her bodily property. No such physical invasion or burden occurs when the state prohibits prostitution or paid surrogate motherhood... In contrast, in passing legislation that bans prostitution and paid surrogate motherhood, the state takes women's power to transfer for value their labor... In order to make out a case for a regulatory taking based on diminished value, the regulation must preclude the property holder from earning a fair rate of return on her property' (*ibid.*, pp. 1649–1650).

[131] For clarity I am not making an argument about this either way, I am merely making an analytical point about the implications of recognising people as self-owners.

(which are essentially Kantian in nature) ought to be given much purchase.

Consider the following quotation from Kant:

> Man cannot dispose over himself because he is not a thing. He is not his own property – that would be a contradiction; for so far as he is a person, he is a Subject who can have ownership of other things. But now were he something owned by himself, he would be a thing over which he can have ownership. He is, however, a person, who is not property, so he cannot be a thing such as he might own; for it is impossible, of course, to be at once a thing and a person, a proprietor and a property at the same time.[132]

Kant believed that to consider persons as property would consign them to the realm of things and that this is impermissible. The main difficulty with such a position, Cohen pointed out, is that it is 'entirely question-begging. . . to one who does not already accept that persons cannot own themselves'.[133] These types of claims merely prompt us to ask *why* it is not possible to simultaneously be considered as a person and a thing (or for part of a person to be a thing while still attached) or as proprietor and property. And even when we delve deeper into possible reasons, we see that these claims are unpersuasive (whether construed as conceptual or normative ones). Let us consider Kant's wider moral philosophy on the freedom of persons (for which read 'free will') in order to do this.

Freedom, for Kant, is the only innate right possessed by persons.[134] The exercise of one's free will must be in accordance with the categorical imperative: 'act only in accordance with that maxim through which you can at the same time will that it become a universal law'.[135] As such, a person's freedom is constrained by the freedom of all other rational beings.[136] Kant offered different formulations of the categorical imperative which were intended to give rise to specific maxims which could then be used as practical guides to action. The second formulation tells us to 'act that you use humanity, whether in your own person or in the person of any other, always at the same time as an end, never merely as a means'.[137] If we look at his comments regarding persons and property in the light of this, the reason for the posited division between persons and things becomes clearer. As Munzer puts it (although he does not endorse it): 'If [persons] had property rights in parts of their body and

---

[132] Kant, *Lectures on Ethics*, p. 157 (LE 27:386).   [133] Cohen, *Self-Ownership*, p. 212.
[134] Kant, *Metaphysics of Morals*, pp. 30–31 (MM 6:237–8).
[135] Kant, *Groundwork*, p. 31 (GW 4:421).
[136] Kant, *Metaphysics of Morals*, p. 30 (MM 6:237).
[137] Kant, *Groundwork*, p. 38 (GW 4:429).

exercised those rights, they would lose that freedom. They would move from the level of free human beings to the level of things or objects.'[138] It is, on this view, morally wrong for persons to make themselves into things, as to do so is to debase themselves by depriving them of their free will. As such, it is contrary to Kantian autonomy.

We can see how this connects with Kant's second formulation where he entreats us to use persons as ends in themselves and never merely as a means.[139] If something exists in the realm of things, there is no moral concern with treating it as a mere means, of subordinating it to our will. But persons qua rational beings must never be treated as such, whether by others or by themselves, since that is to give them reason to act based on external influences rather than in accordance with moral law. To treat a person with free will as a means is to deprive them of their innate right of freedom in the exercise of their will: 'One may dispose of things which have no freedom, but not of a being that itself has free choice.'[140] Because being a thing equates to not having free will, it is permissible to subordinate those entities lacking in free will to our own wants and wishes. However, one ought not to treat rational beings as lacking in free will. For Kant, this meant that persons do not (or ought not to) have property in their own person since this would entail treating themselves as things lacking in free will: 'The body belongs to the self, it constitutes, in conjunction with that, a person; but now one cannot make one's person a thing.'[141]

Kant's position can be viewed as an objection to *being, becoming, or acting as a thing* when you are *something different*; that is, a rational being with free will.[142] His was concerned with the effect on autonomy of acting in a debasing manner. He said that 'a man is not entitled to sell his limbs for money, not even if he were to get 10,000 thalers for one finger'.[143] He followed this by saying that '[i]f a man does that, he turns himself into a thing, and then anyone may treat him as they please, because he has thrown his person away'.[144] It might be correct, as Kant supposed, that those entities truly lacking in free will can be subordinate to the will of those that do. Yet it does not follow that others may treat a person 'as they please' simply because that person acts in a particular manner. Kant

---

[138] Munzer, 'Kant and property', 322.   [139] Kant, *Groundwork*, p. 38 (GW 4:429).
[140] Kant, *Lectures on Ethics*, p. 127 (LE 27:346).
[141] *Ibid.*, pp. 157–158 (LE 27:387). Here he is specifically referring to prostitution, but it serves to highlight Kant's concern with making the self into a thing.
[142] *Ibid.*, pp. 122–177 (LE 27:340–412).   [143] *Ibid.*, p. 127 [LE 27:347].   [144] *Ibid.*

conflates two separate issues: owning oneself and the manner in which persons are treated by *others*.

The move from an observation about how one conducts oneself qua self-regarding action to the conclusion that this entails a complete abandonment of one's personhood is neither logically entailed nor justifiable. It is a complete non-sequitur. Presumably, where the person acts in an allegedly debasing way they treat themselves as if they lacked free will. But acting *as if* one lacks free will is not the same as *actually* lacking it. It is also not obviously the case that a person lacks free will merely because someone else treats them *as if* they do.[145] Even if one allows oneself to be treated as a means, and thus in a manner contrary to moral law, this need not (and does not) necessarily entail a lack of 'freedom to act differently in the future'.[146] Though there might be some loss of freedom involved in not having my autonomy respected when others treat me in such a manner, this does not consist of the complete loss of my personhood or free will.[147] To take Kant's own example of prostitution,[148] it does not follow from the fact that one willingly exchanges sex for money with one person that it is open to others to commit rape. Similarly, to admit property in one's *own* person and body does not allow that *others* can treat you as property. There is nothing in the idea of self-ownership which entails, let alone necessitates, such a move.

Relatedly, restrictions and prohibitions on our treatment of each other as persons do not imply that persons and their bodies cannot be their *own* property. As noted by the Court of Appeal in *Moore*, there is 'a dramatic difference between having property rights in one's own body and being the property of another'.[149] It is not open to me to treat your house, car, or dog in the manner of my choosing. This is not because they are not or could not be property, but because they are not *my* property. Likewise, I could not claim possession of you, or control over you, because you are already the embodiment of your own will; *vice versa*, you could not own me as property for the self-same reason. There is nothing entailed in conceiving of persons as their *own* property which opens up the possibility of *others* being able to have property in them, either as embodied persons, or in parts of their bodies. What the recognition of property rights in oneself does do, however, is to firmly recognise where the locus of control lies: *with the person themselves.*

[145] Munzer, 'Kant and property', 324.   [146] *Ibid.*, 323–324.   [147] *Ibid.*, 324.
[148] Kant, *Lectures on Ethics*, pp. 157–158 (LE 27:386–387).
[149] *Moore*, Court of Appeal at 504.

6   Concluding Thoughts

David Archard has said that 'the value of autonomy is to be found in *the leading of lives*. Whether autonomy is valued intrinsically or instrumentally it is valued within the context of lives rather than in respect simply of isolated decisions.'[150] If there is value in autonomy and in persons leading autonomous lives, then this warrants a degree of prima facie normative protection. This is something that is brought to the fore when we conceive of autonomy as being in operation in different contexts and spheres throughout the lives of persons. One facet of autonomy consists of the liberty to think, choose, act as one pleases and requires restraint from interference by third parties. Another lies in a person's ability and liberty to *exercise* control over their body, actions, and life. In some sense persons need to be the *source of control* over their thoughts, choices, and actions. Conceiving of persons as self-owners is a way of drawing a boundary which we think of as having significant normative force.

The value of recognising persons as being self-owners lies in the autonomy-protecting function of the rights that comprise self-ownership. A person's self-ownership interests are the liberties and powers they have in the use and control of their embodied selves. We may properly call these rights when they entail a duty on all others to refrain from interfering in an individual's personal domain. When this is the case, self-ownership can be thought of as a perimeter of rights which protects an individual's personal domain as located in their own person. These self-ownership rights are underpinned and justified by their strong connection to considerations of autonomy and liberty and are, thus, to be seen as autonomy-protecting.

If we take a rich conception of autonomy as foundational (one which takes into account the interests and lives of persons, as well as their relations with other persons), the rights of use and control which flow from this are to be seen as those of self-ownership. These, however, must be compatible with like rights for other self-owners. In this way, considerations of equality amongst persons serve to draw a boundary around that autonomy. Even so, equal consideration as a person is not the end of the story with regards to the legitimate constraints that self-owners are subject to. Self-ownership is simply a prima facie normative position. Property rights and considerations of ownership, even in relation to the self and our bodies do not exhaust our moral armoury. Rights in themselves are not the baseline moral justification for our treatment of

---

[150] D. Archard, 'Informed consent: Autonomy and self-ownership' (2008) 25 *Journal of Applied Philosophy* 19, 21.

persons. Neither are they the end *conclusions* of moral argument. They are, as Raz maintains, the *'intermediate conclusions* in arguments from ultimate values to duties'.[151] Nevertheless, even though there might be overriding moral considerations which trump claims based in self-ownership, recognising persons as self-owners gives us pause to think carefully about whether, and which, infringements are truly justified.

Ultimately the objections to self-ownership examined in this chapter have been found to be unpersuasive. By and large they require us to already accept as an initial premise that persons cannot have property in themselves. It is exactly this underlying premise that needs to be substantiated if self-ownership as a moral concept and thesis is to be rejected. At the heart of the position of some commentators is the endorsement of a dichotomy between the world of persons and the world of things. In Chapter 5 we saw that this dichotomy forms a central tenet of the law of property. There we saw it clearly expressed in *R* v. *Bentham*: '[o]ne cannot possess something which is not separate and distinct from oneself. An unsevered hand or finger is part of oneself. Therefore, one cannot possess it... What is possessed must under definition be a thing. A person's hand or fingers are not a thing.'[152] In this manner a boundary is drawn around the embodied person. This boundary functions not only as a pragmatic division by which we can more easily categorise and organise various legal rules, it seemingly represents the underlying moral philosophical justification for having such classifications in the first place. Such distinctions may sometimes be useful in terms of the classification of legal rules, but, we ought not to confuse their utility in this respect with undisputed ontological, phenomenological, or moral propositions. This is something which we will see more fully in the next chapter.

---

[151] Raz, 'Nature of rights', 208 [emphasis added]. Rights help us to conceptualise the way we should act towards the holders of those rights. But they can only exist within a more extensive moral reasoning, and they do this as the intermediate conclusions between justification and duties. Thus, other reasoning both provides the underlying moral justification that gives rise to rights and can temper the conclusions of rights-based arguments. Raz warns against using legal rights as a normative basis for moral rights (J. Raz, 'Legal rights' (1984) 4 *Oxford Journal of Legal Studies* 1, 1–5). Note, however, that although rights might be viewed as having their origins in legal theory (see Hohfeld, *Fundamental Legal Conceptions of a Right*), the concept of rights is not exclusively legal. See my comments in Chapter 10, section 3.

[152] [2005] UKHL 18 at [8].

PART III

Beyond Self-ownership

8

Property Rights in Biomaterials

1. Introduction

At the end of Chapter 4 I asked, if biomaterials are *res nullius* while attached to us, upon what basis do they become *our* property once separated from us? The intuitive answer is simply that they are 'ours'. After all they have been removed from *our* bodies. In this respect we could view the origin of the biomaterials as both factually and normatively significant. Yet in determining that such materials are indeed 'ours', we have to be mindful of the reasons why this is so. Legally, the idea of a normative transformation is integral to understanding the transition to being a *res*. When the requisite transformation occurs property rights can be created *de novo*. This we saw in Part I of the book. Nonetheless, what emerged from these earlier chapters was that the relevant law consists of little more than an ad hoc set of principles; for example, the work/skill exception, intention, and so on, with little indication of if or when these might be triggered. We also saw that the various philosophical rationales underlying potential interpretations of the law are not satisfactory. They neither adequately explain nor justify how property rights in biomaterials ought to be generated, nor why they should be allocated to particular parties. Some commentators, as we saw, favour the automatic allocation of such rights to the source of the biomaterials. But while mere separation is attractive, if we are concerned about protecting source interests in biomaterials, more is needed to tell the normative story. This is because where the source of the biomaterials is not considered the owner (at least morally speaking) prior to their removal, we have no prima facie reason for thinking that any new property rights (moral or legal) created upon separation should vest in them. There thus exists an explanatory and justificatory gap if we cling to the idea that the body and newly separated materials are *res nullius*.

The arguments in this chapter suggest that this lacuna can be closed *if* we start from self-ownership. With this in mind, I start by arguing that the moral justification and analytical route to ownership of separated biomaterials is actually quite straightforward. In so doing, I posit the 'no moral magic' principle; to wit, the rights of use and control which persons have pre- and post-separation are normatively contiguous and coextensive. We have no good reason to think that these change in any fundamental way when biomaterials are separated from the body. Following this, in sections 3 and 4, I examine two alternatives to the account given. First, I explore further (and reject) the supposed ontological and moral force of separation in explaining and justifying the creation of *de novo* legal property rights (in biomaterials). Second, I return to labour theory and examine two related philosophical lines of reasoning which might get us to the conclusion that persons own (some of) their separated biomaterials. Ultimately, however, I conclude that when we start from self-ownership we do not need to invoke labour-based rationales.

2   Self-ownership and Continuing Normative Authority

There is a multitude of ways how, and reasons why, biomaterials come to be detached from persons. These include samples removed for diagnostic purposes or as part of clinical treatment, organ donation, storage of blood or gametes for later use, and participation in research projects requiring human tissue. What ought to be the relevance of separation or detachment for the question of source property rights? My suggestion here is that it is of scant relevance *if* we are considered morally to be self-owners.

2.1   The 'No Moral Magic' Principle

There is a rational connection between embodied self-owners and their separated biomaterials. This is a connection which does ordinarily exist between self-owners and other things in the external world, such as land, cars, and so on. I say ordinarily because biotechnological advances mean that there are some instances where this does not hold true. This we will see in Section 3 in relation to, for example, implanted devices such artificial joint replacements (knees, hips, etc.), heart valves, internal pacemakers, and internal cardioverter defibrillators. I will argue that the boundary between persons and things is blurred in such cases, with once external objects becoming part of persons. Even so, biomaterials are the principal example of 'things' in the world which have a *prior connection* to their source.

First, biomaterials are part of the person before being removed (for whatever reason). Second, they are linked to the person via the (genetic) data they frequently contain. Third, and perhaps most significantly, before detachment takes place, there is little (or often no) dispute regarding who has the requisite rights of use and control. As Price has said, 'our bodies are the most intimate, sometimes the only, "possession" we have and our ability to sanction their use is usually beyond dispute except where the outweighing collective interest is overwhelming'.[1] It is not that we could not have similarly intimate connections with extra-personal objects, but that if and when we do, we have to *acquire* them. We do not need to acquire our biomaterials. On the contrary, until such time as something happens to transform our relationship to them, these are already under our possession and control.

Whether organs and tissues are part of the body or detached, what is at stake is the normative authority of the person. For this reason, when biomaterials are separated, the initial presumption of control must be in the source's favour. Since property rights are the primary way in which our control of things in the external world is secured, the source should be accorded property rights in their separated biomaterials. These can be viewed merely as an extension or a reflection of their pre-existing moral rights of self-ownership. On this view there is a moral and conceptual continuity between the rights which govern biomaterials in the embodied and separated states. Self-owners are the ones in a position of ultimate normative authority regarding themselves and their bodies. The rights which comprise self-ownership, as we saw in in the previous chapter, are the logical entailment of each person's autonomy. Our reasons for respecting and protecting this do not routinely change when a living person's organs or tissues are removed.[2]

Hence, unless we think that a person's normative authority as a matter of course stops at the bodily limit, we have little reason to think that the substance of their *rights* over their biomaterials change on separation. We are still fundamentally interested in the person's rights of use and control. Although we could regard the rights in the embodied and separated states as substantively different, this risks invoking overly complex and slippery reasoning (as we will see throughout sections 3 and 4 of this chapter). Essentially, it would entail different sets of rights coming in and out of existence. Upon detachment, the person's self-ownership rights would

---

[1] Price, 'The Human Tissue Act', 821.
[2] They might, but we need good reason for why this is so.

cease and a new altered set of rights in the biomaterials would be created. Such an account would lack coherency. It is analytically neater to simply consider the rights post-separation as being contiguous and co-extensive with those which comprise self-ownership. In this way, the source's entitlements to control the uses of those materials remain intact. The effect of this is that the person's ability to control various aspects of their lives, including their bodies and bodily materials, continues to be protected.

For the reasons just set out, self-ownership creates a strong presumption that ownership of separated biomaterials should vest in the source of those materials. The account is a straightforward one and is premised on the idea that no moral magic vis-à-vis the substance of the rights occurs when biomaterials are separated from their source. That is to say, separation in and of itself does not break the normative continuity between persons and their biomaterials. Thus, unless there are good arguments to the contrary, the use and control that persons exercise over their embodied selves ought to extend to their parts once separated. In this way the property rights (moral and legal) that persons ought to be recognised as having in their biomaterials after separation are a consequence and mirror of their pre-existing (moral) self-ownership rights. Let us consider some potential objections to this view.

2.2   Normative Continuity: Some Possible Objections

2.2.1   Against 'Prior Embodiment'?

The type of account just presented may fall under what Wall has termed a 'prior embodiment' or 'original acquisition' justification'.[3] He says that:

> The problem with the prior embodiment justification is that it does not explain why prior acquisition or possession is a past act or event that can, in the present, impose on others duties to refrain from using the resource. There is no reason to presume that someone's prior relationship with bodily material relates, or is connected, to his or her assertion of rights in the bodily material.[4]

The first thing to say is that, although they could be related, 'prior embodiment' and 'original acquisition' represent distinct ideas which

---

[3] 'The person was, in other words, the first to acquire possession of the materials. This "prior embodiment" or "original acquisition" is considered by some to be sufficient to ground a person's entitlements to use and control his or her material' (Wall, *Being and Owning*, p. 45).

[4] *Ibid.*, p. 46.

ought not to be conflated. The term 'original acquisition' as ordinarily employed in political philosophy means the acquisition of previously (and wholly) unowned things.[5] Some other reasoning is then given to supposedly explain and justify the *mode* by which property rights in the thing are generated and allocated; for instance, first possession or labour-based reasoning.[6] These are modes of original acquisition. In this way, prior embodiment could be construed as a way to acquire ownership, but it is not necessarily so. The coupling of the two concepts is certainly not needed if we are drawing on self-ownership. Instead, within the self-ownership context, prior embodiment is merely a way of understanding the connection to the person of the now-separated biomaterials.

The next difficulty is that we need to be careful where we place the argumentative burden in relation to *biomaterials*. Moreover, we must resist drawing false equivalencies. Wall supports his contention regarding prior embodiment by directing us to John Simmonds' reconstruction of an objection to original acquisition (which Simmonds attributes to Waldron, amongst others):

> [Original acquisition] arguments normally entail that persons can, by their acts of acquisition, deliberately create for others universal moral duties of forbearance and noninterference with respect to holdings of possibly scarce resources. Such a power (to create significant moral burdens for others at will) is 'radically unfamiliar' and 'repugnant' to us, and it is therefore a power of which we should be highly suspicious. Needless to say, we should be equally suspicious of any argument which purports to justify such a power for individuals.[7]

We should note is that Simmonds himself does not agree with Waldron's objection since he thinks that only extreme versions of original acquisition theses would be susceptible to Waldron's critique. The reason for this is twofold. First, he thinks that we can point to numerous instances of

---

[5] This point was also made in Chapter 3 in relation to the different use of the term in Scots law and to explain why the Scots law usage might be somewhat perplexing to political philosophers. See note 153.

[6] For some pieces which include a discussion of these aspects see, for example, Kymlicka, *Contemporary Political Philosophy*, pp. 111–121; R.A. Epstein, 'Possession as the root of title' (1979) 13 *Georgia Law Review* 122; C.M. Rose, 'Possession as the origin of property' (1985) 52 *University of Chicago Law Review* 73; B. van der Vossen, 'What counts as original appropriation? (2009) 8 *Politics, Philosophy, and Economics* 355; and K. Widerquist, 'Lockean theories of property: Justifications for unilateral appropriation' (2010) 2 *Public Reason* 2.

[7] J. Simmonds, 'Original-acquisition justifications of private property' (1994) 11 *Social Philosophy and Policy* 63, 81; Waldron, *Right to Private Property*, pp. 265–267.

unilaterally created duties (either institutionally or non-institutionally mediated); '[f]or instance, I may make a legal will, unilaterally imposing on all others an obligation to respect its terms (which they previously lacked)'.[8] Second he notes that most classical justifications for original acquisition contain 'serious limits on rights of acquisition – so that genuinely onerous obligations could not be unilaterally imposed'.[9]

Waldron's objection is about the ad hoc creation of duties (moral or legal) through the acquisition of things.[10] What is at issue are original acquisition arguments as applied to *unowned* things in the *external* world – land, oil, natural resources, and so on. The general contention is that when it comes to unowned external (and scarce) resources, the normative presumption should be against allowing parties to create new binding duties on others by their acquisition of those things.[11] Now even if it is true that ordinarily we resist the creation of ad hoc duties in relation to external resources, the application of this in the context of separated biomaterials is misguided. The principal difficulty is that persons are neither 'acquiring' their biomaterials nor 'creating' new duties. Until moments before the biomaterials' separation, a person's possession of these (and rights over them) is beyond doubt.[12] What is more, persons already have duties of forbearance and non-interference with respect to all other persons. No new duties are being created upon separation. The duties regarding any newly removed biomaterials are mere continuations of those already in existence.

Although he rejected the idea of self-ownership, this is something which Harris recognised: '[t]hose rules which previously protected the whole of his body crystallize around what is taken from it'.[13] Hence, while

---

[8] Simmonds, 'Original-acquisition justifications', 83.   [9] *Ibid.*, 84.
[10] Waldron, *Right to Private Property*, p. 271.
[11] A further, and likely more pressing, normative concern focuses on egalitarian objections to the acquisition of natural resources; that is, questions of whether such resources are to be conceived of as held in common for all people, and, if so, what would constitute the just acquisition, distribution, and use of these.
[12] At least in the usual sense of the word, as Martin Wilkinson notes in a slightly different context, 'people do not *appropriate* their own bodies, and no problem of justifying appropriation of one's own body arises' (T.M. Wilkinson, 'The confiscation and sale of organs' (2007) 13 *Res Publica* 327, 332 [emphasis added]). I say 'usual' because as Cecile Fabre notes, 'we do depend on social cooperation and thus on other people's efforts, work and deployment of material resources, for the continued growth and health of our body' (C. Fabre, 'Reply to Wilkinson' (2008) 14 *Res Publica* 137, 139). We will return to related points in Section 4 as they have a bearing on labour-based justifications for the creation of property rights in biomaterials.
[13] Harris, *Property and Justice*, p. 360. For a discussion of some of the problems with Harris' broader framing of the issues see Quigley, 'Property in human biomaterials', pp. 679–682.

we do not have prima facie reasons to think that there are pre-existing rights and duties vested in individuals with respect to external resources, this cannot be presumed when it comes to separated biomaterials. Hence, if we are to draw analogies here, a more appropriate one would be with already owned items rather than completely unowned ones. Take my computer, for instance. Should you purloin this from my office, it will do you no good to claim that my prior possession of it 'does not impose on others duties to refrain from using the resource'. In such a scenario, there is at least an initial presumption that I have (and indeed ought to have) moral and legal rights over the computer. And it is the fact of my prior possession of it which raises such a presumption. Even if it turned out that I was not the owner of the computer, the fact of possession would still raise the presumption that I was.

For these reasons, it is incumbent upon those who would argue either for the reallocation or extinction of the requisite rights and duties to make their case. It is not, as Wall's argument suggests, for the source to prove why they should hold on to the rights which they had only moments before. In this context, we should be suspicious not of arguments which seem to justify the power of individuals to create binding duties, but of those which seem to justify *the power to remove already existing ones*. To allow the justificatory burden to fall in the wrong direction would have the type of unpalatable consequences that this book has sought to resist. Not in the least, it constructs a moral and regulatory space where source interests may fail to be protected. Separated biomaterials would become just another commons to be enclosed by third parties in unjust ways.

2.2.2   Redistributing Human Biomaterials?

There may be countervailing moral or policy reasons which speak against the continuing normative authority account given in this chapter. In the main, however, these are either unpersuasive or do not affect the prima facie position vis-à-vis source property rights. Principal concerns are those pertaining to (1) the commodification and commercialisation of human biomaterials and (2) the (re)distribution and use of biomaterials for the greater societal good. Both of these are essentially issues relating to the transfer of bodily materials, which will be dealt with more in-depth in the next chapter. Nevertheless, it is worth making some preliminary

---

In particular, he connected it to his distancing criterion, which will be discussed in Section 3 below.

comments about arguments which centre on the redistribution of resources for societal benefit.

Some version of the (re)distributive concern is evident in, for example, the *Moore* and *Greenberg* decisions. As we saw in Chapter 3, in both cases the courts expressed the worry that recognising source property rights would hinder access to biomaterials and, as such, have a detrimental effect on research.[14] The consequence of the courts' refusal to acknowledge source property rights is that it permits the transfer and redistribution of biomaterials to those conducting research. This redistribution of scarce biological resources, we might argue, serves the interests of society at large. It is in all our interests if researchers have access to the raw materials they need for their research. For this reason, the legal system ought to facilitate it. Such an argument is alas too simplistic and belies the complexity (both motivational and practical) of research involving human biomaterials.

Claims centring on the negative impact on research are not particularly compelling. This is plain when we take into account what the decisions in the two cases mean for how the researchers were subsequently able to use and manage the samples. Via their own property rights in the materials, they were able to restrict access to the materials (and any resulting data and processes). Other third parties wanting to use Moore's splenic cells or the resultant cell lines, for example, would not have been able to do so. No further (re)distribution would have taken place without the agreement of the original researchers (or their institutions). Additionally, in order for the wider societal benefit argument to gain proper purchase, it would need to be shown that the relevant research is in fact being conducted within such a frame and this is doubtful. By this I do not mean that all that needs to be demonstrated is that research *writ large* is good for society and good for the individuals in it. This is not in question. What is questionable is how particular institutions and actors conduct their research. In the two US cases, commercialisation was a significant motivating factor in conducting the research. The resulting processes and products were not made widely or freely available in order to benefit society (the very nub of the dispute in *Greenberg*).

Of course, arguments could be, and indeed have been, made that a fundamental change in the way in which research is conducted is needed; that it ought to be done against a backdrop of genuine concern for the greater public good. This manifests in at least two types of argument. First,

[14] *Moore*, Supreme Court at 144; *Greenberg* at 1070–1071. See Chapter 3, Section 4.1.

some commentators argue that it might be incumbent on us all to contribute to research,[15] with the use of our separated biomaterials constituting just one way in which we could do this. Second, other commentators focus on research outputs and advocate some sort of benefit-sharing model. Such models are most often suggested in the context of bio-bank research. As Heather Widdows explains, benefit-sharing 'does exactly what the name suggests. It provides a mechanism by which to share the benefits of research with the community from which samples, knowledge or other materials or information is derived.'[16] There is not space here to explore any in-depth arguments with respect to these suggestions and I remain open to them. But *even if* we accept the thrust of such proposals, they do not tell against the account given in this chapter (and book as a whole). The reason for this is that neither type of argument need entail denying that the source has prima facie property rights in those materials. Instead, the arguments would be about the redistribution of already-existing rights. It would, therefore, be for those who would redistribute them (and the biomaterials themselves) to make a thoroughgoing argument in this respect.[17]

Let us now move on to consider the first of two potential alternatives to the normative continuity account just given: separation from persons. In so doing, my concern is with the normative significance of 'boundaries'

[15] For arguments related to both sides of the duty to participate in research debate see, for example, J. Harris, 'Scientific research is a moral duty' (2007) 31 *Journal of Medical Ethics* 242; I. Brassington, 'John Harris' argument for a duty to research' (2007) 21 *Bioethics* 160; I. de Melo-Martin, 'A duty to participate in research: Does social context matter?' (2008) 8 *American Journal of Bioethics* 28; R. Rhodes, 'In defense of the duty to participate in biomedical research' (2008) 8 *American Journal of Bioethics* 37; and S. Holm, B. Hofmann, and J.H. Solbakk, 'Conscription to biobank research?' in J.H. Solbakk, S. Holm, and B. Hofmann (eds), *The Ethics of Research Biobanking* (Dordrecht: Springer Science + Business Media, 2009), pp. 255–262.

[16] Widdows, *The Connected Self*, p. 102. See also D. Nicol, M. Otlowski, and D. Chalmers, 'Consent, commercialisation and benefit-sharing' (2001) 9 *Journal of Law and Medicine* 80; G. Haddow, G.T. Laurie, S. Cunningham-Burley, and K. Hunter, 'Benefit-sharing: Public solutions to private interests?' (2007) 64 *Social Science and Medicine* 272; K. Hoeyer, 'The ethics of research biobanking: A critical review of the literature' (2008) 25 *Biotechnology and Genetic Engineering Reviews* 429; and D. Chalmers, M. Burgess, K. Edwards, *et al.*, 'Marking shifts in human research ethics in the development of biobanking' (2015) 8 *Public Health Ethics* 63.

[17] Note, for example, Fabre's argument that living persons are under an obligation to redistribute their organs: ' if one thinks that the badly off have a moral right, as a matter of justice, to the material resources they need in order to lead a minimally flourishing life, then, in some cases. . . one must be committed to conferring on the sick a moral right that the able-bodied supply them the body parts they need in order to lead such a life' (*Whose Body Is It Anyway?*, p. 98).

for arguments regarding the *de novo* creation of property rights in separated biomaterials.

3   Bodies, Biomaterials, and Law's Boundary-Work

Where do property's (outer) boundaries lie? For the law, property's 'things' require separation from the person.[18] As Douglas says, and we saw in Chapter 5, '[w]hen we ask whether a person, A, can hold property rights in human biological material... we are only concerned with material that is *physically separate* from A'.[19] The underlying rationale is exemplified by Lord Bingham's comments in *R* v. *Bentham*: 'One cannot possess something which is not separate and distinct from oneself. An unsevered hand or finger is part of oneself. Therefore, one cannot possess it... What is possessed must under definition be a thing. A person's hand or fingers are not a thing.'[20] Legally, therefore, separation functions as a normative prerequisite for the creation of property rights.[21] A line is drawn around persons, separating them from the external world of things which lies beyond some presumed bodily limit. The law thus embodies a dichotomy between persons as subjects and things as objects.[22] The subject–object distinction offers a seemingly straightforward and pragmatic way of determining whether biomaterials can be objects of property. Viewing it as normatively weighty achieves a particular purpose vis-à-vis property claims. It renders the person (and their body) external to the realm of property, while simultaneously allowing that property rights could exist in biomaterials once separated from the body.

Both the appeal to a person–thing/subject–object dichotomy and its supposed normative work is evident in the positions of numerous commentators. Consider the following:

> There may be a logical problem in saying that we own ourselves. That is, there needs to be a clear separation between 'the owner' and 'the owned'. We can only say we own our bodies if we see a clear distinction between 'us' and 'our bodies'.[23]
>
> Jonathan Herring and P.-L. Chau

---

[18] See Chapter 5, Section 2.1.

[19] Douglas, 'Property rights in human biological material', p. 96 [emphasis added].

[20] *Bentham* at [8].   [21] See chapters 3 and 4.

[22] M. Davies and N. Naffine, *Are Persons Property? Legal Debates about Property and Personality* (Aldershot: Ashgate, 2001), p. 185.

[23] J. Herring and P.-L. Chau, 'My body, your body, our bodies' (2007) 15 *Medical Law Review* 34, 43.

... there must be an owner and there must be something owned, and these two cannot be the same thing.[24]

James Penner

... property requires the notion of thing, and the notion of thing requires separation from self.[25]

Margaret Jane Radin

[P]rivacy theory entitles the body to protection as the physical embodiment of a person, the subject of a privacy interest, whereas property theory reduces the body to a mere object of ownership. . . The distinction lies in the boundary that divides persons from things and subjects from objects.[26]

Radhika Rao

After separation, the necessary distancing between human source and owned object. . . would be present, so there would be no conceptual difficulty in implementing the principle [that the person be considered the owner of the separated part].[27]

James W. Harris

Only those 'things' in the world which are contingently associated with any particular owner may be the objects of property; as a function of the nature of this contingency, in theory nothing of normative consequence beyond the fact that the ownership has changed occurs when an object is alienated to another.[28]

James Penner ('separability thesis')

Although not always explicitly drawn out, each of these commentators takes the *physical* space that separates persons from things as delimiting the *conceptual* and *moral* space that property occupies. Within this we can detect three elements – ontological, moral, and legal – regarding the types of 'things' which can be governed by property (rights). The supposed *ontological* boundary between persons and things takes on a *moral* significance, which, for them, both explains and justifies the structure of certain legal categories and rules. Thus, only those objects which are separate from persons can fall within the ambit of property.

While it seems intuitive that upon removal separated biomaterials cross, as Radin puts it, 'some perceptible boundary',[29] separation and

---

[24] Penner, *Idea of Property*, p. 124.
[25] M.J. Radin, *Reinterpreting Property* (Chicago: University of Chicago Press, 1993), p. 41.
[26] R. Rao, 'Property, privacy, and the human body' (2000) 80 *Boston University Law Review* 359, 455.
[27] Harris, *Property and Justice*, p. 353.   [28] Penner, *Idea of Property*, p. 112.
[29] Radin, *Reinterpreting Property*, p. 41.

the normative consequences which (ought to) flow from it are not entirely clear-cut. Neither is it obvious what the normative significance of 'distancing', 'contingency', or 'separability' ought to be when it comes to persons, bodies, and biomaterials. As we are about to see, the substantive, yet problematic, assumption underlying these positions is that the relevant divide between persons and the external world of things is both ontologically sound and morally significant. As Klaus Hoeyer says, 'technologies using and engaging with "the human body" challenge ideas about body boundaries... [these] are not given and never have been – they are under constant establishment, biologically as well as culturally'.[30] To illustrate, we let us consider two examples: (1) organs and other biomaterials and (2) implanted medical devices. These are illuminating because they draw out the bi-directional nature of the challenges at issue; that is, in the biotechnological world biomaterials and objects move *out of* and *into* the body. Each is also useful in highlighting the boundary-work which takes place within debates regarding biomaterials.[31] By reflecting on the diverse ways in which biotechnological advances challenge our conceptions of the body and the bodily boundary, ambiguities are revealed and we are prompted to confront any moral conclusions which are dependent on such boundaries.

[30] K. Hoeyer, *Exchanging Human Bodily Material: Rethinking Bodies and Markets* (Dordrecht: Springer, 2013), p. vi.

[31] The term 'boundary-work' has its intellectual antecedence in research regarding the problem of demarcating science from non-science. See T.F. Gieryn, *Cultural Boundaries of Science* (Chicago: University of Chicago Press, 1999), p. 27; T.F. Gieryn, 'Boundary-work and the demarcation of science from non-science: strains and interests in professional ideologies of scientists' (1983) 48 *American Sociological Review* 781; M. Lamont and V. Molnar, 'The study of boundaries in the social sciences' (2002) 28 *Annual Review of Sociology* 167. This term can also be used in other ways; for instance, Stephen Wainwright and colleagues discuss how scientists engage in boundary-work which is 'not about differentiating science from non-science, but rather, about drawing boundaries between what is ethically preferable' (S.P. Wainwright, C. Williams, M. Michael, B. Farsides, and A. Cribb, 'Ethical boundary-work in the embryonic stem cell laboratory' (2006) 28 *Sociology of Health and Illness* 732, 739). Here they note that 'the differentiation between science and regulation is itself an accomplishment, partly enacted through boundary-work. The ethical boundary-work that gets done requires *deferral* to non-science – a reversal of Gieryn's formulation where boundary-work serves to *privilege* science' (p. 744). For a recent piece which includes a discussion of boundary-work in the context of health research regulation see S. Taylor-Alexander, E.S. Dove, I. Fletcher, A.G. Mitra, C. McMillan, and G. Laurie 'Beyond regulatory compression: Confronting the liminal spaces of health research regulation' (2017) 8 *Law, Innovation, and Technology* 149.

3.1   Probing Property's Boundaries I: Organs and Other Biomaterials

Advances in medicine and the biosciences mean that a huge variety of biomaterials – from blood to tissue samples to whole organs – are both separable and regularly separated from persons. In this sense, they are very literally only 'contingently associated' with those persons. This is almost entirely a function of advancing technology. The idea of separation or contingency of one's kidney, for example, was moot prior to the existence of the relevant transplantation technology and expertise. Living kidney transplantation has the effect that a kidney, having been part of one person (the donor) and their body, becomes separated. It then becomes part of a different person (the recipient) and their body, having not been so before. The newly transplanted kidney becomes incorporated into (the life of) the recipient.[32] Nevertheless, complications may ensue from the surgery or further down the track. Hence, the kidney remains separable in the sense that it could be removed. It is only contingently associated with the recipient. The fact that the kidney originally resided in one particular person does not affect the fact either of its separability or contingency qua physical separation.[33]

Transplant surgery thus offers a tangible challenge to the subject–object dichotomy and thus to the boundaries constructed within the

---

[32]   Having said this, I am mindful of Shildrick who reminds us that 'the DNA of transplanted material remains unchanged in its new location to the extent that the receiving body perceives it for life as non-self material that should be ejected. Although very high doses of immuno-suppressant drugs may damp down that biological reaction, it remains the case that the "new" organ will never be less than alien, while at the same time providing the *sine qua non* of the self that attempts to reject it' ('Corporeal cuts: Surgery and the psycho-social' (2008) 14 *Body and Society* 31, 40).

[33]   These points are not necessarily at odds with broad thrust of, for instance, Penner's position. He says that if 'science proves capable of disconnecting an organ so that one remains essentially the same person, as is the case with a kidney, we can regard such an organ as a contingent material possession, and therefore one's property' (*Idea of Property*, p. 122). He does not deny that body parts *could* be property. Yet in saying this he moves the goalposts for assessing whether they could in fact be so. The relevant criterion becomes not just about physical separation *tout court*, but the *effect on the person* of the removal of a particular body part.

Elsewhere I have questioned how we should best interpret this. Is it a *personality-affecting* claim, such that property rights are disallowed if constituent parts of a person's personality (emotions, desires, preferences, and so on) change? Or is it a *personhood-affecting* claim? This would be something like the claim that we ought not to regard organs (and other biomaterials) as contingent material possessions subject to property rights where their removal affects the source's status as a person. There I suggest that neither of these is particularly germane to the property question (Quigley, 'Property in human biomaterials', 675–679).

law. Organs which were once an integral part of one subject become separated objects in the external world, only once again to become a fundamental part of another person. Given this, the line in the sand which the subject–object divide represents is shifting and not clear-cut.

This is also the case outwith the transplant context; for instance, biomaterials removed and used for research and other purposes. On these occasions, materials are removed and by crossing the bodily boundary become objects of research entangled in the institutional complex within which such research takes place. Many biomaterials will remain objects in the external world, but not all will. Recall from Chapter 1, Brazier's analysis of humans as medicines. There we noted that persons are no longer mere end-users of medicine, but potential sources and purveyors of it. As Brazier argues, there are ever increasing and 'diverse means by which we ourselves may be used as medicine'.[34] When persons' cells are used to develop and then form part of treatments for particular illnesses (e.g. stem cell therapies), the biomaterials transgress the disputed subject–object dichotomy. In essence, they display a subject–object–subject transitivity as they go from person to research laboratory to clinic and back to other persons.

One response to the foregoing would be to claim that it is an error to talk about the contingency of things, because it is actually the contingency of rights which are at issue.[35] Yet, at least for some commentators, the contingency of the rights themselves is *premised on* the physical separability of the biomaterials from the person. Property rights are those rights which contain the requisite level of contingency; that is, rights regarding things that can be separated (or are separate) from persons. The significance of physical separation is evident in the comments of several authors quoted earlier. Consider these again: 'we are only concerned with material that is *physically separate* from A'[36]; 'the idea of property seems to require some perceptible boundary, at least insofar as the notion of thing requires

---

[34] Brazier, 'Human(s) as medicine(s)', p. 188.

[35] One person who potentially thinks this is Wall. However, this has to be read into his arguments as he does not state it directly. He reminds us that property is about rights and not things and thinks that critiques such as the ones just offered misunderstand the direction and nature of the contingency in question. On this he says: 'It is not that our personalities depend on non-contingent rights (so that the deprivation of a non-contingent right is a drastic event for our "personalities" or "status as persons"). Rather, the existence of non-contingent rights is dependent on the rights-holder (so that the change in the rights-holder would be fatal to the existence and content of the right)' (Wall, *Being and Owning*, pp. 127–128).

[36] Douglas, 'Property rights in human biological material', p. 96 [emphasis added].

separation from self[37]; '[a]fter separation, the necessary distancing between human source and owned object. . . would be present';[38] and '[o]nly those "things" in the world which are contingently associated with any particular owner may be the objects of property'.[39] In all of these, the presumed (meta) physical space between persons and things, subjects and objects, is the (moral) divide upon which legal property rights are premised. Although claims about rights may flow from this, they clearly embody commitments about physical things themselves.[40]

Leaving this aside, rights are central and one argument in this respect is that the character of rights qua property rights is relevantly different to other sorts of rights which persons might hold. Specifically, property rights contain an element of *contingency* that other rights do not. According to Penner:

> What distinguishes a property right is not just that they are contingently ours, *but that they might just as well have been someone else's.* . . The contingency of our connection to particular items of property is such that, in theory, there is nothing special about *my* ownership of [for example] a particular car – the relationship the next owner will have to it is essentially identical.[41]

Further, he says that, in order to determine whether property rights can arise, we need simply ask, 'does a different person who takes on the relationship to the thing stand in essentially the same position as the first person?'[42] Similarly, and adopting Penner, Wall says that 'if a subsequent rights-holder is able to stand in "the same position" with regards to the object or resource as the original rights-holder, then the relationship between the original rights-holder and the object or resource is a contingent relationship'.[43]

Establishing such contingency in relation to human biomaterials is largely unproblematic. Third parties regularly come to stand in the same position as the first person (the source). Medical and biotechnological innovation means that it is not only possible, but an everyday occurrence that many of our biomaterials and even whole organs 'might just as well

---

[37] Radin, *Reinterpreting Property*, p. 41.   [38] Harris, *Property and Justice*, p. 353.
[39] Penner, *Idea of Property*, p. 112.
[40] Indeed, for Penner, the alternative name for his separability thesis is 'the "thinghood" of property' (*ibid.*). That this is his position cannot be in doubt since one of his main objectives is to make the case that 'things' are central to our understanding of property, such that property rights are rights regarding (separated) *things*.
[41] Penn *Ibid.* [emphasis in original].   [42] *Ibid.*, p. 114.
[43] Wall, *Being and Owning*, p. 126.

be someone else's'. This, as we saw, is the entire crux of transplantation.[44] Kidney recipients come to stand in the same position to the kidney as their donors in a number of ways, including the rights which persons have over the organs in question. Organ recipients acquire all the rights of use and control formerly held by the donor. As such, the recipient has essentially the same relationship qua rights, powers, and so on that the donor had; they are now the person with the ultimate rights of use and control regarding the kidney.[45]

In a similar manner, biomaterials which may be used for other purposes, such as for carrying out biomedical tests or research, are only contingently associated with their source. Although, in these cases, those acquiring the biomaterials do not take on the same functional relationship, they do gain the associated rights of use and control. Some or all of those rights which originally attached to the source, now attach to some other person or institution. In these cases the rights themselves are separable from their original holders and can, therefore, be viewed as only being contingent in nature.

Does this mean that we should view *all* rights over biomaterials as contingent and, therefore, as property rights? Wall thinks not. He contends that, unlike the rights we hold as embodied self-owners (to wit, rights of bodily integrity and privacy), the rights which we have regarding our separated biomaterials – like the materials themselves – can be ambiguous.[46] For him, this is because, even after separation, biomaterials may continue to be tied to a person's subjectivity (that is, their lived experience).[47] He says:

> Where the bodily material continues to be unified with the body in terms of a person's task, the bodily material remains functionally equivalent to the body. . . Alternatively, where the bodily material is no longer 'directed towards an existing or possible task' it becomes like any other object in the world, and has only a 'mechanical' or 'instrumental' relationship with the progenitor.[48]

For example, the purpose of storing the sperm for the men in *Yearworth* was to use it in the future should they need to. Here, the sperm can be

---

[44] See also Quigley, 'Property in human biomaterials', pp. 673–675.   [45] *Ibid.*, p. 678.

[46] Wall, *Being and Owning*, p. 186.

[47] As explained by Carolyn Ellis and Michael Flaherty, subjectivity refers to 'human lived experience and the physical, political, and historical context of that experience' (*Investigating Subjectivity: Research on Lived Experience* (London: Sage Publications, 1992), p. 1).

[48] Wall, *Being and Owning*, p. 188. His account draws strongly on phenomenological perspectives, especially that of Maurice Merleau-Ponty. There is not space here to do full justice to his account, but see, in particular, Ch. 2 of *Being and Owning*.

viewed as retaining 'functional unity' with the men's bodies.[49] The sperm when stored continued to be bound to the men's subjectivity. By contrast, if the men had purposefully donated their sperm for research, no such functional unity would be present. Hence, even with respect to the same materials the subject–object dichotomy is not always clear-cut. There are occasions when the boundaries are blurred: 'the bodily material may be a mere object. . . or may be an expression, extension, or representation of the person's subjectivity'.[50]

How does this relate to the idea of non-contingent rights and indeed what counts as a non-contingent right? For Wall, rights over materials which retain a functional unity with the body or are part of a person's subjectivity are non-contingent. On this view, rights over the sperm in *Yearworth* ought to have been viewed as non-contingent because their purpose was to enable preferences and choices which were necessarily tied to the men as persons:

> Property rights are contingent rights since they protect preferences and choices that have no particular relationship with the rights-holder. . . Where there are no normative consequences (beyond mere allocative consequences) following the change in rights-holder then such rights will be contingent rights. . . Our property rights are rights that can exist independently of us.[51]

Although attractive, these criteria are not unproblematic. Rather than giving us clear criteria from which to draw a line between property and other rights, instead they may call any such line into further question.

First, people may have 'particular' relationships with any number of our common or garden chattels. Consider Margaret Radin's example of a wedding ring. She argues that while a ring might be fungible property to a jewellery shop owner, it is more than that for someone who subsequently buys it and makes it their wedding ring.[52] Such objects can be 'integral to

---

[49] *Ibid.*, p. 77. Note that Wall calls the relationship which the men had with their sperm an 'ownership' one, even though he denies that property law was appropriate in the case. This is because, as noted in Chapter 6, he views 'ownership' as a functional, not a legal, relationship. As I argued there, using the terminology of ownership in this way is confusing and arguably not representative of the legal landscape. See Chapter 6, Section 5. We briefly met the idea of functional unity in Chapter 4, where we saw it was considered in *Yearworth*, but rejected as the basis of a personal injury claim (thus itself rejecting the approach taken in a German Bundesgerichtshof case). See Chapter 4, note 5 and accompanying text.

[50] Wall, *Being and Owning*, p. 190.   [51] *Ibid.*, p. 138.

[52] Radin, *Reinterpreting Property*, p. 54.

personal continuity' and constitutive of their personhood, part of their subjectivity.[53] Thus, where those objects which are external by nature become integral to the constitution of the internal self, the boundaries between persons and things becomes blurred.[54] We can think of other instances where this might also be the case; sculptures, paintings, and other works of art perhaps. Artists often put considerable time, effort, and creativity into such pieces. They view the process as quite literally putting themselves into their work. Artwork, therefore, is in some sense 'an expression, extension, or representation of the person's subjectivity'.

Second, there can very clearly be 'normative consequences' beyond mere allocative ones when we transfer ownership or property rights in extra-personal objects (where the property-status is not ordinarily in question). There are normative implications beyond mere allocation when a person has to pawn their wedding ring or sell their most personal piece of art because they need the money. To do so may feel like an injury to them as persons. The preferences and choices they have with regards to those objects are 'particular' to the original wedding ring owner and artist in a way that they cannot be to the pawnbroker or art dealer. Other transfers may have different normative consequences. Forced repossessions of houses, for example, may lead to homelessness where the person has nowhere to go and no safety net.[55] As Harris noted, property is often a mode of wealth distribution. Where property and contract go hand in hand (as we will see in the next chapter) property takes on the dual function of governing the use of things and allocating items of social wealth.[56] As such, there can be very tangible consequences of transfers of the objects and the associated property rights.

My purpose here is not to argue that there are no differences between property rights and other types of rights. Instead it is to draw attention to law's boundary-work regarding bodies, biomaterials, and property rights, and to highlight some philosophical difficulties with the legal rationales underpinning the construction of these boundaries. While we can accept that there are contingency or separation requirements built into the structure of the legal rules (delineating personal from property rights),

---

[53] *Ibid.*, p. 198.
[54] She uses this insight to argue that property can be conceived of as being on a continuum of *fungible* to *personal*. This reliance on the blurring of the subject–dichotomy is somewhat at odds with her statement that the notion of property requires a perceptible boundary.
[55] Quigley, 'Property in human biomaterials', pp. 676–677.
[56] Harris, *Property and Justice*, p. 50.

we need not accept these as being based on an *immutable* ontological or moral reality. In essence the ontological foundations of property law are rendered uncertain by advancing (bio)technologies, something which is further illustrated when we consider implanted medical devices.

3.2   Probing Property's Boundaries II: Everyday Cyborgs

Contemporary biomedicine has made possible both the removal of diseased (and even non-diseased) body parts, as well as the implantation of replacement parts and devices. These replacements range from the simple to the extraordinarily complex; for example, artificial joint replacements, and implanted devices such as pacemakers, internal cardioverter defibrillators (ICDs) (devices which emit an electric shock to restore the heart to its normal rhythm), and the total artificial heart. These parts and devices may be completely artificial, biological, or biohybrid in nature (a mixture of biological and synthetic components). Gill Haddow and colleagues use the term 'everyday cyborg' to describe such linking of the organic, biological person with synthetic, inorganic parts and devices.[57] They conceptualise the 'everyday cyborg' as one where 'modifications are required that quite literally become part of a person and that are automated and beyond individual autonomy'.[58] It is this transgressing of the bodily boundary and the incorporation of these once-external devices which challenges the usual divide between subject and object. Consider the following four ways in which implanted devices can become incorporated into (the lives of) persons: (1) physical internalisation, (2) functional integration, (3) psychological constitution, and (4) phenomenological assimilation (or dissimilation).

Metal hips or knees, heart valves, pacemakers, ICDs, and so on all require surgical procedures to place them inside the body. Although the bodily boundary is broken during these procedures, the wounds heal, rendering these parts and devices internal. In this manner, they are

---

[57] G. Haddow, E. King, I. Kunkler, and D. McLaren, 'Cyborgs in the everyday: Masculinity and biosensing prostate cancer' (2015) 24 *Science as Culture* 484, 486.

[58] *Ibid.*, p. 490. This draws on the original concept of the cyborg as postulated by Clynes and Kline (M.E. Clynes and N.D. Kline, 'Cyborgs and space' (1960) September *Astronautics* 26. There is a wealth of cyborg literature, particularly within science and technology studies, which there is not the space to set out here. However, see D. Haraway, 'A Cyborg Manifesto: Science, Technology, and Socialist-Feminism in the late Twentieth Century' in *Simians, Cyborgs and Women: The Reinvention of Nature* (New York: Routledge, 1991), pp. 149–181. For a discussion of this and other cyborg literature, see Haddow *et al.*, 'Cyborgs in the everyday', 486–490.

literally incorporated into the person. Beyond mere physical internalisation, however, implanted devices are crucial to the functioning of the everyday cyborg. Persons receive these devices when some part of them does not function as it should; for example, hip or knee replacements for osteoarthritis which causes them pain and limits their movement, metal or tissue heart valves when their original ones become 'leaky', and pacemakers when the electrical activity in their hearts becomes disordered or disrupted.

Significantly, the functionality of some implanted devices – such as heart valves, pacemakers, and ICDs – is essential to the recipients' continued existence. Without them the everyday cyborg could not live. Take, for instance, cases of severe aortic stenosis. Here a person's aortic valve in the heart becomes narrowed and the cusps of the valve cannot open and close properly. In its severe form, this can lead to heart failure. Without a replacement valve the heart failure may worsen and become life threatening. Consider also ICDs. When the everyday cyborg's heart beat becomes disordered, an ICD will emit an electric shock which can restore the heart to its normal rhythm. Again, such devices become constitutive of the person's (very capacity for) personhood. Implanted devices, therefore, represent a very tangible (and vital) integration of subject and object. The breaking and remaking of the bodily boundary and these modes of incorporation matter, because they challenge, as Shildrick puts it, 'the fundamental socio-cultural belief in the fixity of corporeal boundaries'.[59]

It goes beyond the purely corporeal, however. Implanted devices can also become psychologically incorporated into persons. They can affect a person's sense of self and identity, becoming part of their narrative about themselves and their lives. This conceptualisation fits with what Haddow calls the 'Triad of I'.[60] The triad comprises image, integrity, and identity. It is a way of thinking about how implanted technologies can affect and disrupt the lives of the everyday cyborg.[61] Image is about the potential disruption of a person's body image. Integrity is deeper and corresponds to the lack of control that the person has over the implanted device. Identity reflects the changes which may occur to the everyday cyborg's sense of self and how the device may (or may not) become integral to this.[62]

---

[59] Shildrick, 'Corporeal cuts', 34.
[60] G. Haddow, *Embodiment and the Everyday Cyborg: Technologies and Altered Subjectivites* (Manchester: Manchester University Press, forthcoming).
[61] Haddow mainly focuses on internal cardioverter defibrillators, but the triad works equally well in thinking about other devices.
[62] See, for instance, Shildrick's comments relating to identity in the context of heart transplantation ('Contesting normative embodiment'). See also M. Shildrick, P.

The Triad of I and incorporation through psychological constitution are related to the fourth mode of incorporation which I posit here, that of phenomenological assimilation or dissimilation. Hoeyer notes, '[t]he body is the phenomenological category par excellence';[63] that is, the body is the site of our experiences (or at least that through which they are mediated). By extension, that which becomes part of us, physically or psychologically, may affect these experiences. We may, for example, be aware of our artificial knee because there is a stiffness present that was not there before (despite the pain of the osteoarthritis being absent). The everyday cyborg's experiences may even be stark and painful; for example, when their ICD emits an electric shock without warning.[64] Conversely, there may be a lack of experience. Once the wounds of the flesh heal, we may lack awareness of implanted parts.

The everyday cyborg illustrates how advancing biotechnology presents challenges for the law. The property-status of implanted devices at least prior to implantation is not contested. They are chattels which exist in the external world which are transferred, traded, and protected via personal property law. If, however, only objects which are separate from persons can be property, what happens to these devices, conceptually, morally, and legally speaking upon implantation? As the focus of this book is on biomaterials which become separated from persons, there is not space to fully explore that question here. Nevertheless, the imagery and actuality of the everyday cyborg gives us a way of understanding the blurring of the subject–object boundary which may occur. It helps us to understand the different modes in which such devices become *incorporated into* (the lives of) persons. Once external objects can become part of us: physically, functionally, psychologically, and phenomenologically. As a consequence, these objects become bound up with persons and the boundary between these becomes blurred. This is especially so where the object in question becomes intimately connected to our functioning as persons, as in the case of pacemakers or ICDs. In such cases once external objects are (or become) constitutive of (or at the very least conducive to) our lives as persons.[65] We, therefore, have good reason to reassess the supposed

---

McKeever, S. Abbey, J. Poole, and H. Ross, 'Troubling dimensions of heart transplantation' (2009) 35 *Medical Humanities* 35.

[63] Hoeyer, *Exchanging Human Bodily Material*, p. 67.

[64] G. Haddow, S.H.E. Harmon, and L. Gilman, 'Implantable Smart Technologies (IST): Defining the 'Sting' in Data and Device' (2016) 24 Health Care Analysis 210, 215.

[65] This account has resonances with Radin's property-for-personhood approach. For her, certain items such as wedding rings and a person's home can be constitutive of their

ontological boundary between subjects and objects; that is, between persons and things.

The conclusion to be drawn from all of this is twofold. First, even though the separation between persons and the external world of things is intuitively appealing, it is not as easy as it first appears to draw a bright line between persons as subjects and things as objects. Shildrick argues that '[t]he body, no less than the self, is a construction in process, and although open to deliberative transformation, it does not necessarily change or develop in predictable ways'.[66] This (re)making of the body and self through medical and biotechnological advances challenges, and will continue to challenge, the boundary which the law has constructed between persons as subject and things as objects (in the external world). Second, if the posited separation between subject and object is blurred, then the philosophical basis for the current legal rationale becomes uncertain. Hence, we ought not to mistake the structure of our legal rules (e.g. differentiating personal from property rights) as deriving from an ever-fixed ontological or moral reality. If this is correct, there is a justificatory challenge for the law. What is the (justified moral) basis for the creation and subsequent allocation of property rights in separated materials? The answer, posited earlier in the chapter, is

personhood and so should garner greater legal protections qua property. She draws on Hegel who considered the acquisition of property to be essential for moral development as a person. Radin argues that, if the Hegelian idea of the actualisation of the will through the possession of and use objects external to the self is taken seriously, then the dichotomy between subjects and objects breaks down since these objects can become constitutive of personhood. Thus, where those objects which are external by nature become integral to the constitution of the internal self, the boundaries between persons and things becomes blurred (*Reinterpreting Property*, pp. 195–196).

For an account relating to biomaterials which is overtly Hegelian see Wall, *Being and Owning*, pp. 50–52 and 128–131. There he builds on what he calls the Hegelian blur to make a case for entitlements in biomaterials: 'A Hegelian basis for entitlements in bodily material would suggest that: (i) where the bodily material acquires an attribute that can only be explained "in terms of the working will"; and (ii) where that attribute introduces an intended state of affairs; (iii) entitlements in the material may arise because the will (or subjectivity) of the individual needs to be expressed through the engagement with the external and physical world' (p. 51).

The blurring of the boundaries between persons and things which I have pointed to is not Hegelian, it is more tangible in nature and occurs directly as a consequence of biotechnological developments. My purpose is also different. I do not point to the blurred boundaries to construct a theory of entitlements, but to challenge the philosophical basis for an ingrained doctrinal position. Indeed, as we saw at the beginning of this section, Radin who herself challenges the subject–object dichotomy, holds on to it for certain purposes: 'property requires the notion of thing, and the notion of thing requires separation from self' (*Reinterpreting Property*, p. 41).

[66] Shildrick, 'Corporeal cuts', 42.

that the initial justification for doing so is grounded in our pre-existing moral rights prior to separation; that is, our self-ownership.

Before concluding this chapter, I turn to examine one further alternative which could potentially provide the moral foundations for the ascription of source property rights in separated biomaterials: labour-based reasoning.

4   Biomaterials as the Fruits of Our Labour?

In Chapter 4 I examined labour, in the form of the work/skill exception, as a basis for *third party* acquisition of property rights in separated biomaterials. There we saw that if it is explanatory, then it is only weakly so and operates post hoc. We also saw that as a justification it is unpersuasive. Further, even if we were to accept that labouring does the moral work some expect of it, we are still left with a major problem with regards to third party acquisition. Morally speaking, the application of labour is not a means to acquire items already owned by someone else. Labouring is supposed to be a means of original acquisition; that is, a way of acquiring title in previously *unowned* things. As such, if biomaterials are already owned by their source, appeals to labouring by third parties become redundant. Distinct from this, however, is the question of *source* property rights, since any such rights would come prior to considerations regarding third party acquisition. Labour, therefore, is potentially relevant to source rights, even if not to third party ones.[67]

A preliminary point to note is that a source labour-based analysis could be construed as compatible with the decision in *Yearworth*. Consider some elements which were emphasised by their Lordships in the case. While they took the negative control bestowed upon the men by the HFE Act as indicative of their property rights, they also noted that the claim relates to 'products of a living human body intended for use by the persons *whose bodies have generated them*'.[68] They state: 'By their bodies, [the men] alone generated and ejaculated the sperm'.[69] This wording has some resonance with neo-Lockean natural rights views of property.[70]

---

[67] In examining this, I do not attempt to answer the larger question of whether labour-mixture is a legitimate general strategy for justifying the creation of property rights in external resources. Instead I focus on whether bodily labour is relevant or necessary to bestow title regarding separated biomaterials upon their source.

[68] *Yearworth* at [45] [emphasis added]. Here they explicitly note that they are not being asked to take a view on products that might be used by third parties.

[69] *Ibid.*   [70] See Quigley, 'Property: The future of human tissue?', 461.

Under such an approach our biomaterials would be regarded as the fruits of our labour and our ownership of them would be thus justified. It is likely correct, as Harmon and Laurie argue, that the 'moral or conceptual foundations' would have been given scant attention by their Lordships in reaching their decision.[71] But even so, a labour theory undercurrent is discernible, whether intentional or not.

Utilising labour-based reasoning may be an attractive *analytical* path for those who wish to claim that persons have property rights in their separated materials. Consider, for instance, Hillel Steiner's position. He is a proponent of self-ownership and advocates general property rights in biomaterials:

> Our bodies are factories. They produce things like blood, skin, hair, etc. Self-ownership gives us the titles to these and protects our liberty to dispose of them, just as it does in the case of our non-renewable types of tissue... Similarly, our bodies produce energy. They convert body tissue into energy, some of which gets expended in our acting. A good deal of this expended energy is simply abandoned by us in the course of this acting... Other portions of our expended energy are infused into parts of the external environment, transforming their features in various ways. Sometimes we claim these things for ourselves as the *fruits of our labour*.[72]

When Steiner says that 'our bodies are factories' we might think that he is simply employing an evocative metaphor, rather than literally invoking labour-based reasoning as the justification for how we come to have title in our biomaterials. This, however, is not the case. For him, labour and bodily ownership are intertwined in a continuous cycle: we use our labour to

---

[71] Harmon and Laurie, 'Property, principles, precedents, and paradigms', 485. Drawing on Jeremy Bentham, they also maintain that in appealing to natural rights such an approach would be 'nonsense upon stilts'. They take this view because they identify such reasoning with theological natural rights claims. They say, 'the natural rights approach views the earth as granted res communis to all humankind by God, and considers that unclaimed material combined with labour gives rise to individual ownership' (485). However, one does not need to rely on the theological version of Locke to see that the wording of the *Yearworth* decision could be seen as stemming from a 'fruits of their labour' type reasoning, as we are about to see. For Bentham's views see J. Bentham, 'Anarchical fallacies' in J. Waldron (ed.), *Nonsense Upon Stilts: Bentham, Burke, and Marx on the Rights of Man* (London: Methuen, 1987), pp. 46–76.

Interestingly, Wall attributes a more Hegelian tenor to this case, saying that '(i) the semen acquired an attribute "which can only be explained in terms of the working will" and (ii) the semen enables an intended state of affairs that would otherwise not exist without the object, the men own the semen since (iii) the will (for genetic parenthood) can only be manifest through the use of the semen' (*Being and Owning*, p. 52, note omitted).

[72] Steiner, *Essay on Rights*, p. 233 [emphasis added].

obtain the things we need to nourish our bodies; this gives us ownership of those bodies and bodily materials, which in turn enables us to produce more labour. This is illustrated in the following example which he gives:

> I own the oranges sold to me by my grocer. And I own the orange juice I make from them with my juicemaking machine and the electricity I have paid for. If I use that orange juice, along with other ingredients and instruments which I own to make a cake, then I own that cake. If, instead, I drink the juice then I own the resultant body tissue which is the joint product of the juice and other bodily ingredients which I own. And I further own one of the main products of that body: namely its labour.[73]

We can see that this exposition, with its focus on the body as producer of the materials, has parallels with the reasoning in *Yearworth*. It is a fruits-of-our-labour claim and contains a two-step parallel claim: first, a person's bodily materials are the fruits of their labour and, second, labour-mixture is the mode by which self-owners gain property rights over things in the external world.[74] These two things are related since the energy produced by our bodies is simultaneously being consumed maintaining our bodies and producing new materials, as well as being expended on the world around us as we go about our everyday activities. Since persons have to expend labour in order to acquire the food that nourishes them then the formation of a person's various bodily materials (cells, tissues, fluids, and so on), on Steiner's view, counts as the fruits of their labour.

One might object to this line of reasoning by arguing that we do not in fact labour to create our bodies and biomaterials. This is Donna Dickenson's view. She says that on Lockean-derived positions, 'we do not have a property in that which we have *not* laboured to create' and 'we do not own bodies because we have not worked to make them'.[75] We can

---

[73] H. Steiner, 'The fruits of bodybuilders' labour' in A. Dyson and J. Harris (eds), *Ethics and Biotechnology* (London: Routledge, 1996), pp. 64–78, p. 66. My thanks to Hillel for discussion of his position over email and for helping to clarify my thoughts with regards to it.

[74] Self-ownership, for Steiner, is one of two original rights held by all persons; the second being the right to an equal portion of the world's raw natural resources. These rights are 'original' in the sense that they represent 'our initial domains – our initial allotted action-spaces' (Steiner, *Essay on Rights*, p. 229). In other words, our legitimate sphere of action is carved out by the scope of our self-ownership, as well as our entitlements to things in the external world. The corollary of this, unsurprisingly, is that any such entitlements are constrained by the rights of other self-owners, including their rights to their fair share of external resources. A substantive focus of Steiner's arguments is in tracing the path from self-ownership to ownership of external things. This, as noted in the previous chapter, is a central part of the libertarian project (right and left) (see Chapter 7, Section 1).

[75] Dickenson, *Property in the Body*, p. 35. See also pp. 40–41.

see why she says this. Given that our bodily processes are largely unconscious, it is questionable whether they count as labour in any morally relevant sense. At the cellular level, or even the level of entire systems of organs, we do not exert conscious effort or work. In the main our bodies do what they do and we are unaware of the processes involved. Cell turnover, hormone production, digestion, breathing, the beating of our hearts, and so on are all largely automatic and reflexive. As such, we do not labour simply by *being*.

Dickenson does, however, argue for a limited exception: extracted ova, drawing a distinction between ordinary bodily processes and the intentional, effortful labour required to produce extracted ova. Unlike ordinary bodily processes, ova extraction involves a great deal of effortful labour. The woman is required to undergo a surgical procedure to remove multiple ova which have been produced after the administration of medication to hyperstimulate her ovaries, all of which produces not insignificant risks and physical side-effects.[76] She thus maintains that women ought to be recognised as having property rights in these:

> These ova are not mere waste or abandoned tissue: they are extracted, in multiple and unnatural quantities, through laborious and risky procedures. Put more properly in the active rather than the passive voice, women labour to produce extracted ova, in the purposeful manner characterising the sort of labour that grounds property rights in Locke.[77]

Nevertheless, it is not entirely clear what labouring amounts to in a Lockean sense. Some of the examples Locke himself offered seem only to involve labour in the very loosest of terms; for example, the gathering of acorns and apples from the forest floor, the drawing of a pitcher of water from a fountain, and drinking water from a river.[78] Such activities do not, on the face of it, represent particularly laborious labour. It is evident, however, from the text as a whole that Locke meant something more by labour than simply acting on the world.[79] The crucial aspect of

---

[76] *Ibid.*, pp. 48–51.

[77] *Ibid.*, p. 41. See also D. Dickenson, 'The lady vanishes: What's missing from the stem cell debate' (2006) 3 *Journal of Bioethical Inquiry* 43.

[78] Locke, *Two Treatises*, pp. 288–291. Of course, context may be important here. Perhaps, for example, we might think that there is a relevant difference between just bending down to pick up fallen apples from the forest floor and the effort involved in searching for the best tree and then climbing that tree to gather the apples.

[79] Feasibly, some of Locke's examples (at least without better context) are just not that appropriate or illuminating. As Cohen insisted, 'unless all acting on the world is to be regarded as labouring', then some examples ought not to be viewed as labour (*Self-Ownership*, p. 75).

this is the idea of something being added[80] -the relevant additions to nature being either *effortful* labour or some kind of added *value*.[81] As such, labour cannot be reduced to an entirely passive function of nature. More is required if the idea of labour is to do the requisite moral work.[82] As Dickenson highlights, labour and work (properly so called) are active concepts. They are doings, happenings, undertakings, and so on. They are also conscious and effortful. It is through the exertion involved in labouring that entitlements are created. Given this active account, we might conclude that automatic bodily processes do not count as morally relevant work and are thus incapable of generally justifying property rights in biomaterials. Such a conclusion would be too hasty.

We can see the counter-objection in Steiner's position already set out above: bodily processes, automatic or not, cannot be viewed in isolation. Whilst many bodily processes themselves are unconscious and automatic, we do in fact labour to *maintain* these. We eat food to fuel our bodies, take exercise to maintain our health, and seek out and provide ourselves with shelter. We also go out and labour in our respective jobs in order to afford to buy the food we eat and so on.[83] The analogy drawn by Steiner is with that of a brick-making machine:

> These automatic processes – like those of brick-making machines – require inputs, including labour inputs like chewing food, locating oneself in a non-lethal environment, etc. The automatic process of a brick-making machine is initiated by the labour of pushing a start-button and by the labour of shovelling in some sand and other chemicals. Cells can't be made from nothing: their precursors need to be labour-supplied with nutrients.[84]

---

[80] Locke, *Two Treatises*, p. 288.

[81] Of land, for instance, he talks of tilling, planting, improving, and cultivating, all of which look more like labour understood as entailing effort and/or added value (*ibid.*, p. 290).

[82] Pun intended.   [83] Steiner, 'Fruits of bodybuilders' labour', p. 66.

[84] Steiner, personal communication, 25 February 2015. Note that he also uses the brick-making analogy in his book. There, however, its purpose is to help interrogate the paradox of universal self-ownership (*Essay on Rights*, pp. 237–248). The paradox, as explained by Katherine Curchin, arises from two claims made by libertarians: '(1) that all individuals are (at least originally) self-owners, and (2) that all individuals own the products of their labour. Libertarians hold that these two claims are consistent with each other, and indeed that (2) can be derived from (1). The difficulty in making both these claims simultaneously becomes apparent when we recognise that self-owning individuals appear to be the products of the labour of other individuals – their parents. If we accept that individuals own the products of their labour, it would follow that parents own their children. The ownership of some persons by others appears to directly contradict the first claim that all individuals are (at least originally) self-owners' (K. Curchin, 'Evading the paradox of universal self-ownership' (2007) 15 *Journal of Political Philosophy*

This wider 'labour-supplied' view of our bodies and bodily materials is certainly plausible. On such a view it is not obvious how significantly different labour expended acquiring the goods which sustain and nourish us is to the labouring involved in having injections to hyperstimulate the ovaries. Both involve intentional effort, albeit of different varieties. It is also not clear, as Dickenson argues, that we might have a 'spectrum of property rights [encompassing a range of biomaterials] based on the criteria for agency, intentionality, labour, and risk-taking'.[85]

Focusing only on immediate or proximate causes of risk and discomfort – such as that involved in ova extraction or donations to a biobank – disregards the wider labour-supplied context in which embodied persons are situated. Although we might think that going to our local supermarket to buy the food to nourish our bodies does not seem particularly laborious, most people will in fact have laboured to acquire the means by which to do this. Some of the ways in which this is done involve the risk and discomfort of hard physical labour. Think, for example, of construction or cleaning work, or of traditional farmers who actively tend to their livestock and plants which they keep for food. This may be in gruelling and harsh conditions, depending on which part of the world the farmer lives in. If discomfort and risk are key, then on a Dickenson-type, labour-derived account they ought to be viewed as having property rights in their bodies. Nevertheless, taking risk and discomfort as the central elements of labouring would be to unnecessarily exclude other sorts of (presumably worthy) labour; for example, that involving skill or time commitments rather than physical or physiological hazards.

Moreover, if, as Dickenson maintains, a person's *agency* is what is significant in understanding why work and labour create entitlements,[86] then we may also be committed to recognising the wider 'labour-supplied' contexts in which this agency operates. At the very least her arguments could be used to support the view that the men in *Yearworth* had labour-derived property rights in their sperm. In making her argument, Dickenson emphasises intentionality and control.[87] Whilst these two elements are clearly present in cases of ova donation, they are also present in cases of sperm preservation. In taking the requisite steps to preserve their sperm, the men displayed both intention and (initial) control over the fate of the

---

484, 484–485). For debate on this, see Steiner and Curchin's pieces just referred too, as well as H. Steiner, 'Universal self-ownership and the fruits of one's labour: A reply to Curchin' (2008) 16 *Journal of Political Philosophy* 350.

[85] Dickenson, *Property in the Body*, p. 118.   [86] *Ibid.*, pp. 35–37

[87] See, for example, *ibid.*, pp. 48, 100, 118, and 123.

samples. Within a general labour-supplied context those acts would be regarded as labour as much as the production of any other biomaterials.[88]

Dickenson's arguments are motivated by a justified disquiet regarding 'the power imbalance between women who "donate" ova and commercial biotechnology companies, stem cell banks, and funded research teams'.[89] It is for this reason that she defends property rights in women's reproductive labour. She sees this as a way to prevent their estrangement from that labour and to make them visible within the context of reproductive research and industry.[90] While this is a legitimate and pressing concern, with seeming explanatory and analytical appeal, there is no easy labour-based line which can be drawn (whether or not it includes risk and discomfort) which would admit extracted ova, but exclude all other bodily materials. On a broad labour-supplied view, we *could*, therefore, be considered as labouring to produce our biomaterials. Nevertheless, appeals to such reasoning are redundant *if* we are already considered to be self-owners.

Labouring, as has already been noted, is a mode of original acquisition; that is, it is a way of justifying the creation and allocation of property rights in resources which are *unowned*. Self-owners already have an open-ended set of use-privileges and control-powers over their embodied selves. This necessarily includes their bodies and biomaterials. The rights in our bodily materials do not, therefore, arise *de novo*. It is our self-ownership which creates title and justifies the allocation. Thus, if biomaterials are already owned, appeals to labouring as generating property rights are not required, whether narrowly or broadly applied. Even on

---

[88] Another reason why we ought to be hesitant about accepting that source labour creates justified property rights only in *selected* biomaterials (i.e. extracted ova) is that it seemingly disregards the labour of others. If labour is morally relevant to property rights in extracted ova, then how ought we to take account of the labouring of those who work at the clinics where the extraction takes place, those who administer the injections, those who do the extractions, those who create stem cell lines from the ova, and so on? Do we see extracted ova as co-produced resources for stem cell science? If the answer is yes, then any property rights must be shared amongst those who expend the labour. One way around this, for those like Dickenson, would be to apply *Bazley*-type reasoning and say that those doing the ova extraction are working as agents of the woman. They labour for her ends whether the ova are being donated for research or stored for future use (for a discussion of *Bazley* see Chapter 4, Section 3.1). Cf. Melinda Cooper and Catherine Waldby's discussion of reproductive labour in the context of regenerative medicine in *Clinical Labor: Tissue Donors and Research Subjects in the Global Bioeconomy* (Durham and London: Duke University Press, 2014), pp. 101–115.

[89] Dickenson, 'The lady vanishes', p. 16.

[90] Dickenson, *Property in the Body*, pp. 41–45 and Ch. 3. This also includes concerns about surrogacy (Ch. 4) and umbilical cord blood donation (Ch. 5).

Steiner's own account, 'fruits of our labour' arguments are not necessary to justify property rights in cells, tissues, organs, and other bodily materials. He says that 'self-ownership is a sufficient basis for creating unencumbered titles to things produced solely from self-owned things'.[91] As such, each person's self-ownership gives them (along with ownership or legitimate acquisition of the materials to nourish their bodies) presumptive title to their biomaterials. Labour (itself a derivative of self-ownership for Steiner) would only be needed to generate (justified) property rights in things which are not previously owned. In the end, therefore, labour-based arguments as applied to the source of biomaterials fall foul of the same general objection as those relating to third party acquisition. For third parties, labour cannot be used to justify the acquisition of biomaterials since they are already owned by the source; whereas for the source, labour-based reasoning is superfluous and, therefore, analytically redundant.

5   Concluding Remarks

Up until relatively recently, premising property rights on the physical separation of the thing from persons raised few difficulties. It is only with scientific and medical advances, which make possible the removal of body parts, organs, and tissues, that this has become an issue. As we have seen throughout this book, it is the conflicts which ensue regarding the use and control of biomaterials which necessitate a re-analysis of the current legal paradigm, as well as its philosophical underpinnings. Prior to these there has been little need for recourse to the law of property for anything other than things in the external world. The consequence of this, as Price has observed, is that legally speaking, the '*conceptual* impossibility of separating a particular thing from the person to whom it belongs is the hallmark of personal as opposed to property rights'.[92] Hence, for the law, property's outer boundaries are to be located at the bodily boundary. A line is drawn around persons which distances them from the external world of things. Difficulties arise when we presume that this legal categorisation has a justified extra-legal ontological and moral basis. Questions are thus raised regarding the normative basis for the creation and subsequent allocation of property rights in separated materials.

In this chapter I rejected both separation and labour-based rationales as either necessary or justified modes for the creation of *de novo* property

---

[91] Steiner, *Essay on Rights*, p. 235.   [92] Price, *Human Tissue*, p. 241 [emphasis added].

rights in separated biomaterials. What we have seen is that biotechnological advances take the separation of biomaterials from the realm of
conceptual impossibility to practical reality. Both biomaterials and rights
over them can exist independently of any particular person. Moreover,
items which unquestionably start life as chattels in the external world can
become integral to a person's life and subjectivity. In this way lines drawn
around persons which are presumed to answer normative questions
become blurred. The consequence of this blurring is that the separation
can no longer do the normative work expected of it.

We also saw that we do not need to invoke labour-based arguments to
reach conclusions about source entitlements over reproductive, or any
other, biomaterials. It is not that labour could not form the justification
for creating *de novo* property rights. It is simply that there is not any *de
novo* creation of such rights taking place. The body and its biomaterials
are not *res nullius*, morally speaking. Hence, any legal property rights
ought not to be conceived of as arising *in virtue of* source labour. Instead
it is the prior connection between embodied self-owners and their separated biomaterials which creates presumptive property rights in those
materials. There is a normative continuity between a person's rights over
themselves, their bodies, and their biomaterials in the embodied state and
those rights which exist upon separation. The initial presumption should,
therefore, be that nothing much changes when biomaterials become
separated from their source. The person (self-owner) remains the source
of control regarding their biomaterials until such time as they waive or
transfer their rights over them. In this vein, the next (and final substantive) chapter examines the issue of the legitimate use and transfer of
biomaterials (and their attendant property rights).

9

Transferring Bodily Property

1 Introduction

When conflicts over human biomaterials arise, determining who has property rights in, or ownership of, these is important. Such a determination is not a trivial matter because in allowing that certain parties can have property rights in, and ownership of, biomaterials, we are granting that they have *control* over those biomaterials. Additionally, in permitting ownership we are also determining who does *not* have rights of use and control over these materials. This becomes apparent when conflicts arise over the use of biomaterials, something we saw in Chapter 3 in relation to the *Moore* and *Greenberg* cases. In *Moore* it was denied that the plaintiff had any property rights in the biomaterials,[1] while in *Greenberg* it was held that any source (property) rights had been extinguished when the tissue samples were voluntarily donated for research.[2] The Court in the latter case saw the source's interests with regards to their biomaterials as ceasing (or being strictly limited) after procurement has taken place. To a certain degree this reasoning is echoed in the later *Catalona* case, which we met in Chapter 1. In classifying the prostate tissue samples as *inter vivos* gifts, the Court accepted that the sources had property in their samples *prior* to donation. But, similar to *Greenberg*, a central issue was whether any proprietary rights were retained after the transfer of the samples. Again, much like in *Greenberg*, the decision of the Court was that no such rights were held by the donors.[3] One issue that was not adequately acknowledged in these cases is that the *initial conditions* under which donations are made will, and indeed ought to, be important. They impact on the legitimacy of the transfer of materials and on their subsequent uses. It is, thus, themes relating to legitimate use and the transfer of bodily materials which thread their way through this final substantive chapter.

---

[1] *Moore*, Supreme Court at 137.   [2] *Greenberg* at 1074–1075.
[3] *Catalona*, Court of Appeals at 673–677.

We can transfer our property rights in numerous ways, such as through abandonment, loans, donations, simple exchanges, or sale. Sometimes this involves the permanent alienation of those rights, and sometimes it may only be temporary. When a person divests themselves of their property rights regarding a particular resource, they are engaging in the ultimate exercise of their use and control. Hence, even though donations, simple exchanges, and sale of biomaterials all represent distinct modes of transfer, essential to each is that they involve the exercise of core property rights. As we have seen throughout this book, biomaterials can be, and indeed regularly are, transferred and alienated in different ways. This chapter examines some of the different modes in which we might transfer our bodily materials, beginning with a defence of the view that, howsoever we transfer them, consent is the means by which this is legitimised. The latter half of the chapter involves an examination of transfer by way of sale. This is because the sale of human biomaterials (by the source) is an especially vexed issue. Objections on this front are usually centred on the possibility that the source might engage in market transactions if they are recognised as having property in their separated biomaterials. Property, however, is not simply (or sometimes at all) about sale. The law of gifts (and thus donations), we will see, is encompassed by the law of property. Importantly, we will also see that sale is not an analytically intrinsic component of property.

2 Consent and Property: Re-orienting the Normative Touchstone

Prior to the current human tissue legislation coming into force, Mason and Laurie asked the question, 'consent or property?'[4] In asking this they draw our attention to the fact that these two frameworks are often dichotomised in debates regarding human tissue. Their conclusion at that time was that a 'properly conceived property model could serve to address many of the issues that currently leave the law and our attitudes to the human body at odds'.[5] Legislators in both England and Scotland did not take such a route and opted instead for consent as the legal (and ethical) benchmark.[6] This,

---

[4] Mason and Laurie, 'Consent or property?' Specifically, they asked this in relation to post-mortem examinations in the aftermath of the organ-retention scandals (although prior to either of the newer Human Tissue Acts).

[5] *Ibid.*, p. 728.

[6] Recall that, although authorisation is the term used in the Scottish Act, I am referring to consent and authorisation collectively as consent. See Chapter 2, Section 3.3.

as we saw in Chapter 2, has left the law in relation to human biomaterials somewhat lacking. Neither the English nor the Scottish Acts give much substance to consent as a guiding principle. The more recent Human Transplantation (Wales) Act fares no better. Interrogating the legislation and the various Codes of Practice reveals little that could substantively answer questions of why consent should be required to use someone's separated biomaterials. There is no definition of consent given in the Acts or the Human Tissue Authority's Codes of Practice. Nothing much is said beyond some well-rehearsed tropes which link consent to the notion of validity (in order to be valid, the consent must be voluntary, informed, and given by someone with capacity). This does not aid us in determining why the consent of the source is required for the use of their separated biomaterials, or, indeed, whether it should be required at all. The law relating to human tissue essentially conflates the consent process with the justification for having such a process in the first place. Consent is presented as an ethical value in and of itself and is insufficiently connected to any principled foundations.[7] The result is free-floating consent, something which cannot adequately protect the gamut of interests that persons might have in respect of their biomaterials. Additionally, as the sperm cases in both the United Kingdom and Australia have demonstrated, something more besides consent is sometimes necessary to resolve novel challenges.

Laurie and colleagues warn that 'we should not be distracted from the property debate by the illusion that consent is the sole, or optimal, ethico-legal solution to the dilemmas thrown up by modern medicine, as many official bodies would have us believe'.[8] Their position is that both models have a role to play in the regulation of human biomaterials: 'consent and property are not mutually exclusive concepts; indeed to the extent that they are both a means of furnishing respect, they should perhaps be made to work together towards a common end'.[9] While I agree with the sentiment behind this statement, my analysis in the previous chapter suggests that we need to go even further. Rather than seeing consent and property as two separate modes of governance, or as two separate frameworks which can guide moral action, we need to reorientate our thinking towards viewing them as two aspects of the same normative story. As we will see below, there are both conceptual and pragmatic reasons for this. Importantly, doing this provides us with a useful and appropriate

---

[7] On this as a general issue in the law see Brownsword, 'The cult of consent' and Chapter 2, Section 4.32.
[8] Laurie, Harmon, and Porter, *Mason and McCall Smith's Law and Medical Ethics*, p. 496.
[9] *Ibid.*, p. 504. See also Mason and Laurie, 'Consent or property', 727.

normative anchor with which to ground consent, as well as to help deal with legal challenges relating to biomaterials.

2.1   Legitimating the Use and Transfer of Biomaterials

When it comes to our biomaterials, consent and property are analytically connected and cannot be easily separated. If the arguments in the previous chapter bear up, one implication is that the usual singular narrative regarding respect for autonomy is not enough to tell the moral or legal story. Specifically, if ownership of separated biomaterials should vest in the source, then consent pertaining to the use of those materials is in part presupposed by the property rights they have in them.[10] If we think about how consent operates this should not be particularly surprising. It is to a certain extent a contextualised notion and, as such, cannot be divorced from the role we want it to play. Our understanding of consent in different situations will be bound up with its function given a particular set of circumstances. As John Kleinig puts it:

> Where called for, consent can sometimes function like a proprietary gate that one opens to allow another's access, access that would be impermissible absent the act of voluntarily opening the gate. Thus, I may consent to another's sexual advance, use of my car, performance of an operative procedure, or dissemination of information concerning myself. Or, sometimes, consent can function like a normative rope whereby one binds oneself to another. Thus, I may consent to another's offer of marriage or request that I give a lecture or join a committee. In each case, whether consent is viewed as opening the gate or as binding oneself, an act or outcome that would not be permissible absent the consent is given *normative sanction.*[11]

It is this idea of normative sanction which is essential to the current enquiry. When it comes to biomaterials, what is it that we are sanctioning? And what happens normatively speaking, be this legally or morally?[12]

---

[10] Deryck Beyleveld and Roger Brownsword argue such a point in relation to the terms of Article 22 of the European Convention on Human Rights and Biomedicine ('My body, my body parts, my property' (2000) 8 *Health Care Analysis* 87).

[11] J. Kleinig, 'The nature of consent' in F.G. Miller and A. Wertheimer (eds), *The Ethics of Consent: Theory and Practice* (Oxford: Oxford University Press, 2010) pp. 3–24, p. 4 [emphasis added].

[12] There are many lovely ways in which the normative question regarding consent has been asked in the literature. I particularly like Hurd's turn of phrase when she examines the 'moral magic of consent', a phrase also picked up by Kleinig. See H.M. Hurd, 'The moral magic of consent' (1996) 2 *Legal Theory* 121.

To answer these questions let us remind ourselves of the analysis of property rights given in Part II of the book. There we saw that our property interests regarding our biomaterials consist of the dual core of the liberty to use the materials and the power to control those uses. When these interests are supplemented by duties of non-interference imposed on all others, we can call them property rights.[13] It is not just the physical samples which are at issue – for example, when individuals donate tissue for research purposes – but the attendant property rights. These rights can be analysed in terms of their Hohfeldian incidents (claims, liberties, powers, and immunities) and their correlatives (duties, no-rights, liabilities, and disabilities). Prior to consenting to donate your tissue samples to the hospital following surgery, you are the property-rights holder with regards to those samples. On a standard Hohfeldian analysis, your *rights* over the samples entail a correlative *duty* on the part of the hospital and its researchers not to non-consensually use (i.e. dispossess you of) those samples. While you are at *liberty* to use (subject to any non-property restrictions) the samples,[14] the researchers have *no-right* to do so. You have the *power* to change the (legal or moral) relations between yourself and the researchers, but the researchers do not. They can be said to have a *liability* in that respect (although the researchers may, of course, elect not to have their position changed; for example, by refusing offers of donated samples). Finally, you have an *immunity* in respect of your rights over the samples. This is because third parties do not have the power to alter your position of normative authority. They thus have a *disability*.[15] Since a person's normative authority over their biomaterials does not cease upon separation, they remain the source of control regarding these until such time as they waive or transfer their rights over them.[16] Consequently, third parties are under an obligation to refrain from interfering with those rights (and the materials themselves) unless, and until, their own normative standing changes.

Consent is the *mode* by which any such change is achieved. In this sense consent is transformative with respect to the relative normative

---

[13] See Chapter 6, sections 2 and 3.

[14] For example, give it to researchers at a different institution rather than the hospital.

[15] For a thoroughgoing explication of the Hohfeldian relations, as well as an analysis of the function of consent on these, see Beyleveld and Brownsword, *Consent in the Law*, pp. 64–81.

[16] Or unless there are compelling countervailing reasons why they ought not to be viewed as the person in the requisite position of normative authority. I also do not discount the possibility that their rights in this respect are liable to expire in certain situations; for example, upon death.

positions of the parties.[17] Specifically, a person's consent alters the rights relations that they have with other persons. When we consent to some third party or other using our biomaterials we are, in effect, consenting to an alteration in our rights with respect to the samples. It functions, as Beyleveld and Brownsword note about consent in general, 'to authorise a change of position within a baseline relationship'.[18] The effect of consent on the rights of the various parties to a transaction may be twofold: 'while consent can function as a defence against a breach of right or duty, it can also function to create new rights'.[19] Indeed it might do both of these things simultaneously. We can appreciate why this is so by thinking about the different incidents.

Liberties and claims, as we saw in Chapter 6, differ from powers and immunities. The former two elements constitute the core of the right, whilst the latter two represent a periphery which can protect or modify that core. In particular, powers can be utilised to alter the normative position of both the rights-holders themselves and third parties, some-thing which is germane to understanding the function of consent as it pertains to property rights. When you consent to the donation of your samples you are actively exercising both your liberties and powers with regards to the sample, the effect of which is to change the normative relations between yourself and the hospital and its researchers. This change may be temporary or it may be permanent depending on the context and the terms of the transaction. The most straightforward case would be one where you donate the tissue for whatever purposes the researchers see fit, and, in so doing, you intend to relinquish any further control over the samples. The consequence of consenting is that the property rights which were vested in you, transfer to the hospital and/or researchers. These parties are no longer under a duty of non-interference with the samples. They have now gained the authority to use and control the samples. Equally, you now are under such a duty of

---

[17] This idea of transformation is one which has come to the fore in recent discussions regarding consent. Franklin G. Miller and Alan Wertheimer, for example, have argued that we need to go beyond valid consent and instead see consent as a morally transfor-mative action between actors. See F.G. Miller and A. Wertheimer, 'Preface to a theory of consent transactions: Beyond valid consent' in F.G. Miller and A. Wertheimer (eds), *The Ethics of Consent: Theory and Practice* (Oxford: Oxford University Press, 2010), pp. 79–106. In the same volume, Kleinig talks of consent as being morally transformative ('Nature of consent'). Meanwhile, Price referred to consent in relation to the donation of organs and biomaterials as being transformative of legal relationships (*Human Tissue*, p. 109).

[18] Beyleveld and Brownsword, *Consent in the Law*, p. 80. [19] *Ibid.*, p. 7.

non-interference, where you were not before. The giving of consent in such situations is the exercise of a power.[20] This is latent until exercised, but the entitlement to exercise it is part and parcel of what it means to have a property *right*. Significantly, the transfer of property rights to the researchers includes the attendant powers. By consenting you divest yourself of the corresponding powers from that point forward. Thereafter you no longer occupy the requisite position of normative authority with respect to those biomaterials. This position is now occupied by the researchers.

Other contexts may give rise to more complex alterations in the normative relations at issue. For example, in cases like *Yearworth*, where samples are being stored for future use by the source, a different picture emerges. Here the intention of those storing the samples was not to irrevocably give up their rights over the sperm. Hence the men did not transfer all of their use-privileges or control-powers. Nevertheless, in agreeing to store their sperm, the men exercised their powers to change the normative positions of other parties. The fertility unit gained rights and duties which it did not have previously. It was at liberty to store the samples (and we could certainly say it had a right to do so) but in accepting the samples they undertook a duty of care in respect of them.

When we give consent we are sanctioning a change in the moral and/or legal relations between ourselves and some other party or parties. In this respect consent is a legitimator. It functions to either authorise certain uses of the materials within the scope of the source's property rights, or, where they wish to give up those rights, as legitimating their transfer. Absent the consent of the source, or other holder of the requisite property rights, and the biomaterials in question could not be legitimately used or transferred. Consent similarly protects the property rights of other users (hospitals, researchers, etc.) once those materials have been *legitimately* transferred to them. As such, it plays an important role in protecting persons in the *exercise* of their property rights.

None of this means that we need to completely abandon the standard autonomy-based narrative regarding consent. Since the exercise (or not) of a person's property rights over their biomaterials is part and parcel of what it is to be autonomous, then these also function to protect their

---

[20] According to Beyleveld and Brownsword, 'consent is implicit in the exercise of a power. . . because the exercise of a power, by (Hohfeldian) definition, is the exercise of will, or choice, by the power-holder. . . if one freely chooses to exercise a power, then one must consent, as it were, to one's own act' (*ibid.*, p. 71).

autonomy in this respect.[21] The key point, however, is that consent does not stand apart as a separate normative obligation. It ought instead to be viewed as an integral part of persons' property rights in their biomaterials. This shift in emphasis ties consent in this domain to firm foundations. The analytical benefit is that it allows us to identify exactly what it is we are consenting to; that is, what it is we are sanctioning. It also means that we can give a detailed account of the normative changes which occur, be they legal or moral. By connecting the consent requirement to underlying property rights we are in a good position to assess potential wrongs, as well as to understand the reasons for these. Recognising the initial proprietorial control of the source would ensure that any transfer of biomaterials (and the accompanying property rights) is done in a legitimate manner; that is, with proper consent.

2.2   Some Observations and Implications

The first thing to note is that the law as it stands can accommodate the reframing of separated biomaterials in the manner advocated in this book. This much has been seen in the sperm cases. Despite its limitations, the decision in *Yearworth* in particular demonstrates how the common law can evolve to meet the challenges wrought by biotechnological change. As such, making property our normative focus qua biomaterials would not require legislative change. While the Human Tissue Acts display an outward commitment to consent and eschewal of property, they are not incompatible with a property approach. As I have argued, the general recognition of source property rights over biomaterials would give the Acts a substance which is otherwise lacking. In relation to the 2004 Act, Price commented that 'neither the Act nor the reform exercise as a whole articulated what, apart from consent, legitimates permissible forms of action'.[22] Yet it is essential that we have some idea of why persons are entitled to control the use and transfer of their tissues. The answer offered in this book is that their self-ownership gives them prima facie property rights (that is, rights of use and control which are good against the world) over their separated materials.

Interestingly, the debate of the House of Commons Standing Committee, which was scrutinising the Human Tissue Bill prior to its enactment, actually suggests ownership as one of the key principles underlying this

---

[21] See parallel arguments regarding self-ownership in Chapter 7, sections 2 and 3.
[22] Price, 'The Human Tissue Act', 815.

piece of legislation. During the debate, Dr Ladyman maintained that the 'fundamental principle that we must apply to interpreting the Bill is that material provided by people from their own body is theirs to *control*, and they must consent to how it is used in the future'.[23] Further, he said that the 'principles of the Bill are that we all own our own bodies, we are entitled to determine how material from our bodies is used, and we should have consented to the use of that material.[24] This, as Price noted, 'is a species of property grounded rationale'.[25] None of the Committee members questioned Dr Ladyman's contentions regarding ownership. Instead the discussions, as reported, seemingly took it as axiomatic that ownership provides the baseline justification for persons' rights to control the uses of their bodily materials.

A second important consideration centres on the effect on research of using a more explicit proprietary framework. In *Moore*, it was claimed that 'companies are unlikely to invest heavily in developing, manufacturing, or marketing a product when uncertainty about clear title exists'.[26] Despite this pronouncement, finding in favour of the plaintiff would not have resulted in any uncertainty, quite the contrary. The message from the Court would have been clear: title vests in the source and it is not acceptable for researchers, their institutions, or biotech companies to illegitimately deal with biomaterials in a manner of their own choosing. Further, if they do, there will be a penalty for so doing. This need not unduly hamper medical research as was claimed by the Court.

If we are worried about the impact on research, we should be as concerned (if not more so) about requiring consent for the use of biomaterials as we are about whether or not the samples are the property of the source.[27] This is so, whether or not we view those consent requirements as premised on the existence of property rights. Consent is a binary transaction. As such, *at the point of donation* persons can either give or withhold their consent, along with the relevant samples of their biomaterials. If they choose the latter path then they prevent their materials from being used in research. This is exactly the kind of restrictive control which bothered the courts in both *Moore* and *Greenberg*.

---

[23] S. Ladyman, Human Tissue Bill, House of Commons Standing Committee G (27 Jan 2004), col. 59.
[24] *Ibid.*, col. 65.   [25] Price, 'The Human Tissue Act', 815.
[26] *Moore*, Supreme Court at 146.
[27] Something that was recognised in the earlier Court of Appeal judgement in *Moore* at 139–140.

Connected to this was a concern in these cases about *continuing* control. There was a mistaken presumption that granting source property rights would somehow allow persons to exert control over their tissue samples beyond the point of donation. A determination of property does not confer (in and of itself) the right to *continue* to direct or restrict the uses of biomaterials once *legitimately* transferred. The key word here is 'legitimate'. Legally, property in chattels can be transferred by deed, delivery, declaration of a trust, or sale.[28] There must also be an intention to transfer.[29] Ordinarily, my control over an item qua property will cease upon transfer. This would be no different for biomaterials than it would for other sorts of moveables. The legitimacy of any transfers, however, is called into question where they are not consensual or where the original consent is vitiated; for example, transfers involving deception, fraud, or coercion.

As it stands, transfer by delivery would be the most significant mode of transfer relevant to the procurement of biomaterials for research. Individuals express their intention to transfer the samples via their consent to donation and these samples are taken into the possession of the researchers or their institution. Physical possession of the samples, along with the attendant property rights, is thus transferred.[30] Problems will not generally arise with the actual delivery aspect of the transaction, but, depending on how the consenting and procurement process is handled, the transfer may be voidable.[31] For instance, if there is fraudulent misrepresentation of the purposes for which the biomaterials will be used, then the transfer of the property rights could be rescinded.[32] We can see why this might be pertinent to cases such as *Greenberg*, where the plaintiffs only consented to the donation of the samples on the understanding that the results of the research would not be restricted or commercialised. If a similar case were to come before the English courts and the source was deemed originally to have property rights in the samples, then they need not reach the conclusion that an individual's rights terminate upon donation. Such a conclusion would depend on

---

[28] See Bridge, *Personal Property Law*, pp. 153–193; R.J. Smith, *Property Law* (Edinburgh: Pearson Education Ltd, 2011), pp. 111–117; and McFarlane, *Structure of Property Law*, pp. 168–179.

[29] Smith, *Property Law*, pp. 112–113; McFarlane, *Structure of Property Law*, pp. 165–168.

[30] For a comparison of abandonment with delivery in the context of human biomaterials see N. Maddox, "Abandonment' and the acquisition of property rights in separated human biomaterials' (2016) 16 *Medical Law International* 229, 242–244 ['Abandonment'].

[31] McFarlane, *Structure of Property Law*, pp. 150–152.   [32] *Ibid.*, p. 150.

whether or not there had been a legitimate transfer of the biomaterials in the first place; a claim which might not be sustainable where donors are misled or inadequately informed about potential uses of their samples.

Let us now move on to examine specific ways in which biomaterials (and their attendant property rights) might be divested. First, I will look briefly at abandonment and gratuitous transfers, before spending the rest of the chapter examining transfers for value (e.g. sale).

3   Abandonment and Gratuitous Transfers

3.1   Abandoning Our Biomaterials?

Although a number of commentators have suggested that separated human biomaterials ought to be considered as abandoned by their source,[33] there has until recently been little in-depth analysis of this contention.[34] Significant amongst those advocating a doctrine of abandonment is the 1995 Nuffield Council on Bioethics report on human tissue.[35] In discussing potential legal claims by persons from whom tissue had been removed, the report stated that the 'likely approach would be that where tissue is removed in the course of treatment, consent to the treatment will entail the abandonment of any claim to the tissue'.[36] In the report, support for this view is located in two US cases: *Venner* v. *State of Maryland*[37] and the *Moore* case. The defendant in *Venner* had swallowed balloons filled with hashish. He was subsequently admitted to hospital after they leaked. A number of balloons were recovered from his stools and taken as evidence by the police. One of the points at issue was whether this constituted an infringement of his Fourth Amendment rights. Neil Maddox explains that 'the Fourth Amendment prohibits certain types of searches and seizures; however, the amendment does not protect against the seizure of abandoned property'.[38] Powers J held that:

> By the force of social custom... when a person does nothing and says nothing to indicate an intent to assert his right of ownership, possession,

---

[33] See, for example, Nuffield Council on Bioethics, *Human Tissue*: Ethical and Legal Issues (London: Nuffield Council on Bioethics, 1995), p. 73. For their general discussion of the abandonment issue see pp. 67–75.

[34] For an in-depth critique see I. Goold, 'Abandonment and human tissue' in I. Goold, K. Greasley, J. Herring, and L. Skene (eds), *Persons, Parts and Property: How Should We Regulate Human Tissue in the 21st Century?* (Oxford: Hart Publishing, 2014), pp. 125–155. See also Maddox, 'Abandonment'.

[35] Nuffield Council, *Human Tissue*.   [36] *Ibid.*, p. 67.   [37] (1976) 354 A 2d 483.

[38] Maddox, 'Abandonment', 236.

or control over [bodily] material, the only rational inference is that he intends to abandon the material. When one places, or permits others to place waste material from his body into the stream of ultimate disposition as waste, he has abandoned whatever legal right he theretofore had to protect it from prying eyes or acquisitive hands.[39]

The Nuffield Council took this to imply that the 'legal presumption is in favour of abandonment'.[40] Meanwhile, although abandonment was not mentioned in *Moore*, the Nuffield Council report stated that 'the court appears to have found that Moore's consent to the operation entailed an abandonment of any claims over the removed tissue'.[41] There are a number of difficulties with the Council's position here, as there are with abandonment claims regarding biomaterials more generally speaking.

Let us first note that theoretically it might be possible to abandon ones biomaterials, be that the 'abandonment of actual or de facto possession of a thing, abandonment of ownership of the thing or abandonment of any claims in respect of the thing'.[42] We might say that a person 'abandons' possession, for example, when they agree to store their gametes or tissues in the hospital freezer. However, where the source does not intend to give up ownership or other claims over the materials, it is not truly abandonment.[43] It is instead some sort of transfer.[44] It may, for example, be a gratuitous bailment, similar to that in *Yearworth*. Here the hospital acquires a number of possessory rights (and responsibilities) regarding the biomaterials for a period of time. This does not entail that the source has given up their ownership of the samples. They would still be the ones in the position of ultimate normative authority in relation to the stored biomaterials. Thus transfers of possession need not (and as we will see shortly, do not ordinarily for the law) entail the abandonment of our ownership or claims regarding our biomaterials.[45]

Actual abandonment can only occur where the source intends to give up 'entirely and irrevocably' their ownership or claims regarding their biomaterials.[46] In the terms in which I have been talking in this book, this means giving up their normative authority with regards to the biomaterials and divesting themselves *in toto* of the relevant use-privileges and

---

[39] *Venner* at 499.   [40] Nuffield Council, *Human Tissue*, p. 69.   [41] *Ibid.*, p. 72.

[42] Maddox, 'Abandonment', 233. Here Maddox is summarising Goold's more extensive discussion of the different meanings of abandonment. Goold, 'Abandonment and human tissue', pp. 126–129.

[43] Goold, 'Abandonment and human tissue', p. 126.

[44] Douglas and Goold, 'Property in human biomaterials: A new methodology' (2016) 75 *Cambridge Law Journal* 478, 486–487.

[45] Goold, 'Abandonment and human tissue', p. 127.   [46] *Ibid.*, p. 126.

control-powers. Moreover, as Goold notes, unlike different types of transfers (e.g. gifting, bailment, or sale), this does not involve the transfer to the biomaterials or attendant rights *to* anyone. Instead, abandonment suggests that, at the point at which the rights are divested, they become free-floating, detached from any one person, being now up for grabs by the world in general. The thing becomes a true *res nullius*.[47] In order for other persons to acquire them, they must then somehow lay claim to them in this free-floating state. Being *res nullius*, the biomaterials would be open to acquisition by some other means such as first occupancy or labour-related routes, whereupon property rights could once again be created.[48] Note, however, that this observation exposes a logical difficulty with abandonment arguments. For property rights over biomaterials to be abandoned, somebody must have had them in the first place.[49] In relation to newly separated biomaterials, that person can only be the source. Yet often those utilising the language of abandonment deny that this is the case, as indeed was the tenor of the 1995 Nuffield Council report.

Leaving aside the issue of the logical flaw, abandonment is still tricky, legally and ethically speaking. A principal issue is that we do not routinely assume that other chattels have been abandoned so it is unclear why we would do so when it comes to biomaterials. Besides, as Goold persuasively demonstrates, English law on the matter is not clear-cut.[50] What support there is comes either from cases relating to theft[51] or the very particularised law of wreck.[52] There is not, therefore, direct authority on the types of civil claims which conflicts over biomaterials tend to give rise to.[53] In any event, satisfying the elements of the doctrine (such as they are) is far from straightforward.[54] Mainly this centres on the question of

---

[47] *Ibid.*, pp. 126–129.   [48] See Price, *Human Tissue*, pp. 251–264.

[49] *Ibid.*, p. 252. Douglas and Goold note that '[i]n order for it to be possible to say that A has either "transferred" his right in the tissue sample to B or abandoned his right to it, then not only must the law recognise a property right in respect of the tissue sample, but it must also allocate it to A' ('Property in human biomaterials', 487).

[50] Goold, 'Abandonment and human tissue', pp. 129–136.

[51] See, for example, *Williams and Others* v. *Phillips* (1957) 41 Cr. App. R. 5; *Bentinck Ltd* v. *Cromwell Engineering Co.* [1971] 1 All ER 33; and *Robot Arenas Ltd and Another* v. *Waterfield and Another* [2010] EWHC 115 (QB). For an analysis of theft and abandonment see R. Hickey, 'Stealing abandoned goods: Possessory title in proceedings for theft' (2006) 26 *Legal Studies* 584.

[52] See, for example, *Pierce* v. *Bemis (The Lusitania)* [1986] QB 384.

[53] Goold, 'Abandonment and human tissue', p. 130. See the discussion generally at pp. 129–136 for an analysis of the case law, including the cases listed above.

[54] *Ibid.*, p. 136.

whether or not someone intended to abandon the thing, and in so doing divest themselves of all their property rights in that respect. This is something which, as Goold puts it, for the law 'will not lightly be found'.[55] Whether or not it is, will depend on context:

> Where an item has value the court will presume that the owner did not mean to abandon it. This is true even of items dropped on the street. As Rolfe B stated in *R v Peters*, 'If I had an apple and dropped it, it might be presumed that I had abandoned it, but if I drop £500 the presumption is that I do not mean to abandon it.'[56]

Directly preceding this, Rolfe B in *R v. Peters* also said:

> If a man is possessed of a chattel, he does not lose the property in it because he places or drops it in a field. Nay, if he drop it in a street, it still remains his property. The only case where a party can be justified in converting it to his own use is, where it has fallen or dropped where a party may fairly say the owner has abandoned it; or if the party cannot be found to whom it belonged.[57]

A pragmatic reason why the law takes this approach is that abandoning ones property rights over an item also entails divesting oneself of any attendant responsibilities. Being easily able to do this is not, from the law's point of view, desirable, since it would entail people simply abandoning their property to avoid duties or liability relating to their arising.[58]

The consequence of all this is that, in the context of biomaterials, we may reasonably challenge abandonment claims. In English law it is difficult to prove abandonment,[59] and it is certainly not as a general rule 'presumed'. We do not ordinarily presume abandonment with other goods so there is little reason why we should do so with biomaterials as the Nuffield Council suggested we ought to. This is especially pertinent given the changing values, outlined in Chapter 1, which attach to human biomaterials. Advancing biotechnology means that low or non-value (monetary or otherwise) cannot simply be assumed.[60] There is little reason, therefore, to suppose that those who have tissue removed in the course of medical treatment (or indeed for other purposes) intend to abandon either the materials themselves or their rights over them.

---

[55] *Ibid.*   [56] *Ibid.*, p. 135, citing *R* v. *Peters* (1843) 174 ER 795.   [57] *R* v. *Peters, ibid.*
[58] Goold, 'Abandonment and human tissue', p. 130.
[59] See S. Thomas, 'Do freegans commit theft?' (2010) 30 *Legal Studies* 98, 104–114.
[60] See Chapter 1, Section 3.

3.2   Donations and Bailments

As already noted, property in chattels can be transferred by deed, delivery, declaration of a trust, or sale. Transfers for value, including sale, will be dealt with in the final part of this chapter and so I leave them aside for now and focus on gratuitous transfers. Gratuitous transfers are voluntary transfers in which no consideration is received in return. These include gifts (between donor and donee) and gratuitous bailments (between bailor and bailee).

The language of gifting or donation is frequently used in relation to biomaterials. When it is, it supposedly fulfils a legitimating function; that is, as Goold comments in relation to the language of abandonment, it is used 'as a means to show how tissue can pass into the control of someone else, usually a medical researcher, who is then legitimately allowed to use it as she wishes'.[61] Consider, for example, a now out-of-date incarnation of the MRC's guidance on the use of human biomaterials in research. It said that:

> We recommend that tissue samples donated for research be treated as gifts or donations, although gifts with conditions attached. This... promotes the 'gift relationship' between research participants and scientists... It also provides a practical way of dealing with the legal uncertainty over ownership, in that any property rights that the donor might have in their donated sample would be transferred, together with the control of use of the sample, to the recipient of the gift.[62]

This has been moderated somewhat in their most recent guidance, simply saying that '[t]he MRC requires that samples of human biological material donated for research are treated as *donations*, although there will sometimes be conditions attached. In this way, a "*gift relationship*" between research donors and researchers can be promoted.'[63] Furthermore, in a footnote they say, '[d]onated samples are often described as "gifts" although it is recognised that donors of samples are not usually regarded as having ownership or property rights in these'.[64]

Note the slight difference between the two iterations of the MRC's guidance. The earlier version seemingly recognises that gifting involves the legal transfer of property rights, whilst the later one suggests that donors do not have any such property rights. This difference perhaps

---

[61]   Goold, 'Abandonment and human tissue', p. 138.
[62]   Medical Research Council, *Human Tissue and Biological Samples for Use in Research: Operational and Ethical Guidelines* (April 2001 – amended 2005), p. 8.
[63]   MRC, *Human Tissue and Biological Samples* (2014), p. 8.   [64]   *Ibid.*, p. 6.

reflects the way in which usage of the term 'gift' from some non-legal discourses, in particular bioethics and social policy, has permeated discussions relating to biomaterials.[65] In these literatures, one of the reasons for the focus on gifting in this context has been to oppose market norms. Gifting has, to this end, been framed as an alternative to property.[66] Commentators, however, have increasingly been emphasising that legally speaking, the law of gifts is part and parcel of the law of property.[67] As such, gifting cannot be used as an alternative to a property approach.

That the donation of biomaterials implies property can be seen in the *Catalona* case. As we saw at the very beginning of this book, the case centred on whether Dr Catalona or participants in his research into prostate cancer *retained* a proprietary interest in the biomaterials which had been donated to a biorepository.[68] The Court referred to the donated samples as *inter vivos* gifts and outlined the elements required: '1) present intention of the donor to make a gift; 2) delivery of property by donor to donee; and 3) acceptance by donee whose ownership takes effect immediately and absolutely.'[69] The connection between donation, gifting, and property for the Court here is unambiguous. In *Yearworth*, Clarke LCJ interpreted the fact that that the tissue in *Catalona* had been donated as

---

[65] Goold and Quigley, 'Human biomaterials', p. 252. For a critique of the 'gift relationship' as utilised by the Nuffield Council in the earlier report see R. Tutton, 'Person, property, and gift: Exploring languages of tissue donation to biomedical research' in O. Corrigan and R. Tutton (eds), *Genetic Databases: Socio-Ethical Issues in the Collection and Use of DNA* (Abingdon: Routledge, 2004), pp. 19–38. Richard Titmuss' social policy work regarding the gift relationship and blood donation has been highly influential with regards to debates around the human body and biomaterials more broadly. See R.M. Titmuss, *The Gift Relationship: From Human Blood to Social Policy* (London: George Allen and Unwin, 1970). Much has been written on this over the years, but for a recent discussion and critique see A.M. Farrell, *The Politics of Blood: Ethics, Innovation, and the Regulation of Risk* (Cambridge: Cambridge University Press, 2012), pp. 56–75.

[66] Thomas Murray, for example, contends that 'our organs and tissues are not exactly property or surplus, but a very special kind of gift' (T. Murray, 'Who owns the body? On the ethics of using human tissue for commercial purposes' (1986) 8 *IRB: Ethics and Human Research* 1, 5). See also H. Marway, S.L. Johnson, and H. Widdows, 'Commodification of human tissue' in H.A.M.J. ten Have and B. Gordijn (eds), *Handbook of Global Bioethics* (Dordrecht: Springer Science and Business Media, 2014), pp. 581–598.

[67] Mason and Laurie, 'Consent or property?', 725; G.T. Laurie, 'Privacy and property? Multi-level strategies for protecting personal interests in genetic material' in B.M. Knoppers and C. Scriver (eds), *Genomics, Health and Society: Emerging Issues for Public Policy* (Canada: Policy Research Initiative, 2004), pp. 83–98, pp. 88–89; Tutton, 'Person, property, and gift', pp. 26–28; Hoppe, *Bioequity*, p. 16; and Goold and Quigley, 'Human biomaterials', pp. 247–254.

[68] See Chapter 1, Section 2.2. [69] *Catalona*, District Court at 997.

meaning that it 'was property capable of passing from the donors to the donee'.[70] Such a position is also a conceptually coherent one since it is unclear how a person could make a gift of something to which they do not hold the requisite property rights. If this is correct, then the locus of attention for donations shifts to whether or not they are legitimate; to wit, whether the donor intended to transfer property rights regarding the biomaterials and whether any such transfers are consensual.

According to Bridge, '[a]n effective gift between a donor and a donee requires that the donor display a clear intention to transfer to the donee his interest in the object that is being given'.[71] It also requires acceptance by the recipient, along with either 'physical delivery or the execution and delivery of a deed'.[72] As noted in Section 2.2, with respect to biomaterials, transfer by delivery would be the most common mode of transfer. This would suffice in cases where materials were being removed by the researcher (or by an employee at the researcher's institution) to whom control over the materials would pass. It would also cover cases of gratuitous transfers between laboratories or institutions where there is no expectation that the biomaterials would be returned (as opposed to bailments where there is such an expectation). A deed of gift can also be used to convey property from a donor to donee; that is, the donor could sign a document, which needs to be witnessed, expressly conveying their intent to make a gift.[73]

Unconditional donations involve no terms being specified in order for the gift to be effective. They involve the complete transfer of property rights over the item to some other party. In this manner, they entail the complete alienation of those rights. Alienation here is to be differentiated from instances where the object of property is temporarily not in our possession because it has been bailed to someone else (e.g. if I have loaned my book to a colleague or store items in a storage facility) or where we do not have immediate use-rights with respect to the object in question (e.g. because I am renting out my house to tenants).[74] As such, an

---

[70] *Yearworth* at [48(e)].   [71] Bridge, *Personal Property Law*, p. 171.

[72] *Ibid.* See also C. Stewart, Lipworth, W., Aparicio, L., *et al.*, 'The problems of biobanking and the law of gifts' in I. Goold, K. Greasley, J. Herring, and L. Skene (eds), *Persons, Parts and Property: How Should We Regulate Human Tissue in the 21st Century?* (Oxford: Hart Publishing, 2014), pp. 25–38, pp. 31–35.

[73] Law of Property (Miscellaneous Provisions) Act 1989, s. 1(2) and (3). See Bridge, *Personal Property Law*, pp. 174–175. Potentially consent forms could fulfil this function.

[74] We alienate our property whenever we *permanently* transfer it. We also alienate it when we exchange it for another item or transfer it for value (such as money). I say this in contradistinction to Christman who does not see exchanges as a form of alienation and

unconditional donation involves the complete transfer of a person's use-privileges and control-powers over the biomaterials in question. By making the unconditional transfer, the moral and legal relations between donors and donees are irrevocably altered.[75] After transfer the donor is no longer the person in the position of ultimate normative authority with respect to the materials, this is now the donee.

Conditional donations on the other hand will specify terms; for instance, tissue donors might consent to the donation of their tissues only if it is used for a particular research project, or on the understanding that it will *not* be used for certain types of research.[76] The conditions may be ones which have to be fulfilled either prior to transfer of ownership or after, and they 'must not be impossible of fulfilment, illegal, or contrary to public policy'.[77] Consider again the situation in *Greenberg*. If the donated samples had in this case been viewed as a gift, then it would have been on condition that the results not be commercialised.[78] It is this negatively permissive character of conditional gifts which Cameron Stewart and colleagues see as an improvement over free-floating informed consent-based models in relation to the use of human biomaterials:

> It focuses on the expressed and implied limits of what is permitted by the donor (for example, 'I donate my tissue to A so long as it is not used for human cloning'). Such limits have the advantage of being capable of expression when the gift is given, unlike a statement by a donor about material risk for research which hasn't been invented yet.[79]

Of course, as argued in Section 1 of this chapter, consent is not redundant. It is the mode by which normative sanction for the transfer is given. The validity of the consent will be dependent upon adherence to the

---

maintains that '[t]o alienate an item of ownership is to unilaterally divest oneself of title to it and to declare an intention that another become the owner (such as with a gift)' (*Myth of Property*, p. 129). My disagreement here may, however, just be linguistic since he makes this distinction to draw a line between control rights and income rights.

[75] Unless, as noted in Section 2.2, the transfer is voidable, such as in cases of fraudulent misrepresentation or coercion.

[76] For a general discussion of the possible application for the law of gifts applied to biobanking (where the analysis is pertinent to biomaterials more generally) see Stewart, Lipworth, Aparicio, *et al.*, 'Problems of biobanking', pp. 35–38. See also C. Stewart, J. Fleming, and I. Kerridge, 'The law of gifts, conditional donation and biobanking' (2013) 21 *Journal of Law and Medicine* 351.

[77] Vaines, *Personal Property*, p. 293. See also Stewart, Lipworth, Aparicio, *et al.*, 'Problems of biobanking', pp. 32–35.

[78] See Hardcastle, *Law and the Human Body*, p. 72.

[79] Stewart *et al.*, 'Problems of biobanking', p. 36.

conditions attached to the transfer. The giving of consent for the transfer of the biomaterials and property rights is also a means of indicating the requisite intent to transfer.

It has been suggested that situations in cases such as *Greenberg* and *Catalona* are more akin to bailment than conditional donations.[80] Although conditions attach to conditional gifts, legal ownership in the item at issue is transferred.[81] In such cases, subject to the particular conditions set by the donor, donees are the ones with normative authority. With bailments, however, such as was the case in *Yearworth*, only possession is transferred. In that case the men retained ownership and were the ones in the position of ultimate normative authority with respect to the sperm samples. The bailor retains the final say-so regarding the items at issue. As Hardcastle notes, a 'bailor can recall possession at any time'.[82] Accordingly, it is debatable whether in *Catalona*, for example, we ought to view the transfer of the samples as a conditional gift or a bailment. The decision described the donations as *inter vivos* gifts and held that any proprietary interests in the samples had passed to Washington University upon donation of the material.[83] It was also remarked that since there could be no expectation of the return of the tissue samples, it must have been donated as a gift.[84] These statements notwithstanding, it is not true that the research participants' interests or control over their samples completely terminated upon the passing of the samples. Specifically, although they may not have physically been able to have their samples returned to them, they could withdraw their consent – and thus their participation in the research – if they so wished.[85] The decision does not indicate exactly what this would have consisted of in this case, but usually it means that no further use would be made of particular samples in the research. Given that such withdrawal would represent an ultimate exercise of powers of control regarding the samples,

---

[80] Hardcastle, *Law and the Human Body*, pp. 157–158 and Goold and Quigley, 'Human biomaterials', pp. 253–254.

[81] For a gift with conditions-precedent, the conditions have to be fulfilled prior to the transfer of ownership. With conditions-subsequent, the conditions attach after the transfer. In the first situation, if the conditions are not met, the gift will not pass. In the second, the existence of the conditions do not encumber the initial transfer of ownership, but they do effect what might happen later if the conditions are not fulfilled.

[82] Hardcastle, *Law and the Human Body*, p. 157.

[83] *Catalona*, Court of Appeals at 673–677.   [84] *Ibid.*

[85] *Ibid.* at 671. The judgment notes that 'absent from the record is any mention the [research participants] ever were informed they could physically withdraw or request the return of their biological samples' (at 676).

the case for viewing such situations as bailments rather than conditional donations is at least arguable.[86]

3.3   Trusts and Biorepositories

One interesting, and sometimes misunderstood, approach worth mentioning is the idea of trusts in the context of biomaterials. This is another method which can be used to convey a gift. A trust is where property is held by a trustee for the benefit of another. The trustee holds the legal property rights in the item, whilst the beneficiaries have a beneficial (also called equitable) interest in the thing.[87] One way to create a trust is for the donor (also referred to as 'settlor' or 'transferor') to transfer the property to a trustee or trustees.[88] The declaration of a trust *inter vivos* in relation to chattels can 'be declared in writing, orally, or by conduct'.[89]

In essence, UK Biobank operates as a trust. Legally, it is constituted as a not-for-profit charitable trust:

> UK Biobank is a major national and international health resource, and a registered charity in its own right, with the aim of improving the prevention, diagnosis and treatment of a wide range of serious and life-threatening illnesses – including cancer, heart diseases, stroke, diabetes, arthritis, osteoporosis, eye disorders, depression and forms of dementia.[90]

David Winickoff and colleagues have argued that this sort of 'biotrust' is an appropriate way of dealing with the procurement, use, and management of biological samples within the context of large-scale biobanks.[91]

---

[86] See Hardcastle, *Law and the Human Body*, p. 158; and Goold and Quigley, 'Human biomaterials', p. 253.

[87] Vaines, *Personal Property*, pp. 301–302; Bridge, *Personal Property Law*, pp. 184–186. Although trustees are referred to as 'legal owners', Lawson and Rudden argue that this 'is both inaccurate and misleading. . . because they cannot treat the property as their own' (*Law of Property*, p. 86). As such, the trustees do not have ultimate normative authority with regards to the property ('[t]hey cannot even neglect, let alone destroy, it' (*ibid.*, pp. 86–87)). Trustees hold the property on trust for the beneficiaries and must manage it in the manner set out under the trust's terms. Nevertheless, whilst their property rights are restricted, they do have better title than all others. So whilst their normative authority is restricted, they are the only ones who can exercise it. They can authorise changes in the normative baseline as it pertains to the items in question subject to the terms under which the trust is set up.

[88] For an outline of trusts in respect of chattels see generally, Vaines, *Personal Property*, pp. 301–304.

[89] *Halsbury's Laws of England* (5th edn 2013), vol. 98, para. 59.

[90] www.ukbiobank.ac.uk/about-biobank-uk/ (accessed 27 November 2017).

[91] D.E. Winickoff and R.N. Winickoff, 'The charitable trust as a model for genomic biobanks' (2003) 349 *New England Journal of Medicine* 1180; and D.E. Winickoff and L.B. Neumann,

Unlike private trusts, specific beneficiaries (or classes of beneficiaries) need not be named with regards to a charitable trust. Instead activities are directed towards the public benefit,[92] and can be for a range of purposes to that end, including the advancement of health, saving lives, and the advancement of science.[93] As such, the charitable trust can provide 'a legal structure for the handling of property rights and the management of donated [samples]... and a social structure aimed at bolstering community participation, representation and trust'.[94]

Commentators are often rightly concerned with issues such as trust, accountability, and transparency in research involving human biomaterials, particularly in the context of biobanks. It is sometimes suggested that a 'trust' model would be an appropriate approach to deal with these concerns and that it provides an *alternative* to a property model for the regulation of human biomaterials. Like with gifting, however, the legal configuration and function of a trust has been misunderstood by non-legal commentators. For instance, Widdows maintains that:

> The trust model – not surprisingly, given its heritage in 'gift' – is clearly a non-property model. Not only are participants not granted property rights in their samples, but the fact that one is contributing to a public shared good... is emphasised... The trust model not only avoids the pitfalls of property, but also introduces and emphasises the importance of social capital and public goods.[95]

Whilst Widdows is correct regarding the importance of research involving human biomaterials for the public good, as the foregoing discussion

---

'Towards a social contract for genomics: Property and the public in the 'biotrust' model' (2005) 1 *Genomics, Society and Policy* 8. Winickoff's focus is often on biobanks conducting genomic research, but the idea is equally applicable to other types of biobanks and bior-epositories. Although for an analysis, including an exploration of trusts, which predates Winickoff and colleagues', see K. Gottlieb, 'Human biological samples and the laws of property: The trust as a model for biological repositories' in R.F. Weir (ed.), *Stored Tissue Samples: Ethical, Legal, and Public Policy Implications* (Iowa City: University of Iowa Press, 1998), pp. 182–197. Interestingly, Gottlieb's piece discusses both bailment and trusts in the context of stored sperm; the former she suggests as appropriate where stored for later personal use, and the latter where it is stored for donation to third parties (pp. 194–195). See also Dickenson, *Property in the Body*, pp. 122–125.

[92] Charities Act 2011, s. 2(1)(b).   [93] *Ibid.*, ss 3(1)(d) and (f).

[94] Winickoff and Neumann, 'Towards a social contract for genomics', 10. See also C. Stewart, L. Aparicio, W. Lipworth, and I. Kerridge, 'Public umbilical cord blood banking and charitable trusts' in I. Goold, K. Greasley, J. Herring, and L. Skene (eds), *Persons, Parts and Property: How Should We Regulate Human Tissue in the 21st Century?* (Oxford: Hart Publishing, 2014), pp. 53–65.

[95] Widdows, *The Connected Self*, pp. 137–138.

has made clear, like gifting, trusts are not an alternative to property. They are an integral part of the law of property. Like with other modes of gifting, persons cannot gift items over which they do not hold the requisite rights of use and control; that is to say, property rights. Hence donations to a trust presuppose that donors have property rights in the items they are transferring.[96] For the law, therefore, biotrusts presume the existence of source property rights in biomaterials which the source can transfer to the trustee or trustees.

Part of the issue is the elision of different meanings of the word 'trust'. Trust is frequently used to mean belief or confidence (or lack thereof) in those carrying out the research or in the governance structures which regulate such research; for example, '[p]articipants agree to trust UK Biobank not to misuse their samples and data'.[97] However, this sense of the word is then imported into related discussions regarding the appropriate *modes* of governance and regulation of biobanks: 'The on-going mechanisms monitor the behaviour of biobanks and ensure that trust is maintained. . . If this is done effectively then participants will still have some say, some control, but *without* invoking property.'[98]

Another potential source of confusion regarding the property issue and UK Biobank may relate to the fact that, to a large extent, it is governed by a policy-led approach. As Graeme Laurie, one of the former chairs of UK Biobank's Ethics and Governance Council, notes, UK Biobank 'developed and operates according to an Ethics and Governance Framework. Such an instrument has no basis in law and yet has played a crucial role in the set up and ongoing management of the resource'.[99] The advantage of this, according to Laurie, is that the system can adapt over time and can respond to scientific and other changes, as well as to lessons learned in partnership with research participants. In this way, he argues, it is a good example of reflexive governance.[100]

---

[96] Winckoff and Neumann, 'Towards a social contract for genomics', pp. 13–14.
[97] Widdows, *The Connected Self*, p. 134. See also A.K. Hawkins and K. O' Doherty 'Biobank governance: A lesson in trust' (2010) 29 *New Genetics and Society* 311; H. Widdows, *Global Ethics: An Introduction* (Abingdon: Routledge, 2014), pp. 222–223; and D. Chalmers and D. Nicol, 'Commercialisation of biotechnology: Public trust and research' (2004) 6 *International Journal of Biotechnology* 116. Also, see generally the contributions in P. Dabrock, J. Taupitz, and J. Ried (eds), *Trust in Biobanking* (Dordrecht: Springer, 2012).
[98] Widdows, *The Connected Self*, p. 138 [emphasis in original].
[99] G.T. Laurie, 'Reflexive governance in biobanking: On the value of policy led approaches and the need to recognise the limits of law' (2011) 130 *Human Genetics* 347, 347.
[100] *Ibid.*, 351–354.

Yet while UK Biobank's Ethics and Governance Framework is 'a living instrument',[101] it operates against and within a particular legal background. Laurie explains that 'UK Biobank is subject to a plethora of existing legal provisions for protecting participants' interests',[102] including being subject to the law of trusts. Given this, and given that the substance of much of the biobanking debate is about the *regulation and governance* of human biomaterials, we cannot disregard the legal property-context in which organisations such as UK Biobank are embedded. Indeed UK Biobank's own documents explicitly note that UK Biobank will be the legal owner of any samples held in the biobank.[103] Importantly, however, they have committed not to sell the samples.[104]

The fact that a trust model *is* a property model is not a disadvantage. As Winickoff and Neumann note, the charitable trust puts 'a legally binding fiduciary obligation on the trustee to faithfully manage the resource according to the charitable purpose and the public benefit defined in the trust instrument'.[105] This has a number of benefits:

> First, it respects the altruistic intent of donors, while ensuring that their goodwill is not exploited. Second, it imposes a duty on the resource managers to make the resource productive. Third, fiduciary law addresses a power imbalance between the settlor/beneficiaries and the trustee, in contrast to the consent model, which has often been criticized for failing to take into account the power imbalance between doctor and patient Fourth,... [it] reduces the conflicts of interest in making prioritization decisions about the resource, enhances the opportunity for ethical review, and encourages interest groups to participate in decision-making. Fifth,

---

[101] *Ibid.*, 352.   [102] *Ibid.*

[103] See, for example, 'Access procedures: Application and review procedures for access to the UK Biobank resource', ss B8.1–B8.3 and 3, available at www.ukbiobank.ac.uk/wp-content/uploads/2012/09/Access-Procedures-2011.pdf. See also 'Material Transfer Agreement for data and/or samples', s. 3.1, available at: www.ukbiobank.ac.uk/wp-content/uploads/2012/09/Material-Transfer-Agreement.pdf (accessed 27 November 2017).

[104] As stated on the website: 'UK Biobank Limited will be the legal owner of the database and the sample collection (see Section III.A.1). Such ownership conveys certain rights, such as the right to take legal action against unauthorised use or abuse of the database or samples, and the right to sell or destroy the samples. Participants will not have property rights in the samples. UK Biobank does not intend to exercise all of these rights; for example, it will not sell samples. Rather, UK Biobank will serve as the steward of the resource, maintaining and building it for the public good in accordance with its purpose' (UK Biobank, 'Ethics and governance framework', version 3.0 (2007), p. https://www.ukbiobank.ac.uk/wp-content/uploads/2011/05/EGF20082.pdf (accessed 27 November 2017).

[105] Winickoff and Neumann, 'Towards a social contract for genomics', 11.

the procedural mechanisms and structures are likely to help mediate among diverse interests implicated by the research.[106]

Of course, much hinges on how the trust is executed and managed on a day-to-day basis.[107] But in principle, the trusts model is a good illustration of how property law can be used to regulate the transfer and use of human biomaterials in a manner that addresses many commentators' concerns.

4 Transfers for Value: On Property Rights and Income Rights

The power to alienate one's property, that is, divest oneself *in toto* of all of one's rights with respect to a particular object, represents the ultimate disposition of our property rights over that object. As we have just seen, this necessarily encompasses gifting, and as such donation, as an exercise of a person's power to transfer. Despite this, objections to property in biomaterials are infrequently objections to transfer per se, but instead to the possibility of the sale of those materials. Further, objections to the sale of biomaterials tend not to be blanket objections to such a practice, but to the possibility that the source of the biomaterials could engage in market transactions with respect to their tissues and cells. Consider, for example, the *Moore* case. Here a disquiet regarding the possibility of the commercialisation of human biomaterials by the source ran through the majority decision. Underpinning this was the implicit acceptance that market transactions are germane to the property question; that is, a determination of property is seen as *including* rights to income or exchanges for value. The consequence of this was that proprietary control of the biomaterials was denied to Mr Moore.

The assumption that property includes the right to derive income can be seen closer to home in the Human Tissue Act 2004. The Act only prohibits from commercial dealings material which has been removed for *transplant purposes*. Biomaterials removed explicitly for research or other purposes are, therefore, not covered. In addition, material which has been removed for transplant purposes may be exempt from the general prohibition where it has become 'the subject of *property* because of an application of skill'.[108] Thus, the Act seemingly views the right to engage in commercial dealings as part and parcel of a determination of property.[109]

[106] *Ibid.*, 12
[107] See generally, *ibid.* See also Laurie, 'Reflexive governance in biobanking'.
[108] s. 32(9)(c) [emphasis added].
[109] This presumption also runs through the academic literature. See, for example, Brenkert, 'Self-ownership, freedom, and autonomy', 53; C.S. Campbell, 'Body, self, and the property

There are two aspects to this type of presumption which will be scrutinised in the remainder of this chapter. The first is the relationship between property and market transactions, and the second is the (misplaced) worry regarding the sphere of activity of the *source* in relation to their biomaterials. What we will see is that the justificatory basis for the right to the receipt of property-related income is separate to the justification for any concomitant powers of transmission. This is the case even though the right to income and the power to transfer are both necessary if one is to engage in an exchange for value. The alienability of one's property (rights) by transfer need not include market alienability.[110] Powers of transmission need not, and do not, imply that there is a right to derive income from such transfers.

4.1   Property, Persons, and Commercialisation

While it can be difficult to disentangle property from market transactions, these are not analytically and irrevocably bound up together. Although some kind of property is a prerequisite for many contracts, as Penner observes, having property does not necessarily entail the right to trade or enter into contractual agreements with other individuals or organisations.[111] Transactions of this sort involve two separate (and separable) areas of law: property and contract. And it does not follow from the general marriage of property and contract, that the right to make either legally or morally binding agreements is part of the *core* of property.[112] Ownership does not analytically demand the right to contract to the transfer of property in exchange for income or some other value in kind. The power (right) to sell is, as Penner contends, a '*hybrid "power"* in which the power to make contracts includes the power to

---

paradigm' (1992) 22 *Hastings Center Report* 34, 41; R.E. Gold, *Body Parts: Property Rights and the Ownership of Human Biological Materials* (Washington: Georgetown University Press, 1996), 2; and L. Skene, 'Arguments against people legally "owning" their own bodies, body parts, and tissue' (2002) 2 *Macquarie Law Review* 165, 165.

[110] See David Price's comments in relation to the Human Tissue Act 2004 ('The Human Tissue Act', 818).

[111] Penner, *Idea of Property*, pp. 91–92. Regarding property and contract, Harris noted that '[b]argaining and contracting in most situations take property for granted. In modern legal systems, the majority of contracts presuppose property. The contractor on one side at least offers to transmit something over which he has ownership privileges and powers, especially money' (*Property and Justice*, p. 50).

[112] This is both an analytical legal claim and a normative philosophical one.

make contracts concerning the power to dispose of property'.[113] We can see why this ought to be the case by thinking about the normative arguments regarding the justifications for property rights and income rights.

In essence, the underlying justification for the right to receive income is different from that underpinning the recognition of property rights. The power to transfer is an integral part of property's dual core of liberties and powers. However, transfers resulting in the accrual of value (such as sales) are different. The core of property (and indeed self-ownership) as we have seen in earlier chapters, centres on use and control, and owners are those in positions of ultimate normative authority regarding particular items. Property rights and established rules within a system of property help to reduce or readily resolve conflicts which might ensue over scarce resources. This in turn decreases instabilities of possession which might occur absent such rights and rules. The usefulness of property rules in these respects, however, is underpinned and justified by 'interests such as liberty, autonomy, and self-determination'.[114] It is for this reason that I defined owners as those in positions of ultimate normative authority. Income rights, by contrast, are not connected with use and control in this manner.

Christman argues that income rights are justified by 'principles that govern the pattern of distribution of goods in the economy, considerations which are not reducible to those individualist interests'.[115] They 'are conceptually tied to the distribution of goods in ways that control rights are not'.[116] This conceptual connection comes from the way income rights can (and do) influence the distribution of resources in society. Transfers for value are both dependent on, and the cause of, the pattern of resource distribution in society. There is a thus a 'dual-causal connection',[117] something which is captured in relation to biomaterials by Wall's example of kidneys and blood:

> [I]f kidneys and blood were both tradable commodities, the income received for the sale of a kidney would be higher than for the equivalent amount of blood because of the scarcity of the resource and the willingness of purchasers to pay for the organ. . . The recognition of income rights in kidneys would lead to a different (for better or worse) allocation of kidneys in society since they could be freely exchanged as a commodity.[118]

---

[113] Penner, *Idea of Property*, p. 153 [emphasis added].
[114] Christman, 'Self-ownership', 30.   [115] *Ibid.*   [116] *Ibid.*, 31.
[117] J. Wall, 'The legal status of body parts: A framework' (2011) 31 *Oxford Journal of Legal Studies* 783, 791.
[118] *Ibid.* Wall also adopts Christman's distinction between control rights and income rights. However, he draws on Guido Calebrsi and Douglas Melamed's view of property and

When an owner engages in market exchanges or trades, the income that accrues to her is dependent on the distribution of resources in the economy at that particular time, be they bicycles, computers, or kidneys. At the same time, the very act of engaging in value-dependent or value-generating transactions affects future distributions of the resources in question.

Income rights are consequent on the very existence of a market, whereas gratuitous transfers are not. The market creates surpluses which are a net benefit to society; it does this through 'efficiencies of stability, information transfer, and economies of scale'.[119] If this is correct, then these extra benefits exist because of the *system as a whole* rather than individual property-holders; in which case no one individual can be said to have a prior claim to control the surplus. In such a situation, society, perhaps through the state, can decide to redistribute any surpluses and, thereby, determine the income rights to be recognised.[120] Thus, income rights are tied to considerations of distributive justice in a manner that rights of use and control are not.[121] This is not to claim that control rights do not have *any* distributive implications. The extent to which owners are permitted to accumulate income consequent on the use and control of their property, they become, as Harris put it, agents of wealth-distribution.[122] However, this dual function of 'governing both the use of things and allocating items of social wealth'[123] does not detract from the fact that these functions are separable and rest on different justifications.

In addition to resting on different justificatory bases, the manner in which property (control) rights generally operate can be substantially distinguished from the way income rights function. There is some overlap, but, as Christman maintains, the latter are conditional or contingent on other persons for their exercise in a way in which control rights need not be.[124] In order for a person to engage in exchanges or trades for value, someone else must also engage in the transaction. An owner can neither transfer her property for value nor accrue any net benefit or income from this if no one is willing to trade with her. No one has a duty to engage in

---

liability rules to argue that the latter are more apt for protecting control rights. For Calabresi and Melamed's account of property, liability, and inalienability rules see G. Calabresi and D. Melamed, 'Property Rules, Liability Rules, and Inalienability: One View of the Cathedral' (1972) 85 *Harvard Law Review* 1089.

[119] Christman, 'Self-ownership', 32.   [120] *Ibid.*, 32–33.   [121] *Ibid.*, 31.

[122] Harris, *Property and Justice*, pp. 26 and 47.   [123] *Ibid.*, p. 26.

[124] See generally Christman, 'Self-ownership', 33–34, and *Myth of Property*, p. 131.

market transactions for the benefit of another.[125] As such, no right to income can be enjoyed in isolation from others. By contrast there are many use-privileges and control-powers that can be exercised over a resource that are not dependent on others for that use and control. Consider, for example, a book. One can read it, refrain from reading it, burn it, use it to prop up a table, etc.; engagement with others in the market or elsewhere is not necessary in order to exercise such use and control.

One could contend that this element of contingency is not just relevant to transfers for value, but to all transfers and, hence to instances of gifting and donation.[126] This strikes me as broadly accurate on a one-to-one interpersonal level; however, exchanges within a market seem crucially different from gratuitous transfers (or even simple exchanges). The 'level of contingency' involved in market transactions is greater than with these other types of transaction.[127] It is the very existence of markets which creates surplus value and, therefore, income rights. A market system is 'contingent on the existence of stable rules of cooperation which govern the exchanges in question'.[128] This requires that our relations with others to be organised on a scale that is not necessary for simpler transactions. Of course, we can, and often do, conduct market transactions between only two actors. However, even in situations where I sell you my pen in a direct transaction, we are dependent on the existence of the market at large, something which is not the case if I just give the pen to you. The market will influence, and perhaps set, the price at which I sell you the item in question. Furthermore, our tokens of exchange (money) are only available to us because of the market. Thus, as well as having different underlying justifications, there is an operational gap between the property rights and any income rights arising from their transfer.

In making this distinction between property rights and income rights it necessarily follows that I reject accounts which either implicitly or explicitly bundle market norms into their conception of property rights. Take, for example, Guido Calabresi and Douglas Melamed's influential exposition which takes an economic analysis of entitlements and their protections. Three categories of rules which could be said to protect entitlements are outlined: 'property rules', 'liability rules', and 'alienability rules':

> An entitlement is protected by a property rule to the extent that someone who wishes to remove the entitlement from its holder must *buy it from*

---

[125] Christman, *Myth of Property*, p. 131.   [126] Thank you to Søren Holm for this point.
[127] Christman, *Myth of Property*, p. 131.   [128] Christman, 'Self-ownership', 33.

him in a voluntary transaction in which the value of the entitlement is
agreed upon by the seller... Whenever someone may destroy the initial
entitlement if he is willing to pay an objectively determined value for it, an
entitlement is protected by a liability rule... An entitlement is inalienable
to the extent that its transfer is not permitted between a willing buyer and
a willing seller.[129]

From this, at least two different aspects of what it means for an entitlement to be protected by a property rule present themselves.[130] First, we
could focus on the voluntary nature of the transaction; that property rules
function 'by inhibiting any taking without owner's (*sic*) consent'.[131] If
this is the case then, in one sense, the analysis would be consistent with
that given in Section 2 of this chapter; that is, a requirement for free and
voluntary consent functions to protect a person's property rights. If this is
the case, then it is unfortunate that the language used predisposes us
towards market-oriented thinking since it could be misleading in driving
us towards a paradigm seen only in such terms.[132] On the other hand, it
could also be interpreted as making the market integral to property
rights.[133]

The main difficulty with this, as noted by Schroeder in relation to
Calabresi and Melamed's analysis, is that it 'confuses the definition of
rights with the enforcement of rights'.[134] Whether or not something
ought to be considered a property right (or entitlement) is a function of
the content of that right, not the manner in which it is protected. The
conceptual locus of proprietary rights is most plausibly to be identified
with rights of use and control, whilst the exact scope of those rights, along
with any remedies for their infringement, are determined by the various

[129] Calabresi and Melamed, 'Property rules', 1092 [emphasis added].
[130] The literature that has sprung up around Calabresi and Melamed's analysis is vast. Just a
few articles are G. Calabresi, 'Remarks: The simple virtues of *The Cathedral*' (1997) 106
Yale Law Journal 2201; M.I. Krauss, 'Property rules vs. liability rules' in B. Bouckaert and
G. De Geest (eds), *Encylopedia of Law and Economics, vol. II* (Cheltenham: Edward Elgar
Publishing, 2000), pp. 782–794; J.E. Krier and S.J. Schwab, 'Property rules and liability
rules: The Cathedral in another light' (1995) 70 *New York University Law Review* 440; A.
Nicita and M. Rizzolli, 'Property rules, liability rules and externalities' (2006) 24 *Journal
of Public Finance and Public Choice* 99; C.M. Rose, 'The shadow of *the Cathedral*' (1997)
106 *Yale Law Journal* 2175; and J.L. Schroeder, 'Three's a crowd: A feminist critique of
Calabresi and Melamed's one view of the cathedral' (1999) 84 *Cornell Law Review* 394.
[131] Nicita and Rizzolli, Property rules, 100.
[132] Thank you to Graeme Laurie for his thoughts on this.
[133] This is the approach taken by Wall in his analysis of property rules. He contends that,
'only property rules are able to protect income rights in a resource' (Wall, 'Legal status of
body parts', 799).
[134] Schroeder, 'Three's a crowd', 410.

rules which exist within a particular legal system. Attempts to conceive of the domain of 'property law' as being a discrete, defined (or even definable), and entirely knowable entity is probably doomed to failure. The law does not operate in neat categories. For that reason, any number of legal rules might operate across categories, but still all be concerned with the business of regulating our use of objects of property and, as such, be seen as 'property law' in a broader sense.[135]

Connected to this is perhaps a more basic point. Something is not a property rule because it relates to the voluntary sale of (entitlements to) objects. To encompass sale, and thus protections for income rights, under the rubric of 'property' rules, is to enshrine an ideological commitment to the market in the very notion of property.[136] Instead, by seeing property rules as an umbrella term, we allow that the protections engendered are broad-ranging, encompassing those rules generally contained within property institutions: trespassory, property-limitation, expropriation, and appropriation rules.[137] Trespassory rules govern trespasses to our property interests and property-limitation rules limit our uses and abuses of our property rights, and so on. Conceiving of property rules in this more straightforward manner is preferable. Doing so not only describes the actual function of the rules, but does not presuppose the presence either way of market mechanisms as the method of enforceability.

The consequence of all this is that, in relation to biomaterials, when income rights are seen as separate from the core use-privileges and control-powers which might govern them, we avoid conflating the power to transfer with any right to accrue value from that transfer. Separating the powers of control from the right to income allows us to admit property, without necessarily having to permit biomaterials to be traded on the market. The difficulty here is that, as we saw in Chapter 1, there is a flourishing global market in tissues, cells, and other biomaterials. Moreover, as noted at the beginning of Section 4, objections in this regard tend not to centre on markets in biomaterials *tout court*, but display a selective moral disquiet about the *source* engaging in

---

[135] R. Nwabueze, 'Body parts in property theory: An integrated framework' (2014) 40 *Journal of Medical Ethics* 33, 35. See also R. Nwabueze, 'Cadavers, body parts, and the remedial problem' in I. Goold, K. Greasley, J. Herring, and L. Skene (eds), *Persons, Parts and Property: How Should We Regulate Human Tissue in the 21st Century?* (Oxford: Hart Publishing, 2014), pp. 157–175, pp. 173–174.

[136] Something which Wall seemingly tried to avoid in his own recognition of the separability of property (control) rights and income rights. Wall, 'Legal status of body parts', 789–792.

[137] Harris, *Property and Justice*, pp. 23–41.

commercial activity. Consider, for instance, Justice Arabian's comments in *Moore*:

> Plaintiff has asked us to recognize and enforce a right to sell one's own body tissue for profit. He entreats us to regard the human vessel – the single most venerated and protected subject in any civilized society – as equal with the basest commercial commodity. He urges us to commingle the sacred with the profane. He asks much.[138]

Concerns of this ilk imply that permitting individuals a portion of the income rights for their tissues is to wrongfully commodify those tissues or the individuals themselves. But if it is an appeal to the wrong of commodification that is at issue, we need to know wherein this wrong lies and why.

4.2   Wrongful Commercialisation and Commodification?

Stephen Wilkinson argues that 'to call something "commodification" [in the normative sense] is to express moral disapproval and refer to a distinctive kind of wrong: the wrong of commodification'.[139] For him, wrongful commodification occurs when things 'are treated as if they are commodities despite their not being (really) fungible or merely instrumentally valuable'.[140] When applied to human biomaterials, this can be resolved into two related aspects. First is a concern that exchanging

---

[138] *Moore*, Supreme Court at 148–149. Justice Arabian either misunderstood or mischaracterised the nature of the claims before him. Moore was not asking that the courts rule that he be allowed to sell his tissues on the open market, but that he be recognised as retaining such control that he could prevent others from doing so non-consensually.

[139] S. Wilkinson, 'Commodification' in R.E. Ashcroft *et al.* (eds), *Principles of Health Care Ethics* (Chichester: John Wiley and Sons, 2007), pp. 285–291, p. 285.

[140] *Ibid.*, p. 286. The conceptual terrain with regards to commodification claims is complex. There is not space here for a thoroughgoing analysis of all of the varied aspects of the debate, but see, for example, M.C. Kaveny, 'Commodifying the polyvalent good of health care' (1999) 24 *Journal of Medicine and Philosophy* 207, 209; M. Nussbaum, 'Objectification' (1995) 24 *Philosophy and Public Affairs* 249, 257; M.J. Radin and M. Sunder, 'Introduction: The subject and object of commodification' in M.M. Ertman and J.C. Williams (eds), *Rethinking Commodification: Cases and Readings in Law and Culture* (New York: New York University Press, 2005), pp. 8–29, p. 8; M.J. Radin, *Contested Commodities* (Cambridge: Harvard University Press, 1996, reprinted 2001), especially Chs 1, 2, 7, and 8; S. Altman, '(Com)modifying experience' (1991) 65 *Southern California Law Review* 293; I.G. Cohen, 'The Price of everything, the value of nothing: Reframing the commodification debate' (2003) 117 *Harvard Law Review* 689; and J.C. Williams and V.A. Zelizer, 'To commodify or not to commodify' in M.M. Ertman and J.C. Williams (eds), *Rethinking Commodification: Cases and Readings in Law and Culture* (New York: New York University Press, 2005), pp. 362–382.

human biomaterials for money represents a form of value incommensurability; that is, the value of human tissue is not (and ought not to be) reducible to a common measure, such as money, which would enable it to be traded. The second is that allowing the source to engage in commercial activity with regards to their biomaterials is to treat as a thing something which ought not to be so treated.[141] Let us examine each of these in turn.

To say that there is a value incommensurability in this area is to say that biomaterials and material gain belong to different, incommensurable spheres of valuation; spheres which ought not to be brought together. It is to claim that there is no true way to trade off (and indeed that we ought not to) the loss of one's tissue with money (or other goods) gained in return. There are two facets to claims such as these: one regarding the nature of the goods and one regarding the nature of the transaction.[142]

We cannot, at least without ruling out a market in biomaterials writ large, think that there is something in the nature of the goods (biomaterials) themselves which makes them incommensurable. Biomaterials are already traded and those who raise concerns about commercialisation do not suggest that all instances of biomaterials markets ought not to be permitted. We concurrently attach diverse (and perhaps divergent) values to a variety of goods, including biomaterials. Market ideals coexist with non-market ones and goods are often, as Radin notes, incompletely commodified.[143] Whether or not particular instances of commodification (incomplete or otherwise) are therefore acceptable may depend on the nature of the transaction; that is, whether it assumes a value equilibrium or fungibility with the goods in question. For this reason, for some, it is the *expressive* nature of certain transactions which may function as a constraint on exchanges of goods belonging to different spheres of valuation.[144]

---

[141] This is similar to one of the objections to self-ownership we met in Chapter 7. For arguments in relation to body parts and biomaterials which touch on both the 'value incommensurability' and 'treating as a thing' aspects see K. Greasley, 'Property rights in the human body: Commodification and objectification' in I. Goold, K. Greasley, J. Herring, and L. Skene (eds), *Persons, Parts and Property: How Should We Regulate Human Tissue in the 21st Century?* (Oxford: Hart Publishing, 2014), pp. 68–87.

[142] Cohen, 'Price of everything', 696–710. See also J. Griffin, *Well-Being: Its Meaning, Measurement and Importance* (Oxford: Clarendon Press, 1986); and R. Chang, (ed.), *Incommensurability, Incomparability, and Practical Reason* (Cambridge: Harvard University Press, 1997).

[143] Radin, *Contested Commodities*, pp. 103–114. She says that '[s]ocial policy reflects our understandings of the meaning(s) of human interactions... it becomes simplistic to think of [these] choice[s] as binary: either complete commodification or complete non-commodification' (p. 103).

[144] Cohen, 'Price of everything', 707–710.

The expressive concern is one about the communicative effect of treating things from one sphere of valuation *as if* they are commensurable with those from another. In relation to biomaterials, it is a concern about the value equivalence of those biomaterials with money. The difficulty with this is that we ought not to elide moral concerns about our treatment of separated biomaterials with those regarding our treatment of persons. When we speak of separated biomaterials we cannot think that those items are wrongly commodified in and of themselves; that they are not capable of being objects or things in the relevant sense. Third parties can, and do acquire these materials, whereupon they are treated as things and are subsumed into the market. They are, thus, commodified. Nonetheless, the commodification of biomaterials does not necessarily imply commodification of the person. If arguments from commodification are to have any bite then the relevant moral objection must centre on cases where the *person* from whom the particular biomaterial has originated is somehow wrongfully commodified.

In this respect, it is worth considering Martha Nussbaum's account of objectification. She outlines several features which may be present when claims about objectification are made:

1. *Instrumentality*: The objectifier treats the object as a tool of his or her purposes.
2. *Denial of autonomy*: The objectifier treats the object as lacking in autonomy and self-determination.
3. *Inertness*: The objectifier treats the object as lacking in agency, and perhaps also in activity.
4. *Fungibility*: The objectifier treats the object as interchangeable (a) with other objects of the same type, and/or (b) with objects of other types.
5. *Violability*: The objectifier treats the object as lacking in boundary-integrity, as something that it is permissible to break up, smash, break into.
6. *Ownership*: The objectifier treats the object as something that is owned by another, can be bought or sold, etc.
7. *Denial of subjectivity*: The objectifier treats the object as something whose experience and feelings (if any) need not be taken into account.[145]

The common thread running through these characterisations is that they all involve a third party treating the person objectified in an objectionable

---

[145] Nussbaum, 'Objectification', 257. Objectification here is 'a relatively loose cluster-term' (*ibid.*). Those who use it often mean to capture more than one of several features (258), with commodification being a subset of objectification (284).

manner. And this gets to the nub of the issue regarding the use and sale of biomaterials.

As Wilkinson observes, 'one of the main ways in which we fail to treat (autonomous, competent) people as ends is by doing things to them (or that involve them) without requiring their valid consent'.[146] We can see why this would be the case. Consent is a means of respecting the autonomy of persons. If this is done in a substantive sense, we do not use persons as mere means since we are acting in line with their autonomous goals and interests. Hence we wrongfully commodify persons, and treat them as a mere means, where we permit third parties to *non-consensually* acquire either use or income rights (or both) in biomaterials, while simultaneously denying them to the source of those materials.

Although arguments from commodification are used in attempts to justify the exclusion of the source from market transactions regarding their biomaterials, it is not clear that they do the requisite normative work in this area, or, if they do, why they should apply solely in relation to the *source* of those materials. Given that a market in tissue commodities already exists,[147] it may be unreasonable to protect third parties in this respect, while excluding the very source of the tissue. We cannot coherently worry about the commodifying effect of recognising property and income rights in the source, while protecting those self-same rights in third parties. Therefore, unless good reasons to the contrary can be found, the presumption ought to be in favour of permitting the source both the property and income rights in relation to their bodies. As Laurie and colleagues argue:

> It is entirely reasonable to hold that some financial reward should also be given to the source of the valuable sample while, at the same time, accepting that the majority of the spoils should return to those who have done the work in creating a patentable invention. It is *not* reasonable to exclude completely from the equation the one person who can make everything possible.[148]

---

[146] Wilkinson, 'Commodification', 290.

[147] Here as in elsewhere the issue of boundary-setting looms large. In this case, the demarcation of market from non-market, and the purposes for which such boundaries are drawn. For a critique which questions the assumption of any such boundary, as well examining attempts to at demarcation see Hoeyer, *Exchanging Human Bodily Material*, especially Chs 2 and 5.

[148] Laurie, Harmon, and Porter, *Mason and McCall Smith's Law and Medical Ethics*, p. 494. Dickenson puts it well in her discussion of Cooper and Waldby, saying, '[t]hey view the no-property rule about extracted bodily tissue as aiding and abetting the seizure of surplus economic value from human research subjects' (*Property in the Body*, p. 45). See Cooper and Waldby, *Clinical Labour*, p. 8.

Indeed, we should be wary of arguments which support, prima facie, such exclusion.

For instance, drawing on Harris, Maddox argues that income rights in separated biomaterials ought to be viewed as 'windfall wealth'. This is 'a new item of social wealth to which no-one in the community has a better claim than anyone else'.[149] He contends that '[i]f one accepts this argument that income rights in these materials are windfall wealth, they do not vest in the hospital or research institute by virtue of their abandonment or gift by their source. They are a new right and were not the source's to give.'[150] The broad point that Maddox is making is that windfall wealth ought to accrue to the community rather than private organisations. Nevertheless, whilst there is merit in such a position generally speaking, it is not obvious, in the specific case of biomaterials, that 'no-one in the community has a better claim than anyone else'. Despite the separation between property and income rights which I have argued for in this chapter, we are still talking about income rights over materials which are owned by the source. In this respect, they have at least a prima facie claim to the income. We might agree that on the balance there are countervailing reasons why the commercial benefit ought to accrue to the community, but this is not the same as saying that the initial rights ought not to vest in the source.

There may sometimes be practical, policy, and other reasons why we might not want to grant income rights to the source of biomaterials. Context, in this arena, may make all the difference. The kinds of considerations which may figure in our deliberations in this regard include 'the kind of body part or material at issue; whether the property right benefits the progenitor, and the social consequences and symbolic meaning of granting the right'.[151] Even so, when conflicts over the uses of biomaterials arise, and where the courts decide that individuals cannot have property in biomaterials (and/or income rights in these), *but* third parties can, they wrongly shift the focus of judicial protection from the source and from their use and control over the materials.

5   Conclusion: Legitimating the Use of Biomaterials

In this chapter I was concerned with the *legitimate* use and transfer of separated biomaterials. What we saw is that when we reorientate our

---

[149] Maddox, 'Abandonment', 246.   [150] *Ibid.*, 247.
[151] K. Greasley, 'Property rights in the human body', pp. 68–87, p. 87.

normative touchstone away from a free-floating consent regime and towards property, we can be properly attentive the interests of the source. Consent is the mode by which persons give normative sanction to the use and transfer of their biomaterials. Importantly, the control-powers which are exercised when they do so are part and parcel of their core property rights. Consent does not stand apart from those rights. In this manner, consent is a legitimator, functioning to authorise a change in the normative baseline and altering the moral and/or legal relations between persons and some other party or parties. Others can acquire the ownership of separated body parts; however, this must happen via a process of legitimate transfer. Whether this takes the form of donations or sale, the relevant feature is the consensual agreement by the original owner (or their proxy) to the transfer of their property and the property rights held therein.

Along with Imogen Goold, I have noted elsewhere that '[w]e already deal with body parts and biomaterials as we do many other things that are accepted as property. Blood, organs, and various biomaterials are donated to others for transplant, and to researchers for use in studies. They are sometimes sold, sometimes stolen, and often stored.'[152] In this chapter, we saw that various ways of dealing with biomaterials logically presuppose source property rights. Although sometimes discussed as alternatives to a property approach, here we saw that both gifting and trusts form part of the law of property. They cannot, therefore, be used in order to deny either the existence of property rights in biomaterials themselves (that is, to say biomaterials are *res nullius*) or the source's prima facie claims over them. While transfers for value, including sale, raise a number of concerns for some, following Christman, I argued that the power to transfer (a feature of core property rights) and income rights are analytically separable. As such, we could accept that persons have property rights in their biomaterials without also permitting them to receive income in respect of them. Such a determination, however, would need further defence since it is not obvious why income rights ought to be permitted to accrue to third parties to the exclusion of the very source of the valuable materials.

---

[152] Goold and Quigley, 'Human biomaterials', p. 232. On the breadth of these uses, and the various parties with interests in human bodily materials, see I. Goold, 'Why does it matter how we regulate the use of human body parts?' (2014) 40 *Journal of Medical Ethics* 3.

10

The Future of Human Biomaterials?

1 Introduction

In the opening chapter of this book, I noted that Lord Judge CJ, in *Yearworth*, said that 'developments in medical science now require a re-analysis of the common law's treatment of and approach to the issue of ownership of parts or products of a living human body'.[1] This book has provided that. In it, I have given a new defence, underpinned by self-ownership, of the position that persons ought to be seen as the prima facie holders of property rights in their separated biomaterials. The general motivation for the analysis given stems from a broader interest in how the law can and ought to deal with challenges raised by advancing biotechnology. Human biomaterials provide an illuminating illustration of such challenges. A more specific motivation is connected to concerns regarding the generally asymmetrical approach of the law to resolving conflicts involving biomaterials; that is, the tendency to permit third parties to acquire property rights in biomaterials, while denying those self-same rights to the source of those materials.

Three main insights have emerged from the discussion. First, despite the challenges posed for the law by novel disputes involving biomaterials, the common law can evolve to deal with them. This we saw in relation to cases such as *Yearworth, JCM v. ANA, Clarke v. Macourt,* and *Arora*. Second, this evolution has required, and will continue to require, the law to confront and move boundaries which it has constructed; in particular, those which serve to delineate property from non-property in relation to biomaterials. This is the nature of biotechnological developments in general. They expose gaps and inadequacies in the law's approach, which then necessitates a reappraisal of these within the law. Third, biotechnological advances, and resultant legal challenges, help us to re-evaluate the philosophical basis of the law's approach, including the boundary-work which has led to the law as it currently stands.

---

[1] *Yearworth* at [45].

Advances in relation to biomaterials prompt us not only to reconsider the normative significance of the presumed boundary between persons and things, subjects and objects, but also to question the philosophical foundations and boundaries of property law itself.

2   Human Biomaterials and the Property (r)Evolution

As we saw in Part I of the book, biomaterials can now be put to a multitude of uses not envisaged in the past. In the biotechnological world, the body and its parts have become enormously valuable in diverse ways, including scientifically and commercially. We have become 'humans as medicines'.[2] Entire tissue economies have developed in order to exploit the latent biovalue in our bodies and biomaterials.[3] This biovalue is harnessed through a multifaceted, complicated (and often globalised) institutional complex. Within this system, biomaterials are acquired, handled, processed, used, and transferred. A further facet of the practical institutional complex is that activities involving biomaterials tend only to occur within organisations where there are particular domains of expertise (e.g. research laboratories). Moreover, they can only legitimately take place within the legal institutional limits placed on them (e.g. the requirements of the two Human Tissue Acts). Indeed, the latter has a significant impact on the former. In the context of the Human Tissue Act 2004, for instance, only establishments licensed by the Human Tissue Authority are permitted to store, procure, process, test, distribute, or import/export relevant materials.[4]

One consequence of all this is that conflicts can arise regarding the use and control of biomaterials, something brought into sharp focus throughout the book by cases such as *Moore*, *Greenberg*, and *Catalona*. The challenges for the law, however, are not confined to conflicts arising solely out of commercial or quasi-commercial interests. This we saw in sperm cases. Together the cases discussed expose the difficulties which attend the law when called upon to deal with novel challenges in relation to biomaterials. Insofar as the law was previously focused on the 'no property' rule and consent-based approaches, it was not well-equipped to deal with these. The law of consent forms the bulwark of protections accorded to individuals regarding their bodies and separated biomaterials.

---

[2] Brazier, 'Human(s) as medicine(s)'.   [3] Waldby and Mitchell, *Tissue Economies*.
[4] See Human Tissue Authority, Do I need a licence? at: www.hta.gov.uk/policies/do-i-need-licence (accessed 27 November 2017).

But it has proved insufficient to resolve novel disputes since it cannot protect the multitude of interests that living individuals might have in their biomaterials.

Where property has been used, the piecemeal development of the law in relation to the body and biomaterials led to problematic (property) principles becoming embedded; that is, the no property baseline and the work/skill exception. The sperm cases aside, a striking consequence of this is the exclusion of the source from the ownership of biomaterials. This is concerning because, as Hoppe puts it:

> Human tissue and body products are already being treated in a proprie-tary fashion and property rights are granted to those who take the tissue but not those who possess the tissue initially... This leads to the possibi-lity of exploitation by others, which in turn remains unsanctioned because the initial refusal to grant property rights to the source means that no civil remedies are available and no criminal sanctions in relation to the dis-honest appropriation are possible.[5]

It is of course true that the source may not be the only person who has interests in biomaterials, nor are they the only party who could have their rights in respect of these infringed. Researchers or other legitimate possessors of biomaterials also have an interest in being protected in their use and control of these.[6] But, as Price argued, '[w]hilst *researchers'* key interest is the knowledge generated by the donated specimen this is by no means the whole story for donors, who are also concerned with their contribution to certain types of research by way of their own bodily materials'.[7] He also said that '[t]he primary moral right of control is broader than simply a right not to be *harmed...* The primary wrong is committed where a person is disenfranchised from exercising their right to control the future use of the tissue per se.'[8] In being excluded from the protections offered by the law of property, when third parties such as researchers are not, persons are rendered vulnerable to unjustified dis-possession. They also lack adequate remedial avenues for damage and other wrongs done. In being consent-focused, the two Human Tissue Acts and the HFE Act are ill-equipped to deal with the different types of interests and challenges at stake. Moreover, although the 2004 Act, for example, makes it an offence to use biomaterials for scheduled purposes without appropriate consent, the relevant provisions are limited. They only cover (relatively minor) criminal sanctions for infringement. As

---

[5] Hoppe, *Bioequity*, p. 137.   [6] Goold and Quigley, 'Human biomaterials', p. 258.
[7] Price, *Human Tissue*, pp. 178–179.   [8] *Ibid.*, p. 178.

Yearworth and other cases demonstrate, something more is needed to complement existing human tissue legislation. Hence, the more recent openness to property approaches in a number of jurisdictions is promising.

Property law gives us a pragmatic and established framework for dealing with things.[9] It already has a comprehensive set of doctrines and rules for dealing with the transfer of chattels. Via its system of rules we can manage many of the varied problems which may arise regarding biomaterials; from unconsented interferences such as theft to illegitimate transfers to negligent damage. Property law can thus provide a means to protect source interests in biomaterials, not just those of third parties who might acquire them. If human biomaterials are obtained illegitimately (that is, non-consensually or without proper disclosures being made) then property law provides a framework for redress. Transfers may be voidable and remedies available which can deal with a variety of misappropriations or misuses of these materials, something which is not available within the framework of the free-floating consent-based regimes inherent in the current legislation.

It has been suggested by Jonathan Herring that new legislation is needed to regulate human biomaterials and to deal with the novel challenges raised by advancing bioscience.[10] However, developing *sui generis* legislative regimes is not without its difficulties. Lyria Bennett Moses has outlined some of the problems with such an approach:

> (1) the problem of completeness (or the creation of 'gaps' in the law); (2) the problem of administrative costs associated with creating (and amending and interpreting) multiple legal regimes, possible additional bureaucracy, and the need for the community (especially the legal profession) to navigate multiple legal regimes; (3) the risk that a *sui generis* regime might be overtaken by technological change to the extent it makes assumptions based on the technological landscape at the time of its creation; and (4) the risk that *sui generis* legislation will be distorted by special interest politics.[11]

For these reasons, drafting new legislation which could anticipate novel challenges in relation to human biomaterials is unlikely to be satisfactory.

---

[9] Goold and Quigley, 'Human biomaterials', pp. 245–259. See also Douglas and Goold, 'Property in human biomaterials', 502.

[10] J. Herring, 'Why we need a statute regime to regulate bodily material' in I. Goold, J. Herring, L. Skene, and K. Greasley (eds), *Persons, Parts and Property: How Should We Regulate Human Tissue in the 21st Century?* (Oxford: Hart Publishing, 2014), pp. 213–229.

[11] Bennett Moses, 'The problem with alternatives', p. 200.

It is also unnecessary. A more explicit recognition of source property rights in biomaterials would supplement the current statutory provisions in a significant way. Accordingly, when further unforeseen novel challenges arise (which they inevitably will), these could be dealt with within the existing legal framework: human tissue legislation plus property law.

3   Questioning Boundaries and Philosophical Foundations

The recent evolution which has taken place in the common law with regards to property in biomaterials necessitated the revision of previously presumed boundaries; principally, this entailed a shift from the old – and seemingly entrenched – no property rule. In Chapter 3, we saw that, given the no property baseline, the idea of normative transformation became key for the law. If biomaterials are to be admitted to the realm of property, something must happen to facilitate a change in legal status from *res nullius* to *res* – a normative boundary must be crossed. For a time, the work/skill exception fulfilled this role. However, as we saw in detail in that chapter, the exception is lacking on a number of levels. On a practical level, interpreting its scope and application is far from straightforward. Moreover, the supposed rationales which could be said to trigger or underpin it are lacking at either an explanatory or a justificatory level. In Chapter 4, we saw that with *Yearworth* the death knell of both the no property rule and the work/skill exception has been tolled (although only future cases will reveal whether or not they are actually dead). There I argued that the law appears to be moving towards viewing mere separation as being normatively transformative vis-à-vis human biomaterials and property. Nevertheless, we saw that separation from persons does not (and cannot) on its own, give us a prima facie justification (moral or legal) for allocating property rights to the source, or for that matter to third parties. Something more is needed to both explain the change in normative legal status upon separation (*res nullius* to *res*) and to justify the (initial) allocation of any property rights created.

The principal arguments in this regard were given in chapters 7 and 8. There we saw that the law engages in significant boundary-work, attempting to demarcate persons from things and non-property from property. This is evident in the way in which distinctions and dichotomies are constructed. The lines drawn are presumed to answer normative questions regarding whether or not something ought to be considered as property. For the law, and numerous commentators, the line between person and thing is seen as having both ontological validity and normative force (morally and legally speaking). Yet, as we have seen, it is not that simple. Fluids, cells, tissues, organs, as well as synthetic or biohybrid materials, move in and out of us, either because of natural biological processes or medical intervention.[12] In this manner, the posited separation between person and things is challenged, something which the discussion of everyday cyborgs in particular illustrated. Given this ontological fluidity, we ought not to see moral and legal categories, and the normative assumptions contained within them, as being forever fixed and immutable. Our normative conclusions cannot be fixed, because the construction (literal and otherwise) of our bodies is not fixed.[13] It is thus difficult, in the biotechnological world, to maintain a normative bright line between persons as subject and things as objects for the purposes of a property analysis. The blurring of the subject–object boundary creates a moral justificatory challenge for the law. If the person–thing dichotomy is called into question, then notions such as distancing and separability cannot do the normative work asked of them, rendering uncertain the philosophical basis for the current legal approach. Given this, upon what basis ought property rights in separated biomaterials be created and allocated?

The position argued for in this book is that the moral justification for, and analytical route to, ownership of (and property rights in) separated biomaterials is quite straightforward, *if* we start with self-ownership. As outlined in Chapter 7, a person's self-ownership interests are those interests that they have regarding themselves, their bodies, and their lives. They are best viewed as the prima facie set of use-privileges and control-powers which persons have with regards to their embodied selves. This was defended not just as a descriptive claim regarding the interests that persons have regarding themselves and their bodies, but also as a normative statement about the moral force of those interests. Self-ownership rights are those which persons ought to be accorded in virtue of their autonomy and which, when duly recognised (and enforced), can be seen as forming a perimeter of normative protection

---

[12] Hoeyer, *Exchanging Human Bodily Material*, pp. 5 and 166.

[13] Shildrick has said, '[o]nce it is acknowledged that a human body is not a discrete entity ending at the skin, and that material technologies constantly disorder our boundaries, either through prosthetic extensions or through the internalization of mechanical parts, it is difficult to maintain that those whose bodies fail to conform to normative standards are less whole or complete than others' ('Why should our bodies end at the skin?', 24). She makes this comment specifically in the context of a discussion on prosthetics and people with disabilities.

around their personal domain. Recognising that individuals have interests in the use and control of themselves and their bodies firmly anchors autonomy to considerations of self-ownership, such that the normative force of the rights of self-ownership, and the correlative duties of third parties, can be seen as autonomy-protecting.

Self-ownership thus creates a strong presumption that ownership of separated biomaterials should vest in the source of those materials. Unless there are good arguments to the contrary, the use and control that persons exercise over their embodied selves ought to extend to their parts once separated. The property interests (moral and legal) that persons ought to be recognised as having in their biomaterials after separation are a consequence and mirror of their pre-existing (moral) self-ownership interests. If this is correct, then separation, in and of itself, ought not to be viewed as either a necessary or justified mode of creating *de novo* property rights in separated biomaterials. This is because no *de novo* rights are in fact being created. Far from newly separated biomaterials being considered nobody's thing (as *res nullius* requiring normative transformation to *res*), they are already somebody's: the person's from whom they have been removed. The rights which persons have over their biomaterials are a normatively contiguous and co-extensive with those they have in their embodied selves; that is, those they have as self-owners. The normative authority they have in this respect does not automatically change upon separation (the 'no moral magic' principle).

In presenting my account of self-ownership, I drew on the account of property and ownership given in chapters 5 and 6. There I argued that property rights are entitlements which carry corresponding and enforceable duties on the part of others. They are *in rem* rights and, as such, are good against the world. Property interests, and the core of property rights, are comprised of a set of open-ended use-privileges and control-powers. Related to this, a person ought to be considered to be an owner when their rights with regards to the thing in question are better than all others *and* when they are the one with the power to authorise a change in the normative baseline.

In characterising self-ownership as I have done, as being the use-privileges and control-powers which persons have with regards to their embodied selves, I run the risk of being charged with attempting to derive morally normative positions and claims from fundamentally legal concepts. Admittedly, this is a danger that all debates regarding self-ownership face. This is because it is 'expressed in juridical terms – the language of rights and privileges whose structure is borrowed from legal contexts in which they are also operative'.[14] Yet it is not the case that the language of rights, property, and ownership is exclusively legal. There are moral dimensions which transcend (and underpin) their legal ones. In this respect, while the account of the core of property given in the book might be reflected in the very specific legal structure and rules which comprise the law of property, it is essentially extra-legal. It is an account of the general moral interests which we have in controlling the uses of things. Consequently, although it is compatible with interpretations of the legal structure of property as being broadly located in the right to exclude or duties of non-interference, it is not to be identified (solely) with them.

Likewise, I have not offered a legal concept of self-ownership. Christman has argued that 'to understand the true contours of [self-ownership] rights, it is necessary to probe the moral considerations which make them important, to utilize concepts which... are closer to the root ideas that principles such as self-ownership express'.[15] In this manner, the view of property and ownership developed earlier gets us close to the roots of the moral idea at issue. As such, it is conceptually useful. Even if the account of self-ownership given borrows from legal concepts, it has unmistakeable normative moral dimensions. The interests which comprise it are morally weighty and make moral demands on each of us.

Some readers may remain unpersuaded that persons ought to be seen as self-owners and as having property in their bodies and biomaterials prior to any separation taking place. This need not hinder them, however, from accepting that persons ought to be presumptively allocated legal property rights over their separated biomaterials. It is the idea of the person's prior normative authority and corresponding rights of use and control which are important (whether or not the label of self-owner is accepted or not). If, as I have argued, there is no interruption in the continuity of a person's normative authority and rights upon physical separation, then this ought to be enough for legal property rights over their biomaterials to be created and allocated to them. The principal manner in which the law protects the use and control of things in the external world is via the law of property. As such, it represents an existing, established, mechanism with a set of comprehensive rules for the protection of these 'new' extra-personal things.

---

[14] Christman, *Myth of Property*, p. 151.   [15] *Ibid.*

4 A Final Word: Philosophic Deadwood?

In this book I have given a philosophically grounded analysis of the justification for vesting individuals with ownership of themselves and their separated parts. In this respect, I have argued that each of us ought to be considered (morally) to be self-owners and, consequently, as having property rights (moral and legal) in our separated parts and products. Even there might be, as noted in Chapter 7, overriding moral or policy considerations which trump putative claims based in self-ownership. However, recognising persons as self-owners, and consequently as owners of their separated parts, gives us pause to think carefully about whether, and which, infringements are truly justified. Harris referred to self-ownership as 'philosophic deadwood wood [which] must be cut away',[16] claiming that *if* we were to recognise a person's ownership interest in their bodies, '[i]t would have to be conceded that the relevant ownership interest was well down the ownership spectrum, far below the full-blooded ownership which applies to other chattels'.[17] I hope that this book has shown that, in relation to persons, their bodies, and their separated biomaterials, nothing of the sort need be conceded.

---

[16] Harris, *Property and Justice*, p. 13.   [17] *Ibid.*, p. 187.

BIBLIOGRAPHY

Ackerman, B.A., *Private Property and the Constitution* (New Haven: Yale University Press, 1977)

Altman, S., '(Com)modifying experience' (1991) 65 *Southern California Law Review* 293

Andrews, L., 'My body, my property' (1986) 16 *Hastings Center Report* 28

Anonymous, 'Alistair Cooke's bones "stolen"' *BBC News* (22 December 2005), http://news.bbc.co.uk/1/hi/4552742.stm

Anonymous, 'The rape of the lock: Is it larceny?' (1961) 25 *Journal of Criminal Law* 163

Archard, D., 'Informed consent: Autonomy and self-ownership' (2008) 25 *Journal of Applied Philosophy* 19

Arneson, R., 'Lockean self-ownership: Towards a demolition' (1991) 39 *Political Studies* 36

Attas, D., 'Fragmenting property' (2006) 25 *Law and Philosophy* 119

Attas, D., *Liberty, Property, and Markets* (Aldershot: Ashgate Publishing Ltd, 2005)

Baron, J., 'Rescuing the bundle of rights metaphor in property law' (2014) 82 *University of Cincinnati Law Review* 57

Becker, L.C., 'The moral basis of property' in J.R. Pennock and J.W. Chapman (eds), *Property: Nomos XXII* (New York: New York University Press, 1980), pp. 187–220

Becker, L.C., *Property Rights: Philosophic Foundations* (London: Routledge and Keegan Paul, 1980)

Bennett Moses, L., 'The problem with alternatives: The importance of property law in regulating excised human tissue and *in vitro* human embryos' in I. Goold, J. Herring, L. Skene, and K. Greasley (eds), *Persons, Parts and Property: How Should We Regulate Human Tissue in the 21st Century?* (Oxford: Hart Publishing, 2014), pp. 197–214

Bentham, J., 'Anarchical fallacies' in J. Waldron (ed.), *Nonsense Upon Stilts: Bentham, Burke, and Marx on the Rights of Man* (London: Methuen, 1987), pp. 46–76

Berlin, I., 'Two concepts of liberty' in H.E. Hardy (ed.), *Liberty, Incorporating 'Four Essays on Liberty'* (Oxford: Oxford University Press, 2002), pp. 166–217

Beyleveld, D. and Brownsword, R., *Consent in the Law* (Oxford: Hart Publishing, 2007)

Beyleveld, D. and Brownsword, R., 'My body, my body parts, my property' (2000) 8 *Health Care Analysis* 87

Birks, P., *Unjust Enrichment* (Oxford: Clarendon Press, 2005)

Blackstone, W., *Commentaries on the Laws of England*, 1st edn (Oxford: Clarendon Press, 1765–1769)

Block, B.P., 'A Tissue Act not to be sneezed at' (2004) 168 *Justice of the Peace* 291

Blumberg, B.S. *et al.*, 'Ted Slavin's blood and the development of the HBV vaccine' (1985) 312 *New England Journal of Medicine* 189

Brassington, I., 'John Harris' argument for a duty to research' (2007) 21 *Bioethics* 160

Brazier, M., 'Human(s) as medicine(s)' in S. McLean (ed.), *First Do No Harm* (Aldershort: Ashgate Publishing Ltd, 2006), pp. 187–202

Brazier, M., 'Patient autonomy and consent to treatment: The role of the law?' (1987) 7 *Legal Studies* 169

Brazier, M., 'Retained organs: Ethics and humanity' (2002) 22 *Legal Studies* 550

Brazier, M. (ed.), *Clerk and Lindsell on Torts*, 17th edn (London: Sweet and Maxwell, 1995)

Brazier, M. and Cave, E., *Medicine, Patients and the Law*, 6th edn (Manchester: Manchester University Press, 2016).

Brazier, M. and Miola, J., 'Bye-bye Bolam: A medical litigation revolution?' (2000) 8 *Medical Law Review* 85

Brazier, M. and Ost, S., *Bioethics, Medicine and the Criminal Law: Medicine and Bioethics in the Theatre of the Criminal Process* (Cambridge: Cambridge University Press, 2013)

Breakey, H., 'Who's afraid of property rights? Rights as core concepts, coherent, prima facie, situated and specified' (2014) 33 *Law and Philosophy* 573

Brenkert, G.G., 'Self-ownership, freedom, and autonomy' (1998) 2 *Journal of Ethics* 27

Bridge, M., *Personal Property Law*, 4th edn (Oxford: Oxford University Press, 2015)

Bristol Royal Infirmary Inquiry, *Inquiry into the Management of Care of Children Receiving Complex Heart Surgery at the Bristol Royal Infirmary: Interim Report* (London: The Stationery Office, 2000).

Brownsword, R., 'The cult of consent: Fixation and fallacy' (2004) 15 *King's College Law Journal* 223

Brownsword, R., 'Property in human tissue: Triangulating the issue' in M. Steinman, P. Sykora, and U. Wiesing (eds), *Altruism Reconsidered: Exploring New Approaches to Property in Human Tissue* (Aldershot: Ashgate Publishing Ltd, 2009), pp. 93–104

Brudner, A., 'The unity of property law' (1991) 4 *Canadian Journal of Law and Jurisprudence* 3

Calabresi, G., 'Do we own our bodies?' (1991) 1 *Health Matrix* 5

Calabresi, G., 'Remarks: The simple virtues of The Cathedral" (1997) 106 *Yale Law Journal* 2201

Calabresi, G. and Melamed, D., 'Property rules, liability rules, and inalienability: One view of the Cathedral' (1972) 85 *Harvard Law Review* 1089

Campbell, A.V., McLean, S.A.M., Gutridge, K., and Harper, H., 'Human tissue legislation: Listening to the professionals' (2008) 34 *Journal of Medical Ethics* 104

Campbell, C.S., 'Body, self, and the property paradigm' (1992) 22 *Hastings Center Report* 34

Cane, P., 'Causing conversion' (2002) 118 *Law Quarterly Review* 544

Carel, H., *Phenomenology of Illness* (Oxford: Oxford University Press, 2016).

Carey Miller, D.L., *Corporeal Moveables in Scots Law* (Edinburgh: W Green and Son Ltd, 2005)

Chalmers, D. and Nicol, D., 'Commercialisation of biotechnology: Public trust and research' (2004) 6 *International Journal of Biotechnology* 116

Chalmers, D., Burgess, M., Edwards, K., Kaye, J., Meslin, E.M., and Nicol, D., 'Marking shifts in human research ethics in the development of biobanking' (2015) 8 *Public Health Ethics* 63

Chang, R. (ed.), *Incommensurability, Incomparability, and Practical Reason* (Cambridge: Harvard University Press, 1997)

Chattin, T.M.K., 'Property rights in dead bodies' (1969) 71 *West Virginia Law Review* 377

Cheney, A., *Body Brokers: Inside America's Underground Trade in Human Remains* (New York: Broadway Books, 2006)

Christman, J., *The Myth of Property: Toward an Egalitarian Theory of Ownership* (Oxford: Oxford University Press, 1994)

Christman, J., 'Self-ownership, equality, and the structure of property rights' (1991) 19 *Political Theory* 28

Christman, J. and Anderson, J. (eds), *Autonomy and the Challenges to Liberalism* (Cambridge: Cambridge University Press, 2005)

Claeys, E., 'Bundle-of-sticks notions in legal and economic scholarship' (2011) 8 *Econ Journal Watch* 205

Clarke, A., 'Use, time, and entitlement' (2004) 57 *Current Legal Problems* 239

Clynes, M.E. and Kline, N.D., 'Cyborgs and space' (1960) September *Astronautics* 26

Coggon, J., 'Varied and principled understandings of autonomy in English law: Justifiable inconsistency or blinkered moralism?' (2007) 15 *Health Care Analysis* 235

Coggon, J. and Miola, J., 'Autonomy, liberty, and medical decision-making' (2011) 70 *Cambridge Law Journal* 523

Cohen, G.A., 'Once more into the breach of self-ownership: Reply to Narveson and Brenkert' (1998) 2 *Journal of Ethics* 57

Cohen, G.A., *Self-Ownership, Freedom, and Equality* (Cambridge: Cambridge University Press, 1995)

Cohen, I.G., 'The price of everything, the value of nothing: Reframing the commodification debate' (2003) 117 *Harvard Law Review* 689

Coke, E., *The Third Part of the Institutes of the Laws of England: Concerning High Treason, and Other Pleas of the Crown, and Criminal Causes*, 4th edn (London: A. Crooke, 1669)

Conboy, K., Medina, N., and Stanbury, S. (eds), *Writing on the Body: Female Embodiment and Feminist Theory* (New York: Columbia University Press, 1999)

Cooper, M. and Waldy, C., *Clinical Labor: Tissue Donors and Research Subjects in the Global Bioeconomy* (Durham and London: Duke University Press, 2014)

Curchin, K., 'Evading the paradox of universal self-ownership' (2007) 15 *Journal of Political Philosophy* 484

Dabrock, P., Taupitz, J., and Ried, J. (eds), *Trust in Biobanking* (Dordrecht: Springer, 2012)

Dan-Cohen, M., 'The value of ownership' (2001) 1 *Global Jurist Frontiers* 1

Davies, M., 'Queer property, queer persons: Self-ownership and beyond' (1999) 8 *Social and Legal Studies* 327

Davies, M. and Naffine, N., *Are Persons Property? Legal Debates about Property and Personality* (Aldershot: Ashgate, 2001)

Davis, L., 'Comments on Nozick's entitlement theory' (1976) 73 *Journal of Philosophy* 836

Day, J.P., 'Locke on property' (1966) 16 *The Philosophical Quarterly* 207

de Melo-Martin, I., 'A duty to participate in research: Does social context matter?' (2008) 8 *American Journal of Bioethics* 28

Department of Health, *Human Bodies, Human Choices: The Law on Human Organs and Tissues in England and Wales* (London: The Stationary Office, 2002)

Department of Health, *Learning from Bristol: The Report of the Public Inquiry into Children's Heart Surgery at the Bristol Royal Infirmary 1984–1995* (London: The Stationary Office, 2001)

Department of Health, *Reference Guide to Consent for Examination or Treatment*, 2nd edn (Crown Copyright, 2009)

Devaney, S., *Stem Cell Research and the Collaborative Regulation of Innovation* (Abingdon: Routledge, 2014)

Devaney, S., 'Tissue providers for stem cell research: The dispossessed' (2010) 2 *Law, Innovation, and Technology* 165

di Robilant, A., 'Property: A bundle of sticks or a tree?' (2013) 66 *Vanderbilt Law Review* 869

Dickenson, D., *Body Shopping: The Economy Fuelled by Flesh and Blood* (Oxford: One World Publications, 2008)

Dickenson, D., 'The lady vanishes: What's missing from the stem cell debate' (2006) 3 *Journal of Bioethical Inquiry* 43

Dickenson, D., *Property in the Body: Feminist Perspectives*, 2nd edn (Cambridge: Cambridge University Press, 2017)

Douglas, S., *Liability for Wrongful Interferences with Chattels* (Oxford: Hart Publishing, 2011)

Douglas, S., 'Property rights in human biological material' in I. Goold, J. Herring, L. Skene, and K. Greasley (eds), *Persons, Parts and Property: How Should We Regulate Human Tissue in the 21st Century?* (Oxford: Hart Publishing, 2014), pp. 89–108

Douglas, S., '*Kuwait Airways Corporation v Iraqi Airways Company* [2002]' in S. Douglas, R. Hickey, and E. Waring (eds), *Landmark Cases in Property Law* (Oxford: Hart Publishing, 2015), pp. 205–226

Douglas, S. and Goold, I., 'Property in human biomaterials: A new methodology' (2016) 75 *Cambridge Law Journal* 478

Douglas, S. and McFarlane, B., 'Defining property rights' in J. Penner and H. Smith (eds), *Philosophical Foundations of Property Law* (Oxford: Oxford University Press, 2013), pp. 219–243

Dworkin, G., *The Theory and Practice of Autonomy* (Cambridge: Cambridge University Press, 1988, reprinted 1991)

Dworkin, G. and Kennedy, I. 'Human tissue: Rights in the body and its parts' (1993) 1 *Medical Law Review* 291

Dworkin, R., 'Rights as trumps' in J. Waldron (ed.), *Theories of Rights* (Oxford: Oxford University Press, 1984), pp. 153–167

Dworkin, R., *Taking Rights Seriously* (London: Duckworth, 1977)

Dworkin, R., 'What is equality? Part 1: Equality of welfare' (1981) 10 *Philosophy and Public Affairs* 185

Dworkin, R., 'What is equality? Part 2: Equality of resources' (1981) 10 *Philosophy and Public Affairs* 283

East, E.H., *Pleas of the Crown*, vol. 2 (London: Butterworth and Cooke, 1803)

Eiseman, E. and Haga, S.B., *Handbook of Human Tissue Sources: A National Resource of Human Tissue Samples* (RAND Corporation, 1999)

Eleftheriadis, P., 'The analysis of property rights' (1996) 16 *Oxford Journal of Legal Studies* 31

Ellickson, R., 'Two cheers for the bundle-of-sticks metaphor, three cheers for Merrill and Smith' (2011) 8 *Econ Journal Watch* 215

Ellis, C. and Flaherty, M., *Investigating Subjectivity: Research on Lived Experience* (London: Sage Publications, 1992)

Epstein, R.A., 'Possession as the root of title' (1979) 13 *Georgia Law Review* 122

Erin, C., 'Who owns Mo? Using historical entitlement theory to decide the ownership of human derived cell lines' in A. Dyson and J. Harris (eds), *Ethics and Biotechnology* (Routledge: London, 1994), pp. 157–178

Erin, C. and Harris, J., 'A monopsonistic market: Or how to buy and sell human organs, tissues, and cells ethically' in I. Robinson (ed.), *Life and Death under High Technology Medicine* (Manchester: Manchester University Press, 1994), pp. 134–153

Erskine, J., *An Institute of the Law of Scotland* (Edinburgh: Legal Education Trust, 1st edn 1773, reprint)

Fabre, C., 'Reply to Wilkinson' (2008) 14 *Res Publica* 137

Fabre, C., *Whose Body Is It Anyway? Justice and the Integrity of the Person* (Oxford: Oxford University Press, 2006)

Faden, R. and Beauchamp, T., *A History and Theory of Informed Consent* (Oxford: Oxford University Press, 1986)

Farran, S., 'Storing sperm in Scotland: A risky business' (2011) 2 *European Review of Private Law* 258

Farrell, A.M., *The Politics of Blood: Ethics, Innovation, and the Regulation of Risk* (Cambridge: Cambridge University Press, 2012)

Farrell, A.M. and Brazier, M., 'Not so new directions in the law of consent? Examining *Montgomery v Lanarkshire Health Board*' (2016) 42 *Journal of Medical Ethics* 85

Feinberg, J., *The Moral Limits of the Criminal Law: Harm to Others* (Oxford: Oxford University Press, 1984)

Feinberg, J., *The Moral Limits of the Criminal Law: Harm to Self* (Oxford: Oxford University Press, 1986)

Flathman, R., 'On the alleged impossibility of an unqualified disjustificatory theory of property rights' in J.R. Pennock and J.W. Chapman (eds), *Property: Nomos XXII* (New York: New York University Press, 1980), pp. 221–243.

Fletcher, R., Fox, M., and McCandless, J., 'Legal embodiment: Analysing the body in healthcare law' (2008) 16 *Medical Law Review* 321

Ford, M., A property model of pregnancy' (2005) 1 *International Journal of Law in Context* 261

Forst, R., 'Political liberty: Integrating five conceptions of autonomy' in J. Christman and J. Anderson (eds), *Autonomy and the Challenges to Liberalism* (Cambridge: Cambridge University Press, 2005), pp. 226–242

Fox, D., 'Relativity of title at law and in equity' (2006) 65 *Cambridge Law Journal* 330

Fried, B.H., 'Left-libertarianism: A review essay' (2004) 32 *Philosophy and Public Affairs* 66

Fuller, D., 'Ownership as authority' (2014) 5 *King's Student Law Review* 16

Gaus, G.F., 'The place of autonomy within liberalism' in J. Christman and J. Anderson (eds), *Autonomy and the Challenges to Liberalism* (Cambridge: Cambridge University Press, 2005), pp. 272–306

Gieryn, T.F., 'Boundary-work and the demarcation of science from non-science: strains and interests in professional ideologies of scientists' (1983) 48 *American Sociological Review* 781

Gieryn, T.F., *Cultural Boundaries of Science* (Chicago: The University of Chicago Press, 1999).

Glister, J. and Glister, T., 'Property in recyclable artificial implants' (2013) 21 *Journal of Law and Medicine* 357

Gold, R.E., *Body Parts: Property Rights and the Ownership of Human Biological Materials* (Washington: Georgetown University Press, 1996)

Goldberg, J.D., 'Involuntary servitudes: A property-based notion of abortion' (1991) 38 *University of California Los Angeles Law Review* 1597

Goold, I., 'Abandonment and human tissue' in I. Goold, K. Greasley, J. Herring, and L. Skene (eds), *Persons, Parts and Property: How Should We Regulate Human Tissue in the 21st Century?* (Oxford: Hart Publishing, 2014), pp. 125–155

Goold, I., 'Sounds suspiciously like property treatment: Does human tissue fit within the common law concept of property?' (2005) 7 *University of Technology Sydney Law Review* 62

Goold, I., 'Why does it matter how we regulate the use of human body parts?' (2014) 40 *Journal of Medical Ethics* 3

Goold, I. and Quigley, M., 'Human biomaterials: The case for a property approach' in I. Goold, K. Greasley, J. Herring, and L. Skene (eds), *Persons, Parts and Property: How Should We Regulate Human Tissue in the 21st Century?* (Oxford: Hart Publishing, 2014), pp. 231–262

Gorr, M., 'Justice, self-ownership, and natural assets' (1995) 12 *Social Philosophy and Policy* 267

Gottlieb, K., 'Human biological samples and the laws of property: The trust as a model for biological repositories' in R.F. Weir (ed.), *Stored Tissue Samples: Ethical, Legal, and Public Policy Implications* (Iowa City: University of Iowa Press, 1998), pp. 182–197

Gray, K. and Gray, S., *Elements of Land Law*, 5th edn (Oxford: Oxford University Press, 2009)

Greasley, K., 'Property rights in the human body: Commodification and objectification' in I. Goold, K. Greasley, J. Herring, and L. Skene (eds), *Persons, Parts and Property: How Should We Regulate Human Tissue in the 21st Century?* (Oxford: Hart Publishing, 2014), pp. 68–87

Green, S., 'An introduction to wrongful interference actions' in D. Nolan and A. Robertson (eds), *Rights and Private Law* (Oxford: Hart Publishing, 2011), pp. 525–551

Green, S. and Randall, J., *The Tort of Conversion* (Oxford: Hart Publishing, 2009)

Grey, T.C., 'The disintegration of property' in J.R. Pennock and J.W. Chapman (eds), *Property: Nomos XXII* (New York: New York University Press, 1980), pp. 69–85

Griffin, J., *Well-Being: Its Meaning, Measurement and Importance* (Oxford: Clarendon Press, 1986)

Grotius, H., *The Rights of War and Peace*, ed. and trans. A.C. Campbell (London: Hyperion Reprint Edition, 1979)

Grubb, A., '"I, me, mine": Bodies, parts and property' (1998) 3 *Medical Law International* 299

Grunebaum, J., *Private Ownership* (London: Routledge and Keegan Paul, 1987)

Haddow, G., *Embodiment and the Everyday Cyborg: Technologies and Altered Subjectivities* (Manchester: Manchester University Press, forthcoming)

Haddow, G., Harmon, S.H.E., and Gilman, L., 'Implantable Smart Technologies (IST): Defining the 'Sting' in Data and Device' (2016) 24 Health Care Analysis 210

Haddow, G., King, E., Kunkler, I., and McLaren, D., 'Cyborgs in the everyday: Masculinity and biosensing prostate cancer' (2015) 24 *Science as Culture* 484

Haddow, G., Laurie, G.T., Cunningham-Burley, S., and Hunter, K., 'Benefit-sharing: Public solutions to private interests?' (2007) 64 *Social Science and Medicine* 272

Halsbury's Laws of England (5th edn, 2015)

Haraway, D., 'A cyborg manifesto: Science, technology, and socialist-feminism in the late twentieth century' in *Simians, Cyborgs and Women: The Reinvention of Nature* (New York: Routledge, 1991), pp. 149–181

Hardcastle, R., *Law and the Human Body: Property Rights, Ownership, and Control* (Oxford: Hart Publishing, 2009)

Harmon, S.H.E., '*Yearworth v. North Bristol NHS Trust*: A property case of uncertain significance?' (2010) 13 *Medicine, Health Care, and Philosophy* 343

Harmon, S.H.E. and Laurie, G.T., '*Yearworth v. North Bristol NHS Trust*: Property, principles, precedents, and paradigms' (2010) 69 *Cambridge Law Journal* 476

Harris, D.R., 'The concept of possession in English law' in A.G. Guest (ed.), *Oxford Essays in Jurisprudence* (Oxford: Oxford University Press, 1961), pp. 69–106

Harris, J., 'Scientific research is a moral duty' (2007) 31 *Journal of Medical Ethics* 242

Harris, J.W., *Property and Justice* (Oxford: Oxford University Press, 2001)

Harris, J.W., 'Who owns my body?' (1996) 16 *Oxford Journal of Legal Studies* 55

Hart, H.L.A., 'Are there any natural rights?' (1955) 64 *Philosophical Review* LXIV 175, reprinted in J. Waldron (ed.), *Theories of Rights* (Oxford: Oxford University Press, 1984), pp. 77–90.

Hart, H.L.A., 'Between utility and rights' (1979) 79 *Columbia Law Review* 828, reprinted in A. Ryan (ed.) *The Idea of Freedom: Essays in Honour of Isaiah Berlin* (Oxford: Oxford University Press, 1979), pp. 77–98

Hart, H.L.A., 'Definition and theory in jurisprudence' (1954) 70 *Law Quarterly Review* 37

Hart, H.L.A., *Essays on Bentham: Studies in Jurisprudence and Political Theory* (Oxford: Clarendon Press, 1982)

Hawes, C., 'Property interests in body parts: *Yearworth v North Bristol NHS Trust*' (2010) 73 *Modern Law Review* 119

Hawkins, A.K. and O' Doherty, K., 'Biobank governance: A lesson in trust' (2010) 29 *New Genetics and Society* 311

Haworth, L., *Autonomy: An Essay in Philosophical Psychology and Ethics* (New Haven: Yale University Press, 1986)

Hegel, G.W.F., *Outlines of the Philosophy of Right*, trans. T.M. Knox (Oxford: Oxford University Press, 2008)

Herring, J., 'Why we need a statute regime to regulate bodily material' in I. Goold, J. Herring, L. Skene, and K. Greasley (eds), *Persons, Parts and Property: How Should We Regulate Human Tissue in the 21st Century?* (Oxford: Hart Publishing, 2014), pp. 213–229.

Herring, J. and Chau, P-L., 'My body, your body, our bodies' (2007) 15 *Medical Law Review* 34

Hickey, R., 'Dazed and confused: Accidental mixtures of goods and the theory of acquisition of title' (2003) 66 *Modern Law Review* 368

Hickey, R., 'Stealing abandoned goods: Possessory title in proceedings for theft' (2006) 26 *Legal Studies* 584

Hodson, J., 'Mill, paternalism, and slavery' (1981) 41 *Analysis* 60

Hoffmaster, B., 'Between the sacred and the profane: Bodies, property, and patents in the Moore case' (1992) 7 *Intellectual Property Journal* 115

Hohfeld, W.N., *Fundamental Legal Conceptions of a Right as Applied in Judicial Reasoning* (New Haven: Yale University Press, 1919, reprinted 1966)

Holm, S., Hofmann, B., and Solbakk, J.H., 'Conscription to biobank research?' in J.H. Solbakk, S. Holm, and B. Hofmann (eds), *The Ethics of Research Biobanking* (Dordrecht: Springer Science + Business Media, 2009), pp. 255–262

Honoré, A.M., 'Ownership' in A.G. Guest (ed.), *Oxford Essays in Jurisprudence* (Oxford University Press 1961), pp. 107–147

Honoré, A.M., 'Rights of exclusion and immunities against divesting' (1960) 34 *Tulane Law Review* 453

Hoppe, N., *Bioequity: Property and the Human Body* (Farnham: Ashgate Publishing Ltd, 2009)

Hoeyer, K., 'The ethics of research biobanking: A critical review of the literature' (2008) 25 *Biotechnology and Genetic Engineering Reviews* 429

Hoeyer, K., *Exchanging Human Bodily Material: Rethinking Bodies and Markets* (Dordrecht: Springer, 2013)

Hurd, H.M., 'The moral magic of consent' (1996) 2 *Legal Theory* 121

Hyde, A., *Bodies of Law* (Princeton: Princeton University Press, 1997)

Independent Review Group, *Retention of Organs at Post-Mortem Final Report* (Edinburgh: The Stationery Office, 2001)

Ingram, A., *A Political Theory of Rights* (Oxford: Clarendon Press, 1994)

International Consortium of Investigative Journalists, *Skin and Bone: The Shadowy Trade in Human Body Parts* (Centre for Public Integrity, 2012)

Jennings, B., 'Autonomy' in B. Steinbock (ed.), *The Oxford Handbook of Bioethics* (Oxford: Oxford University Press, 2007), pp. 72–89

Johnston, D., 'The renewal of the old' (1997) 56 *Cambridge Law Journal* 80

Jones, M.A. (ed.), *Clerk and Lindsell on Torts*, 21st edn (London: Sweet and Maxwell, 2014)

Jones, P., *Rights* (Basingstoke and London: MacMillan Press, 1994)

Kant, I., *Grounding for the Metaphysics of Morals*, trans. J. Ellington (Indianapolis and Cambridge: Hackett Publishing Company Inc., 1993)

Kant, I., *Groundwork of the Metaphysics of Morals*, trans. M. Gregor (Cambridge: Cambridge University Press, 1997)

Kant, I., *Lectures on Ethics: The Cambridge Edition of the Works of Immanuel Kant in Translation*, trans. P. Heath (Cambridge: Cambridge University Press, 1997)

Kant, I., *The Metaphysics of Morals*, trans. M. Gregor (Cambridge: Cambridge University Press, 1996)

Katz, L., 'Exclusion and exclusivity in property law' (2008) 58 *University of Toronto Law Journal* 275

Katz, L., 'The regulative function of property rights' (2011) 8 *Econ Journal Watch* 236

Kaveny, M.C., 'Commodifying the polyvalent good of health care' (1999) 24 *Journal of Medicine and Philosophy* 207

Kent, J., *Regenerating Bodies: Tissue and Cell Therapies in the Twenty-First Century* (London and New York: Routledge, 2012)

Khamsi, R., 'Bio-engineered bladders successful in patients' *New Scientist* (4 April 2006)

Kleinig, J., 'The nature of consent' in F.G. Miller and A. Wertheimer (eds), *The Ethics of Consent: Theory and Practice* (Oxford: Oxford University Press, 2010), pp. 3–22

Korobkin, R., '"No compensation" or "pro compensation": *Moore v. Regents* and default rules for human tissue donations' (2007) 40 *Journal of Health Law* 1

Kramer, M., 'Rights without trimmings' in M. Kramer, N.E. Simmonds and H. Steiner (eds), *A Debate over Rights: Philosophical Enquiries* (Oxford: Oxford University Press, 1998, reprinted 2002), pp. 60–101

Kramer, M., Simmonds, N.E., and Steiner, H. (eds), *A Debate over Rights: Philosophical Enquiries* (Oxford: Oxford University Press, 1998, reprinted 2002)

Krauss, M.I., 'Property rules vs. liability rules' in B. Bouckaert and G. De Geest (eds), *Encylopedia of Law and Economics, vol. II* (Cheltenham: Edward Elgar Publishing, 2000), pp. 782–794

Krier, J.E. and Schwab, S.J., 'Property rules and liability rules: The Cathedral in another light' (1995) 70 *New York University Law Review* 440

Kuflik, A., 'The inalienability of autonomy' (1984) 13 *Philosophy and Public Affairs* 271

Kuzenski, W.F., 'Property in dead bodies' (1924) 9 *Marquette Law Review* 17

Kymlicka, W., *Contemporary Political Philosophy*, 2nd edn (Oxford: Oxford University Press, 2002)

Ladyman, S., Human Tissue Bill, House of Commons Standing Committee G (27 January 2004), cols 59 and 65

Lamont, M. and Molnar, V., 'The study of boundaries in the social sciences' (2002) 28 *Annual Review of Sociology* 167

Laurie, G.T., *Genetic Privacy: A Challenge to Medico-Legal Norms* (Cambridge: Cambridge University Press, 2002)

Laurie, G.T., 'Privacy and property? Multi-level strategies for protecting personal interests in genetic material' in B.M. Knoppers and C. Scriver (eds), *Genomics, Health and Society: Emerging Issues for Public Policy* (Ottowa: Policy Research Initiative, 2004), pp. 83–98

Laurie, G.T., 'Reflexive governance in biobanking: On the value of policy led approaches and the need to recognise the limits of law' (2011) 130 *Human Genetics* 347

Laurie, G.T., Harmon, S.H.E., and Porter, G., *Mason and McCall Smith's Law and Medical Ethics*, 10th edn (Oxford: Oxford University Press, 2016)

Lawson, F.H. and Rudden, B., *The Law of Property* (Oxford: Oxford University Press, 2002)

Leach Scully, J., *Disability Bioethics: Moral Bodies, Moral Difference* (Plymouth: Rowman and Littlefield Publishers, Inc., 2008)

Lee, J., 'The fertile imagination of the common law: *Yearworth v North Bristol*' (2009) 17 *Torts Law Journal* 130

Lennon, K., 'Feminist perspectives on the body' in E.N. Zalta (ed.), *The Stanford Encyclopedia of Philosophy* (Fall 2014 edn)

Liddell, K., 'Beyond a rebarbative commitment to consent' in O. Corrigan *et al.* (eds), *The Limits of Consent: A Socio-Ethical Approach to Human Subject Research in Medicine* (Oxford: Oxford University Press, 2009), pp. 79–98

Liddell, K. and Hall, A., 'Beyond Bristol and Alder Hey: The future regulation of human tissue' (2005) 13 *Medical Law Review* 170

Lindley, R., *Autonomy* (London: MacMillan Education Ltd, 1986)

Locke, J., *Two Treatises of Government*, ed. Peter Laslett (Cambridge: Cambridge University Press, 1988)

McBride, N.J., 'Rights and the basis of tort law' in D. Nolan and A. Robertson (eds), *Rights and Private Law* (Oxford: Hart Publishing, 2012), pp. 331–365

McFarlane, B., *The Structure of Property Law* (Oxford: Hart Publishing, 2008)

McFarlane, B., '*Keppell v Bailey* (1834); *Hill v Tupper* (1863): The *numerus clausus* and the common law' in N. Gravells (ed.) *Landmark Cases in Land Law* (Oxford: Hart Publishing, 2013), pp. 1–32

McHale, J., '"Appropriate consent" and the use of human material for research purposes: The competent adult' (2006) 1 *Clinical Ethics* 195

McHale, J., 'The Human Tissue Act: Innovative legislation – fundamentally flawed or missed opportunity?' (2005) 26 *Liverpool Law Review* 169

Mack, E., 'Self-ownership and the right of property' (1990) 73 *The Monist* 519

Mackenzie, C. and Stoljar, N. (eds), *Relational Autonomy: Feminist Perspectives on Autonomy, Agency, and the Social Self* (Oxford: Oxford University Press, 2000)

Mackie, J.L., 'Can there be a right-based moral theory?' in J. Waldron (ed.), *Theories of Rights* (Oxford: Oxford University Press, 1984), pp. 129–142

MacLean, A., *Autonomy, Informed Consent and Medical Law: A Relational Challenge* (Cambridge: Cambridge University Press, 2013)

McLean, S.A.M., *Autonomy, Consent, and the Law* (London: Routledge-Cavendish, 2010)

McLean, S.A.M., Campbell, A.V., Gutridge, K., and Harper, H., 'Human tissue legislation and medical practice: A benefit or a burden?' (2006) 8 *Medical Law International* 1

Macpherson, C.B. (ed.), *Property: Mainstream and Critical Positions* (Oxford: Basil Blackwell, 1978)

Maddox, N., 'Abandonment' and the acquisition of property rights in separated human biomaterials' (2016) 16 *Medical Law International* 229

Magnusson, R., 'Proprietary rights in human tissue' in N. Palmer and E. McKendrick (eds), *Interests in Goods* (London: Lloyd's of London Press, 1993)

Manson, N., 'Consent and informed consent' in R.E. Ashcroft *et al.* (eds), *Principles of Health Care Ethics* (Chichester: John Wiley and Sons, 2007), pp. 297–303

Manson, N. and O' Neill, O., *Rethinking Informed Consent in Bioethics* (Cambridge: Cambridge University Press, 2007)

Maqsood, M.I., Matin, M.M., Bahrami, A.R., and Ghasroldasht, M.M., 'Immortality of cell lines: Challenges and advantages of establishment' (2013) *Cell Biology International* 1065

Markby, W., *Elements of Law Considered with Reference to Principles of General Jurisprudence*, 3rd edn (Oxford: Clarendon Press, 1885)

Marway, H., Johnson, S.L., and Widdows, H., 'Commodification of human tissue' in H.A.M.J. ten Have and B. Gordijn (eds), *Handbook of Global Bioethics* (Dordrecht: Springer Science and Business Media, 2014), pp. 581–598

Mason, C., Brindley, D.A., Culme-Seymour, E.J., and Davie, N.L., 'Cell therapy industry: Billion dollar global business with unlimited potential' (2011) 6 *Regenerative Medicine* 265

Mason, C. *et al.*, 'Cell therapy companies make strong progress from October 2012 to March 2013 amid mixed stock market sentiment' (2013) 12 *Cell Stem Cell* 644

Mason, J.K. and Laurie, G.T., 'Consent or property? Dealing with the body and its parts in the shadow of Bristol and Alder Hey' (2001) 64 *Modern Law Review* 710

Mason, J.K. and Laurie, G.T., *Mason and McCall Smith's Law and Medical Ethics*, 9th edn (Oxford: Oxford University Press, 2013)

Matthews, E.H., 'Merleau-Ponty's body-subject and psychiatry' (2004) 16 *International Review of Psychiatry* 190

Matthews, P., 'The man of property' (1995) 3 *Medical Law Review* 251

Matthews, P., 'Whose body? People as property' (1983) 36 *Current Legal Problems* 193

Medical Research Council, *Human Tissue and Biological Samples for Use in Research: Operational and Ethical Guidelines* (April 2001, amended 2005)

Medical Research Council, *Human Tissue and Biological Samples for Use in Research: Operational and Ethical Guidelines* (November 2014)

Merleau-Ponty, M., *Phenomenology of Perception* (London: Routledge and Kegan Paul, 1962)

Merleau-Ponty, M., *Signs*, trans. R. McCleary (Evanston: Northwestern University Press, 1964)

Merrill, T.W., 'Property and the right to exclude' (1998) 77 *Nebraska Law Review* 730

Merrill, T.W., 'Property as modularity' (2012) 125 *Harvard Law Review* 151

Merrill, T.W. and Smith, H.E., 'Optimal standardization in the law of property: The *numerus clausus* principle' (2000) 110 *Yale Law Journal* 1

Merrill, T.W. and Smith, H.E., *Property: Principles and Policies*, 3rd edn (Foundation Press, 2012)

Metzger, E., 'Acquisition of living things by specification' (2004) 8 *Edinburgh Law Review* 115

Mill, J.S., *On Liberty and Other Essays*, ed. J. Gray (Oxford: Oxford University Press, 1991)

Miller, F.G. and Wertheimer, A., 'Preface to a theory of consent transactions: Beyond valid consent' in F.G. Miller and A. Wertheimer (eds), *The Ethics of Consent: Theory and Practice* (Oxford: Oxford University Press, 2010), pp. 79–106

Miller, F.G. and Wertheimer, A. (eds), *The Ethics of Consent: Theory and Practice* (Oxford: Oxford University Press, 2010)

Montgomery, J. and Montgomery, E., 'Montgomery on informed consent: An inexpert decision? (2016) 42 *Journal of Medical Ethics* 89

Morales, F.J., 'The property matrix: An analytical tool to answer the question, is this property' (2013) 161 *University of Pennsylvania Law Review* 1125

Moyle, J.B., (trans.), *Institutes of Justinian* (Oxford, 1911)

Munzer, S.R., 'A bundle theorist holds on to his collection of sticks' (2011) 8 *Econ Journal Watch* 265.

Munzer, S.R., *A Theory of Property* (Cambridge: Cambridge University Press, 1990)

Munzer, S.R., 'Kant and property rights in body parts' (1993) VI *Canadian Journal of Law and Jurisprudence* 319

Murray, T., 'Who owns the body? On the ethics of using human tissue for commercial purposes' (1986) 8 *IRB: Ethics and Human Research* 1

Naffine, N., 'The legal structure of self-ownership: Or the self-possessed man and the woman possessed' (1998) 25 *Journal of Law and Society* 193

Narveson, J., *The Libertarian Idea* (Philadelphia: Temple University Press, 1988)

Narveson, J., 'Libertarianism vs. Marxism: Reflections on G.A. Cohen's *Self-Ownership, Freedom and Equality*' (1998) 2 *Journal of Ethics* 1

Nedelsky, J., 'Law, boundaries, and the bounded self' (1990) 30 *Representations* 162

Nedelsky, J., 'Property in potential life? A Relational approach to choosing legal categories' (1993) VI *Canadian Journal of Law and Jurisprudence* 343

Newman, C.M., 'Bailment and the property/contract interface' (2015) George Mason Legal Studies Research Paper No. LS 15–12, 1. Available at SSRN: https://ssrn.com/abstract=2654988

Nicita, A. and Rizzolli, M., 'Property rules, liability rules and externalities' (2006) 24 *Journal of Public Finance and Public Choice* 99

Nicol, D., Otlowski, M., and Chalmers, D., 'Consent, commercialisation and benefit-sharing' (2001) 9 *Journal of Law and Medicine* 80

Nozick, R., *Anarchy, State, and Utopia* (Oxford: Basil Blackwell, 1974)

Nuffield Council on Bioethics, *Give or Take? Human Bodies in Medicine and Research* Consultation Paper, April 2010

Nuffield Council on Bioethics, *Human Bodies: Donation for Medicine and Research* (London: Nuffield Council on Bioethics, 2011)

Nuffield Council on Bioethics, *Human Tissue: Ethical and Legal Issues* (London: Nuffield Council on Bioethics, 1995)

Nussbaum, M., 'Objectification' (1995) 24 *Philosophy and Public Affairs* 249

Nwabueze, R., *Biotechnology and the Challenge of Property: Property Rights in Dead Bodies, Body Parts, and Genetic Information* (Aldershot: Ashgate Publishing Ltd, 2007)

Nwabueze, R., 'Biotechnology and the new property regime in human bodies and body parts' (2002) 24 *Loyola of Los Angeles International and Comparative Law Review* 19

Nwabueze, R., 'Body parts in property theory: An integrated framework' (2014) 40 *Journal of Medical Ethics* 33

Nwabueze, R., 'Cadavers, body parts, and the remedial problem' in I. Goold, K. Greasley, J. Herring, and L. Skene (eds), *Persons, Parts and Property: How Should We Regulate Human Tissue in the 21st Century?* (Oxford: Hart Publishing, 2014), pp. 157–175

O' Neill, O., *Autonomy and Trust in Bioethics* (Cambridge: Cambridge University Press, 2002)

O' Neill, O., 'Nozick's entitlements' (1976) 19 *Inquiry* 468

O' Neill, O., 'Some limits of informed consent' (2003) 29 *Journal of Medical Ethics* 4

Otsuka, M., *Libertarianism without Inequality* (Oxford: Oxford University Press, 2003)

Palmer, N. (ed.), *Palmer on Bailment*, 3rd edn (London: Sweet and Maxwell, 2009)

Pattinson, S., *Medical Law and Ethics*, 2nd edn (Sweet and Maxwell: London, 2009)

Penner, J.E., 'The "bundle of rights" picture of property' (1996) 43 *UCLA Law Review* 711

Penner, J.E., *The Idea of Property in Law* (Oxford: Oxford University Press, 1997)

Pitt, E., *Hansard* HC Deb (1960), vol. 632, cols 1231–1258

Pollock, F. and Wright, R., *An Essay on Possession in the Common Law* (Oxford: Oxford University Press, 1888)

Priaulx, N. 'Managing novel reproductive injuries in the law of tort: The curious case of destroyed sperm' (2010) 17 *European Journal of Health Law* 81

Price, D., 'From Cosmos and Damian to Van Velzen: The human tissue saga continues' (2003) 11 *Medical Law Review* 1

Price, D., 'The Human Tissue Act 2004' (2005) 68 *Modern Law Review* 798

Price, D., *Human Tissue in Transplantation and Research* (Cambridge: Cambridge University Press, 2010)

Pufendorf, S., *The Political Writings of Samuel Pufendorf*, ed. C.L. Carr, trans. M.J. Seidles (Oxford: Oxford University Press, 1994)

Quigley, M., 'Propertisation and commercialisation: On controlling the uses of biomaterials' (2014) 77 *Modern Law Review* 677

Quigley, M., 'Property: The future of human tissue?' (2009) 17 *Medical Law Review* 457

Quigley, M., 'Property and the body: Applying Honoré' (2007) 33 *Journal of Medical Ethics* 631

Quigley, M., 'Property in human biomaterials: Separating persons and things?' (2012) 32 *Oxford Journal of Legal Studies* 659

Quigley, M. and Skene, L., 'Human biomaterials and property: Is the law still an ass?' in C. Stanton, S. Devaney, A.M. Farrell, and A. Mullock (eds), *Pioneering Healthcare Law: Essays in Honour of Margaret Brazier* (Abingdon: Routledge, 2016), pp. 156–167

Quong, J., *Liberalism without Perfection* (Oxford: Oxford University Press, 2010)

Radin, M.J., *Contested Commodities* (Cambridge: Harvard University Press, 1996, reprinted 2001)

Radin, M.J., *Reinterpreting Property* (Chicago: University of Chicago Press, 1993)

Radin, M.J. and Sunder, M., 'Introduction: The subject and object of commodification' in M.M. Ertman and J.C. Williams (eds), *Rethinking Commodification: Cases and Readings in Law and Culture* (New York: New York University Press, 2005), pp. 8–29

Rao, R., 'Property, privacy, and the human body' (2000) 80 *Boston University Law Review* 359

Rawls, J., *A Theory of Justice* (Oxford: Oxford University Press, 1971, rev. 1999)

Raz, J., 'Legal rights' (1984) 4 *Oxford Journal of Legal Studies* 1

Raz, J., *The Morality of Freedom* (Oxford: Clarendon Press, 1986)

Raz, J., 'On the nature of rights' (1984) XCIII *Mind* 194

Raz, J., 'Right-based moralities' in J. Waldron (ed.), *Theories of Rights* (Oxford: Oxford University Press, 1984), pp. 182–200

Reid, E.C., 'Delictual liability and the loss of opportunity of fatherhood: Holdich v Lothian Health Board' in A. Simpson, R. Paisley, and D. Bain (eds), *Northern Lights: Essays in Private Law in Honour of David Carey Miller* (Aberdeen: Aberdeen University Press, forthcoming); Edinburgh School of Law Research Paper No. 2015/30, 1–19. Available at SSRN: https://ssrn.com/abstract=2663063

Reid, K.G.C., 'Body parts and property' in A. Simpson, R. Paisley, and D. Bain (eds), *Northern Lights: Essays in Private Law in Honour of David Carey Miller* (Aberdeen: Aberdeen University Press, forthcoming); Edinburgh School of Law Research Paper No. 2015/25, 1–18. Available at SSRN: https://ssrn.com/abstract=2644303

Reid, K.G.C. *The Law of Property in Scotland* (Edinburgh: Butterworths/Law Society of Scotland, 1996)

Rhodes, R., 'In defense of the duty to participate in biomedical research' (2008) 8 *American Journal of Bioethics* 37

Riddall, J.G., *Jurisprudence*, 2nd edn (Oxford: Oxford University Press, 2005)

Rodgers, M.E. 'Human bodies, inhuman uses: Public reactions and legislative responses to the scandals of bodysnatching' (2003) 12 *Nottingham Law Journal* 1

Rose, C.M., 'Canons of property talk, or, Blackstone's anxiety' (1999) 108 *Yale Law Journal* 601

Rose, C.M., 'Possession as the origin of property' (1985) 52 *University of Chicago Law Review* 73

Rose, C.M., 'The Shadow of *the Cathedral*' (1997) 106 *Yale Law Journal* 2175

Rostill, L., 'The ownership that wasn't meant to be: *Yearworth* and property rights in human tissue' (2013) 40 *Journal of Medical Ethics* 14

Rostill, L., 'Relative title and deemed ownership in English personal property law' (2015) 35 *Oxford Journal of Legal Studies* 31

Rothbard, M., *The Ethics of Liberty* (Atlantic Highlands: Humanities Press, 1982)

The Royal Liverpool Children's Inquiry Report, HC 12–11 (London: The Stationery Office, 2001)

Rothbard, M., *For a New Liberty: The Libertarian Manifesto*, rev. edn (New York: Libertarian Review Foundation, 1978)

Rudden, B., 'Economic theory versus property law: The *numerus clausus* problem' in J.M. Eeklaar and J. Bell (eds), *Oxford Essays in Jurisprudence* (Oxford: Clarendon Press, 1987), pp. 239–263

Russell, D., 'Embodiment and self-ownership' (2010) 27 *Social Philosophy and Policy* 135

Ryan, A. (ed.), *The Idea of Freedom: Essays in Honour of Isaiah Berlin* (Oxford: Oxford University Press, 1979)

Satz, D., *Why Some Things Should Not Be for Sale: The Moral Limits of Markets* (Oxford: Oxford University Press, 2010)

Schroeder, J.L., 'Three's a crowd: A feminist critique of Calabresi and Melamed's one view of the cathedral' (1999) 84 *Cornell Law Review* 394

Scottish Executive Health Department, *Human Tissue (Scotland Act) 2006: A Guide to Its Implications for NHS Scotland* (2006)

Scottish Law Commission, Memorandum No. 28, *Corporeal Moveables: Mixing Union and Creation* (31 August 1976)

Sheach-Leith, V.M., 'Consent and nothing but consent? The organ retention scandal' (2007) 29 *Sociology of Health and Illness* 1023

Sheehan, D., *The Principles of Personal Property Law* (Oxford: Hart Publishing, 2011)

Shildrick, M., 'Contesting normative embodiment: Some reflections on the psycho-social significance of heart transplant surgery' (2008) 1 *Perspectives: International Postgraduate Journal of Philosophy* 12

Shildrick, M., 'Corporeal cuts: Surgery and the psycho-social' (2008) 14 *Body and Society* 31

Shildrick, M., '"Why should our bodies end at the skin?": Embodiment, boundaries, and somatechnics' (2015) 30 *Hypatia* 13

Shildrick, M., McKeever, P., Abbey, S., Poole, J., and Ross, H., 'Troubling dimensions of heart transplantation' (2009) 35 *Medical Humanities* 35

Simmons, A.J., *The Lockean Theory of Rights* (Princeton: Princeton University Press, 1992)

Simmonds, A.J., 'Original-acquisition justifications of private property' (1994) 11 *Social Philosophy and Policy* 63

Simonite, T., 'Lab-grown cartilage fixes damaged knees' *New Scientist* (5 July 2006)

Singer, J. and Beerman, J., 'The social origins of property' (1993) 6 *Canadian Journal of Law and Jurisprudence* 217

Skegg, P.D.G., 'Human corpses, medical specimens and the law of property' (1976) 4 *Anglo-American Law Review* 412

Skegg, P.D.G., 'Medical uses of corpses and the no property rule' (1992) 32 *Medicine, Science, and the Law* 311

Skene, L., 'Arguments against people legally 'owning' their own bodies, body parts, and tissue' (2002) 2 *Macquarie Law Review* 165

Skene, L., 'The current approach of the courts' (2014) 40 *Journal of Medical Ethics* 10

Skene, L., 'Proprietary interests in human bodily material: *Yearworth*, recent Australian cases on stored semen and their implications' (2012) 20 *Medical Law Review* 227

Skene, L., 'Proprietary rights in human bodies, body parts and tissue: Regulatory contexts and proposals for new laws' (2002) 22 *Legal Studies* 102

Skloot, R., *The Immortal Life of Henrietta Lacks* (London: Pan Books, 2010)

Skloot, R., 'Taking the least of you', *New York Times Magazine* (16 April 2006)

Smit, M., 'Alistair Cooke body snatch leader pleads guilty', *The Telegraph* (18 March 2008)

Smith, H.E., 'Exclusion versus governance: Two strategies for delineating property rights' (2002) 31 *Journal of Legal Studies* 4S53

Smith, H.E., 'Property as the law of things' (2012) 125 *Harvard Law Review* 1693

Smith, R.J., *Property Law* (Edinburgh: Pearson Education Ltd, 2011)

Steele, J., *Tort Law: Text, Cases, and Materials* (Oxford: Oxford University Press, 2014)

Steiner, H., *An Essay on Rights* (Oxford: Blackwell, 1994)

Steiner, H., 'The fruits of bodybuilders' labour' in A. Dyson and J. Harris (eds), *Ethics and Biotechnology* (London: Routledge, 1996), pp. 64–78

Steiner, H., 'Universal self-ownership and the fruits of one's labour: A reply to Churchin' (2008) 16 *Journal of Political Philosophy* 350

Stewart, C., Aparicio, L., Lipworth, W., and Kerridge, I., 'Public umbilical cord blood banking and charitable trusts' in I. Goold, K. Greasley, J. Herring, and L. Skene (eds), *Persons, Parts and Property: How Should We Regulate Human Tissue in the 21st Century?* (Oxford: Hart Publishing, 2014), pp. 53–65.

Stewart, C. *et al.*, 'The problems of biobanking and the law of gifts' in I. Goold, K. Greasley, J. Herring, and L. Skene (eds), *Persons, Parts and Property: How Should We Regulate Human Tissue in the 21st Century?* (Oxford: Hart Publishing, 2014), pp. 25–38

Stewart, C., Fleming, J., and Kerridge, I., 'The law of gifts, conditional donation and biobanking' (2013) 21 *Journal of Law and Medicine* 351

Sumner, L.W., *The Moral Foundation of Rights* (Oxford: Clarendon Press, 1989)

Swadling, W.J., 'Ignorance and unjust enrichment: The problem of title' (2008) 28 *Oxford Journal of Legal Studies* 627

Swadling, W.J., 'Property: General principles' in A. Burrows (ed.), *English Private Law*, 3rd edn (Oxford: Oxford University Press, 2013), pp. 219–402

Taylor, R.S., 'Self-ownership and the limits of libertarianism' (2005) 31 *Social Theory and Practice* 465

Taylor-Alexander, S., Dove, E.S., Fletcher, I., Mitra, A.G., McMillan, C., and Laurie, G.T., 'Beyond regulatory compression: Confronting the liminal spaces of health research regulation' (2017) 8 *Law, Innovation, and Technology* 149

Thomas, S., 'Do freegans commit theft?' (2010) 30 *Legal Studies* 98

Titmuss, R.M., *The Gift Relationship: From Human Blood to Social Policy* (London: George Allen and Unwin, 1970)

Tuckness, A., 'Locke's political philosophy' in E.N. Zalta (ed.), *The Stanford Encyclopedia of Philosophy* (Winter 2012 edn), section 3.

Tutton, R., 'Person, property, and gift: Exploring languages of tissue donation to biomedical research' in O. Corrigan and R. Tutton (eds), *Genetic Databases: Socio-Ethical Issues in the Collection and Use of DNA* (Abingdon: Routledge, 2004), pp. 19–38

UK Biobank, 'Access Procedures: Application and review procedures for access to the UK Biobank Resource' (2011)

UK Biobank, 'Material Transfer Agreement for data and/or samples' (2012)

UK Biobank, 'Relationship with Researchers' (2016)

Vaines, C., *Personal Property* (London: Butterworths, 1967)

Vallentyne, P., 'Introduction' in P. Vallentyne and H. Steiner (eds), *Left-Libertarianism and Its Critics* (Basingstoke: Palgrave, 2000), pp. 1–22.

Vallentyne, P., 'Left-libertarianism and liberty' in T. Christiano and J. Christman (eds), *Contemporary Debates in Political Philosophy* (Oxford: Blackwell Publishers, 2009), pp. 137–151.

Vallentyne, P., 'Libertarianism' in E.N. Zalta (ed.), *The Stanford Encyclopedia of Philosophy* (Fall 2010 edn)

Vallentyne, P., 'Robert Nozick: Anarchy, state and utopia' in J. Shand (ed.), *The Twentieth Century: Quine and After (Central Works of Philosophy Vol. 5)* (Quebec: Acumen Publishing, 2006), pp. 86–103

Vallentyne, P. and Steiner, H. (eds), *Left-Libertarianism and Its Critics* (Basingstoke: Palgrave, 2000).

Vallentyne, P., Steiner, H., and Otsuka, M., 'Why left-libertarianism is not incoherent, indeterminate, or irrelevant: A reply to Fried' (2005) 33 *Philosophy and Public Affairs* 201

van der Vossen, B., 'What counts as original appropriation?' (2009) 8 *Politics, Philosophy, and Economics* 355

van Erp, S., 'A numerus quasi-clausus of property rights as a constitutive element of future European property law?' (2003) 7.2 *Electronic Journal of Comparative Law*

van Erp, S. and Akkermans, B., *Cases, Materials and Text on Property Law* (Oxford: Hart Publishing, 2012)

Wainwright, S.P., Williams, C., Michael, M., Farsides, B., and Cribb, A., 'Ethical boundary-work in the embryonic stem cell laboratory' (2006) 28 *Sociology of Health and Illness* 732

Waldby, C., 'Stem cells, tissue cultures and the production of biovalue' (2002) 6 *Health* 305

Waldby, C. and Mitchell, R., *Tissue Economies: Blood, Organs and Cell Lines in Late Capitalism* (Durham and London: Duke University Press, 2006)

Waldron, J., 'Moral autonomy and personal autonomy' in J. Christman and J. Anderson (eds), *Autonomy and the Challenges to Liberalism* (Cambridge: Cambridge University Press, 2005), pp. 307–329

Waldron, J., *The Right to Private Property* (Oxford: Clarendon Press, 1988)

Waldron, J. (ed.), *Theories of Rights* (Oxford: Oxford University Press, 1984)

Wall, J., *Being and Owning: The Body, Bodily Material, and the Law* (Oxford: Oxford University Press, 2015)

Wall, J., 'The legal status of body parts: A framework' (2011) 31 *Oxford Journal of Legal Studies* 783

Wall, J., 'The trespasses of property' (2014) 40 *Journal of Medical Ethics* 19

Webster, A. 'Stem cell research and society: Lessons from social science' *Bionews* (18 August 2008)

Weir, R.F., Olick, R.S., and Murray, J.C., *The Stored Tissue Issue: Biomedical Research, Ethics and Law in the Era of Genomic Medicine* (Oxford: Oxford University Press, 2004)

Weiss, G., *Body Images: Embodiment as Intercorporeality* (New York: Routledge, 1999)

Wellman, C., *A Theory of Rights: Persons Under Laws, Institutions, and Morals* (Totowa: Rowman and Allanheld, 1985)

Wenar, L., 'The nature of rights' (2005) 33 *Philosophy and Public Affairs* 223

Wenar, L., 'Rights' in E.N. Zalta (ed.), *The Stanford Encyclopedia of Philosophy* (Fall 2011 edn)

Whitty, N., 'Rights of personality, property rights, and the human body in Scots law' (2005) 9 *Edinburgh Law Review* 194

Widdows, H., *The Connected Self: The Ethics and Governance of the Genetic Individual* (Cambridge: Cambridge University Press, 2013)

Widdows, H., *Global Ethics: An Introduction* (Abingdon: Routledge, 2014)

Widerquist, K., 'Lockean theories of property: Justifications for unilateral appropriation' (2010) 2 *Public Reason* 2

Wilkinson, D. and Savulescu, J., 'Should we allow organ donation euthanasia? Alternatives for maximising the number and quality of organs for transplantation' (2012) 26 *Bioethics* 32

Wilkinson, S., *Bodies for Sale: Ethics and Exploitation in the Human Body Trade* (London: Routledge, 2003)

Wilkinson, S., 'Commodification' in R.E. Ashcroft *et al.* (eds), *Principles of Health Care Ethics* (Chichester: John Wiley and Sons, 2007), pp. 285–291

Wilkinson, T.M., 'The confiscation and sale of organs' (2007) 13 *Res Publica* 327

Williams, J.C. and Zelizer, V.A., 'To commodify or not to commodify' in M.M. Ertman and J.C. Williams (eds), *Rethinking Commodification: Cases and readings in Law and Culture* (New York and London: New York University Press, 2005), pp. 362–382

Wilson, D., 'A troubled past? Reassessing ethics in the history of tissue culture' (2016) 24 *Health Care Analysis* 246

Winickoff, D.E. and Neumann, L.B., 'Towards a social contract for genomics: Property and the public in the "biotrust" model' (2005) 1 *Genomics, Society and Policy* 8

Winickoff, D.E. and Winickoff, R.N., 'The charitable trust as a model for genomic biobanks' (2003) 349 *New England Journal of Medicine* 1180

Winterton, R., *Hansard* HC Deb (2004), vol. 423, col. 115

Wittgenstein, L., *Philosophical Investigations*, trans. G.E.M. Anscombe (Oxford: Basil Blackwell, 1968)

Witting, C., *Street on Torts*, 14th edn (Oxford: Oxford University Press, 2015)

Wolff, J., *An Introduction to Political Philosophy*, rev. edn (Oxford: Oxford University Press, 2006)

INDEX

CPSIA information can be obtained
at www.ICGtesting.com
Printed in the USA
LVHW081100160419
614331LV00008B/381/P